Group Discussion

Theory and Technique

Group Discussion
Theory and Technique

R. VICTOR HARNACK
THORREL B. FEST
both of University of Colorado

New York:
APPLETON-CENTURY-CROFTS
Division of Meredith Publishing Company

PRINTED IN THE UNITED STATES OF AMERICA

E41270

TO MARTHA AND LUCILLE

Foreword

An ancient sage said that of the making of books there was no end. Without feeling any need to justify his paradoxical behavior, he expressed his complaint in a book which he himself was writing! In the preface to this present work, however, the authors offer their reasons for adding to the already extensive literature of their subject. Admittedly, the field of discussion has been so well tilled that anyone producing another textbook inevitably must face the challenge of making a bona fide contribution to theory and practice. Harnack and Fest pass this test; in their work the informed reader will find an approach and an emphasis quite different from those in any of the other good books on discussion.

This textbook reports a study in depth of the processes and techniques of purposeful, problem-solving communication in small, face-to-face groups. Although the authors' point of view and basic concepts are consonant with the best traditions in the teaching of discussion, their treatment of philosophical, psychological, and sociological principles far transcends any simple, supposedly sure-fire gimmicks.

In their analysis of the roles of participants and leaders in discussion, the authors provide a new and stimulating frame of reference for this vital form of communicative behavior. In my judgment this textbook constitutes a definite breakthrough to a deeper understanding of the nature and function of discussion in the ongoing life of a democratic society. It will bring to discussion as an aca-

demic discipline new dignity and respect among scholars outside
as well as within the field of Speech.

A. T. Weaver
Madison, Wisconsin

Preface

Millions of words purporting to help people discuss more productively in small groups have found their way into print. Since we propose to add more words to this supply, we feel some description of our motivation is in order. Discussion is a vitally important subject, but we cannot justify addition to its literature by the importance of discussion as a subject alone. Our direct experience in the field, which began when we enrolled as freshmen in college, is extensive. The two of us have studied, observed, experimented with, written about, participated in, and taught group discussion for a combined total of more than fifty years. Justification for writing a book, however, should be based upon more than a long acquaintance with the subject, indispensable though such acquaintance may be. Why, then, have we written?

Speech teachers can trace their heritage back twenty-four centuries to Aristotle, Isocrates, and Plato. The stream of rhetorical principles and techniques, which began with those men, has been constantly broadening and deepening. Its main current has been effective speaking on the public platform. Another stream, more recent but parallel, is the scientific study of small-group behavior. Speech educators, psychologists, sociologists, and businessmen who describe and analyze what happens to people engaged in small-group discussion aim to channel currents of this stream toward improved human relations. We believe it is now necessary to help currents from both of these streams to partial confluence at least.

The engineering is not easily achieved. One current in the rhetorical stream, techniques of discussion, is not identical with the consociate current, techniques of platform speaking. And techniques for promoting desirable human relations, which are essential in discussion groups, can easily swamp discussion with "life adjustment" approaches. Indeed, something of a split exists between those who turn to rhetoric or "dialectics" and those who look to group behavior and hope for improved human relations. Today, however, research has provided means to blend profitably currents from these two great streams.

We assume that enhancement and growth of the individual himself is the fundamental value of any interpersonal association. At times individual betterment is accomplished in groups whose primary purposes are to help individuals realize personal goals; at other times individual betterment is a by-product of working for more impersonal, task-oriented, goals. The theory on which we have proceeded is thus goal-oriented; it utilizes the concept of a "bargain" struck between the individual and his group. "Techniques" are consequently designed to implement the process of bargaining, whatever may be the goals of the group.

It will be obvious to the reader that, rather than content ourselves with describing issues to be resolved and with presenting relevant evidence for doing so, we have for the most part chosen to take a stand on many points of controversy concerning discussion theory or technique. We certainly do not expect all scholars working in this area to agree with us in every particular. We do, however, believe our views are provocative and soundly based in research and observation. The more inconclusive the evidence, the more tentative are our conclusions. If readers disagree with our conclusions, we hope they will at least find our assumptions, evidence, and reasoning clear and defensible.

A book of this sort should do more than present sound and useful information; it should also challenge the reader to go beyond its pages. We have made liberal use, therefore, of footnotes and bibliographies. Everyone should find sufficient variety and scope in these additional sources to encourage him to read further. The exercises at the ends of chapters are also designed to stimulate the student to adopt perspectives other than our own. Many of the exercises are conceived as experiments by which the reader may not only test the arguments in the book but also utilize his own experience and observation to supplement what he reads. Such exercises place heavy demands upon the reader's interest, originality, and imagination. If in performing them he discovers evidence that seems to modify or change any of our conclusions, we will be more delighted than dismayed. Research is changing the field of discussion too rapidly to justify any final answers.

Perhaps we should say a word about some matters, normally covered in books of this sort, that we have either left out or relegated to subordinate positions. For example, we have not included a chapter describing how to select topics for discussion; it is our belief that the exercises *show* how to create profitable discussion. Again, although we do not include a chapter on evaluating discussion, we refer to sources that describe various kinds of rating schemes. The exercises, moreover, as well as the functions and techniques listed in the chapters themselves, suggest ways of devising evaluation procedures for specific purposes. Finally, we have placed little stress on how to conduct public discussions from the platform or over radio and television. An abundance of literature that will answer any needs not answered satisfactorily by common sense adaptations of the material in this book is readily available in the platform-speaking tradition.

Although we see a rationale in the arrangement of the parts and chapters of this book, teachers may wish to change the order of presentation for their own instructional purposes. Some may prefer, for example, to assign chapters in Part IV ahead of those in Part III.

No authors can claim to have written a book completely unaided. We are obviously indebted to hundreds of scholars and writers who have preceded us and whose thoughts and observations we have used. Wherever possible we have indicated our indebtedness by proper citation. We wish also to acknowledge especially our debt to those who have influenced us personally—teachers, colleagues, students. They have argued with us, stimulated us, listened to us, and been tolerant of our mistakes. As the reader will discover, we have drawn heavily upon such experiences with others, and we are grateful for our opportunities to do so. Even though we cannot begin to name everyone who assisted in shaping our thoughts, we must mention three individuals who stand out in the memory of one or both of us.

In his classroom and home, Franklyn S. Haiman greatly helped one of us to understand something of the humanity as well as the substance of group discussion. For the other of us the late Henry L. Ewbank was a wise, patient teacher and an endearing friend. We are both uniquely indebted to John W. Keltner. In his classroom one of us was launched upon a career. As a colleague and friend he has constantly criticized and encouraged us while stimulating our imagination and understanding with his own intelligence and deeply human insights.

For direct assistance in the preparation of this book we are especially indebted to Andrew T. Weaver, who read the entire manuscript and unerringly put his finger upon weaknesses. Any shortcomings that remain are attributable only to us. We are grateful also to Barbara Schindler, who read most of the manuscript and helped us find ways to improve many a sentence; to Eloise Pearson, who did much more than any typist should be expected to do in preparing a manuscript; and to many publishers, who allowed us to use material from their books. Proper acknowledgments are given to sources where quotations or paraphrases appear.

R. V. H.
T. B. F.

Contents

xiii

Group Discussion

Theory and Technique

PART I

A Point of View

CHAPTER 1

The Individual vs. the Group:
A Conflict in Communications

> Ah, but a man's reach should exceed his grasp,
> Or what's a heaven for? . . .
>
> Robert Browning*

This book is intended to help people work more productively in discussion groups, keeping in mind that such productivity is, in itself, only a means to an end. But to what end, and why should we concern ourselves with improving our ability in the give-and-take of discussion groups?

The only reasonable justification of group activity is that it can provide an opportunity for the individual to develop his ability and capacity. Indeed, this is the only justification of any activity in a democratic society. Far too many forces in the world seem intent upon degrading human beings rather than helping them realize their full potential. Any realistic ethic argues there can be no justification of a society that does not regard the individual human being and his rights as its *raison d'être*.

This enhancement of the individual person may take many forms. The group may protect the individual from others; the group may allow the individual free rein in certain areas; the group may

---

* *Andrea Del Sarto.*

require some to make sacrifices for others, as in the case of war;
but when any group ceases to serve the individual and degrades
him, the usefulness of that group has ended. The numerous instances in which an individual has made heroic, noble, and unselfish
sacrifices for the group may seem to belie our contention that the
enhancement of the individual provides the greatest good. Such
actions, however, do not negate the thesis, for the act of making
such a sacrifice may be the epitome of the individual's accomplishment and ultimate enhancement.

Increasingly we are concerned about attacks upon and criticisms
of group behavior and collaborative activity that have been voiced
during recent years. Many responsible people are alarmed about
what they perceive to be a subversion of the fundamental ethic we
have just discussed. Men such as David Riesman, Walter Lippmann,
Erich Fromm, and William Whyte have made devastating diagnoses
of ways in which the individual has become submerged by the
group.[1] Some of the attacks have been less than temperate, such
as that which refers to the teacher and practitioner of discussion
as the "Man with the grey flannel mouth." [2]

The chief point that has troubled us is the inadequacy of the
answers that these writers offer for the problem they have described.
Most of them suggest a return to some form of rugged individualism. Some, like Riesman, rather wistfully hope for the emergence
of a new type of personality such as an "autonomous man" who will
be capable of coping with the pressures put upon him by his society.
*It is our contention that an answer to this problem is to be found in
improving the individual's ability to communicate.*

In this chapter we will examine some of the attacks against
the group and the processes that create and maintain it as well as
the circumstances that have given rise to the attacks. We shall
attempt to develop further what we mean by the democratic ethic
of the individual, and we shall show why we believe this dilemma
of the individual vs. the group is a conflict of communications. In

---

[1] David Riesman, with Nathan Glazer, and Reuel Denney, *The Lonely
Crowd; A Study of the Changing American Character* (Garden City, N.Y.:
Doubleday, 1953). Walter Lippmann, *The Public Philosophy* (Boston: Little,
Brown, 1955). Erich Fromm, *Escape from Freedom* (New York: Holt, Rinehart
and Winston, 1941). William H. Whyte, *The Organization Man* (Garden City,
N.Y.: Doubleday, 1957).

[2] Hugo Hellman, "The Man with the Grey Flannel Mouth," *The Quarterly Journal of Speech*, Vol. 44 (February, 1958), pp. 56-60.

the remainder of the book, we hope to show how an individual can enhance his individualism and that of others in the group by a greater understanding of the nature of group processes and the skills of thought and communication necessary to implement those understandings.

A HISTORY OF MEN AND GROUPS

Man's history is a story of his struggle to be an individual and to relate himself meaningfully to others. These two fundamental needs —to be an individual and to relate himself meaningfully to others— have been well described by Erich Fromm in his book, *Escape from Freedom*.[3] Fromm asserts the desire for freedom is a basic human drive since the condition of freedom is essential to growth. Restrict an arm and that arm atrophies; restrict the freedom of a man and that man "dies" for want of psychological growth.

Freedom, however, has a dialectical aspect. A man's freedom may be freedom "from" external restrictions, or it may be freedom "to" relate himself in a spontaneous and creative fashion to the rest of the world. Fromm argues that modern man has not realized the full meaning of freedom "to" and is therefore unable to bear the awful aloneness engendered by freedom "from." How, then, have these two human needs fared in the history of man?

Man has always had to depend upon groups. As we know, the family and the tribe existed long before recorded history, and we are all aware of the role that these groups played in the nurture of man. For centuries tradition dictated an implacable social structure. Serf was bound to lord, slave to master in a structure that allowed no freedom to either party. Birth determined destiny and an omnipotent church presided over all. It is extremely important to note that neither the slave nor the master was free in any genuine sense. The life roles of both were determined by their station in life and from this we have both the notion of *noblesse oblige* and the responsibility of slave to master. The idea of the individual free to determine his own destiny was, with rare exceptions, unknown until "modern" times.

In such circumstances the individual was involved in little conflict because his role in the social structure was fixed and unalterable. He was provided a security in life by the social structure and

[3] Erich Fromm, *op. cit.*

promised a posthumous equality and tranquility. There was little room for anxiety or doubt in such a society.

But a thought, an idea, began to emerge. One manifestation of this idea occurred on June 15, 1215, on the plains of Runnymede, where a historic document was signed. This document declared that there was law which transcended all men—even kings—and men, as individuals, could repair to this law without fear. Every schoolchild knows that the men who forced King John to sign the Magna Charta did not have the welfare of the "common man" in mind when they phrased the document; they had in mind baronial prerogatives as opposed to those of the king. But they had to justify their claims in language which made generalization to include all men almost inevitable.

Events moved slowly at first but soon gathered momentum. The Renaissance began to free artists, poets, philosophers and scientists. Rather than regarding man *on earth* as of no importance, the hopes and aspirations of man now became paramount. Along with this new emphasis upon man the development of man's individual capacities became important.

Economic changes also helped alter the concept of man. Merchants, draftsmen, and traders, stimulated by the possibilities demonstrated in the Crusades, began to crack the class boundaries and suggest that a man could improve his station in life. This idea was indeed radical and took considerable time to gain currency. The significant aspect, however, was the beginning of discontent with a society that preordained for every man a given niche in life and excluded most men from all chance to prove themselves capable of greater accomplishment.

This discontent with the established order became manifest in religious thought, and the Reformation and Counter-Reformation were born. These movements tended to give man freedom in religion —freedom, that is, not from his God, but from the organizational requirements of how he was to relate himself to his God. Vernon Parrington felt that the concept of the "priesthood of all believers" made inevitable the concept that man was capable of governing himself.[4] If he could govern his religious life, he could certainly govern his civic life.[5]

---

[4] Vernon Louis Parrington, *Main Currents in American Thought* (New York: Harcourt, Brace & World, 1930).

[5] Roman Catholics and others contend, of course, that, while a man can

Triumphant men began to proclaim new discoveries and ideas, hesitantly at first, and then with increasing vigor. Galileo, Copernicus, Newton, and others began to question accepted notions about the nature of the world. They began to test new ideas in a fashion unknown since the height of the Greek civilization, and, despite considerable resistance, began to announce their discoveries and ideas to the world at large.

The terrible hopes and the equally terrible consequences of individualism are reflected in the Faust legend born during this period. Here is the story of a man daring to defy even his God to enhance himself as an individual. In successive periods Marlowe, Goethe, and Gounod produced dramatic versions of the Faust legend. "The Devil and Daniel Webster" and *Damn Yankees* are two of the American versions of the same theme.

Colonial America became a haven for the nascent individualism of which we have spoken. Here, religious freedom became a reality for most people. Although leaders such as Cotton and Increase Mather, Governor Winthrop and others denied religious freedom in the Massachusetts Bay Colony for Protestant sects other than their own, men such as Roger Williams, Jonathan Edwards and George Whitefield worked to achieve religious freedom because they recognized it as inseparable from any other freedom.

Accompanying the rise of religious freedom was the economic freedom engendered by independent farmers who owned their own farms and by independent merchants and craftsmen in the towns. The well known story of Benjamin Franklin demonstrates accomplishments which were considered completely impossible a century or two earlier in Europe. Few men wore another's collar and in 1776 the real and fancied oppressions of the British monarch were rejected.[6]

---

govern his civic life, he is not his own authority in matters of faith and morals. Our concern is not with the correctness of any position taken by one or more religious faiths, but to demonstrate how completely the established society, of which the Catholic Church was a part, was challenged by the emergence of the idea of individual freedom.

[6] The French Revolution obviously is more responsible than the American Revolution for creating the changes leading to the development of individualism. Writers such as Montesquieu, Locke and Rousseau provided a rationale for these changes. We are using the American Revolution to date the peak of individualism rather than arguing that it caused the development of the individual.

INDIVIDUALISM AT ITS PEAK

With the American and French Revolutions, the individual, in the
United States at least, came of age. Our own country was built upon
these individuals who were independent politically, religiously, and
economically. Looking back to the Magna Charta, we wrote a constitution and declared proudly that we were a government of laws
and not of men.

Before we overpraise the individualism of that era, let us look
a bit more closely to see what produced it and what its consequences were.

Thomas Jefferson and Daniel Webster understood very well
what had produced the individualism of their day. Jefferson pinned
his hopes upon the agrarian society. He called cities "sores on the
body politic" and hoped that men would prefer to remain upon the
farm where they belonged to a largely self-sustaining economic unit
based upon the family. In the light of this fundamental premise,
Jefferson's famous dictum, "That government is best which governs
least," is easily understood. Since the family farm was almost completely independent of anyone else for basic necessities, the government had to do little except protect the farmer from hostile attack
and insure that such commerce as was needed operated without
unnecessary interference.[7] Webster pinned his hopes upon property
as the cornerstone of liberty, contending that only the individual
who possessed property could be truly free and therefore an individual into whose hands public responsibility could safely be placed.
Framers of our state governments thus limited the electorate to
white, free, adult, male, property holders as the only citizens qualified to vote responsibly.

Individualism flourished at this time for several reasons, but a
primary reason was that people did not need others very much for
the ordinary pursuits of life. To be sure, people needed one another
for a host of things such as the building of roads and harbors and
so on. Fundamentally, however, they were their own economic mas-
ters. The fact that the government did not interfere with the activities of the majority of citizens did not *cause* individualism. The

[7] *The Life and Selected Writings of Thomas Jefferson,* Adrienne Koch and
William Peden, eds. (New York: Modern Library, 1944).

relatively inconspicuous role of the government was made possible because of the small need for collaborative action.

In such a society, with its loss of feudal relations, with its primitive economy based upon the power of horse, sail and human muscle, relationships among individuals on all levels remained largely clear and meaningful. The family, which was generally large, was, of course, the basic unit of cultural and personal interchange. Voluntary and spontaneous cooperation of various families to build a barn, thresh the grain, or husk the corn was fairly frequent. Communities were often composed of people drawn from a comparatively small number of families who had intermarried extensively and who shared many common bonds and interests.

THE FALL OF THE INDIVIDUAL

Even as individualism was coming of age, the tide of events began to destroy it. The "group" began to assert control almost immediately.[8] Industrial growth forced Northern factory owners to bring together groups of laborers; the Southern plantation holders sought slaves as their workers. Despite the hopes of Washington and virtually all of the framers of our Constitution, political parties came into being. In today's political scene we frequently forget that political parties such as we see were not provided for in the planning of most of our founding fathers. They fervently hoped that the government could operate without faction and contending interests, that the people would exercise sober judgment from time to time as to the stewardship of those entrusted to operate the government which was supposed to work in the interests of the people.[9] But parties appeared nonetheless.

As everyone knows, the causes of the Civil War went far beyond the issue of slavery. The economic situations developing in the North and the South were creating sharply different kinds of relationships between workers and employers, farmers and businessmen and, in general, the people and their government. The Civil

[8] The word *group* at this point is being used in the broadest possible connotation. We will define and describe groups extensively in many places throughout this book. Here, the connotation of any physical bringing together of individuals will suffice for the definition of the word.

[9] For an example of this thinking, see George Washington's *Farewell Address*, September 17, 1796.

War doomed the group structure developing in the South and accelerated the collaborative efforts for economic sufficiency developing in the North.[10] Farmers' sons moved to cities to work for others, labor unions were born, private ownership began to give way to corporate ownership. In the past decade we have seen the last of the great personal dynasties pass from the scene when the Ford Motor Company incorporated. The small merchant began to give way to the chain store.

Today we do almost everything in groups. The work day begins with a car pool, struggles through committee meetings, pauses for the local service club, continues with more meetings, and ends with a civic association meeting in the evening to build a bigger and better club that in turn can build a bigger and better club. Students both study and date in groups. The number of groups that a student can join on a college campus is as staggering as the number of groups claiming the attention of a citizen in any community. We decide in groups, sometimes for the sake of improving the decision, and sometimes for the sake of avoiding responsibility for our acts. We exert influence by means of groups. Clay Malick points out that since 1945 approximately 1,500 groups that support long-range policies supposedly good for the country have been formed. They are backed by millions of citizens who seek to influence legislation and governmental behavior.[11]

We could go on multiplying the instances in which people participate in groups to accomplish their purposes. One way to bring this matter closer to home is to make a list of the various groups of which you are a member and to count the time you spend in some kind of collective activity during the week. The amount of collaborative activity in which we all engage is amazing. Going to class, attending church, eating with family or friends should not be overlooked for they are all forms of collaborative activity.

GROUPS CAN BE DANGEROUS

Erich Fromm's analysis of pre-World War II Germany, in his celebrated book, *Escape from Freedom,* offers frightening proof of our

[10] The best account of this point of view is that of Charles A. and Mary R. Beard, *The Rise of American Civilization* (New York: Macmillan, 1954).
[11] Clay P. Malick, "These New Citizen Lobbies," *The Western Humanities Review,* Vol. 13, No. 4 (Autumn, 1959).

assertion that groups can be dangerous.[12] The awful aloneness, he contends, engendered by "freedom from" external restraints of government drove the people of Germany to "escape from freedom." Their escape led them into one of the most brutal authoritarian structures the world has ever seen. But it was "meaningful" to them since every man knew exactly where he stood. Fromm argues that the basic character structure of the German people was such that they preferred authoritarian relationships to the more fluid relationships of democracy.

An experiment that demonstrates clearly the potential danger of groups is the one performed by Solomon Asch.[13] To examine the effect of group pressure upon individual judgment, he designed an experiment involving the perception of relative lengths of lines. Seven to nine individuals, all college students, were grouped in a classroom while an experimenter explained the perceptual test to be administered. On a blackboard in front of the room were two white cardboards; the one at the left bore a single, vertical, black line. This was the standard. The one at the right bore three vertical, black lines that differed in length from each other; only one of the three was equal to the standard. A sequence of twelve such test cards was used. The standard line was always at the left and the other three lines always at the right. The standard line, incidentally, was always exactly forty inches from the correct test line.

It should be noted that the perceptual distinctions were fairly obvious. A set of control subjects erred only 7.4 per cent of the time in making their judgments. (Control subjects were those shown the sets of test cards without the experimental variation described below.)

Experimental variation was produced in the following manner: All of the group, with the exception of one critical subject, were told how they should behave in the experimental circumstances. They were to choose unanimously a wrong line in the third, fourth, sixth, seventh, ninth, tenth, and twelfth trials and the correct line in the remaining trials. The critical subject was placed so that he responded in the last or the next to last position. In seven out of

[12] Fromm, op. cit.
[13] Solomon E. Asch, Social Psychology (Englewood Cliffs, N. J.: Prentice-Hall, 1952).

the twelve situations, therefore, *he heard a unanimous majority contradict the evidence of his senses.* A series of such experiments was performed using a different critical subject in each one. These were the results. *One-third of the responses of the critical subjects were errors, identical to the majority trend.* That is, in one-third of the instances the critical subjects denied the evidence of their senses and conformed to majority pressure. Questioning of the yielding subjects revealed that some actually had their perception altered by the relentless pressure of the majority opinion; some, feeling that they could not be logically right with a unanimous majority opposing them, altered their judgments; and some, preferring to avoid ridicule and embarrassment by going along with the majority, altered their opinions. All of the subjects, whether they yielded to majority pressure or not, were considerably disturbed by the contradiction between what they saw and what they heard the others saying.

This experiment is particularly significant because no direct and overt pressures were exerted to secure conformity. Many who did resist the pressures brought about by the majority opinion reported that their logic led them to believe the group was probably right, but they reported honestly what they thought they saw. They would undoubtedly have been much more likely to go along with the majority if the situation were an actual one rather than an experiment in which they could afford the luxury of adhering to their opinions regardless of what the "right" answer might have been. Also they would probably have been more likely to change had the majority discussed the matter with them and tried to get them to alter their judgments.[14]

David Riesman and his associates, writing what we consider to be a most significant recent book, describe the basic character emerging today as the "other-directed man."[15] They describe the previous character types as "tradition-directed" and "inner-directed." The former character type, dominant in Western Europe up to and through the Middle Ages, accepts the "established order of things" and lets it determine what he shall do and think. The

[14] *Ibid.,* chap. 16. Cf. pp. 205-206 in Chapter 8. We cover the matter of altering judgments in the next chapter.
[15] Riesman, *op. cit.*

atter character type, produced by the Renaissance and the Refornation, internalized the standards of conduct and thought and thus appeared to be independent of the judgments of others about him. This is the type of personality upon which Freud built his psychology. A third and historically more recent character type is the "other-directed man." He possesses no standards handed down from tradition nor any standards that he internalized early in life. He operates instead as if he had a radar system to send out and receive signals reflected from others and is thus able to determine what he should think and feel. The "other-directed man" is tremendously dependent upon the group because his definition of what is right is determined by what is considered right by his peers. His actions and thoughts are conditioned primarily by what others think and feel toward him and his behavior. Our Constitution was framed by inner-directed men who believed that what an individual thought concerned that individual alone, but the "other-directed" man feels compelled to adjust, not only his behavior to group expectations, but his thoughts and feelings as well.

To the extent that Riesman is right concerning the basic character type emerging in the United States today, the situation is frightening. We, like Riesman, make no pretense of admiring the inner-directed man, for he was often bound by standards that were totally inappropriate to the situation he was facing at the time. That is, when the situation he was confronting was different from the situation in which he had learned his values, the inner-directed man lacked appropriate standards. None of these character types was free in any genuine sense, but we do share Riesman's apprehension about a society dominated by people whose main concern is to discover what is presently popular to think and feel, whose only goal in life is getting more and more of what society thinks the successful man ought to acquire, and who believe that the pathway to "heaven" is found by "getting on the team." Our position is well described by Frederick Mayer who writes:

The great tragedies of American life are not found in financial failures but are expressed by the oppressive hold of the community, whether it be Winesburg, Ohio, Boston, or the Gopher Prairie of Sinclair Lewis. These communities are not just physical symbols, they are states of mind

and conditions of the soul. They uphold artificial standards and create
a domination of the spirit by killing individuality and creativity.[16]

Whyte's "organization man" is told where to live, with whom
to associate, and what groups to join, as well as what kind of grey
flannel suit to wear.[17] Vance Packard points out the ways in which
this anxiety is used to foist products upon an unsuspecting public.[18]
In some schools the "curve-buster" is an object of disdain because
he dares to depart too far from the accepted standards of medioc-
rity. Sanity is defined by many as "adjustment" to the group; cooperation as "getting together on the team." And parents everywhere
seem to abdicate to the child's peer group.

It is not difficult to understand why the group has assumed such
a tremendous hold upon people. To begin with, the society in
which we live is extremely complex. More stimuli impinge upon
the nervous system of each of us, more judgments must be made,
and fewer standards for making such judgments exist than ever
before. Further, as is evident from our analysis thus far, the tasks
to be performed today involve considerably more collaborative
effort than did the simpler tasks of an earlier day. One person
seldom produces directly for himself much more than a small bit
of what he consumes. The family farm, once largely a self-sustaining
economic unit, today produces only a small part of its own food
supplies, none of its clothes, and little, if any, of its shelter. The
farmer is dependent upon others for these things. Collaborative
effort of a more direct kind is obvious in most areas. Finally, we
have become a nation composed primarily of white collar workers
who do not produce anything tangible. Many of us are teachers,
lawyers, doctors, salesmen, public relations men, or managers, whose
only tangible products are likely to be pieces of paper containing
certain ideas, the value of which appears to lie only in approbation
of our peers.

We are thus forced on the one hand into collaborative effort, and
at the same time often ignored and threatened as individuals in a
society pledged to assure individual freedom for all of its members.

[16] Frederick Mayer, "India and the Western Mind," *Saturday Review*
(July 30, 1960), p. 11.
[17] Whyte, *op. cit.*
[18] Vance Packard, *The Hidden Persuaders* (New York: McKay, 1957).

How can anyone resolve this dilemma and achieve both individualism and meaningful relationship with others?

TO RESOLVE THE DILEMMA

Resolution of this dilemma can only begin by understanding oneself, the groups to which one belongs, and the process of communication. Then one can begin to become an *individual* and to relate oneself meaningfully to others.

1. Understand Oneself

"Know thyself" is a dictum honored more in the breach than in the observance. Too many college freshmen seem to have no concept of their own goals beyond attending college and getting a degree. And too many citizens join groups that have no apparent purpose other than making themselves ever bigger. These people do not lack goals; their goals are not realistic. Mayer finds the root of modern man's inadequacies in his Faustian concept of life: "We want too much; we have too many expectations. We are like the characters in an O'Hara novel who are bound to be unhappy whether they achieve their goal or not." [19]

To be sure, groups can help the individual in the therapeutic task of learning to reappraise himself and his values and thereby to know himself.[20] This task, however, remains primarily an individual one and thus must be accomplished largely without help from any group. The individual does not really need a group in order to read a book however much book-study clubs may help him. He does not need a group to listen to music, to observe the beauties of the world about him, to think, reflect, or pray. In order to do any of these important things, an individual must learn to live with himself. The injunction, "Love thy neighbor as thy self," assumed a man had some healthy conception of himself which he could love. For modern man, one might well reverse the injunction to read, "Love thy self as thy neighbor." The story of the two psychiatrists meeting on the street may contain more truth than fiction. Said the first, "You're feeling fine; how am I?"

The pessimism expressed by many of the writers we have cited

[19] Mayer, *op. cit.*, p. 11.
[20] See p. 43, Chapter 3.

seems, nonetheless, basically unwarranted. Men have shown and continue to show ability to work more closely toward the twin goals we have thus far described. Initiative for all such progress must begin with the individual, however, since no appeal to a corporate mind can modify the nature of groups on behalf of the individual. Rather must an appeal be made to what Toynbee calls the "creative minority;" that is, to individuals who generate the great developments that shape the course of the world.[21] This book neither advises how to accomplish knowledge of self nor how to reshape the world. It does aim to help the individual in learning to know the group and to communicate effectively in group situations.

2. Understand Groups

If one does not understand the nature of groups and the ways in which men think and act together, he is likely to be incapable of relating himself meaningfully to others while at the same time retaining his individuality. Such understanding cannot merely be a textbook understanding; it must instead be an understanding developed as one relates principles of group behavior to actual group experiences, as one feels the forces in a group situation, recognizes them, and gives them labels. A substantial part of this book is devoted to a discussion of principles of group behavior and to suggestions for actually testing and observing these principles at work.

3. Understand and Use Principles of Communication

Interpersonal relationships can only be established and maintained through the medium of communication. Obvious as this truism is, it is frequently neglected by those who wish to be effective in group situations. Such effectiveness must begin with an understanding of rational thought and continue with an understanding of the principles and methods for transmitting and receiving ideas and feelings. Although we now know a good deal more about this than we once knew, much still remains to be discovered. Testimony of officials at the North American Air Defense Command, the Federal Mediation and Conciliation Service, the United States Chamber of

---

[21] A brief but excellent description of the need and nature of the "creative minority" may be found in William Norwood Brigance, *Speech, Its Techniques and Disciplines in a Free Society,* 2nd ed. (New York: Appleton-Century-Crofts, 1961), pp. 12-13.

Commerce, the Colorado AFL-CIO, and countless other groups, as well as students on the campus, indicates that knowledge and skill in the art of communication may well be everyone's most valuable asset.[22]

Evidence suggests that the kind of training we are discussing offers promise. One example of this evidence, pointed out by Clay Malick, argues that the rise and success of responsible pressure groups that seek to influence governmental laws and behavior is caused, to a considerable extent, by "the unparalleled growth within the citizen body of those who have a college education or better." [23] A college education, of course, does not automatically qualify anyone for successful dealings with groups. But certainly the goals of training in the broad areas of the humanities and social sciences and the more specialized training in such fields as communication and group behavior are to equip a person with the understandings and skills we have been describing.

It is no accident that two of the fastest growing disciplines in colleges and universities throughout the nation are psychology and speech. People have begun to value more highly the understandings and skills proper to these fields, and are seeking their assistance. Although dozens of illustrations could be offered, we shall give but two. In 1950 the United States had only four hundred individuals who had achieved doctoral degrees in all the fields of speech arts; ten years later it had almost two thousand.[24] When the Colorado AFL-CIO approached the University of Colorado for assistance in developing a union training program in 1959, they placed training in group processes and parliamentary procedure at the head of their list of needs.

These three steps—understanding oneself, understanding groups, and understanding communication—are neither panaceas nor easily achieved. The nature of man and his relationships to his fellows have long fascinated and frustrated respected scholars in many disciplines. Yet a disturbingly large number of people believe they

---

[22] We have served as consultants to all of these organizations as well as to others, among them the Western Conference on Research in Nursing, the National Congress of American Indians, the U. S. Civil Service Commission, the Veterans Administration, and the National Committee of the Democratic Party.

[23] Malick, *op. cit.*, p. 422.

[24] *Speech Monographs,* Vol. 28 (August, 1961), p. 193.

have attained high skill in the art of communication and great facility in dealing with others. Because of this unfortunate popular attitude, sound instruction has often had to plead for support in formal curricula, and superficial training has all too frequently usurped its place, both within and without the schools.

We have posed a dilemma that faces modern man, traced it historically, and examined it in its present-day context. We have already suggested a way to resolve it and will, at least in part of the remainder of this book, elaborate this resolution further. The humane and scientific spirit revealed clearly by Elmer Davis has guided thus far our inquiry and will continue, we hope, to do so not only for us but for everyone.

To admit that there are questions which even our so impressive intelligence is unable to answer, and at the same time not to despair of the ability of the human race to find, eventually, better answers than we can reach as yet—to recognize that there is nothing to do but keep on trying as well as we can, and to be as content as we can with the small gains that in the course of ages amount to something—that requires some courage and some balance.[25]

EXERCISES

1. Compile a list of specific situations where the social pressures on the individual were interpreted incorrectly (a) by the individual, or (b) by another member of the group. Select some of the cases from your observations and others from your personal experiences.

2. Prepare a six hundred word case history of the relationships that developed between the group and the individual in one of the situations you list in Exercise 1.

3. For your own benefit, make a list of those beliefs, actions, policies, attitudes, or standards in which you would be willing to conform to social pressure. Make a second list of the ones where you would not conform to social pressure.

4. What forces in contemporary society tend to foster individualism? What forces tend to foster group conformity?

5. Select one or more of the problems, situations, or forces listed in Exercise 3 and organize an informal discussion with members of the

[25] Elmer Davis, *But We Were Born Free* (New York: Bobbs-Merrill, 1954), p. 190.

class. It would be wise to limit your discussion to some aspect of policies, social affairs, attitudes, and the like, and examine both the areas in which the group members would be willing to conform to social pressure and the areas in which the group members would not conform to social pressure.

6. Follow the procedure of Exercise 5, using forces listed for Exercise 4.

7. Join with several other members of the class to conduct an informal survey among friends or, perhaps, residents of selected areas concerning their (a) vocations, (b) the two or three things they most desire in life, and (c) the organizations or clubs to which they belong. Is it possible to find any relationships among the three sets of data? Report your findings and conclusions to the class.

8. Attempt to avoid all group activity and association for at least half a day. Try not to engage in conversation; remain alone. For your own benefit, record how you felt during this period and also how you felt later when you reestablished your group relationships. Note how difficult it is to isolate yourself in our contemporary society.

9. Examine your own attitudes and beliefs with respect to the philosophy of this chapter. To what extent do you agree or disagree? Compare and contrast your views with those of others by means of either informal conversation or class discussion.

SELECTED READINGS

Fromm, Erich, *Escape from Freedom*. New York, Rinehart, 1941.

Lippmann, Walter, *The Public Philosophy*. Boston, Little, Brown, 1955.

Riesman, David, with Nathan Glazer, and Reuel Denney, *The Lonely Crowd; A Study of the Changing American Character*. Garden City, N. Y., Doubleday, 1953.

Whyte, William H., *The Organization Man*. Garden City, N. Y., Doubleday, 1957.

CHAPTER 2

Values and Limitations
of Discussion as a Method

> For God's sake hold your tongue, and let me love . . .
> John Donne*

"Shall we call a meeting," the businessman asks, "or assign this problem to different individuals?" "Would discussion or lecture be the better way," the teacher asks, "to get this material across to the class?" Should we call a meeting? If we call a meeting, who should be asked to participate? These are the questions this chapter seeks to answer.

Collaborative behavior is obviously necessary, as seen in the last chapter, but sometimes individual behavior is more desirable. Collaborative behavior obviously takes several forms. People may collaborate by pooling their money for some purpose such as financing a corporation; they may collaborate by voting for the same candidate for public office; workmen may collaborate by performing several functions in a factory. This book is concerned, however, with that form of collaboration which is called *discussion*. Though discussion takes several forms, too, they will not be evaluated here. Our question is simply, What are the relative advantages and limitations of discussion *as a method* as compared with individual behavior?

* *The Canonization.*

Discussion is the process whereby two or more people exchange information or ideas in a face-to-face situation. The end result may be increased knowledge, agreement leading to action, disagreement leading to competition, or perhaps only a continuation of the status quo. This is, admittedly, a rather general definition of discussion. Many writers have attempted to define it in a much more specific fashion, including such restrictions as: "under the direction of a leader," or "following a pattern of reflective thinking." Little is gained by such restrictiveness. This book will run the risk of being overly inclusive rather than arbitrarily limited.

With these definitions in mind, then, let us examine some of the advantages and limitations of discussion as a method of collaboration. This examination deals with discussion as employed by reasonably able, mature, sensitive, and objective people. There is no magic in assembling a group of the unfit around a conference table in order to pool their ignorance. Neither the list of advantages nor the list of limitations is definitive, but the more important factors are included here.

VALUES OF DISCUSSION AS A METHOD

Two Heads Are Frequently Better Than One

Early research in discussion was primarily an attempt to compare the relative advantages of individual and collaborative work. The main concern of those studies was with the outcomes or products of discussion groups as compared with individual effort. A whole host of experiments and tasks was employed to test this question. Were individuals, after discussion, better able to estimate the number of beans in a bottle? Were time estimations, ethical judgments, aesthetic judgments, and the like improved after discussion? [1] The majority of these experimental tasks involved making judgments or expressing preferences. According to Dickens and Heffernan, the major conclusions that can be derived from most of these

[1] For more complete descriptions of earlier studies, see: G. B. Watson, "Do Groups Think More Efficiently Than Individuals?" *Journal of Abnormal and Social Psychology*, Vol. 23 (1928), pp. 328-336; John W. Keltner, "What Do We know About Group Discussion?" *The Debater's Magazine*, Vol. 3, No. 3, pp. 154 ff.; and Milton Dickens and Marguerite Heffernan, "Experimental Research in Group Discussion," *Quarterly Journal of Speech*, Vol. 35 (1949), pp. 23-29.

studies are: (1) Extreme judgments tend to become less extreme. (2) Judgments tend to improve. (3) The majority influences the individual judgments. (4) Right answers are supported more tenaciously than wrong answers.[2]

Much of this earlier research offers little support for the claim that two heads are frequently better than one. Results were rather ambiguous and in many cases showed that *averaged* individual judgments were probably as good as, and perhaps superior to, the judgments made after discussion.

A very interesting research by Shaw provided something of a clue to the problem.[3] She had her subjects engage in what she called "the rational solution of complex problems." In the experiments the subjects had to create and evaluate various hypotheses as to how the problems might be solved. Groups seemed to be assured of a much greater proportion of correct solutions than did individuals.

The recent work of Barnlund clearly confirms these earlier findings.[4] He engaged his groups in the solution of reasoning problems that involved arguments in which personal feeling was likely to be strong. In order to eliminate the possibility that group superiority might be caused by the more able members bringing the others up to their level, he placed in each group subjects who had been matched according to ability. His results showed an unmistakable superiority for groups as compared to individuals in the solution of the problem.

In the earlier research that failed to show any advantage for group behavior, judgmental or preference tasks were employed, but Shaw and Barnlund used problem-solving tasks. In the first situation, the individuals are asked to make judgments and then try to affect the judgments of others. For example, no real problem-solving or data-gathering activity can precede the making of a judgment concerning the number of beans in a bottle. The accuracy of the group judgment can sometimes be impaired by the influence exerted by one or more of the individuals in the group.

[2] Dickens and Heffernan, *ibid.*

[3] Marjorie E. Shaw, "A Comparison of Individuals and Small Groups in the Rational Solution of Complex Problems," in T. M. Newcomb and E. L. Hartley, eds., *Readings in Social Psychology* (New York: Holt, Rinehart and Winston, 1947), pp. 304-315.

[4] Dean C. Barnlund, "Comparative Study of Individual, Majority and Group Judgment," *Journal of Abnormal and Social Psychology* (January, 1959).

In the problem-solving situation, however, the individuals must propose hypotheses and present a rationale to defend them. The reasons for the advantage of the group now begin to become clearer. First, the group will probably be able to suggest more hypotheses and bring more knowledge to bear upon the solution of the problem than any one individual. Second, the combined critical thinking of everyone in the group is much more likely to catch and correct deficiencies in evidence and reasoning than an individual might. And finally, group interaction seems to have a stimulating effect upon the performance of the individuals.

Another point about the differences between the judgmental activity and the problem-solving activity should be noted. We must make a sharp distinction between the *making of judgments* and the *creation of the criteria* upon which the judgments are to be based. Creating criteria is essentially a problem-solving activity. Thus we assign to legislative bodies responsibility for developing and stating criteria against which the behavior of individuals is to be measured. We call such criteria laws. We assign to a different class of individuals responsibility for determining whether specific behavior violates the established criteria. We term these persons judges. The application extends beyond political life. Speech teachers long ago discovered that the best practice was to average out individual judgments of critics at speech contests, but, at the same time, to have clinics, conferences and conventions for group discussion of the criteria upon which the judgments should be based.

People Tend to Carry Out Decisions
They Have Helped to Form

Critics of the group discussion method may frequently concede the first advantage of group discussion we have cited. Of course, they say, a group of experts may produce a better solution than any one of those experts working individually, but one expert will be far superior to any group of nonexperts. The expert should make the decision and have the ability to compel those affected by it to conform to the decision and carry it out.

The authoritarian action implied in the above stand raises philosophical as well as practical questions which will be discussed later.[5] But quite apart from whether people have any "right" to

[5] See Chapter 10 particularly.

participate in the making of decisions which involve them, there are other demonstrable advantages of having them participate in the decision-making process.

To demonstrate the assertion that people tend to carry out those decisions they have helped to form we turn to the widely cited experiment performed by Coch and French at the Harwood Manufacturing Company.[6] The factory produced garments and employed mostly women. Although the management was liberal and progressive and always had the best type of labor relations, great difficulty occurred whenever new production techniques or equipment necessitated changing a worker's job. The company had consistently adopted the procedure of deciding upon the change to be made and assigning to an expert, such as a time-study man, the task of determining how the change was to be effected and what the new piece-rate was to be.

The experiment by Coch and French consisted of using different approaches with three groups of workers whose job procedures were about to be changed. The first method was called the "no participation" method in which the employees had no voice in the planning of the change although an explanation for the change was given to them. This, as has been stated, was the standard procedure employed by the company in the past. The second method involved "participation through representation" of the workers. In this method a few representatives of the employees worked with the time-study man in establishing both the most effective procedures and the new piece-work rates. The third method involved the "total participation" of the workers. Their ideas and opinions were sought and used by the time-study man. In all of the variations the decision to make a change was made by the management.

The results were rather dramatic. The "no participation" group behaved as similar groups of workers had in the past. Both the "participation through representation" and the "total participation" groups relearned their jobs significantly more rapidly and soon surpassed the standard sixty unit production level. The "total participation" group was slightly superior to the "participation through representation" group. The difference between the "participation"

[6] Lester Coch and John R. P. French, Jr., "Overcoming Resistance to Change," in D. Cartwright and A. Zander, eds., *Group Dynamics: Research and Theory*, 2nd ed. (Evanston, Ill.: Row, Peterson, 1960), pp. 319-341.

groups and the "no participation" group was attributed to the fact that the former had helped set the new standards and had consequently adopted the new standards as their own. Thus, the workers' "own" pressures were added to the "management-induced" pressures to attain a higher standard of work.[7]

Several factors are worthy of note in connection with this application of the discussion method. First, the management of the Harwood Company did not give to the workers the total responsibility for managing the enterprise. The decision to make a change, to introduce new machinery, to alter the product remained a management responsibility. Thus, we can identify *areas* or *levels* of responsibility. For this reason, we do not contend that every aspect of every decision that affects a given individual ought, by right or necessity, to be given to that individual to determine in conference with others. Our complex interdependent society makes such a position impossible. While not contending that it is always possible to identify properly those areas or levels of responsibility in which the individual has a right to participate in the decision-making process, we do contend that a reasonable effort to locate, differentiate, and accept these areas will improve both the morale and the productivity of those concerned.

Another factor to note is the importance of distinguishing between making policy and implementing that policy. We will call these *legislative* and *executive* functions respectively. The legislative or policy-making function is properly given to those most affected by the policy. The executive or implementing function is properly assigned to selected individuals or subgroups. This matter will be discussed at greater length throughout the book because it is one of the most important and least understood aspects of group discussion procedure.

This advantage of group discussion that has been examined

[7] This interpretation is not the only one which can be placed upon results such as these. Arensberg, for example, contends that such results can be understood only in the framework of an "institutional analysis." The change in the institutional structure of which the small group is a part is the more likely agent, he contends, since that change was a necessary prerequisite to the different type of small group interaction in situations such as the one that Coch and French describe. For further discussion of this problem of interpretation see: Conrad M. Arensberg, "Behavior and Organization: Industrial Studies," in J. H. Rohrer and M. Sherif, eds., *Social Psychology at the Crossroads* (New York: Harper & Row, 1951), Part V, 14.

has become so well accepted that many top-level management consulting firms are insisting on the right to employ worker participation in decision-making as part of the consulting contract.

The specific operation of this principle is illustrated in the way
one church proceeded with a major building program. The members felt that they needed expert assistance to carry out a successful
financial drive. They turned to the national headquarters of their
church and were furnished an expert in conducting financial drives
for churches. They did not, however, by this act surrender their
right to make decisions, nor did the expert seek to make them do so.
The expert provided data and experience while acting as a resource person. He also helped to stimulate them to activity by
describing successful campaigns of a similar nature in which he had
worked. The members of the church retained the authority to make
their decisions since they were the ones who had to carry out the
campaign and pay the bill. The result was a successful campaign
illustrating that there is no necessary conflict between the expert
and the layman and that the layman need not abandon his right to
make decisions because he is in the presence of an expert.

Discussion Can Change Individual Attitudes and Behavior

In addition to offering opportunities for the creation of quality
solutions to problems and the successful carrying-out of such solutions, discussion may be of considerable value when the objective
is modifying individual attitudes and behavior. This objective involves an element of persuasion, and some may argue that it has
no place in the discussion process. Discussion, they would contend,
should be objective and objectivity means that one has no fixed
opinions upon the subject for discussion. Such a view is extremely
narrow and completely ignores the realities of actual discussion
situations.

In the chapters dealing with participant and leader behavior,
objectivity will be discussed at greater length. For now, we point
out that it is inconceivable that one who has studied or thought
about a question for any length of time could have no opinions
concerning it. Every teacher in a classroom seeks to modify the
attitudes of his students toward the subject matter. Certainly in a
labor-management negotiation session, the participants do not come
to the meeting without opinions or goals. *Objectivity, therefore, con-*

sists primarily in seeking all relevant information on a subject, evaluating this as logically as possible and being honest and frank both with oneself and others concerning the resulting conclusions and beliefs.

Every discussant, therefore, has two obligations—the obligation to challenge and, if necessary, change the beliefs of others, and the obligation to allow his own beliefs to be challenged and, if necessary, changed. Such a climate in a discussion group is not easily attained. Like most desirable objectives, this one requires understanding and skill to attain. Such an objective, however, is much more realistic and desirable than the objective of trying to deny or conceal our beliefs.

For evidence concerning the assertion that discussion is frequently a desirable method of changing individual attitudes and behavior, we turn to the classical study done by Kurt Lewin and his associates at the University of Iowa during World War II.[8]

During the Second World War meats were rationed and most kinds of meats were in short supply. Beef hearts, sweetbreads, and kidneys, however, were in plentiful supply. Lewin's experiment in changing food habits, therefore, had practical as well as scientific objectives. Housewives were simply not using these intestinal meats despite their nutritional values and despite the fact that people in many other countries consider them delicacies.

The experiments were conducted using six groups of Red Cross volunteers organized for home nursing. In three of these groups, ranging from thirteen to seventeen members, attractive lectures were given that pointed out the nutritional values of the meats and the desirability of cooperating with the war effort, as well as means of preparing the meats to avoid objectionable characteristics of odor, texture, appearance. The lecturer distributed recipes and described ways in which she had prepared these meats for her own family.

In the remaining three groups the discussion method was employed. After an introduction which linked the problem of nutrition to the war effort, the housewives participated in discussion about whether "housewives like themselves" could be induced to use these meats. The women naturally raised questions about the objectionable characteristics of the meats and asked how these obstacles could be

---

[8] Kurt Lewin, "Group Decision and Social Change," in T. M. Newcomb and E. L. Hartley, eds., *op. cit.*, pp. 330-344.

overcome. The same information about recipes and menus was given to these women, *but only after the women themselves had raised the problems.* At the end of the meeting the women indicated by a show of hands whether they were willing to try one of these meats within the next week.

The follow-up revealed that only three per cent of the women exposed only to the lecture actually served one of the meats they had never before served, but *thirty-two per cent of the women participating in discussion served a meat never before served.*

Another study was conducted by Levine and Butler, but in this case the subjects consisted of twenty-nine supervisors of 395 workers in a large manufacturing plant.[9] These supervisors were overrating those working in the higher job grades and underrating those in the lower grades. This seemed to suggest that they were rating the job as well as the performer. The problem was to devise a method of getting these supervisors to change the basis for the ratings so that a more equitable system would prevail. The twenty-nine supervisors were divided at random into a control group, a discussion group, and a lecture group. The results indicated a clear supremacy for the discussion method of producing change.

Many other studies deal with the effect of discussion upon attitudes. We cannot report them all, but two particularly interesting ones are the studies done by Simpson and Robinson. Simpson found that discussion produced significant shifts: "(1) Toward certainty of the rightness of individual positions on issues considered. (2) Toward disagreement with the statements discussed." [10] In Karl Robinson's study the attitudes of his subjects changed significantly as a result of the discussions. An interesting conclusion, however, was that attitudes changed more from reading than from discussion.[11]

How do we account for the change that was produced by Lewin and Levine and Butler? Lewin contended that the discussion produced a higher degree of involvement than the lecture

[9] Jacob Levine and John Butler, "Lecture vs. Group Decision in Changing Behavior," in D. Cartwright and A. Zander, eds., *Group Dynamics: Research and Theory* (Evanston, Illinois: Row, Peterson, 1953), pp. 280-286.

[10] Ray H. Simpson, "Attitudinal Effects of Small Group Discussions," *Quarterly Journal of Speech,* Vol. 46 (December 1960), pp. 415-418.

[11] Karl F. Robinson, "An Experimental Study of the Effects of Group Discussion upon the Social Attitudes of College Students," *Speech Monographs,* Vol. 8 (1941), pp. 34-57.

situation where the audience was essentially passive. But this alone would not suffice since presumably the involvement factor was comparable in the other studies. He contended that the act of making a group decision was probably the more significant factor since it tended to release one of the sets of pressures against change.[12]

Discussion Can Frequently Develop the Individual

The evidence supporting this last main advantage of discussion is rather less precise than the evidence presented in support of its preceding three advantages. Some personality types, for instance, do not seem to profit at all from participation in discussion. But both experimentation and experience support the assertion that most people profit personally from discussion participation.

First, the individual may learn from participation. In many ways this can be more effective than learning from reading or listening to lectures because the information and ideas contributed by others are considered in the dynamic framework of problem analysis and solution. If the individual participates fully in the discussion process, the ideas he acquires should have greater meaning for him since they were generated under circumstances which involved him more completely. Considerable evidence suggests that learning can readily take place in discussion. Studies such as Paul Rickard's show that even factual information can be more readily learned through discussion than through lecture.[13]

Second, participating in the discussion process will probably improve the discussant's skills in relating himself more meaningfully to others. It seems to us that it would be very difficult for an individual participating in a good discussion to fail to respond to the others in the communicative situation of which he is a part.

Finally, he will probably learn more about the people with whom he participates in the discussion process. An intensive discussion about a vital matter will reveal a good deal about the individuals themselves. Since facility in taking the role of the other is of prime importance in the development of the individual, it follows

[12] See Chapter 9 for a more complete discussion of the concept of forces for and against change.
[13] Paul B. Rickard, "An Experimental Study of the Effectiveness of Group Discussion in the Teaching of Factual Content," (Unpublished Ph.D. dissertation, School of Speech, Northwestern Univ., 1946).

that a greater understanding of other people in action should be of considerable benefit to an individual. Considerable time is spent studying the nature of man in courses such as psychology, sociology, and anthropology. This study can be extended by effective participation in discussion.

Let us turn our attention for a moment to some of the factors which may operate to lessen or modify the benefit that the individual may receive from participation in discussion. First, the authoritarian personality will not find participation in most types of discussion situations a rewarding experience. He becomes so obsessed with the rules and procedures that he finds the give and take of most informal discussion procedures frustrating. He often prefers a session governed by parliamentary procedure, prefers an authority or expert to a group of his peers, and desires the stability that seems to come from clearly established policy. The type of relationship with others which he desires makes it impossible for him to have any real kind of individual freedom. He would probably concede only the first of our advantages of discussion as a method, and then only under rigorously controlled circumstances.

The "other-directed man" also would not benefit greatly from participation in the discussion process. This may seem like a strange assertion since the "other-directed man" wants so badly to do things with others. However, he may become so obsessed with harmonious relationships that he fails to follow the substance of the discussion, and it would not be expected that he would learn much from a discussion since his primary focus is on personal and social adjustment. The generation and analysis of ideas, plus the real and potential conflict involved in testing them, are things he avoids. Social acceptance may be easier and more comfortable than the hazards of exploring reality with consequent threat of alienation.[14]

Thus the benefits to be derived from participation in discussion are a function of the goals for which the individual is striving. If a supervisor in a factory delegates a part of his decision-making capacity to the workers (as in the Harwood experiment), he gives

[14] Golembiewski offers support for these conclusions. Experimentation with the effect of discussion participation upon individuals has yielded contradictory results. Golembiewski's explanation closely parallels ours. See Robert T. Golembiewski, *The Small Group* (Chicago: Univ. of Chicago, 1962), pp. 245-247.

up the goal of dominating the decision-making process in favor of the goal of securing the greater productivity of the workers. Most of the time the goal choices are not so specific as they appear in this example, but it is easy to see that the insecure person (and we call both the authoritarian personality and the "other-directed man" fundamentally insecure) would have considerable difficulty profiting in any way from the discussion situation. The goals he would have to modify or postpone would seem too immediate and precious to permit his profitable participation.

LIMITATIONS OF DISCUSSION AS A METHOD

Already limitations are suggested in the examination of the personality types that cannot profit by discussion. Really these are not limitations of discussion as a *method*, but rather limitations of certain individuals. There are, however, factors which can actually be called limitations upon the method of discussion. No attempt is made in the following discussion to rank them in order of importance.

Discussion Takes Time

All have voiced the complaint that we spend the better part of our lives in committee meetings. There is no question but that a great deal of time is thus consumed. Even under the best of conditions, discussion usually takes more time than individual effort. In the Barnlund study, for example, the groups were held to the same total time as the individuals, but even with this restriction a group of five will take five times the man hours that one individual will use.[15] When high-salaried executives meet, the actual cost of time invested in one conference may be in the thousands of dollars.

Time may be saved in a variety of ways by increased knowledge and skill in discussion procedures. The material in this book will help the reader to effect time savings in his discussion groups, and at this point we will discuss specifically one time-saving and morale-building principle. That is the distinction between legislative and executive functions touched upon earlier in this chapter.

If a group is careful to separate its legislative (policy-making) functions from its executive functions, considerable time may be saved from the group activity. Prediscussion arrangements, fact find-

[15] Barnlund, *op. cit.*

ing, and carrying out of group decisions are typical of a broad class of executive functions. Much time is wasted in groups when the group busies itself prematurely in trying to work out the details of implementing a policy. Sometimes, it is true, the execution of a policy will decidedly affect the very nature of that policy itself. It may be questionable under such circumstances whether the executive function can be separated or completely delegated, but some compromise can frequently be effected.

When executive functions are delegated to an individual, he may find that he has to make rather broad interpretations of group policy in order to execute the decision. For example, a department head, when authorized by the group to hire a certain individual, may find that the conditions of hiring have changed since the group decision was made. He may find he has to make a decision immediately and, consequently, has to use his best judgment on whether or not to hire. His responsibility does not stop here, however; he must make a full accounting to the group for his actions so that new policy may be established, if necessary, to cover further comparable circumstances.[16]

Discussion Spreads Responsibility

At first glance, this may seem to be an advantage of discussion, and in certain ways it is in that it provides for many points of view, and that those involved in the decision help in its formulation. The limitation, however, arises from the fact that the spread of responsibility means that there is frequently less compulsion upon each member to produce something of value. A person cannot afford to be ill-prepared when presenting a speech or briefing. A discussant, however, can frequently come to the group with little preparation. Since the total responsibility is not upon his shoulders, he is tempted to let the others carry the ball while he merely observes and evaluates the contributions of others. If a sizable segment of a group adopts this attitude, the quality of the group discussion is considerably reduced.

There are means of dealing with this problem. In groups such as executive committees where each person has a peculiar responsibility, the rest of the group will be looking to him for a specific

[16] Cf. Chapter 12, pp. 330-333.

contribution just as in a speech situation. In such a committee the tax attorney should be prepared to give expert opinion concerning the way the proposed plan involves the tax laws, the production manager should be prepared to present data concerning production aspects of the problem, and so on. Comparable solutions can be found in other groups by delegating certain responsibilities to the members. In many cases, however, delegation is not completely possible and the limitation remains.

Conflicting Value Systems May Limit Decision-Making Potential

This matter was touched upon in the examination of the potential value of discussion for the individual. Sharply differing value systems limit the decision-making potential of the group since the members may find it impossible to agree upon common goals. With reference to the material contained in Chapter 1, for example, a typical Communist who has accepted the concept of dialectical materialism would find it impossible to engage in a problem-solving discussion with us since the ethic we propose simply is not comprehensible to him.

The ideal type of discussion group is composed of heterogeneous participants in order to provide varied sets of experiences and knowledge in the discussion of the problem. This should not be confused with the limitation that may result from the differing *value* systems.

If the group discovers that the value systems of its members differ sharply, then two courses of action are left open. The first is to attempt to reconcile the differing value systems. Under this course, even a political conservative and a political liberal may be able to find a number of areas of common ground among their individual goals and proceed to solve the problems involved in reaching those goals.

The second alternative is to abandon attempts to solve the problem and try to learn as much as possible about the value systems that are involved. One need look no further than the "solutions" produced at Yalta, Teheran, and Potsdam to discover the futility of attempting to arrive at solutions before some genuinely common goals are agreed upon. In passing, note the differences between these results and the results obtained when the goal was the military defeat of a common enemy. Here the goal was sufficiently clear and desirable to make the problem-solving task comparatively simple despite the varying value systems.

Emergencies May Preclude the Use of Discussion

It is obvious that if a hostile air attack were in progress, there would be little opportunity to discuss possible alternatives. Decisions would have to be made in an authoritarian fashion. Time pressure in many other instances seems to preclude the effective use of discussion.

This, however, is one of the least severe limitations upon the discussion process. To begin with, many problems can be anticipated and most groups can preplan at least the skeleton of a policy which could guide them during an actual emergency. Second, most emergencies can be handled with some type of group action if proper communication channels are established in advance.[17] Finally, the executive, who finds himself in a situation where an emergency decision must be made, should make his decision and later voluntarily submit to the group for its examination the wisdom of both his decision and his assumption of an emergency situation. Such action will protect him from the unpleasant repercussions that may follow if the group begins to challenge his behavior.

Status Differences Among Participants
May Limit Effective Discussion

All have observed this limitation in operation. In teacher-student committees, teachers have frequently inhibited the potential contributions of the students; employer-employee conferences frequently fail for the same reason. The writers have observed many instances in which groups composed of military men of different ranks tended to restrict free discussion. The presence of the colonel frequently inhibited valuable contributions from the captains.

The causes of this limitation, of course, lie in the participants themselves and the degree to which they are affected by status differences. Some people seem to be particularly cowed in the presence of those of higher status, and some of those who possess

[17] See Chapter 8, pp. 210-211.

this higher status seem to be afraid it will be overlooked. If the subject for discussion bears any relationship to the status levels of the various participants, those of higher status should be more competent to discuss the subject. For this reason, the opinions of those of higher status might be assumed to "carry more weight." But it is not to this legitimate respect that the limitation refers; it refers to the participants' assumption that pronouncements of those with high status automatically obviate the necessity for further analysis and verification.

Relief from this limitation must generally come from those possessing the higher status. Having mentioned observing many discussions wherein the presence of the colonel inhibited the contributions of the captains, we should hasten to add that we have also observed many instances wherein the colonel was able to dispel a great deal of the reluctance to contribute by demonstrating that he was capable of drawing people out and of listening to, as well as contributing to, free and objective discussion. However, such behavior requires security, insight, skill, and tact that are too often lacking.[18]

Other Factors that Limit Effective Discussion

Majority Pressure May Limit Effective Discussion. Discussed at considerable length in the previous chapter, this limitation should already be clear. Remedying it is, in one sense, the purpose of this entire book. Only one further study which bears on the matter will be mentioned here. Maier and Solem found that an effective discussion leader can help a minority to make itself felt in the discussion.[19] A designated leader is not the only means of protecting the minority, but certainly *leadership* is needed. This whole matter

[18] When the person of higher status also possesses power to reward or punish those under him, the problem is further complicated. Kirk Porter, in his article, "Department Head or Chairman?" *American Association of University Professors Bulletin,* Vol. 47 (December, 1961), pp. 339-342, contends that a university or college department head can never be truly democratic because of the fact that he submits salary, promotion, and dismissal recommendations. This limitation can be modified, but it obviously cannot be eliminated.

[19] Norman R. F. Maier and Allen R. Solem, "The Contributions of a Discussion Leader to the Quality of Group Thinking: The Effective Use of Minority Opinions," in D. Cartwright and A. Zander, eds., *Group Dynamics: Research and Theory* (Evanston, Ill.: Row, Peterson, 1953), pp. 561-572.

will, of course, be discussed at considerably greater length in later chapters.

Discussion Requires Skill. This may be said to be a limitation of the discussion method because untrained individuals will not necessarily profit from participation in discussion to the same degree as those who are trained. We have all obesrved inept discussions. These frequently are conducted by people who assume that little, if any, training is required to make effective use of discussion. Such people assume that discussion is simply talking over a matter with others.

We would like to offer one illustration of this limitation and its remedy. In our contacts with the commissioners of the Federal Mediation and Conciliation Service, one factor seemed to appear with remarkable frequency. Successful labor-management negotiations, the commissioners contended, were primarily a function not only of the skill of the mediator but also of both labor and management representatives. They maintained that many of the bitter labor difficulties of the 1930's and 1940's were the result of poor ability in negotiation, particularly on the part of labor which was just beginning to find its place at the bargaining table. One commissioner summed it up very nicely when he said: "Today the location of a settlement within the area of 'equitable agreement' is not so much a function of the relative power of the contending parties as it is a function of the skill in negotiations which they possess." Bitter experiences have often forced people to become skillful in negotiation.

The Prior Commitments of Discussion Participants May Limit Effective Discussion. Diplomats at international conferences are limited by commitments to their own countries; legislators are limited by commitments to their constituents. Whenever the membership of the discussion group is composed of those who represent others not present, this limitation is operative. It arises not only from the fact that the prior commitment may blind the representative to alternative ways of looking at the problem; it also means he must return to the group that he represents and justify his behavior or secure further directions. Without the benefit of the discussions which have influenced their representative to modify the position they commended to him prior to the discussion, the members of the represented group may reject both the proposal and their representative. Thus, the union business agent who cannot "sell the membership" stands to lose both the contract and his job. Lord Chesterfield once observed that the first duty of a statesman is to be elected. Thus, a given discussion may be limited by the prior commitments of those representatives who wish to *stay elected* in order to accomplish their long-range objectives for the group they represent.

SUMMARY

This examination of the values and limitations of collaborative behavior in discussion groups set forth four major advantages: (1) groups are generally superior to individuals in problem solving; (2) groups are more likely to carry out a group decision or solution; (3) group activity provides an effective means of modifying individual attitudes and behavior; and (4) individuals gain personally from group participation.

The limitations of discussion must be recognized: It (1) consumes time; (2) spreads responsibility for quality contribution; (3) may be limited by diverse and conflicting value systems of participants; (4) is poorly suited for providing emergency decisions; (5) may be unable to cope with effects of status differences within the group; and (6) is sometimes subject to distortion from majority pressures, prior commitments of participants, or lack of understanding of and skill in the process.

Two things should be clear in this chapter. First, discussion is a valuable method of handling a variety of problems. This should be tempered by a realistic appraisal of the limitations as well as the advantages of discussion. The case presented here contains a preponderance of evidence and argument to show that the advantages of intelligent discussion far outweigh the disadvantages that may be present in many situations.

Second, effective discussion is no accident. Simply gathering people around the table won't do. Ideally, all, and certainly some, of the participants should understand the nature of discussion and be skillful in participation. Discussion is the most difficult form of communication which men use, and therefore merits serious study in order to realize its potential advantages. If these conclusions are acceptable and sound, read further as we attempt to examine those understandings and skills necessary for successful discussion.

EXERCISES

1. Attend a meeting of a student governing body, a city council, a local school board, or some similar legislative body. Prepare a four hundred to six hundred word analysis of the meeting based on the information in this chapter.

2. Using either radio or television, listen to two contrasting network or regional programs that employ discussion or some variations of discussion. Prepare a four-minute analysis of the two in which you comment on such elements as:

 a. Purpose.
 b. Content.
 c. Form.
 d. Value to both participants and listeners.
 e. Degree to which each approaches discussion as this chapter defines it.

Programs may be chosen from offerings such as "The Nation's Future," "Wisdom," "The Today Show," "Meet the Press," but need not be limited to this specific list. It may be well to choose one program designed primarily to convey information and another intended to explore values, feelings, or aesthetic reactions. Other possible contrasts are entertainment and controversy, or propaganda and education.

3. Organize a discussion group, or perhaps a number of groups, to consider such problems as the following:

 a. What are the potential uses for discussion in the classroom?
 b. To what extent do the principles of this chapter apply to labor-management relations?
 c. To what degree can a military staff use discussion?
 d. To what extent are the values and limitations stated in this chapter modified when the group members differ significantly in such matters as age, ability, experience, authority, or education?

4. Compile a list of realistic or practical problem situations where you feel discussion could be used profitably. Describe the situation in one paragraph and in a second paragraph justify your choice.

5. Compile a list of cases or situations you have observed where you believe discussion was improperly used or should not have been employed. For each case describe the situation in one paragraph and follow it with a one-paragraph explanation or analysis of the causes of failure.

6. What are the implications of the trend in our political life to substitute organizational for individual communications to our elected representatives? For example, the present tendency would be for the Isaac Walton League to write a congressman rather than to have individual fishermen communicate with that same congressman. Does this have any special relationship to the limitations of discussion?

7. Consider what specific policies or actions can be adopted by a discussion *leader* to minimize the limitations of discussion we have noted.

8. In view of the cultural and social forces to which the individual is subject, what potential exists for overcoming the limitations of discussions?

SELECTED READINGS

Barnlund, Dean C., and Haiman, Franklyn S., *The Dynamics of Discussion*. Boston, Houghton Mifflin, 1960, Chaps. 15 and 16.

Group Dynamics: Research and Theory, 2nd ed., D. Cartwright, and A. Zander, eds. Evanston, Ill., Row, Peterson, 1960, Part III.

Readings in Social Psychology, T. M. Newcomb, and E. L. Hartley, eds. New York, Holt, Rinehart and Winston, 1947, Part VII.

CHAPTER *3*

The Functions
of Discussion in Our Society

A rose by any other name . . .

Shakespeare

All interpersonal communication contains the opportunity for personal improvement, and discussion is especially rich in this possibility. It is the primary means whereby an individual relates himself to the others with whom he is concerned. Discussion is found in the family, in business and professional groups, in government, in neighborhood activity. In short, it is pervasive and important. We attempt to capture the essence of its function by saying that discussion is a *means of self-determination.*

The purpose of this chapter is to examine the nature of discussion in our society by identifying the purposes and circumstances of modern discussion. In the previous chapters we attempted to put value judgments upon our analyses of discussion and the individual participants. Here the emphasis is on description rather than on evaluation. Rather than describing how discussion *ought* to function, we describe how it *does* function today.

An examination of the functions of discussion in our society can best proceed by asking two questions: Why do people discuss? Under what circumstances do they discuss? The first question refers to the purposes, goals and objectives that may be inferred from observing a given discussion. The second question refers to the conditions under which the group meets. The last portion of this chapter is a brief glossary of discussion terms and descriptions which will be used in later portions of the book. Some of these terms may be new to the reader and others will be used in a different sense from that to which he is accustomed.

Before proceeding to an examination of the purposes and circumstances of discussion, here are two warnings. First, there is no magic in naming something. Giving something a name does not result in any physical change in the thing that is named, but often it affects our perception of the thing or the idea. Assigning a name can serve a useful function if we understand the basis for the classification and if that classification helps make meaningful distinctions in the way in which we behave.

The second warning is that the classifications of purposes and circumstances are not mutually exclusive; nor does a given discussion usually have only one purpose, but several. The reason for the classification is to enable the observer to discover the central tendencies of the discussion in order to judge the bases for analysis and treatment of the discussion process.

DISCUSSION PURPOSES

A convenient way of describing purposes for discussion is to group them according to those which are essentially *personal* and those which are essentially *task*.[1] Such a division is neither exhaustive nor mutually exclusive but it provides a helpful way of viewing the process. Understanding this, *personal* purposes are to be considered as those having their origins primarily within the individual and relating most directly to the satisfaction of ego-centered needs or drives. In contrast, *task* purposes are those of a more objective and impersonal character. They tend to be external in origin (although they may come to have a large personal component) and relate to the substance of the discussion.

[1] In Chapter 9 we will discuss this distinction in greater detail since it forms the basis for analyzing the forces that operate upon a discussion group. In order to avoid duplication, we have refrained from introducing all of the concepts of Chapter 9 at this point. The distinction we make here is sufficiently precise for examining discussion purposes, but will be amended in Chapter 9.

Personal Purposes

1. Social. Sometimes people engage in group discussion for what are primarily social purposes. Most discussions over coffee, back-fence exchanges, office analyses of baseball, party talk, and the like are examples of discussions with primarily social purposes. Individual goals in such discussions range from those of whiling the time away as pleasantly as possible to deliberate attempts to strengthen interpersonal relationships, promote status, and secure good will. Many of the social aspects of business relationships, with the attendant expense account and executive fringe benefits, are intended to create situations which allow for social discussion.

Beware of the tendency to sneer at this type of discussion by labeling it as "the production of socially acceptable noises" or by confining the examination of it to some aspect of etiquette. The substance of most social discussions is of little moment, but it is equally true that social discussion is often the prelude to considera-tions of more significant subjects. The establishment of a climate which is conducive to effective decision making is not an unimpor-tant objective. Further, social discussion which has no ulterior motive is still an important means of attaining that significant goal of man which we examined in Chapter 1—the establishment of meaningful relationships with others.[2]

The concern with social discussion in this book is primarily with its use as a part of, or prelude to, discussions which include task-oriented purposes. However, much that is said of establishing favorable group climate and interpersonal relations could apply easily to discussions whose primary or sole objective is social.

2. Cathartic. Closely related to social discussion is cathartic discus-sion, the purpose of which is to allow the individual an opportunity to relieve his tensions, fears, gripes, apprehensions, and aspirations in a group. Bull sessions or counseling interviews are examples of such discussions. Cathartic discussions differ from social discussions in that they exist primarily to deal with personal rather than *inter*-personal problems. Cathartic discussions may lead to nothing more than an expression of personal feelings, but often, like social dis-

[2] Bronislaw Malinowski gave the name *phatic communion* to this form of communication.

ussions, they are a prelude to personal or collaborative problem solving.

Care must be taken not to dismiss cathartic discussion lightly either. The invitation to "get it off your chest" is one which most people need and often seek. Surely it is preferable for people to talk out their grievances than to fight them out, and, frequently, the very airing of a grievance is sufficient to remove the cause.[3] For example, marriage counselors report that many a marriage has come apart because the husband and wife could not find a way to let one another know how they felt or what was troubling them. When they were able to talk about the problems, perhaps aided by some counselor, they found a basis for understanding that made further problem solving either easier or unnecessary.

Since the solving of a problem is often preceded by cathartic discussion, it is of more direct concern than social discussion. Certainly the skills and attitudes necessary to establish favorable circumstances for useful cathartic discussion are an important part of the skills and attitudes necessary for most effective problem solving.

3. *Therapeutic.* As the examination of cathartic discussion might suggest, it is often difficult to distinguish between cathartic and therapeutic discussions. The aim of therapeutic discussion is to help people alter their attitudes, feelings, or behavior about some aspect of their personal life and therapeutic discussion thus comes under the headings of psychotherapy, counseling or psychiatric treatment. Stimulated by the work of Carl Rogers and others, group therapy has become a sizable field for study and practice. This book does not pretend to deal directly with this aspect of discussion, though much of what it has to say is related to group therapy, of course.[4]

4. *Learning.* Certainly one of the most important reasons for par-

[3] Wendell Johnson went so far as to contend that completely verbalizing one's problem is sufficient to solve it. See Wendell Johnson, *People in Quandaries* (New York: Harper & Row, 1946).

[4] For further insights into group therapy, the reader may consult one or more of these sources: Carl R. Rogers, *Client-Centered Therapy* (Boston: Houghton Mifflin, 1951). Margaret E. Bennett, *Guidance in Groups: A Resource Book for Teachers, Counselors, and Administrators* (New York: McGraw-Hill, 1955). R. G. Hinkley and L. Hermann, *Group Treatment in Psychotherapy* (Minneapolis: Univ. of Minnesota, 1951). F. B. Powdermaker and J. D. Frank, *Group Psychotherapy* (Cambridge: Harvard Univ., 1953).

ticipating in discussion is the opportunity for learning. Thousands of classes employ discussion as a primary tool of learning. Other examples of the use of learning discussion include "Great Books" discussion groups, professional seminars, Bible study classes and radio-TV roundtables. Obviously, learning discussion is an important part of our communicative efforts. Its value was briefly defended in Chapter 2 and in most of the book the examination of discussion principles will apply with equal force to learning discussions and to problem-solving discussions.

Before moving to the next group of discussion purposes, there is an important distinction to be made between two types of learning discussion. In most of the discussion types referred to above, the learning discussion was for the benefit of those participating in the discussion. These may be called *private* discussions. Often, however, a discussion is carried on for the benefit of observers. Such learning discussions may be called *public* discussions. Obviously, almost all radio-TV discussions and those discussions carried on in the presence of an audience should be classified as public. The difference between the two types is stressed because of the confusion that has arisen from earlier literature that studied discussion largely as public discussion and attempted to extrapolate from public discussion the principles and skills necessary for private discussion. Public discussion should be largely evaluated as any public speech, but private discussion normally is evaluated by sharply different standards.

Task Purposes

1. Decision Making. One of the most important and pervasive purposes for discussion is that of decision making. Almost every enterprise that requires collaborative effort also utilizes collaborative decision making to some degree, and it is unnecessary to detail examples here. The prevalence of this form of discussion has already been noted in the first chapter and defended in the second, so little need be added at this point save to note that the bulk of this book deals with decision-making discussion.

2. Action. Frequently one group makes the decision and other groups are empowered to translate that decision into action. When preparing for a college homecoming, for example, the main committee usually decides upon the theme and the major events to be held; a dance or other committee must secure the band, the decorations, and the refreshments. Sometimes the action group has rather broad interpretative power, sometimes only executive power. In the latter case, the group's task is primarily to round up the people and resources necessary for the job and to persuade, or order, people to assume the necessary responsibility. It is often difficult to distinguish the action group from the decision-making group, but the distinction is made between decision-making and action groups for the same reason that the distinction between legislative and executive functions was made in the previous chapter. Attention to this principle can have much effect upon both efficiency and morale.

3. Appraisal. Some groups are organized primarily for the purpose of examining a situation, for example, fact-finding boards, committees of inquiry, and juries. Appraisal may either take place *before the fact,* in which case it is usually a prelude to policy formation, or *after the fact,* in which case it is usually intended to set a value judgment upon something that has happened.

One of the best-known examples of the appraisal group is the congressional investigating committees. These committees are often creatures of a parent committee and have been assigned the task of collecting information on some particular subject to form the basis for legislative action. Often such groups have gone well beyond the function of investigation and have arrogated to themselves the functions of lawgiver, prosecutor, judge, and jury, but the majority have been effective instruments for securing necessary information on which to base helpful legislation.

An appraisal group combines some of the characteristics of both the decision-making and the action groups. Appraisal groups often recommend action to be taken or decisions to be made as a result of their investigations, but the difference lies in the fact that the appraisal group is seldom directly responsible for the decision. For example, a fact finding commission may be called in to investigate a labor-management dispute. This group may recommend a solution to the dispute, but it is not in the same economic or psychological position as the labor-management committee that has been wrestling with the problem. The same distinction exists between a management consultant and a manager.

As a result of this distinction, the criteria for effective speaking in the decision-making or action groups are sharply different from the criteria for effective speaking in appraisal groups.[5] This is not the place to examine these criteria since much of what follows does just that. But here the basis for the distinction is made clear.

4. Advisory. The last purpose which we shall examine is that of the advisory group which performs most of the functions of the decision-making or the action group, but does not have the power to make a decision. The advisory group also differs from the appraisal group in that the advisory group is not so much concerned with investigation and attack or defense as it is with policy making.

This type of discussion group is very prevalent and has received far too little attention in discussion literature. Almost all military staff meetings, many business and professional committees, and many student and faculty committees perceive themselves and are, in turn, perceived as essentially advisory groups. Such a group may operate as if it had the power to decide and may assume that its recommendations carry great weight. It is important, however, for advisory groups to remember that someone other than the members of the group holds the decision-making power and bears the responsibility. The military commander calls his staff together to discuss a problem of logistics, for example. The group proceeds as if it were going to make a decision on the matter; they gather data, examine the nature of the problem, create possible solutions, debate the merits of the solutions, *but* the commander decides which, if any, of the solutions to accept.

This type of group is distinguished from the other three types of task-oriented groups because of the peculiar forces that operate upon its members. They are usually affected by the decision; they have an opportunity to speak their minds about the problem, assuming that the chief tolerates free speech; but they cannot decide.

---

[5] Aristotle recognized this matter clearly when he sharply differentiated between the nature of the audience receiving a deliberative (advice-giving) speech and the audience receiving a forensic (attack or defense) speech. That is, audiences receiving deliberative speeches are similar to decision-making or action groups in that they have to make decisions and live with them, while juries, for example, have to make decisions, but they do not have to live with them. Lane Cooper, *The Rhetoric of Aristotle* (New York: Appleton-Century-Crofts, 1932). Note particularly, Book I.

This is not necessarily a disadvantage since the responsibility for a decision frequently cannot be rightfully shared, but it certainly creates problems that the chief and members can not ignore. A clever advisory group can often have things largely its own way, but this must be accomplished by its members' persuasion or subterfuge, or both, rather than as a matter of their right.

DISCUSSION CIRCUMSTANCES

Let us turn now to the problem of classifying discussion groups according to the circumstances which brought them together. In the previous classifications several purposes often operated in a given group. In this set of classifications there is less overlapping of circumstances, however a group which begins under one set of circumstances often continues or develops under a different set of circumstances.

Three kinds of circumstances operate to bring together the members of a discussion group. Groups form under (1) *casual* circumstances, (2) as a result of *voluntary association,* or (3) as a result of some *organizational requirement.* Let us examine each type in turn.

Casual Circumstances

The group formed under casual circumstances is virtually self-evident and requires little elaboration. A group can be called *casual* if its meeting is primarily the result of chance and if the group is not organized or self-perpetuating. Clearly, the *purpose* of such a group may be one or a combination of any of the above purposes. During the course of a day, for example, a man may meet a couple of his associates and ask them to give him their reactions to an article he is writing, and an advisory group exists; later he might have coffee with some other friends and discuss baseball, and a social group exists; still later, he might join other colleagues in contending that a given organizational requirement ought to be changed, and a cathartic group exists; that cathartic group might turn into an appraisal group, or, if they possessed the power, into a decision-making or action group. Such examples can obviously be multiplied, and you may wish to note the number of casual groups you join during the course of a normal day.

Voluntary Association

An organized group whose members enlisted of their own voli-
tion for one or more of the purposes listed above would be one of
the voluntary association type. This type of group differs from the
casual group in that the meeting has been designed and a structure
and identity exist. Clearly, a casual group can grow into a voluntary
association group, and the point at which it changes character may
be quite hazy; but the main criteria should be clear.

Dozens of examples of this kind of group can be offered, of
which churches, service clubs, book study clubs and dance clubs
are a few. Sometimes membership in such organizations borders
on the mandatory for individuals seeking certain kinds of status
within a community. However, in the strictest sense, association in
such a group is voluntary.

Organizational Requirement

Within any organization, whether voluntary, a place of employment,
or whatever the circumstances of initial membership, one usually
finds a number of groups which exist to maintain and further the
objectives of the larger organization. Such subgroups exist as a
result of organizational requirement and will be called *organizational* groups.

Reasons for Membership. An individual may find himself a member
of such a discussion group for one or both of two reasons. The subgroup may exist as a part of the larger organization, its membership
resulting from the *dictates of the organization.* On the other hand,
the individual may form a group within a larger structure or enlist
in an existing one because he believes that his best interests demand
it. We would call such membership the result of *personal dictates.*

Let us consider some examples. A professor of history at a
university usually finds himself a member of the history department
whether or not he wishes it. Within his department he may be appointed, as a dictate of the organization, to a variety of committees
such as a curriculum committee. However, he may offer to make
himself a candidate for the university budget committee because
of the dictates of his own conscience. We are persuaded that most
of the meaningful memberships of discussion groups result from

the dictates of conscience rather than the dictates of the organization. Many people hold nominal membership in literally dozens of groups, but they hold genuinely active membership in fewer, largely as a result of the requirements the individuals levy upon themselves.

More important here than the reasons for an individual's membership in an organizational group is the relationship that the discussion group bears to the rest of the world. Most voluntary and casual groups exist in a kind of formal organizational vacuum. That is, they have little responsibility for adapting to requirements levied by a larger organization. The amount of external adaptation required varies, of course, with different groups, but generally most voluntary and casual groups do not approach the amount of external adaptation required of an organizational group. External requirements levied upon the organizational group compose a distinctly different set of forces operating upon the members from the forces operating upon those of voluntary and casual groups.

Differences Between Voluntary and Organizational Groups. The members of a discussion class would be considered as a voluntary group. If they set themselves the task of discussing some problem concerning the United Nations, their responsibilities to the external world *for the substance* of their decision are very limited. True, they have to satisfy their instructor that they are proceeding according to accepted principles of discussion, and if they attempt to represent delegates of several countries, they can approximate something of the feeling of external responsibility. Contrast, then, the forces operating upon this group with those operating upon the actual Security Council of the United Nations. Here, the members have responsibilities both to the world community and to their respective governments. They cannot act as they might wish.

Voluntary groups tend to focus more upon personal goals while organizational groups tend to focus more upon task purposes, but, confining ourselves to task purposes, here is one more example of the differences. A service club deciding upon a project is not subject to the same external forces as is the sales department of a corporation when deciding upon a new sales campaign.

Much of the discussion group research has utilized voluntary groups as subjects, probably because it is usually easier to form voluntary groups experimentally than to create organizational groups for experimental purposes. As a result, much of the theoretical data about discussion groups has not been fully applicable to organizational groups. This book attempts to account for the different forces that operate upon organizational groups, particularly as these forces affect the problems of leadership.

A GLOSSARY OF DISCUSSION FORMS

In the literature of discussion there occur a variety of terms identifying discussion forms that the student should know. This section attempts to define some of the more common terms and concepts.

Panel

A panel discussion is usually a public discussion in which the members examine some problem or issue under normal discussion give and take. Anywhere from three to twelve members may be found on a panel, but the ideal number for coherent discussion is usually about five.

Symposium

A symposium resembles a panel in that it is a public discussion with approximately the same number of participants, but, rather than discussing back and forth, the members give prepared speeches on different phases of the question. Following the speeches, the members may operate for a time as a panel, or they may open the discussion for questions and comments from the audience.

Forum

This word formerly designated the public place or market place of a city. Since the Romans used such a place to hold open discussions on questions of public concern, the term has come to refer to audience participation in discussion. This usually provides a period when members of the audience may ask questions of speakers or make observations on the issues. When describing a program, the word *forum* is usually hyphenated with the word describing the speaking which gives rise to the audience participation, for example, *lecture-forum, panel-forum, symposium-forum.*

Colloquy

The colloquy is an arrangement similar to a panel which utilizes a number of audience "representatives" on the same platform with a number of "experts." These audience representatives question or raise issues with the experts. This method is often used when one or more outside experts are brought into some organization. In order to sharpen the focus of the contribution that such experts make, the colloquy proceeds at once to the questioning of the experts rather than allowing the experts to give prepared speeches that may or may not deal directly with the particular problems of concern to the audience.

The *interview* program that is quite popular on radio and TV embodies most of the principles of the colloquy. The interlocutor takes the position of asking questions and making observations which he feels the members of his audience would like to ask if they had the opportunity.

Debate

A debate is frequently referred to as a form of discussion and thus should be mentioned here. By arranging speakers on opposite sides of a proposition, a debate provides an organized method of illuminating a subject or of persuading an audience. Sometimes, as in the case of the 1960 Presidential Debates, the speakers proceed without benefit of a stated proposition, usually producing something that can more rightly be called a symposium. When controversy dominates a discussion, some people say the discussion has turned into a debate. However, most good discussions generate considerable controversy, so we do not wish to call controversy the antithesis of discussion.

A typical debate will have one or two speakers on a side. Alternating speeches of a set length will be given for and against the proposition, with the speakers favoring the proposition having the right to speak both first and last.[6]

[6] For a good distinction between discussion and debate see Henry Lee Ewbank and J. Jeffery Auer, *Discussion and Debate: Tools of a Democracy* (New York: Appleton-Century-Crofts, 1951).

Committee

The term committee may refer to any group organized or appointed to accomplish some given task. It often refers to a group created by some legislative body. This kind of committee has the task of investigating problem areas and producing motions which can be examined by the parent body. A legislative committee is distinguished from the legislative body which uses parliamentary rules in that the committee can investigate a problem without having before it a motion, while the legislative body is restricted to debating motions. If the parent body wishes to investigate and deliberate without a motion, it must resolve itself into a *committee of the whole*.

Case Discussion

The case method of study has gained considerable popularity over the past years.[7] Applicable to a wide range of problems, it consists of presenting a discussion group with a description of a situation which the members are first to examine and then to suggest procedures for handling. Sometimes the group simply examines or evaluates the behavior of someone in the situation. You will note a number of cases for discussion at the ends of chapters in this book.

Buzz Group

A convenient method of providing for a large number of people to participate in discussion is the buzz group technique. It consists of: breaking up a larger group into subgroups of approximately six members each; giving each subgroup some set time for discussion, usually five or ten minutes; and then having a representative from each subgroup report back to the larger group. This method is often used following a lecture, panel, symposium, or the like, as a means of generating questions from the audience while giving everyone a chance to participate in the formulation of these questions. It is managed, usually, by a chairman who designates the composition of the several groups, indicates the matter they are to consider, and tells them how they are to make known the results of their discussion. Sometimes counting off or similar techniques are used to ensure

[7] The Harvard Business School has been particularly instrumental in popularizing this method of learning. It has also become popular in some types of adult education.

heterogeneity of subgroups. Sometimes the matters for discussion are predetermined and distributed to each of the subgroups.

Role Playing

A very effective method of discussion training involves role playing. It consists simply of having the discussants assume characters other than their own during the discussion. Such roles may be worked out in advance in order to illustrate some particular problem, or the roles may be created by the discussants on the spur of the moment in order to examine and experience some aspect of interpersonal relationships. We leave the examination of the techniques of effective role playing for a more detailed consideration in Chapter 11.

EXERCISES

1. Keep a record of the nature and length of all the discussions in which you engage for a full week. What subjects or topics were discussed? How would you classify the discussions as to purpose? Do many subjects reappear in discussions having different purposes? Do you find any pattern of relationship between topics and purposes?

2. Having classified your discussions in Exercise 1, try to view these through the eyes of the other participants. Do you feel that any of these persons would assign different purposes to some of the discussions from those you assign? If you find differences, how would you account for them? If possible, check with some of the participants to see how they viewed the discussion.

3. Learning is considered an important discussion purpose. Consider the similarities and differences between the examples given in this chapter and the conduct of the conventional classroom. Organize a discussion group to explore the potentials and problems of using discussion as a teaching method.

4. In the daily conduct of business, education, government, social organizations, and related aspects of human affairs, many people engage in many discussions. How useful do you believe it would be if these groups understood and applied the distinctions made between discussion purposes? Compare the possible values of such understandings in relation to personal and to task purposes.

5. Compare and contrast the orientation, procedures, and problems of representative decision-making groups with those of similar advisory groups. Are there any particular misconceptions or distortions of perception to which advisory groups may fall victim? If so, how may such errors be avoided?

SELECTED READINGS

Barnlund, Dean C., and Haiman, Franklyn S., *The Dynamics of Discussion.* Boston, Houghton Mifflin, 1960, Chap. 2.

Cortright, Rupert L., and Hinds, George L., *Creative Discussion.* New York, Macmillan, 1959, Chap. 2.

Garland, J. V., *Discussion Methods: Explained and Illustrated.* New York, Wilson, 1951.

PART II

Thinking Together

CHAPTER 4

Problem Solving:
The Pattern of Thought

"I don't think they play at all fairly," Alice began, in a rather complaining tone, "and they all quarrel so dreadfully one can't hear oneself speak—and they don't seem to have any rules in particular; at least, if there are, nobody attends to them—and you've no idea how confusing it is all the things being alive; ..."

Lewis Carroll*

THE NATURE OF THINKING

This chapter and this unit deal with a subject which has fascinated man for centuries—the human mind. We have no idea how many volumes have been written about the nature of thinking, and it would be presumptuous for us to suggest that our analysis in these three chapters could adequately delineate the scope of what is known or conjectured about thought. Our aim is to organize and present the essentials so that they are useable in actual discussions. The reader who wishes to explore this subject further will find at the end of each of the chapters a list of readings which will serve as a starting point for a rewarding investigation.[1]

---

* *Alice's Adventures in Wonderland.*
[1] Particularly fascinating are some of the recent attempts by psychologists

A book about discussion should include a section on thinking. Some people believe that thinking is largely an individual matter and that its adaptation to group discussion should be treated in connection with such matters as group structure or communication. There are reasons for disagreeing with this position. It is disturbing to note the number of people who do not seem to apply the same rigorous standards to their thinking in discussion groups as they do in other situations. Such people may hold themselves to strict standards in a research project, an essay, or a speech, but may exhibit the most casual reasoning in a discussion. As pointed out in Chapter 2, the process of thinking seems to be affected by participation in discussion. From the early social facilitation experiments of F. H. Allport to present studies of conforming and deviate behavior, evidence for this has been accumulating. Finally, the process of thinking is essentially a social one. This point deserves further elaboration.

The best statement of this point of view is found in the works of George H. Mead.[2] In the introduction to *Mind, Self, and Society*, Charles W. Morris puts Mead's position succinctly:

Mind is the presence in behavior of significant symbols. It is the internalization within the individual of the social process of communication in which meaning emerges. It is the ability to indicate to one's self the response (and implicated objects) that one's gesture indicates to others, and to control the response itself in these terms. . . . Instead of beginning with individual minds and working out to society, Mead starts with an objective social process and works inward through the importation of the social process of communication into the individual by the medium of the vocal gesture. The individual has then taken the social act into himself. Mind remains social; even in the inner forum so developed, thought goes on by one's assuming the roles of others and controlling one's behavior in terms of such role-taking. Since the isolation of the physical thing is for Mead dependent upon the ability to take the role of the other, and since thought about such objects involves taking their roles, even the scien-

---

to study thinking processes in laboratory settings. In addition to the readings mentioned, an imposing research project has been undertaken at the University of Colorado by Kenneth Hammond and his associates dealing with inferential behavior in a probabilistic environment. It is our hope that some of this research may have been published by the time this book is printed.

[2] George H. Mead, *Mind, Self and Society* (Chicago: Univ. of Chicago Press, 1934). Copyright 1934 by the University of Chicago.

tist's reflection about physical nature is a social process, though the objects thought about are no longer social. [3]

We do not argue that thinking takes place only in groups or even that the *best* thinking takes place in groups. Much of what is productive, valuable, and rewarding is a product of solitary work. The point here is threefold: (1) it is difficult to discuss the materials in the rest of the book without reference to the nature of thinking; (2) thinking is better understood as an interactive process, both between individuals and between individuals and the objective world; and (3) certainly, effective groups require effective thinking. Most of the advice given in these three chapters will apply equally to individuals working alone or to groups of individuals thinking together, and, as indicated earlier, much of what has been written about thinking, apart from group considerations, will enrich the understanding and skill of the reader who wishes to pursue the subject beyond the bounds of these three chapters.

THE NATURE OF PROBLEM SOLVING

Thinking and pseudo-thinking may be described and classified in a variety of ways. Cognition is interpreted by psychologists as including sensation, perception, inference, judgment and discrimination. The concern here is with that form of thinking which may be called problem solving, not because it exhausts the area of cognition, but because it is the functional approach to a study of thinking.

A Conception of Problem Solving

John Dewey made problem solving virtually synonymous with thinking.[4] Here the concern is not particularly with whether or not problem solving can or should be equated with thinking, but with examining the nature of problem solving itself. Following Dewey's analysis, we can set forth the following characteristics of problem solving: [5]

[3] Charles W. Morris, "Introduction," in *ibid.*, p. xxii.
[4] See particularly John Dewey, *How We Think* (Boston: Heath, 1933).
[5] Dewey went so far as to insist that thinking involved a transaction between the individual and the environment which invariably resulted in a changed environment. This concept is probably a bit difficult to sustain. For a further examination of Dewey's position, see the *University of Colorado*

1. *Problem-Solving Thinking Involves Forming Connections Between Ideas.* That form of "thinking" which involves only a kind of kaleidoscopic assortment of ideas and associations is not problem-solving thinking. Apparently, the majority of our mental time is occupied with some form of activity which is little more than being aware of sensations and notions with no attempt to form patterns. Walking down a street, we notice the sights, sounds, and smells, and perhaps we are pleased or disturbed by them, but we do not consider such awareness *thinking.*

2. *Problem-Solving Thinking Aims at a Conclusion.* That is, it is purposeful. During the walk just mentioned, we might notice that a particular smell of the trees reminds us of some place where we used to live and we might form mental images of the place and our reactions to it. We thus have the connection between ideas, but our thinking is not aimed at any conclusion. Most social and cathartic discussions, for example, may involve thinking which forms connections between ideas, but this thinking usually does not aim at a conclusion. On the other hand, most of the other types of discussion groups will seek conclusions as a part of their thinking.

3. *Problem-Solving Thinking Presupposes a Perceived Disequilibrium.* Suppose a man gets into his car some morning in order to drive to work. When he turns the key, he discovers that the car refuses to respond and his normal routine has suffered a jolt. What does he do? He decides that he must either get the car working again or find some other means of getting to. He perhaps tries the former, and a check of his watch confirms his suspicion that he hasn't the time to call the garage and have them send someone out to fix the car. He checks under the hood to see if he can spot the source of trouble, but his mechanical skills are not equal to the task. How else might he get to work? The bus has just gone; he cannot take the time to call a taxi; and it will obviously take too much time and energy to walk. However, some of his neighbors work where he does and others drive nearby. He decides to walk

Studies: Series in Philosophy, No. 2 (Boulder, Colorado: Univ. of Colorado, August, 1961). Note particularly the article by Paul Henle, "Dewey's Views on Truth and Verification."

to the intersection and hope that a cooperative neighbor will drive by. When one does, and he gets a ride, his problem is solved and the disequilibrium has been removed.

The important point in the previous example is that the problem-solving process had to be triggered by some discrepancy between desire and capacity. Had the car started and functioned normally, the man would have had no problem and consequently would have done no problem-solving thinking.

The Elements of a Problem

Let us shift our attention from the characteristics of problem-solving thinking to the problem itself. In order to understand problem solving, there must be a more precise understanding of what is involved in that disequilibrium which we mentioned a moment ago. A problem has three elements which must all be present before it can be a problem.[6] As will be evident in a moment, each irritation or annoyance which may be encountered is not necessarily a problem.

1. *Goal.* A goal is any condition which an individual perceives will remove the effects of an undesirable situation. Clearly, if anyone is content with the situation in which he finds himself, he will have no problem. But if he envisions some condition different from the present one, the first element of a problem is present. The goal may be simply one of escaping from a given situation, or it may be one of attaining some specific condition or thing which the individual wants. A goal may be a genuine gain to the individual seeking it, or it may prove to be no more satisfying than the present situation. *Good* problem solving, therefore, will not treat goal selection casually. Later in this chapter goal selection will be discussed more carefully.

Before proceeding further, there is need for a clear distinction between motives, drives, needs, on the one hand, and goals, objectives, desired ends, on the other. Much of the literature on this subject tends to confuse the two. Perhaps one reason for the confusion is that the need or drive is frequently stated *in terms of the goal.* Barnard speaks directly to this point of confusion:

[6] For this analysis we are indebted to research done by John W. Keltner. The results of his research and further sources are indicated in his book, *Group Discussion Processes* (New York: Longmans, Green, 1957).

Motives are usually described in terms of the end sought. If the action of a man is to obtain an apple, we say the motive of the action is to obtain an apple. This is misleading. The motive is rather the satisfaction [reduction] of the "tension" resulting from various forces; and often we recognize this. . . . In most cases the end sought or the action taken represents motives of composite origin—social and physiological. This cannot be determined, and is usually unknown to the person whose action is involved. [7]

Similarly, when writers speak of the "need for belonging," they are stating an assumed social need arising from a multiplicity of factors in terms of the goal, a condition involving certain relationships with other individuals. The drive or tension, however, is not the same thing as the goal being sought.

2. *Status Quo.* The status quo is the situation in which an individual finds himself in relation to his goal. Determining the status quo involves asking the question, Where am I in relation to the goal? How far must I go? One can think of dozens of examples of groups whose sole task is to determine the status quo of a problem, for example, auditing committees, fact-finding committees, inquiry groups. An individual advised to take stock of himself is being told to determine precisely his status quo.

First comes the listing of the resources available for use. What ideas, energies, relationships, materials, people and potentials can be commanded, arranged, energized to make movement toward the goal possible? Second comes the task of evaluating these actual and potential resources, both alone and in combination, to determine their value in relation to goal attainment. In short, the individual must answer two questions: What are my resources? Are they appropriate for the task? Clearly, if the former are nonexistent or undiscovered, the goal is unattainable.

Two of the factors which determine the degree of tension or disequilibrium are the degree to which a given situation is important to an individual or group and the discrepancy between the goal and the status quo. An analysis of this sort leads to a study of motivation which, if complete, would be beyond the scope of this book.

[7] Chester I. Barnard, *The Functions of the Executive* (Cambridge, Mass.: Harvard Univ., 1938), p. 18.

Though aspects of motivation are dealt with in various portions of the book, for now a mention of the sources of the concept should be sufficient.

3. *Obstacles.* An obstacle is any condition or thing which prevents or hinders an individual from reaching his goal. Even though there may be a discrepancy between the goal and the status quo, there may be no problem if no particular effort or ingenuity is required to reach the goal. A man driving to work does not recognize the existence of a problem unless his car breaks down and he is prevented from reaching his goal. A source of constant amazement is the number of "problems" that disappear when the goal and the status quo have been clearly identified. Of course when this happens, the individual has discovered one of two things: either his goal was different from what he had imagined it to be or he was closer to his goal than he had imagined.

Once the goal(s), the status quo, and the obstacle(s) have been identified, a further process of evaluation and integration begins. The problem solver has two fundamental courses of action open to him. First, he may try to find some way of overcoming or circumventing the obstacle in order to reach the goal. If he can find no way to get around the obstacle, or if all ways are too expensive, involved, or time-consuming to make it worthwhile, he must change the goal. Of course, he may keep the goal and postpone resolution of the problem until he has mustered sufficient resources but that is essentially changing the goal since it has been changed from an immediate matter to a long-range one. Suppose that a high school graduate wishes to go to college in September (goal) and finds that he is qualified in all respects except that his financial resources are far from what will be required (status quo). His obstacles are obviously those circumstances preventing his acquisition of the necessary funds. He casts about for various means of raising the money (scholarships, loans, and part-time jobs) and discovers that he will not be able to manage. He may then decide to work for a year or two to save up enough money to make up the difference. He has changed his goal slightly by making it read *college in two years* and has devised a potential means of achieving that goal. The steps whereby this problem was solved constitute the structure of problem solving to which we now turn.

62# 64

THINKING TOGETHER

The Structure of Problem Solving

As we proceed to examine the structure of problem solving, let us recognize that verbalizing and doing have somewhat different dimensions. Many of the concepts appear to be easily understood. Almost all students will be able to talk and write about them clearly and correctly. But we have heard sincere and able men and women from many different occupations and backgrounds, who clearly understood and believed in the concepts, yet were *incapable of applying them in actual discussion.* That is, actually applying the concepts is often a painful discipline.

There are essentially two phases to the structure of problem solving.[8] They are the *problem description* phase and the *problem solution* phase. Within each phase are a series of three steps whose sequence as well as content are important.[9] The three steps in the problem description phase are identified as *D-1, D-2, D-3;* the steps in the problem solution phase as *S-4, S-5,* and *S-6.* Now let us discuss the steps and then turn attention to the critical junctures within the sequence.

D-1. Problem Formulation. In this initial stage the discussants should attempt to identify the elements of the problem confronting them. Having described the elements of a problem above, further elaboration is not needed. Note, however, that the process of identifying the elements of the problem usually involves defining critical terms as the problem is developed.

D-2. Problem Analysis. At this point the goals, status quo, and obstacles must be examined to determine the requirements of any proposed solution. Several aspects of this step are worthy of note.

Most problems have a variety of goals and a variety of obstacles. Discussants must take special pains to apply the most rigorous standards of reasoning and treatment of evidence to determine exactly what must be solved. Since evidence and reasoning are

---

[8] Several different names are used to describe this process. Reflective thinking, the scientific method, pragmatism, and extensional thinking are all names used in the literature. For our purposes they all mean about the same thing.
[9] This pattern is essentially the same as Keltner's, *op. cit.* Others specify very similar series of steps.

examined in the next two chapters, it is sufficient to insert the caution that evaluating a solution is difficult if the requirements of the solution are hazy. For example, solutions to the problem of economic inflation are considerably hampered by lack of understanding of and agreement concerning the causes of inflation and the relative effects of such alleged obstacles as wage increases, price increases, market expansion.

A more immediate, and sometimes personal, situation confronts the college student about to "flunk out." The goal is obvious: higher grades and now! The status quo is also simply determined—the current grade average he just received from the dean's office. Careless problem solving may proceed by casually assuming that the obstacle has been insufficient study. Solution? Study more. But in fact, the obstacle may be the student's lack of capacity for abstract thinking and a solution may be difficult or impossible. Or the obstacle may be study *methods* instead of study *time,* and a solution may involve a critical examination of how time is spent.

One should be careful to remember that the status quo, the obstacles, and even the goal are seldom fixed; they are often changing. When examining the status quo, for example, one must not only note where he is in relation to his goal, but he must also estimate where he will be if no significant change is made. When examining the obstacles, he must not only be aware of the existence of the obstacle and its immediate effect, but he must determine whether or not it will continue in its present stage if nothing is done. The same sort of analysis is required for the goal. Let us illustrate each of these in turn.

In discussions of the problem of racial integration, disputes usually arise between "liberals" and "moderates" or "conservatives." "Liberals" insist that, unless certain measures are taken, there will be no perceptible improvement in the problem. "Moderates" or "conservatives," on the other hand, usually insist that the normal evolution of the status quo will remove the problem in due time without "revolutionary" changes. Similarly, when discussing problems of military preparedness, the relative strength of the United States *vis-a-vis* the Soviet Union cannot be regarded as static. Hundreds of people are employed in several intelligence agencies in the military and elsewhere to study the constantly changing threat posed by the Soviet Union and other nations. When the first Sputnik was launched, most Americans were chagrined and dismayed to discover that American supremacy had been severely challenged. The evidence of Russia's development had been available, but it received little publicity and most Americans preferred to ignore it.

Parents are familiar with the numerous "phases" through which children are supposed to pass as they grow and mature. In the course of a child's development many obstacles to desirable behavior are noted. The wise parent seeks to discover which obstacles will disappear in time, which need corrective action, and which need some modification in order to lay the groundwork for appropriate further development.

Finally, consider the changing nature of the goal. At first glance it seems to be static since it is set by the discussants and is not beyond their control. However, the goal must be considered as dynamic both because of changing obstacles and status quo *and* because of changing desires of the problem solver(s). Consider the case of a couple deciding what kind of house to buy. They must include in their thinking anticipated family growth, changes in the neighborhood, and changes in the economic situation. They must also consider changes in their own desires which are predictable on the basis of others' experience.

D-3. Problem Reformulation (if necessary). If the analysis in steps *D-1* and *D-2* indicates a need to rearrange the nature of the problem to be solved, this is the step during which it is accomplished. Actually, this step may intrude at almost any point in the problem-solution sequence. It frequently is undertaken after solutions have been proposed, tested, and discarded and the discussants begin to become frustrated with their efforts.

A problem statement is, after all, a question which is raised in order to direct inquiry. The more we know about something, the better questions we may be able to ask about it. Good problem solvers are often reformulating their problems in the light of their discoveries. The story is told of an automobile manufacturing company which was concerned because they were running out of drying sheds in which to store their cars while the paint dried. At first the problem seemed to be simply the need to build more sheds. Land was expensive; buildings were expensive; and construction was time-consuming. But one person had an idea: If the paint dried faster, more cars could be accommodated in the existing sheds. This problem reformulation led to the discovery of faster drying paint so that the company was able to expand its production without building more drying sheds.

S-4. Solution Proposal. Unwary discussants are often tempted to make this the first step in problem solving. The logical advantages of delaying solution proposal are obvious. Not until the problem has been clearly understood does it pay to become concerned about the solutions. But when the problem is clear and the solution proposal step is in order, it is wise to introduce as many solutions as possible that bear upon the problem.

Many beginners have great difficulty separating solutions from goals. When asked the question, "What should be done about ....?" they tend to respond, "We should do............" They then assume that their goal is to achieve this solution rather than to recognize the solution as a means to a goal. In the previous example about automobile paint the goal for the first problem was more drying sheds; the solution was a means of finding the land and money to build them. In the second problem, the goal was accommodating more cars in the existing space over a twenty-four-hour period; the solution was faster drying paint.

Because of prediscussion commitments to given solutions, some discussants tend to regard their particular solution as a goal to be achieved. Such thinking short-circuits the problem-solving process and turns potential inquiry into debate over proposed solutions without benefit of genuine problem analysis. Such problem description and analysis as the discussants may do is often a means of "stacking the deck" in favor of their particular solution. Prediscussion preferences are neither unusual nor necessarily bad. Difficulty arises only when discussants confuse the real problem goals and solutions they favor, consequently failing to look at the problem objectively.

S-5. Solution Testing. In this step the various solutions proposed must be measured to determine which one, or which combination, will most nearly achieve the goals without creating additional problems. Again, this requires the application of sound evidence and reasoning. In addition, a number of psychological problems are involved in coming to a decision.[10]

S-6. Action Testing. A solution must be put into action and this is properly the final step in the problem-solving process. Problems have a habit of recurring, since solutions are seldom perfect or lasting, and consequently the whole problem-solving process should be regarded as a cycle rather than a one-way, one-time process. Some people seem to be unduly frustrated by this fact and act as if they wished that problems could be settled once and for all, but life is seldom that way. This cyclical process can be stimulating and challenging rather than frustrating.

CRITICAL REQUIREMENTS OF PROBLEM SOLVING

In the description of the structure and the elements of problem solving, a number of requirements were indicated. The purpose of this section is to note three critical aspects of problem solving which are not necessarily related to particular points in the structure. These requirements are highlighted because the success of problem-solving efforts depends upon a clear realization of them. The three requirements are: (1) the *question for discussion*, (2) *goal-setting*, and (3) *creativity*.[11]

The Question for Discussion

Discussions must begin somewhere and problem-solving discussions usually begin with a question about some problem. The discussion question does not pose as many considerations of structure and phrasing as the debate proposition, but the group is not therefore relieved of responsibility for formulating such questions carefully and reexamining them frequently. In this continuous activity are several important considerations the problem solver would do well to note.[12] Unlike a debate proposition, for example, the discussion

---

[10] These are considered in Chapter 14 so they will not be considered here.

[11] A fourth requirement, *judgment,* is esentially the subject of the next two chapters.

[12] As an example, see Austin J. Freeley, *Argumentation and Debate: Rational Decision Making* (Belmont, Calif.: Wadsworth, 1961), Chap. 2.

question may shift (as we noted when discussing problem reformulation) during the discussion. The question which actually launches discussion may be substantially different from the one finally answered. This shifting should not disturb anyone so long as everyone knows just what question is being discussed at the moment. Thus, when we speak of the question for discussion, we do not restrict ourselves to the question which launches discussion. Let us turn to the criteria.

1. *The Question for Discussion Should Focus Attention Upon the Real Problem.* Many discussions are launched by taking note of some manifestation or symptom of a real problem. Most public discussions use these symptoms for the topic of the discussion in order to attract public interest. But good problem solving demands questions that focus attention upon the problem itself. A community recently became very disturbed when a school board ruling prohibited certain types of Christmas pageants and activities on the assertion that they violated the concept of separation of church and state. Many discussions were held with topics such as, "Keep Christ in Christmas!" and, "What should be done about the school board ruling?" Such topics miss the point. The problem dealt with the issue of establishing criteria by which religious or semireligious activities could be related to school functions. A better question would have been, What should be the criteria by which teachers can determine the appropriateness of religious activities in the school?

2. *The Question for Discussion Should Specify Whose Behavior Is Subject to Change.* Sometimes this is understood, but frequently it needs to be spelled out. If a production committee tackles the problem, How can production be improved? it might be understood that they are talking about their own job efficiency, but machinery and raw materials involving other departments might have been intended. A more specific question is, What management practices should be adopted in order to increase worker efficiency? This question focuses attention upon the problem—worker efficiency—and specifies the group whose behavior is directly affected by the solution—the managers. Some additional examples will illustrate both this concept and the previous one.

What should be done about juvenile vandalism? may be a good question to launch a discussion, but it should not be the question finally answered. Let us note several additional ways in which this question might be phrased. What should be done (by parents) about (limiting the occurrence of) juvenile vandalism? The phrase *by parents* specifies whose behavior is to be changed, and the phrase *limiting the occurrence of* focuses attention upon the real problem to be examined. The question might also have read: What should be done (by the courts) (to juvenile vandals)? The phrase *by the courts* specifies whose behavior is to be changed, and the phrase *to juvenile vandals* focuses attention upon the problem. Our first question could ultimately be phrased in perhaps a dozen different ways. Each phrasing would modify to some extent the problem being examined and the scope and nature of possible solutions.

3. *The Question for Discussion Should Not Suggest Potential Solutions.* If a question asks the discussant to agree or disagree with a particular solution, the problem solving process has been short-circuited. Unfortunately, many questions which purport to stimulate problem solving are phrased so that they include solutions. The question, Should the Federal Government Adopt a Program of Compulsory Health Insurance? is simply a debate question. If discussants attempt to examine the problem for which federal compulsory health insurance is a proposed solution, they do so with a view of accepting or rejecting this particular solution rather than *creating* a solution to the problem of the nation's health. A better question for the purposes of stimulating problem solving is, What should be the role (if any) of the federal government in providing for the health costs of the American people?

Often a particular group is not expected to begin at the beginning and proceed all the way through a problem. Sometimes one group will study the problem and may propose one or more solutions to it. Another group may begin the discussion at step S-5 (solution testing) in which case a question specifying a solution is appropriate.

Many discussion groups are not expected to deal with the entirety of the problem. Learning groups and appraisal groups usually do not examine an entire problem, and, of course, social and cathartic groups seldom make any pretense of dealing with the entire problem. Learning groups examine such questions as: What *has been* the role of the federal government in providing for the health costs of the American people? and What is the present state of juvenile delinquency? Appraisal groups are frequently assigned the task of determining whether or not a problem actually exists before a decision-making or action group is handed the task of solving the problem. Thus whenever the scope of the discussion group is limited, the scope of the discussion question should be similarly limited.

Goal Setting

The most critical aspect of the entire discussion process is goal setting. It is important for both problem solving effectiveness and desirable interpersonal relationships. At this point we shall consider only those aspects of goal setting that influence problem-solving effectiveness, leaving consideration of the relation of goal setting to interpersonal relationships until later in the book.

At first glance goal setting may seem to be the easiest of the several steps in problem solving, but a closer look will reveal how difficult it really is. For instance, look at the present international situation facing the United States. Tradition and old ways of solving problems offer little help in the space age. Prior to World War II one of our national goals was simply to remove any threat to our existence by defeating an enemy in battle. We then dismantled our military resources and returned to peaceful pursuits, and when another threat appeared, we could mobilize rapidly enough to render a sizable peace-time military force unnecessary. Today we are uncertain. Most people believe that our national goal is to defeat Communism, but few believe that war is the means we should use. Thus, "defeat Communism" must mean something different from conventional military defeat. What is the goal? Is it a scientific struggle in which the winner is to be determined by a race to the moon? Is it a popularity contest to be settled by votes in the United Nations General Assembly? Is it an economic contest with the impoverishment of the other side the goal? Is it a spiritual contest with maintenance of national sanity the goal? Perhaps these all should be goals or perhaps none should be, but evidently we, as a nation, have not decided what the goal should be, and we are expending vast resources working toward a number of goals hoping that the achievement of one or more will restore national equilibrium.[13]

Business goals may seem much more clear. Make money! But again complications appear for, while making money may be the appropriate long-range objective, the question of the short-range goals must be settled. Should the goal be production efficiency and lower costs or should it be creating mass demand and a new "image"? Or both? Should the company attempt to lead public taste, or should it adapt to established trends? Then consider the research goals. William Whyte contends that business organizations often seek to mold their research scientists so that they conform to the goals of the organization and produce immediately practical results.[14] But these very goals are self-defeating, he contends. Allowing the research scientists to pursue their hunches might result in more desirable long-range gains. As cases in point, he cited General Electric and Bell Laboratories as both outstanding in industry and among the only research laboratories where scientists were given virtually free rein.

Bring the matter down to the individual. Many college students seem not to know why they are in college. Going to college seemed the thing to do, so they went. Presumably such students seek a degree (although some rank the acquisition of a mate higher than a degree) and most are rather convinced that an education will not be harmful. One of the authors had an experience some years ago which was very enlightening on this point. He had posted the final grades for the semester and recorded a C+ for one student. This student came in to discuss his grade and for some time the author was confused because he thought the student was protesting the fact that he had not received a B for the course. It developed that the student was angry because he did not know his work had been adequate and would have studied less had he known that his C was virtually assured when he went in to take the final exam!

[13] One of the most interesting bipartisan projects today is the program called "Goals for Americans." This was launched by President Eisenhower when he commissioned a group of outstanding individuals to investigate American goals. The project was continued by President Kennedy, who sponsored discussions called "Goals for Americans," utilizing the report of the President's Commission. See *Goals for Americans* (Englewood Cliffs, N. J.: Prentice-Hall; A Spectrum Book, 1960).

[14] William H. Whyte, Jr., *The Organization Man* (Garden City, N. Y.: Doubleday, 1957).

How may goal setting affect the discussion group? If the discussants are either uncertain of their goal or divided as to its nature, this confusion will be reflected in the quality of the solution. We have observed countless discussions after which the discussants thought they were clear about their goals and thought that the others were of the same opinion only to discover that post discussion analyses revealed considerable difference of opinion concerning the goals. When the discussion record was examined, the discussants were amazed to discover that they had said little, if anything, about the goals although they were certain that goals were discussed and agreed upon. How do intelligent people fall into such traps? One tendency is to assume the existence of common, clear, mutually accepted goals. Another is to assume that other group members rank these supposedly agreed upon goals in the same order. It is both easy and reassuring to view the goals through only one pair of eyes, and thus discussants bring to the process limited experience and less skill in stating, testing, and adjusting goals in a group situation. Thus they feel uncertain and uncomfortable when engaged in exploring or defending goals, and the circle of avoidance remains unbroken. Perhaps such experiences are simply evidence of essentially autistic tendencies, but group goal selection can and should be better. It is difficult for a group to spend too much time setting its goals.

Two questions must be asked about the goal. Is it *desirable?* and, is it *attainable?* The more important question is the first. If the goal is not one which would relieve the tensions the group is examining, there is little point in asking the second. The first question should be answered early in the discussion; the second may not be answered until the group has reached step S-6 (action testing). Too many desirable goals have been brushed aside because people were either too lazy or not sufficiently ingenious to overcome the damning effect of that assertion, It can't be done. Since so many things that are routine today couldn't be done yesterday, it is better to err by attempting the impossible rather than to reject, out of hand, the desirable.

Creativity

The most baffling aspect of thinking is creativity. We know quite a bit about such aspects as judgment and discrimination, for many standardized tests have been constructed to measure such skills.

But such tests cannot measure creativity.[15] They present the test-taker with two or more choices and ask him to choose the correct or better answer. But the *test-maker* rather than the *test-taker* must create the alternatives. In problem-solving discussion, however, discussants must both create the answers and judge between them.

Creativity is needed particularly at two points in the problem-solving sequence—goal setting and solution proposal. Determining the obstacles and status quo is largely the process of discovery. Analyzing effects and relationships is reasoning. Judging proposed goals and proposed solutions is again a matter of reasoning. But obtaining goals and proposed solutions to analyze and judge requires creativity.

A major study is now being conducted at the University of California at Berkeley to determine why some persons are more creative than others. Writing in the *Saturday Review,* Donald W. MacKinnon reported some of the tentative conclusions which he and his colleagues reached about creative people. MacKinnon first warns that paths toward the development of an individual's creative potential are many and varied. Characterizing the creative person is, therefore, extremely difficult, but MacKinnon's tentative conclusions suggest that the creative person is marked by

His high level of effective intelligence, his openness to experience, his freedom from crippling restraints and impoverishing inhibitions, his esthetic sensitivity, his cognitive flexibility, his independence in thought and action, his high level of creative energy, his unquestioning commitment to creative endeavor, and his unceasing striving for solutions to the ever more difficult problems that he constantly sets for himself. [16]

As MacKinnon indicates, it is extremely hazardous to attempt to pin down the characteristics of creativity in some convenient little formula, but we can highlight some that seem to recur again and again in the literature. Three fundamental characteristics seem useful in focusing attention upon the nature of creativity. The first two

[15] Two of the best tests designed to measure problem-solving ability and critical thinking are respectively: The "Johnson Test," Alma Johnson, "An Experimental Study in the Analysis and Measurement of Reflective Thinking," *Speech Monographs,* Vol. 10 (1943), pp. 83-96; and the "Watson-Glaser Test," Edward M. Glaser, *An Experiment in the Development of Critical Thinking* (New York: Teachers College, Columbia Univ. Press, 1941).

[16] Donald W. MacKinnon, "What Makes a Person Creative?" *Saturday Review* (February 10, 1962), p. 69.

are suggested by Erich Fromm and the third is our deduction from the literature and our own experience.[17]

The Capacity to be Puzzled. Creativity is characterized by the capacity to be puzzled. If discrepancies in what one observes are brushed aside, if experience is routinized, if "accidents" are not noted, a person is not likely to be creative. Intelligence, curiosity, sensitivity to experience, freedom from restraint, and flexibility are all implied by the capacity to be puzzled. Both studies of creativity and anecdotes about creative people and their acts are replete with illustrations of the capacity to be puzzled. Some of the most revealing examples of the capacity to be puzzled are found in Wertheimer's *Productive Thinking* which we strongly recommend to the reader.[18]

The Ability to Concentrate. Creativity is characterized by the ability to concentrate. As Fromm points out, this ability is all too rare in a society filled with so many distractions and with work days so segmented. Many people who possess the capacity to be puzzled, as well as the intelligence and dedication required for concentration, find it well nigh impossible to create the environment necessary for sustained concentration. Concentration, however, requires more than available time and freedom from interruption. It also requires a capacity for reasoning and close examination of details and differences.

The Ability to Complete. Finally, creativity is characterized by the ability to complete. The individual who possesses the ability to be puzzled and the ability to concentrate may still be an intellectual dilettante without the ability to complete. Rollo May uses the term *encounter* to describe essentially what we have included under these three abilities.[19] The encounter must be a genuine experience that involves the whole of the individual and carries with it a concept

[17] Erich Fromm, "The Creative Attitude," in Harold H. Anderson, ed., *Creativity and Its Cultivation* (New York: Harper & Row, 1959).

[18] Max Wertheimer, *Productive Thinking,* enlarged edition, Michael Wertheimer, ed. (New York: Harper & Row, 1959). See also Max Black, *Critical Thinking: An Introduction to Logic and the Scientific Method,* 2nd ed. (Englewood Cliffs, N. J.: Prentice-Hall, 1960).

[19] Rollo May, "The Nature of Creativity," in Harold H. Anderson, ed., *Creativity and Its Cultivation* (New York: Harper & Row, 1959).

of fulfillment. He includes a particularly revealing anecdote about a person who constantly stood on the verge of genuine creativity but was never able to bring a project to fruition because he sought his gratification in bringing to the attention of others, particularly mother surrogates, his creative potential and literally feared finishing any project.

Despite the stress placed upon intelligence, creativity does not imply highly intellectualized unemotional activity. Running throughout these investigations is the idea that creativity involves the total self without any artificial dichotomy between intellect and emotion. May uses the term *ecstasy* to describe the nature of his encounter, and suggests that ". . . reason works better when emotions are present. . . ."[20] Of course, emotion and emotionalism are not the same, nor are excitable name calling and comparable outbursts conducive to effective reasoning or creativity. Genuine creativity, rather, involves the whole person whether working alone or with others.

This is a very brief sketch of the characteristics of the creative person. It is regrettable that more specific and objective information is not available. A major study now being supported by the Carnegie Foundation may provide greater insight than we now possess. Another research project is being carried out by Getzels and Jackson. Their research is beginning to suggest means whereby creativity may be both identified and controlled.[21]

COLLECTIVE THINKING

The final task of this chapter is to examine thinking as it takes place in the group situation. Most of what has been said earlier would apply with equal force to individuals or groups, but the remainder is intended to be a guide to effective use of the concepts of thinking in the group. Three aspects of thinking in the group are examined: discovering problems, organizing thinking, and encouraging creativity.

Discovering Problems

Some people may feel that they have enough problems already and wonder why anyone needs to go around looking for more. The title

---

[20] *Ibid.*, p. 65.
[21] Jacob W. Getzels and Philip W. Jackson, *Creativity and Intelligence* (New York: Wiley, 1962).

of this section might indicate that we have so few problems that we feel left out. Such statements are usually made facetiously since it is obvious that *discovering* a problem is not the same thing as *creating* a problem. There are a number of people however, who spend most of their lives ignoring, evading, or escaping real problems that should be faced and solved. Still others seem to perpetually try to create problems where none exist. We have no suggestions for the kind of person whose behavior has become pathological in either fashion, but intelligent groups can be of real value in discovering problems that affect the group or its members. It is a sad fact, however, that many groups foster problem evasion or problem creation rather than problem discovery.

Insulated Groups. People who wish to evade problems often join with other like-minded persons. Such groups are usually voluntary groups with social or cathartic purposes. Members of such groups seem to feel that assuring one another that "God is in His heaven, and all's right with the world," is one way to make it so. Many of the groups that have sprung up around the country in response to pressures for racial integration seem to be examples of insulated groups. They spend much time arguing that most Negroes don't really want integration, that the trouble is caused by "radical" elements such as the NAACP and "outside" agitators, that if "outsiders would only leave us alone, they would discover that there were few problems and that time would take care of what problems there might be." [22]

Insulated groups are found in all walks of life—in churches, in businesses, in politics, and in "Academia." This book does not attempt a personality analysis of such people; there are other sources more appropriate. [23] But realistic people who find themselves in too many groups that seem to be insulating themselves against problems of the day will do well to take a strong second look and

[22] We do not argue that all groups who oppose racial integration are as unrealistic as the ones we describe. *Though our sympathies lie with the supporters of integration, we recognize that there are those who honestly and realistically oppose integration.*

[23] Three of the most interesting sources for more information about personality characteristics are: T. W. Adorno, *et al., The Authoritarian Personality* (New York: Harper & Row, 1950); O. J. Harvey, David E. Hunt, and Harold M. Schroder, *Conceptual Systems and Personality Organization* (New York: Wiley, 1961); and Milton Rokeach, *The Open and Closed Mind* (New York: Basic Books, 1960).

perhaps find different associates if group tendencies cannot be changed.

Witch-hunting Groups. At the other end of the spectrum are groups which drain time and energy away from real problems to imaginary or petty problems. Such groups are always demanding investigations of one sort or another, are certain that the country's moral fiber is decaying, and seem to spend half their time writing letters to editors. Most super patriotic groups, we believe, fall into this category, but, like insulated groups, witch-hunting groups are found almost everywhere.

People who gravitate to insulated groups very probably do so for quite the same reasons that others join witch-hunting groups. In both cases real problems frequently are ignored, in the first case by not seeing them, and in the second by creating diversionary problems. Perhaps the individual whose name leaps immediately to mind as archetype of witch-hunters is the late Senator McCarthy of Wisconsin. In their excellent book, *McCarthy and the Communists,* Rorty and Decter point out how McCarthy nearly paralyzed a nation with his tactics, and when he did stumble across what might have been a genuine problem, he showed no inclination to follow up his widely publicized accusations.[24]

Realistic Groups. Those individuals and groups who manage to maintain a sensitivity to genuine problems are most necessary ingredients of our society. As is usually the case, it is hard to find a distinctive label for what is sober and intelligent, and the label *realistic* is not very colorful. However, such groups are essential, if not exciting, and perhaps the reader can think of a better term.

Realistic groups are generally free from restraint, catholic in interests, and information-oriented. Realistic individuals resemble very much the creative individual we discussed a moment ago. Realistic groups come to grips with problems that demand solution, and they seldom waste their time and energy as do insulated and witch-hunting groups.

Some of the clues that realistic groups use to discover problems can be described as *differences that matter:*

[24] James Rorty and Moshe Decter, *McCarthy and the Communists* (Boston: Beacon, 1954).

1. Discrepancies between expectation and results are signs of
ɔotential problems. One can expect to overshoot the mark on occa-
ion, but persistent or gross miscalculations should prompt inquiry.
)id we expect that the new office building would permit better
vork, only to discover that the money seems to have been spent in
ain? A classic case of discrepancy between expectation and result
s the attempt over the past several years to reduce agricultural pro-
luction in order to boost prices. Each year fewer farmers produce
nore and the surpluses continue to pile up. Something is wrong!

2. Unexplained by-products are signs of potential problems. For
ears, managers of industries assumed that the annual Christmas
ɔonuses were the epitome of enlightened labor-management rela-
ions. But some managers began to notice considerable resentment
ɔn the part of the workers and finally discovered that the men re-
enṭed the paternalistic manner in which the gift was given; they felt
he "gift" should be theirs by right in their salaries. Could some
trikes have been averted had this problem been noticed earlier? [25]

3. New developments are signs of potential problems. United
Itates' military planners constantly note new military developments
n the military capacity of our potential enemies. The problems such
levelopments pose are obvious, but interestingly enough, not all the
levelopments that cause concern are those of others. Our own mili-
ary developments cause concern because the planners figure that if
ve are able to invent a new weapon, it is only a matter of time before
ɔur enemies will produce something similar that we must prepare to
lefend against.

4. Fluctuations in the reliability of old measuring sticks are
igns of potential problems. All of us use, more or less habitually, a
ıumber of guides to predict things. The Dow-Jones Average, for ex-
ımple, has long been a barometer of the stock market trends. "As
√laine goes, so goes the nation," used to be a favorite election night
ɔarometer. Recently, however, these old political barometers have
ıot been functioning very smoothly. Watch on TV computers
truggling during election nights with data that are supposed to be
ʒood indicators of the final outcome of the election. During the 1960

[25] Interestingly enough, the National Labor Relations Board ruled that
ɔonuses, gratuities, stock-sharing plans, etc., if repeated, are to be classed as
xpected and, hence, subject to bargaining by the unions. This decision was
ıpheld by the case of Inland Steel vs. the N. L. R. B. in the Seventh Circuit
Court, 1948, and later upheld by the Supreme Court.

presidential election, for example, the computers were making early
predictions for a landslide Kennedy victory; by morning, however
the Kennedy margin had become paper thin. Of course, these miscalculations did not approach the famous fiasco of 1948 when Truman's upset victory over Dewey left most of the political predict...
red-faced and admitting that their old barometers were faulty.

There are other clues to the presence of problems, but the four
just named are among the best. Realistic groups will discover more
that are particularly suited to their own needs. The point to be re
membered is that a group does no one a favor by concealing prob
lems or diverting attention from them.

Organizing Thinking

Everyone who has worked systematically through a problem is
aware of the difficulty of keeping his own thoughts focused upon the
problem and avoiding profitless thought diversions. To keep several
minds focused upon problems is obviously more difficult. Therefore
some kind of structure is necessary if group thinking is to be some
thing more than a collection of random thoughts. Let us examine
some of the issues involved in organizing group thinking.

Agendas. Many people feel that an agenda is sufficient to organize
group thinking. We agree that agendas are helpful, but an agenda is
only a listing of the topics which a group wishes to discuss in the
tentative sequence in which they will be examined.[26] Each item on
an agenda normally constitutes one or more problems which the
group must examine. The order of items on the agenda may be a
matter of rules, such as parliamentary agendas, or a matter of preference, but an agenda is not a *structuring of thought.*

The Problem-Solving Sequence. If the agenda is not sufficient to
structure group thinking, the logical alternative is the problem-solving sequence presented in this chapter. However, the problem of
organizing group thinking is not solved so simply. There are several
questions to ask before recommending that every group follow this
sequence each time it confronts a problem. (1) Can groups learn to
use the problem-solving sequence? (2) If groups can learn to use it,

[26] We are not going to discuss at this point how the agenda should be
drawn up or who should do it. These are questions that are more properly related to leadership and group structure. See Chapter 12, pp. 327-330.

does it improve the quality of their thinking? (3) If both questions one and two can be answered affirmatively, does it follow that the sequence should always be used?

Considerable evidence, from both experiment and experience, shows that groups *can* learn to follow a problem-solving sequence and that it will improve the quality of their collective thinking. The experiments of Keltner and Douglas reveal this quite clearly.[27] Many teachers, discussion leaders and students of psychology can draw on their experience and observation in the classroom, the committee meeting, the training program, the planning group, or the study club to confirm the assertion that groups can and do learn to use the sequence with profit. Why, then, not simply advocate its universal use and be done with the issue?

Barnlund and Haiman devote considerable attention to whether or not the application of structure will be overly restrictive and consequently resented and rejected by the participants. They put the issue as follows:

If a group finds that the method is too demanding or discovers that members are giving more attention to maintaining their agenda than to the problem—and in the course of doing so are becoming increasingly irritated with the restrictions it places on them—then the time may have come to jettison the method. On the other hand, this may mean surrendering too easily to the blandishments of the superficial, ill-informed, or irrational members of the group. The "easiest way out" is not often the path to mature decision-making. [28]

Each individual will consciously or unconsciously adopt some kind of structure which may be no more than to "set up" the group for some preconceived solution to the problem. The issue is whether there needs to be some concerted approach to solving problems or whether a more intuitive approach is healthier. Because of the logical advantages of the problem-solving sequence, we believe that the normal course should be to follow at least the main guide posts

[27] John W. Keltner, "An Experimental Study of the Nature and Training of Skill in Problem Recognition and Formulation for Group Discussion," (Unpublished Ph.D. dissertation, School of Speech, Northwestern Univ., 1947). Jack Douglas, "An Experimental Study of Training in Problem-Solving Methods" (Unpublished Ph.D. dissertation, School of Speech, Northwestern Univ., 1951).

[28] Dean C. Barnlund and Franklyn S. Haiman, *The Dynamics of Discussion* (Boston: Houghton Mifflin, 1960), p. 96.

in the sequence. *Of course, social groups, cathartic groups, learning groups, and therapy groups will often not want to (or need to) follow the sequence since the purposes of such groups are primarily individual, but decision-making, action, advisory, and appraisal groups should normally follow the sequence.*

The problem solving sequence should be flexibly applied, however, for several reasons:

1. A group does not always have the whole problem to examine. Sometimes a group has been given the task of recommending solutions to an already defined problem. Sometimes the group is expected to go no further than to examine goals, in which case the application of the whole sequence is obviously not called for.

2. A group that works together regularly often finds repeating the problem description steps a waste of time, since they already understand what is needed. In such cases it is usually desirable to plunge immediately into the solutions. But such groups should be cautious. The nature of the problem may have changed without their being collectively aware of what has happened, or their own goals may have changed and their problem solving has ground to a halt. In other words, even these groups should occasionally work through the whole sequence.

3. Sometimes allowing a group to skip back and forth among the various steps in the sequence will improve the overall thinking of the group. Often solution proposals suggest changes in the goals or a need to reexamine obstacles. A discussant who proposes a solution when the group is still in the problem description stage should not be batted down by the others for this act alone. If the group knows what is being done, and if the solution proposal can be used to clarify the problem, positive advantages may be gained. If the group is unaware of what is happening, or if they blithely go ahead skipping essential steps in problem description, their product will usually be less than satisfactory.

4. Finally, occasional pursuit of tangents is often a very necessary release for the group and, not infrequently, produces ideas or dimensions worth noting. Rigid adherence to the sequence may choke off profitable excursions.[29]

---

[29] The psychological advantages of such pursuits will be discussed in later chapters. Here we simply note that people are not machines and that occasional lapses from a pattern should not be equated with stupidity or lack of motivation. See Chapters 12 and 14 particularly.

Encouraging Creativity

A discussion group that wishes to accomplish as much as possible should do its best to attract first-rate people as members. There are wide variations in creative potential, however. Everyone has some measure of creativity, and it is more to the point to examine ways that problem solving can be conducted to use as much creativity as possible.

Brainstorming. Many regard brainstorming as the best means of releasing the creativity of a group. Alex Osborn originated the concept and set out four basic rules: (1) don't criticize any ideas; (2) no idea is too wild; (3) quantity is important; and (4) seize opportunities to improve or add to ideas suggested by others.[30] In practice one group does nothing but brainstorm a problem, producing as many ideas as possible with no concern for the validity of the ideas, and another group or individual judges between the ideas suggested.

The capacity for judgment of existing information and recognized relationships, however, is not necessarily accompanied by the capacity to generate new and useful concepts. Such creativity may be another matter. People who practice brainstorming report dozens of exciting examples of its effectiveness, particularly in circumstances which had baffled the experts. Housewives have brainstormed ideas that have revolutionized supermarket practices. Osborn reports an instance in which a sailor suggested a way for a ship to avoid being blown up by mines that were floating toward it. The ship was in a position where it could not maneuver, and all normal techniques for dealing with mines were useless. In some desperation the captain called for a brainstorming session. A sailor suggested that the mines be diverted around the ship by pushing them away with streams of water from the ship's hoses. It worked.

While brainstorming has proved very effective in many situations, it has some important drawbacks. Osborn points out that the problem has to be specific, simple, and preferably familiar.[31] Many problems that a group confronts do not possess these characteristics. Further, some observation suggests that the chain reaction of ideas

[30] Alex F. Osborn, *Applied Imagination: Principles and Procedures of Creative Thinking* (New York: Scribner's, 1953), pp. 300-301.
[31] Osborn, *op. cit.*, p. 303.

may in some cases inhibit different directions of thought rather than release ideas of a different cast.

One of the authors conducted a rather large-scale experiment to determine whether an initial period of brainstorming could be used as a technique to increase individual involvement in the task and sharpen the quality of group thinking. The experiment also tested whether the same group could both brainstorm and later judge rather than assigning these two functions to different groups. Groups of college freshmen were assigned the task of suggesting a plan whereby a high school student could best prepare himself for college work. Each group was led by a trained discussion leader. The leaders took half of the groups through the problem-solving sequence outlined earlier in this chapter; the other half of the groups began with a ten-minute brainstorming session and then doubled back to the beginning of the problem-solving sequence. Results showed no advantage for either method. Groups were scored from top to bottom on the rating form used in both the brainstorming-first condition and in what we called the "conventional" condition.

Our conclusion concerning the advantages of brainstorming is similar to the one reached by R. S. Robbins:

Brainstorming, then, is no substitute for creativity; but by inducing more careful definition of the problem at hand in all its aspects and dimensions, brainstorm sessions facilitate the creative act on the part of some one individual either during or after the meeting. [32]

Brainstorming works well when the problem is "specific, simple, and familiar," *and when the brainstorming group does not have the additional task of solving the problem.* When problems become more complex, and when groups must decide as well as suggest solutions, we should seek additional means of releasing the creative potential of group members.

Conflict. Paradoxically enough, conflict is one of the best means of encouraging creativity. Turning again to Fromm's article, we find:

Another condition of creativeness is the *ability to accept conflict* and *tension* resulting from polarity, rather than to avoid them. This idea is very much in contrast to the current climate of opinion, in which one

---

[32] R. S. Robbins, "Brainstorming Re-Evaluated," *The Journal of Communication,* Vol. 10 (September, 1960), p. 152.

attempts to avoid conflict as much as possible. All modern education tends to spare the child the experience of conflict. Everything is made easy, everyone is tolerant. Ethical norms are leveled out in such a way that there is rare occasion to experience conflict between desire and norm. There is a general superstition that conflicts are harmful, and that hence they should be avoided. The opposite is true. Conflicts are the source of wondering, of the development of strength, of what one used to call "character." If one avoids conflicts, one becomes a smoothly running machine, where every affect [emotional response] is immediately leveled off, where all desires become automatic, where all feelings become flattened out. [33]

Conflict, properly used, is one of the highest forms of cooperation.[34] Improperly used, conflict will cause the more timid to retire into obscurity and encourage the more vocal to engage in fruitless wrangles. One of the chief advantages of discussion is the opportunity to have one's ideas tested by conflict with others, thus stimulating better ideas.

While recognizing the virtues of conflict, it must not be forgotten that self-repression stifles creativity. Fear of criticism is frequently a condition of self-repression. For this reason, the problem-solving sequence seeks to separate problem formulation from problem analysis and solution proposal from solution testing. People should have a chance to propose their ideas as freely as possible, and conflict that is a part of analysis and evaluation should not force the creator of an idea to defend it just because it is his brainchild.[35]

Individual Thought. Finally, we suggest that when a group is faced with a knotty problem, it will be wise not to attempt to solve the problem in one sitting. If the group members progress through step four and stop, retracing their steps when they meet again, members will often demonstrate amazing creativity during the interval. Many of the half-formed notions stimulated by the first session will be

[33] Erich Fromm, "The Creative Attitude," in Harold H. Anderson, ed., *Creativity and its Cultivation* (New York: Harper & Row, Publishers, 1959), p. 51.

[34] See Chapter 7, pp. 171-176 for a discussion of the nature of cooperation.

[35] This is not the place in the book to deal with the procedures for creating a permissive climate nor with the communication problems that are an inevitable part of expressing one's ideas. See, particularly, Chapters 13 and 16. Here it is simply suggested that the structure of the problem solving should contribute toward creativity by encouraging *ex*pression rather than *re*pression.

worked out and articulated by the time the group meets again, and totally new ideas may also be forthcoming.

EXERCISES

1. Arrange for a group of four to ten individuals to explore the nature and perception of problems. Ask each person first to compile his own list of problems which he feels are both important and possible of solution. Have him group these into three categories: those of a personal nature, those related to his organization or work or related activities at the local level, and finally, those of a city, state or regional nature. Meet as a group to compare lists and explore agreement as to the existence of the problems, the importance of the problems, the frequency of mention of both specific problems and also types of problems. Attempt to state clearly and concisely several of the problems about which there appear to be differences of opinion as to existence or importance. What results do you observe? Attempt the same careful statement for one or two problems regarding which there seemed to be general agreement. Does this attempt to state the problem in concise terms affect the perception of the problem? What does this experiment suggest concerning creating problems as compared to discovering problems?

2. Pair off with one or two of your close friends or acquaintances and discuss a semipersonal or limited problem of mutual concern. Make a tape recording of your discussion. Next, each person should think back over the discussion and jot down specific points or reactions to the problem-solving procedure. Then play back the recording, comparing your initial individual evaluations to those you form after hearing the playback. What do you conclude individually and collectively?

3. Consider how you feel when a problem of importance to you is unsolved or a decision is withheld or delayed. What accounts for this? Sample the attitudes and feelings of several other persons to see how they react to such a situation. One possible approach is to formulate a series of hypothetical situations in which they might conceivably find themselves. Then ask whether they would prefer an immediate or delayed decision and the reason for their response. With a little creativity you can even introduce into some of the situations the potential for a more favorable decision if the subject will accept delay. What are the implications for problem solving by individuals? By small groups? To what extent do you feel this might affect broad social and political behavior?

4. Choose some personal habit, mannerism or routine which you will attempt to change—the route you follow from one place to another,

the pocket in which you carry your wallet or purse, the place or time at which you eat breakfast or take a coffee break. Make careful note of your reactions and experiences. What problems do you encounter? How do you feel? What are the implications for individual and collective problem solving? (It may be both interesting and helpful to ask a friend to observe your efforts but to refrain from commenting on them or assisting you until your planned activity has been concluded.)

5. Plan a short experiment to illustrate the effects of various approaches to problem solving. Choose a problem which will challenge the interest and abilities of a group of 15 to 20 cooperating participants, and for which constructive solutions might be developed within a period of 30 to 45 minutes. Separate the large group into thirds, giving each person a written statement of the problem and any directions required, including the time available. Ask the first third to attack the problem by group discussion, using the pattern developed in this chapter; ask the second third to attack the problem by brainstorming; and for the final third, have each person formulate his suggestions or solutions individually and independently. Ask each group, as well as each of the persons working individually, for a short written summary, including all the ideas generated. Bring the subgroups together for reports from each relative to: participants' feelings of satisfaction, the procedures employed, the number of proposals generated, and judgments as to quality of proposals or solutions. The results might form the bases for a discussion by the entire group.

6. The experiment outlined in Exercise 5 may be modified or expanded by choosing a problem to which there is a specific or clearly preferred solution. Numerous ones will come to mind. Helpful suggestions may be found in references on reasoning, logic, psychology, science, and mathematics. Max Black, *Critical Thinking* (New York: Prentice-Hall, 1946) lists some possibilities; see pp. 10-11, and Chapter 14, "Inquiry At The Common-Sense Level," pp. 247-264. Marjorie Shaw's study (cited on p. 22 of Chapter 2) includes the descriptions for the problems she used.

7. Prepare a case study of an actual problem-solution situation in which you have participated or which you have been able to observe. Describe and analyze what took place in chronological sequence from recognition through action. Indicate the degree to which you consider each of the following was either a positive or negative factor in the process: location and statement of the problem, goal determination and acceptance, and originality or creativity. Do you believe the process and/or the solution could have been improved? If so, what suggestions would you offer?

8. Evaluate both the quality of the decision and procedure used to reach it for six or eight decisions arrived at by several groups of which you are a member. Attempt to limit your consideration to those deliberations with which you are quite familiar and which have taken place within the past three or four months. For each rating, use a scale ranging from 1 to 10. In judging *quality* of decision, consider 1 as "very poor" and 10 as "very good." In judging *procedure* used in arriving at the solution, consider 1 as representing "habitual, conventional or stereotyped" methods, and 10 as representing "original, imaginative or creative" approaches. First rate each decision as to quality and then follow with the ratings of procedure. Study each set of ratings separately. Compare the two ratings for each decision and the two sets of ratings in general. What do you conclude about the effectiveness of the various groups in solving problems? How would you explain your conclusions? How do you believe improvement could be achieved most effectively? (It might happen that you rate one group high on quality of decision and low on procedure, or vice versa. What accounts for the discrepancy?)

9. Plan a discussion to explore the question: What are the implications for problem solving when people are placed into small groups?

10. In our efforts to stimulate originality and creativity in each group member, how shall we insure some degree of order in the discussion and progress to a practical solution of the problem? Consider steps that the individual group member may take to enhance his creative contribution to discussion. How may he aid others in this respect?

11. Consider the effect of authoritarian organization and relationships on the patterns of individual thought and on group efforts at problem solving. Make a study of this in some unit such as a family, a club, an organization (educational, business, religious, military), a system of government, or a culture.

12. Consider the effects which our patterns of daily life and thought have on our problem solving and the reciprocal or circular nature of this relationship. Consider the actual and potential effects such conventional behavior may have on our approach to social, economic, and political problems.

13. Some conflict is inevitable in productive discussion. Conflict almost always does violence to customs. Starting from these two statements, conduct a discussion (or a series of discussions) to consider the nature of conflict, its potentials, and the possibilities of managing it to insure productivity.

14. Biologically and psychologically, man has changed little if any in the last 3,000 years. However, his society and its technology have literally exploded in terms of knowledge and complex interrelationships. What, if

any, problems does this situation present? How can we proceed to adjust most satisfactorily? What assumptions must we make?

15. Most competent observers of our contemporary scene agree that one of man's greatest needs is to improve his use of human resources, particularly the intellectual and motivational ones. In what areas of human activity could these be used most productively? What are the potentials? How should we proceed to release and utilize these resources?

16. Peoples and nations engage in problem solving and decision making just as do individuals and small groups. This is a never-ending process and the person familiar with government and history, interested in sociology, knowledgeable about psychology, or a student of persuasion may wish to study the manner in which national and international groups have attempted to solve problems and the role *small groups* within these large groups played in formulating and securing the acceptance (or, in some cases, imposing) the solution or group of solutions. Many possibilities will suggest themselves of which the following are representative of several contrasting philosophies and procedures:

    a. American efforts to cope with the economic depression of the '30's.

    b. Hitler's rise and leadership of the German people.

    c. Mussolini's rise and leadership of the Italian people.

    d. England's response to the rise of the German and Italian dictatorships.

    e. America's policy toward the war prior to the attack on Pearl Harbor.

    f. The development of Japan's imperialism during the '30's.

    g. English or European approach to economic rebuilding following World War II.

    h. Development of the European Common Market—and the United States' relationship to it.

    i. Emergence of a spirit of nationalism and self-determination among the undeveloped countries of the world.

    j. American response to the Communist challenge.

    k. American approach to determining a policy for public education.

SELECTED READINGS

Barnlund, Dean C., and Haiman, Franklyn S., *The Dynamics of Discussion*. Boston, Houghton Mifflin, 1960, Chaps. 4 and 5.

Cortright, Rupert L., and Hinds, George L., *Creative Discussion*. New York, Macmillan, 1959, Chap. 4.

Creativity and Its Cultivation, Harold H. Anderson, ed. New York, Harper & Row, 1959.

Dewey, John, *How We Think.* Boston, Heath, 1938.

Keltner, John W., *Group Discussion Processes.* New York, Longmans, Green, 1957, Chaps. 3, 4, 5, and 6.

MacKinnon, Donald W., "What Makes a Person Creative?" *Saturday Review* (February 10, 1962).

McBurney, James H., and Hance, Kenneth G., *Discussion in Human Affairs.* New York, Harper & Row, 1950, Chaps. VI and VII.

Osborn, Alex F., *Applied Imagination: Principles and Procedures of Creative Thinking.* New York, Scribner's, 1953.

Rorty, James, and Decter, Moshe, *McCarthy and the Communists.* Boston, Beacon, 1954.

Von Fange, Eugene K., *Professional Creativity.* Englewood Cliffs, N. J., Prentice-Hall, 1959.

Wertheimer, Max, *Productive Thinking,* enlarged ed., Michel Wertheimer, ed. New York, Harper & Row, 1959.

CHAPTER 5

Evidence:
The Basis of Thought

> Having eyes, see ye not? and having ears, hear ye not?
> and do ye not remember?
>
> Mark 8:18

Whether we rely upon divine revelation or upon the results of carefully controlled experimentation, we must have some evidence to use as we think and draw conclusions. Evidence is the building blocks of belief—the basis of thought. To provide that basis, we define evidence, examine the process of discovering evidence, study the ways that an individual or a discussion group may evaluate the evidence that is discovered and presented for consideration, and, finally, look at the way evidence may be systematically brought to the group.

DEFINITION OF EVIDENCE

Black's Law Dictionary defines evidence as:

Any species of proof, or probative matter, legally presented at the trial of an issue, by the act of the parties and through the medium of witnesses, records, documents, concrete objects, etc., for the purpose of inducing belief in the minds of the court or jury as to their contention.[1]

[1] *Black's Law Dictionary*, 3rd ed. (St. Paul, Minnesota: West, 1933), p. 695.

This starting point provides a basis to spell out the nature of evidence. Note the important phrase, "for the purpose of inducing belief." Facts and opinions exist independently of the use to which they may be put; the moment they are used to induce belief, they become evidence and must be examined as such.

Kinds of Evidence

Evidence may be conveniently classified under three headings: fact, statement of observation, and inference. Each is defined briefly and then compared and contrasted. Finally, the importance of making the distinctions is illustrated.

Fact. A fact is any observable, nonverbal object or act. The term *observable* does not restrict the definition to what may be observed by the unaided senses. Some instrument of observation may be needed, such as a telescope or microscope. The nonverbal characteristic of the definition may cause much confusion if it is not properly understood. The book you hold in your hands (including the print on its pages) is a fact. When you turn to a friend and talk about it ("This is a book." "Harnack and Fest wrote it." "Here is an interesting idea."), the existence of the book remains a fact, but your talk about it is *not* a fact from your friend's point of view. The reference here is to the substance or "meaning" of your talk, not to the fact that you uttered words. You could have simply handed him the book and let him observe. The moment you talk about it, gesture about it, or otherwise structure the circumstances under which he observes the book, you are communicating about it and have added verbal factors to condition his observation.

Statement of Observation. A statement of observation is a report of an alleged observation. That is, a statement of observation is an attempt to represent a fact by some set of symbols. Usually when people speak of the need to "get the facts" before making decisions, they mean that they want *symbols*—statements of observation.

Even when made as accurately and conscientiously as possible, a statement of observation is only, at best, a guide to the facts reported and not a substitute for the facts themselves. The observer must, of necessity, leave out many or most of the characteristics of the fact. That is, he must abstract from the many things that might be reported and concentrate upon what he considers the "important" or "essential" characteristics. Further, many of the characteristics are simply "unspeakable." That is, the reporter does not possess any conventionally used symbols to represent what he observed. Most men, for example, have much more difficulty discriminating in words between various colors than do their wives. For another example, consider the difficulty of reporting a performance of an orchestra. Here words are slippery and grossly inadequate as anyone who has attempted to write critical reviews will testify. One could use a copy of the score, and this would be an improvement over the words, but still it falls short of reproducing the experience of hearing the actual performance. (The score would be of no help at all if the person reading the score were uninstructed in such symbols. And, of course, the score says nothing about the orchestra's interpretation.) Perhaps the best statement of observation would be a sound-motion picture of the performance, but, as every hi-fi addict will testify, much is still left out, and other sensations such as odors, temperature, and ventilation which were a part of the original observation are left out altogether.

Inference. An inference is a statement which goes beyond observation and asserts that which has not been (or cannot be) observed by the one who makes the statement. All statements about the future must be classed as inferences since the maker of the statement cannot observe what has not occurred. All statements about causal relationships must also be classed as inferences since one can observe proximity in space or time, but not the relationship itself. And, of course, conclusions, judgments, and interpretations must be classed as inferences. Every decision that we make during the course of living is therefore an inference. When we decide to wear our brown suit, we infer that it will be appropriate in comfort and appearance for our activities. When we drive down a street, we infer that the other drivers will pay reasonable heed to driving regulations.

One use of inferences is not so apparent. *We must make inferences even when we attempt to report a fact.* We infer that some characteristics are more important than others and abstract them for the purposes of our report. Every reader of detective stories is familiar with that crucial clue which was overlooked by everyone except the master detective who made the appropriate inferences about its importance.

Comparison of Fact, Statement of Observation, and Inference. Using concepts developed by Irving Lee, Haney suggests the following criteria for distinguishing the making of statements of observation from the making of statements of inference: [2]

Statements of Observation	*Statements of Inference*
1. Can be made only *after* observation.	1. Can be made at any time.
2. Must stay with what one has observed—must not go beyond.	2. Can go beyond observation—well beyond. We can infer to the limits of our imaginations.
3. Can be made only by the observer.	3. Can be made by anyone.

Haney's criteria for making statements of observation suggest that, if the maker of the statement abides by these criteria, the statement of observation will presumably be valid. The same is not true of the criteria for statements of inference. The next chapter will develop in detail the methods for assessing the degree of probable truth that our inferences possess.

The late Irving J. Lee of Northwestern University was fond of using this example to make the distinction between facts, statements of observation, and inferences.[3] He would bring an apple to class and, showing it to the class, ask them if there were seeds in the apple. Most people said that there were, if they could assume that it had not been tampered with. Lee would then ask if it were a fact that there were seeds in the apple, and again most people said it was

---

[2] William V. Haney, *Communication Patterns and Incidents* (Homewood, Ill.: Irwin, 1960), p. 21. Haney adds a fourth pair of distinctions which he calls a "helpful, but not essential, contrast: Statements of observation approach 'certainty.' Statements of inference involve only degrees of probability."

We would agree that this pair of statements is not essential for it is possible to demonstrate that many statements of inference have been shown to possess higher degrees of probability than do many statements of observation. This is discussed in the next chapter.

[3] Lee used the term *statement of fact* for what we have termed statement of observation. We are following Haney's practice in this matter.

a fact, but a few would begin to hedge. Finally, he would cut open the apple and point out that only then could statements of observation be made about the seeds. The seeds themselves were facts; talk about them, when they could be observed, were statements of observation; and talk about them, when they were hidden in the apple, were inferences.

General semanticists insist that we should be careful to avoid two fundamental confusions. First, statements of observation are not the same as that which is observed. The word or symbol is an arbitrary convention used to "stand for" a fact, but it is not the fact itself. Second, inferences should not be confused with statements of observation. These confusions can result in much misevaluation, if one is not careful to separate the three kinds of evidence.

The insistence upon separating facts, statements of observation, and inferences is because three fundamentally different methods are used to verify them. Facts simply exist; they are neither true nor false. Verification of their existence is determined by independent observations of their presence, in which case statements of observation may be made about the facts, or by independent observations of their effects, in which case inferences may be made concerning their existence. Statements of observation may be verified by others using the statement as a guide or "map of the territory described" to determine whether the map guides one with reasonable accuracy to the fact. If, for example, you say that your house is located at 15th and Pine, your statement becomes a literal "map" which can be verified by looking. If this is not possible, the statement of observation must be assigned a degree of probability by making inferences about the one who reported the statement. Inferences are assigned a degree of probability by examining the reasoning process which led the maker of the inference from his observation to his conclusion or from one inference to another, and are finally verified by observing the outcome of predictions made by inference.[4]

----

[4] This is a very brief account of considerable work done by general semanticists and logicians. Chapter 6 contains a much more detailed explanation of the reasoning process by which inferences are evaluated and the whole concept of probability is examined in some detail. Later in this chapter we examine tests for evaluating the various types of evidence. The reader is urged to examine further the works of general semanticists and we have cited several works at the end of this chapter. The authors representing this field are Bois, Haney, Hayakawa, Lee, and Weinberg.

Reporters of Evidence

When facts and statements are considered as evidence, we must look at how a group receives the evidence. When a group is examining a problem, the evidence seldom "presents itself." Individuals must bring the evidence to the group and often it must pass through many interpretations before it becomes available for consideration. Sometimes the observation or inference is formulated to be used as evidence, and sometimes the evidence already exists. Let us look at the three kinds of evidence in light of how each kind may be brought to the attention of the discussion group.

Reporters of Fact. The group may often want to observe the facts directly rather than simply acting upon statements of fact. Thus, a group considering slum clearance will usually want to go out and look at the slums to be cleared and possibly examine successful slum clearances elsewhere. In other cases, the object to be observed may be brought to the group, as when documents, records, letters, and similar matters are presented for first-hand observation.

Usually someone brings the facts to the attention of the group. When that happens, we must concern ourselves with the communications surrounding the presentation of the fact or the circumstances under which it was observed. Communication about an object can affect our perception of it as in the following illustration. Does it make any difference whether we say, "Look at the vase," or whether we say, "Notice the two faces"?

The issue here is not the variability of perception. We are simply underscoring the observation that words affect our perception. Carmichael, Hogan, and Walter conducted a very interesting experiment a number of years ago. They presented subjects with a series of stimulus figures representing nothing in particular. To one group of subjects they presented one set of identifying words just before showing the figures; to the other group of subjects they presented a different set of identifying words just before showing the same set of figures. The subjects were then asked to draw the figures observed. The difference between the two sets of drawings was remarkable. The authors concluded: ". . . to some extent at least, the reproduction of forms may be determined by the nature of words presented

FIGURE 5.1

orally to subjects at the time that they are first perceiving specific visual forms." [5]

The conditions under which an object is perceived can clearly affect the perception of it. The kind of light available, the relation of the object to other objects or events, and so on will influence perception and in some cases will create such dramatic confusions as reversing black and white.

Reporters of Statements of Observation. The statements of observation used by a group may be either furnished firsthand by one of

[5] L. Carmichael, H. P. Hogan, and A. A. Walter, "An Experimental Study of the Effect of Language on the Reproduction of Visually Perceived Form," in Irving J. Lee, ed., *The Language of Wisdom and Folly* (New York: Harper, 1949), p 258.

the members of the group or may be reported 2nd, 3rd, . . . nth-hand to the group. The number of times a statement of observation is removed from the original observation does not affect its classification as a statement of observation, when we consider it as evidence, but it does affect the verification of the statement because of the number of layers that must be uncovered before we reach the original. The way in which a simple observation can be distorted by the "rumor mill" should be enough to caution us about this matter.

Reporters of Inferences. When inferences are used as evidence, most people think that they must be inferences made by some authority *outside* of the group. But often members of a discussion group introduce their own inferences as *evidence* rather than as *reasoning* based upon information commonly available to all. The head of a department, for example, may meet with the president of the college and discuss with him the accepted bases of promotions within the organization. The head may return to his executive committee and report his inferences that certain kinds of promotion justifications will not be accepted by the front office. He may further infer that if the group sends up a promotion request for Mr. X, it will almost certainly be denied because of the kinds of justifications the group has available. Someone else on the executive committee may have talked to the president or to another high-ranking official and come back with a contrary set of inferences. The committee must decide which set of inferences possesses the greater degree of probability, and consequently decide which, if either, they will accept as evidence. They may wish to accept neither but insist upon further examination.

As with statements of observation, the inference may be reported firsthand by some member, or some outside authority, or it may be reported 2nd, 3rd, . . . nth-hand to the group. The same problems of evaluation are presented by successive removals from the primary source.

THE DISCOVERY OF EVIDENCE

How do people perceive potential evidence? Evidence, as we have seen, usually exists and remains to be discovered or developed. Sometimes the evidence is created by inference or experimentation conducted by members of the group. But, regardless of how the evidence comes into being, there must be an initial step of discovery. Existing evidence must be located; facts forming the basis of the inference must be observed; or the hypothesis guiding the experiment must be formulated. Every so often, we literally or figuratively stumble over evidence that may be of use to us or our group, but usually discovery is the fruit of purposeful seeking and no accident. In the discussion of creativity in the previous chapter, some of the conditions necessary for discovery were implied. This chapter extends these observations to the specific task of uncovering needed evidence. Six factors increase the likelihood of evidence being discovered and enhance the possibility of its being valuable.

Competence

First and foremost the evidence seeker must be competent.[6] Discoveries by the incompetent are rare and usually run-of-the-mill. We will briefly discuss competency under two headings—general competency and specialized competency.

General Competency. More and more frequently, organizations are seeking the broadly trained and generally competent individual in preference to the narrowly trained specialist because they recognize the potential versatility and flexibility of such a generalist. A case in point occurred recently when a well known employers' association, seeking people as candidates for positions as contract negotiators, asked us to recommend some liberally educated people who had had courses and experience in debate, discussion, and other public speaking activities. The association representative added that specific training in areas such as labor law and economics was desirable but not essential since the person could learn about such matters if he were broadly trained and skilled in communication.

The growing importance of interdisciplinary research has placed even more emphasis upon the broadly qualified person. The work that received the Monograph Prize of the American Academy of Arts and Sciences for the year 1959 in the field of social sciences, for

---

[6] The person bringing evidence to a group performs two functions. He first must discover or formulate the evidence. When he does this, we call him a *researcher*. Next, he must bring the evidence to the attention of someone else. When he does this, we call him a *reporter* as we did above.

example, was a book called *Bargaining and Group Decision Making*. The authors, Sidney Siegel and Lawrence E. Fouraker, are professors of psychology and *economics* respectively.[7]

Specialized Competency. Contempt for the specialist is not implied here. The ideal person would be a "broadly trained specialist," without being facetious. The generalist will seldom be able to do much more than scratch the surface with his research unless he possesses specialized skills.

Specialized competency obviously includes knowledge of the field of the particular research. It also includes ability in the research skills peculiar to a given field. The skills needed by the historian are different from those needed by the chemist; the physicist needs skills different from those of the psychologist.[8]

Not infrequently the skilled researcher is not highly skilled in group communication. But his contribution should not be ignored by those more knowledgeable in the field of group deliberation. Ideally, the inarticulate researcher should develop competence of at least a general nature in group deliberation, and others should be especially careful to seek patiently the researcher's contribution.

Tools of Research

The most competent researcher is helpless in many fields if he does not possess the tools required for discovery. For this reason billions of dollars have been spent on laboratories and instruments of observation such as microscopes. Further elaboration here would merely be a list of such tools. Competence should enable the researcher to know what tools he requires.

Access to Potential Evidence

Another indispensable requirement of research is access to potential evidence. The researcher must be in a position to observe; he must

[7] Sidney Siegel and Lawrence E. Fouraker, *Bargaining and Group Decision Making: Experiments in Bilateral Monopoly* (New York: McGraw-Hill, 1960).

[8] The skills required for most fields of research are described by texts appropriate to the field. For the field of speech there is J. Jeffery Auer, *An Introduction to Research in Speech* (New York: Harper & Row, 1959). A broader approach to the behavioral sciences is found in Leon Festinger and Daniel Katz, eds., *Research Methods in the Behavioral Sciences* (New York: Holt, Rinehart and Winston, 1953). The reader will find many others in various fields.

have the books and other sources of information available. Again this point requires little emphasis except for one very significant development in our contemporary society—the institution of the *security clearance.*

This relatively recent development presents two significant problems pertaining to acquiring of evidence. First, for many people access to evidence they need is delayed, denied, or both. Second, the process of gathering the evidence necessary to justify a security clearance may raise questions concerning the competence of the person supplying information to the investigator.

Because of the precarious international situation today, several million people have had to obtain security clearances in order to perform their jobs in such fields as nuclear physics, electronics, space and aeronautics research. Because of the nature of their research, these people must have a security clearance to obtain access to evidence they need. More than one capable researcher, for example, Robert Oppenheimer, has been denied a security clearance. Even though security investigations may be carried out more responsibly today than during the McCarthy era, people are asked to make judgments about others when they often do not have, nor could reasonably be expected to have, access to sufficient evidence to support the conclusion. This problem requires much sober thought about the methods of determining loyalty.

Will to Observe

One of the requirements for creativity is the ability to complete.[9] Creativity is no passive process in which one waits for lightning to strike; discovery of evidence requires no less dedication. Some people have potential evidence "right under their noses" and still do not have the will to observe, and hence, pass it by. Others seem to be too lazy to look.

There are, doubtless, many reasons why some potential researchers lack the will to observe. The astronomers of Galileo's day who refused the invitation to look through the telescope for themselves did so because they believed that the very act of looking constituted heresy. Today such cases are rare and we therefore con-

[9] See Chapter 4, pp. 75-76.

sign to the study of motivation the problem of the potential researcher who lacks the will to observe.[10]

Flexibility to Observe

Even if the researcher possesses the attributes just described, he may still be incapable of first-rate discovery if he is not *flexible* enough to observe potential evidence. Flexible does not mean weak-willed. The researcher must be capable of perceiving distinctions that are meaningful.

Flexibility of Language. Our symbol system conditions, to a considerable extent, what we see. We tend to notice what we can label, and lacking the labels, tend to be blind. All of us have probably had the experience of learning a new name for something, a bird perhaps, and then being astonished to discover how many birds of this type seemed suddenly to appear. The birds had been there all the time, of course, but we had not noticed them until we learned the name, and then it seemed as if the species had suddenly multiplied.

An essential part of competence in a field is the knowledge of the symbol system of that field. To the extent that the symbols are varied and flexible, the researcher is aided in his perception of potential evidence. The novice in a field usually possesses only general terms which tend to obscure differences by concentrating upon the characteristics which individual members of a species hold in common. The horticultural novice, for example, may believe that the word *rose* is sufficiently definitive, but a dedicated rose grower will have dozens (and perhaps hundreds) of names for different roses. He also knows the names and distinctive signs of various rose diseases and pests that are unknown to the novice. As a result, the rose specialist will be able to spot with assurance the early signs of red spider infestation, for example, while the novice might not detect the presence of such pests until his plants begin to defoliate.

Some Eskimos apparently have as many as seven different words to identify what most of us simply refer to as snow. Their experience with snow has led them to make distinctions, and to label those distinctions, with much greater precision than most people find neces-

---

[10] For more information concerning the problem of motivation, see M. Sherif and H. Cantril, *The Psychology of Ego-Involvements* (New York: Wiley, 1947).

sary. A skiing enthusiast in the United States, however, will be able to make distinctions between various conditions of snow even though he may have to rely more upon qualifying adjectives when labeling the distinctions. Again, he has a greater requirement to differentiate than most people have.

Previously existing symbols are not necessary to make distinctions, but a researcher needs a broad and flexible language and he must be personally capable of going beyond the bounds set by his language, or the scope of his discovery will be restricted. Since some aspects of what one observes are difficult to express, we must be concerned with identification and, if possible, with the creation of labels to communicate the knowledge of the new discovery.

Freedom from Attitudinal Blind Spots. An elderly man, who had spent all his life in the fertile farm country of the Mid-west, visited Colorado and looking upon the marvelous mountains and rugged countryside said, "Humph! Won't grow much corn." His attitude toward land blinded him from seeing such beauty. Similarly, many regard the sight of row upon row of green corn sprouting from rich black earth as a beautiful sight; to many others, the same sight is merely dreary.

Most people tend to look for virtues in their friends and flaws in their foes. Further, people tend to be suspicious of what they do not know and, consequently, are quite certain they will not like it. Most parents are familiar with the child who is convinced he does not like a certain food even though he admits he has never tasted it. Most children outgrow this tendency to dislike foods they have never tasted, but other types of ignorance-produced dislikes are more pernicious. Many people are quite uncertain about what a university is and what goes on within its sphere, yet they are quite certain that they do not like it and seize upon scraps of evidence that, they believe, offer proof that universities abound with "reds," "intellectuals," and people of low moral character. They then spend remarkable energy writing letters to editors and otherwise denouncing the university and its practices.

Possibly no aspect of modern life is more emotion-packed than the matter of race relations. We should like to offer two examples of attitudinal blindness drawn from this area.

A few years ago Sherif and Hovland conducted an experiment designed to measure the effect that attitude had upon the perception of statements.[11] The subjects were given 114 statements about Negroes. Each statement was typed upon a separate card. The subjects were instructed to sort the cards into eleven piles ranging from those statements that were very favorable to Negroes to those that were very unfavorable to Negroes. In another version of the experiment, the subjects were told to arrange the cards as before, but with no restriction as to the number of categories into which the cards were to be sorted. The results showed that both the subjects who admitted to being strongly prejudiced *in favor of* Negroes and those who admitted to being strongly prejudiced *against* Negroes tended to polarize their judgments. That is, the subjects tended to perceive a fairly large number of statements describing their own position, very few neutral statements, and a large bulk of statements strongly opposing their own position. When the number of categories was unspecified, the strongly prejudiced subjects often used only three categories and, even in these cases, they put more statements in each extreme pile than they put in the neutral pile. Subjects whose feelings were not extreme tended to level off the number of statements in each pile and tended to use more categories when the number was unspecified. As might be expected, given cards showed up in a variety of positions on different scales. The conclusions were that those who feel strongly about an issue will tend to see things as black or white. They perceive that people are either for them or strongly against them—not neutral.

One more example is taken from a study conducted by Allport and Postman.[12] The following picture was one of several shown to subjects who were asked to look at the picture for a few seconds. The experimenter then turned the picture face down and asked the subjects to report what was in the picture. In a distressing number of reports, the Negro was perceived as the probable aggressor, and as being shabbily dressed, while the white man was seen as well dressed, and the razor even found its way into the Negro's hands in many of these distorted reports.

[11] Muzafer Sherif and Carl I. Hovland, "Judgmental Phenomena and Scales of Attitude Measurement: Placement of Items with Individual Choice of Number of Categories," *Journal of Abnormal and Social Psychology*, Vol. 48 (1953), pp. 135-141.

[12] Gordon W. Allport and Lee Postman, *The Psychology of Rumor* (New York: Holt, 1947), pp. 64-74.

FIGURE 5.2

From the *Psychology of Rumor* by Gordon Allport
and Lee Postman. Copyright 1947 by Holt, Rinehart and Winston, Inc. Reprinted by permission of
Holt, Rinehart and Winston, Inc.

All of us are subject to attitudinal blindness in one form or
another. One of the main advantages of discussion is that, unless all
members of the group have the same blind spot, they can frequently
help one another to become aware of the blind spots.

Developing freedom from attitudinal blindness in ourselves is
difficult. The injunction, "Be objective," is of no more help to the
researcher-discussant than is the injunction, "Just relax," to the
speaker suffering stage fright. First, we must be aware of our attitudes and the potential effect they may have upon our behavior.
Second, we must work to modify attitudes which appear to run
counter to available evidence. Third, we must develop an attitude of
skepticism about our feelings when we do not know much about the
object of our attitude. The personal characteristics necessary to
accomplish the above steps are our next concern.

Security to Learn [13]

The characteristic of security is closely related to what we have just been discussing, but with this important difference. The personal characteristics involved in competence: will to observe, language flexibility, and attitudes, were primarily object-oriented. That is, we talked about competence *in a given field,* the will to observe *something,* the symbols which identified *that which we observed,* and attitudes about *something.* Here our concern is with an individual's own *belief system*—the way in which the individual organizes, assimilates, and utilizes the information he receives. That is, the focus is now upon the *relationship* between the individual and the object. An example of such focusing is furnished by Harvey, Hunt, and Schroder:

Let us consider the cases of an avid atheist and a zealous believer in God: in terms of many behavioral criteria or attitudinal classifications, these two persons might be viewed as opposites. . . . If they were considered according to . . . their ways of relating to God, the atheist and the zealous believer might be seen as very similar to each other, more similar in fact than either would be to a person to whom the object, God, had a little personal relevance. [14]

Any given belief of an individual can be said to be grounded at one or more points along a "reality continuum" ranging from "objective reality" at one end to "social reality" at the other. The belief in the equality of races, for example, may be grounded in objective

[13] Our prime concern in our own research at this time is with the personal characteristics of those who enjoy and profit from discussion. We confess that our ideas on this subject here and elsewhere in the book are largely speculative. We hope that we will soon be able to present experimental evidence of our own bearing upon this question rather than having to depend upon extrapolations from other research. The theoretical framework which we are building is best described by the term *security*. That is, we believe that only those who are sufficiently secure personally can participate with profit in the give-and-take of discussion, and it follows that similar characteristics are necessary to participate with profit in the give-and-take of interaction with the world in which we discover our evidence.

[14] O. J. Harvey, David E. Hunt, and Harold M. Schroder, *Conceptual Systems and Personality Organization* (New York: Wiley, 1961), p. 2.

TABLE 5.1

THE REALITY CONTINUUM

Objective Reality	Social Reality
The individual perceives that his belief is amenable to objective measurement, that the belief is relatively independent of the beliefs of others.	The individual perceives that his belief may be verified only by reference to the beliefs of others or to intuitive or supernatural sources.

evidence and further substantiated by the beliefs of others such as the virtually unanimous opinion of anthropologists.

One of the most important characteristics of the secure individual is his tendency to rely upon objective reality as the basis for beliefs. This is the only characteristic discussed here since it is primarily relevant to the process of discovering evidence. This tendency has several important consequences.

1. The secure individual perceives a greater possibility for utilizing objective reality. Obviously, not all beliefs can be grounded in objective reality. Many situations are vague or ill-defined, and objective standards of measurement are either unknown or simply not applicable. However, the whole objective of scientific inquiry has been to move from right to left on the reality continuum. Not long ago, historically speaking, the practice of medicine was governed almost entirely by beliefs grounded in various forms of social reality. Diseases were generally assumed to be caused by the devil; charms, incantations, or other forms of magic seemed to be the means of curing disease. The dramatic advance in medicine was made possible by a few who were secure enough to believe that the causes and cures of diseases could be objectively measured. Until recent years, almost every advance in medicine was fought by those who preferred to ground their beliefs in social reality.

2. When forced to rely upon social reality, the secure individual's confidence in his beliefs will vary in proportion to his confidence in the people who provide the conclusions he is asked to accept. A given individual may not possess the competence, tools, or

access to evidence necessary to observe for himself the objective reality necessary to ground a belief. However, others may, and there is clearly no basis for rejecting a belief simply because one cannot look for himself. If the credentials of those who claim to be able to observe are adequate, one can assign a degree of probability to the evidence presented. If the secure individual is forced to rely entirely upon social reality as the basis of his belief, and if he must act upon such evidence, he will hold such beliefs tentatively rather than dogmatically.

3. Finally, the secure individual is not personally distressed by contradiction. Knowing the uncertainties of observation and the hazards of inference, he is not upset to discover that new evidence or different interpretations of old evidence tend to shake old beliefs. Whether he accepts or rejects the new evidence will not be a function of its novelty. The acceptance will, rather, be a function of weighing the two sets of evidence against appropriate criteria of believability. These criteria constitute the next section.[15]

BELIEVABILITY OF EVIDENCE

The previous section discussed those circumstances and personal characteristics that increase the likelihood that the researcher can discover valuable and pertinent evidence. This section's concern is with the means whereby the *receivers* of the evidence, the members of the discussion group, evaluate the evidence they are asked to accept. Some of the criteria[16] of believability closely parallel the criteria of discovery, and some will be discussed in greater detail elsewhere.

Even when facts themselves constitute the evidence, some individual is the reporter of the evidence. Thus, a reporter is assumed in each criterion. In those infrequent instances in which the group observes a fact without an intervening agency, the criterion of verification by independent observation is open to the group.

[15] Our discussion of the problems of discovering evidence bears a relationship to the famous "Idols" conceived by Francis Bacon. A short description of these may be found in Will Durant, *The Story of Philosophy* (New York: Simon and Schuster, 1953). For a more detailed description, see one of the various editions of Bacon's *Novum Organum*.

[16] We do not endorse some of the criteria, though we present them because almost all people use them at one time or another. We shall indicate the shortcomings of such criteria when we describe them.

The criteria of believability are grouped around Aristotle's famous "canons of invention." The terms are adapted somewhat in order to avoid unnecessary definitions.[17]

Logical Believability

The criteria in this category are those that assess believability somewhat independently of the personal characteristics of the reporter or the hopes and desires of the group members. Such criteria are toward the objective reality end of the continuum, and are generally to be preferred over other criteria of believability.

1. *Opportunity to Observe.* This criterion is obviously similar to access to evidence. When using this criterion, the group should ask, "Did the originator of the evidence have the opportunity to observe?" When a statement of observation is presented as evidence, the originator must have had this opportunity. When inferences are presented as evidence, the maker of the inference may have personally observed the facts which gave rise to the inference, or he may have been utilizing observations of others. In the latter case, the group must inquire whether the maker of the statement of observation had opportunity to observe, and whether the maker of the inference had access to reliable reports of the observation.

2. *Tools of Observation.* This needs no elaboration since it is essentially the same as the "Tools of Research" criterion discussed on p. 100. The qualifications for statement of observation and statement of inference are the same as above.

3. *Removal from Firsthand.* How close the evidence is to firsthand reports is the issue here. Care must be taken to insist that there is no one-to-one correlation between the number of minds and interpretations through which the evidence has passed and its believability. Evidence passed along by word of mouth is chiefly suspect because of our knowledge of the possibilities of rumor distortions. Evidence coming to us from most news stories or from journals which make a practice of condensing the information is also suspect. With the current demand for up-to-date news and the speed with

[17] Lane, Cooper, *The Rhetoric of Aristotle* (New York: Appleton-Century-Crofts, 1932).

which such news must be gathered and printed, and with the tendency to select and highlight information so as to capture reader attention, newspaper reports are often wrong or misleading.[18] If the group has not the time, inclination, or opportunity to get the original report, the character, rather than just the number, of the intervening reports must be examined. The personal characteristics examined in the next category of criteria present the means whereby this is done.

4. *Effective Reasoning to Produce Inferences.* Often the inference that constitutes the evidence is supported by a description of the reasoning process which led to the inference. When this is done, the group members may examine the reasoning and thus decide the believability of the inference for themselves.[19]

Personal Believability

The criteria in this category assess the believability of evidence by examining the characteristics of the reporter, the originator of the evidence, any additional channels through which the evidence has passed, or any combination of the three. As is evident from the discussion of logical believability, the logical tests are difficult and often impossible to apply. The secure individual prefers to ground his beliefs directly in objective reality, but when such grounding is not possible or desirable, he prefers to turn to people in whose capacities for observation and judgment he has confidence. Such grounding falls somewhere along the middle of the reality continuum. Three criteria can help the group to examine personal believability:

1. *Personal Qualifications.* When discussing the competence of the researcher, we noted how competence is achieved. Here the question is, How can the members of the group assess the competence of the person in question?

If the reporter is a member of the group or is well known to the members of the group, the degree of his competence is probably well known. However, the group should be especially careful to distinguish between the person's *status* in the members' eyes and

---

[18] Weekly news journals such as *Newsweek, Time,* and others tend to minimize this difficulty because of their greater opportunity to sift information.

[19] The means for checking the reasoning process are described in the next chapter.

his actual competence to provide the evidence they are examining.[20]

If the reporter is unknown to the members of the group, his qualifications are usually determined by a knowledge of his training and experience in the field of concern. The group may learn about the reporter's qualifications from someone who knows the reporter well and is, himself, qualified to judge. External evidences of qualification such as degrees earned and articles published may help the group assess the reporter's qualifications. And, of course, the reporter may seek to qualify himself. One who introduces a speaker, for example, usually takes pains to point out why the speaker is qualified to talk about the subject. External evidences of qualification can often be obtained from such sources as *Who's Who In America*, a regional *Who's Who, Dun and Bradstreet Reports, Directory of American Scholars*, and others. Any librarian can suggest dozens of such references. Even such sources as positions held in an organization can suggest qualifications.

The reporter who is concerned about the persuasiveness of his evidence will usually take pains to indicate his qualifications as a part of his report. In this book, for example, we have mentioned our experiences a number of times in order to lend believability to our statements.

One strong warning should be inserted here. The fact that an individual may be qualified in one field does not automatically mean that he is qualified in another. Recently a number of highly qualified military men have given advice and drawn inferences in fields such as education and politics, fields in which many of them are essentially laymen. Yet, because of their admitted contributions to the military, the public accords their evidence unwarranted believability. Such prominent individuals are entitled to their opinions; yet sometimes they are not qualified to offer certain evidence as *authorities*.

2. *Personal Bias.* This refers to bias toward either the evidence itself or toward the group for which the evidence is intended, and may be both positive and negative. Having already discussed the effect that attitudinal blindness can have upon observation, let us examine how bias may be detected and accounted for.

If the reporter is biased *in favor of* the group which is to receive

[20] This was discussed as one of the limitations of discussion in Chapter 2.

the evidence, there is reasonable assurance that he will attempt to provide the best evidence possible. The opposite holds true for reporters biased *against* the group. For example, the state central committee of a national political party may ask a county chairman to assess the party's chances in the coming election. Assuming that the chairman is qualified for his position, he will probably give an accurate report to the state central committee. This report may be considerably less encouraging than the optimistic statements that the chairman had been releasing for the local press. The reporter's attitudes toward a group may be determined from his statements professing his attachment, but more likely by looking at his record of reliability, consistency, and accuracy. As in the case of disarmament negotiations with the Soviet Union, we usually insist that deeds speak louder than words when we are trying to assess reliability.

Considering bias toward the evidence itself, we must ask the question, "What has the reporter or the researcher to gain if the evidence is believed?" If our answer is, "Nothing except a reputation for accuracy," we usually are inclined to say that the person is "disinterested" and that his evidence is probably accurate (again, assuming his qualifications). Advertisers are fond of citing studies made by "independent research laboratories." If the laboratories are indeed independent, we should expect that their evidence is probably believable. However, we question the advertiser by asking, "What have you left out of the laboratory's report, and have you confused your own statements of observations with your own inferences, or encouraged us to make further inferences?" For this reason, many people prefer to turn directly to reports from independent laboratories such as *Consumer's Reports*. The Better Business Bureau in your community can probably cite dozens of instances in which advertisers have distorted perfectly valid evidence so much that they have received official Bureau censure.

When the reporter has much to gain if his evidence is believed, the evidence is almost worthless unless we are able to find other means of assessing its believability. However, in one case evidence from a biased source may be a proverbial gold mine. When the evidence reported by a biased source, if believed, may be used counter to the reporter's interests, it is called *"admission against interest."* Thus, in a court of law when a known enemy of the accused offers testimony tending to show the innocence of the accused, such evidence is more persuasive than if presented by a neutral witness.

3. *Evidence of Scholarship.* A good report of evidence should be effectively presented in either writing or speaking, well documented, and well qualified. We call such matters evidence of scholarship because they are the commonly used criteria of good research reporting in any respectable field.

Effective presentation includes good organization so that the pieces of evidence are seen in proper sequence. It also includes the use of language, statistics, tables and illustrations that are intelligible and meaningful to the reader or hearer.[21] The inclusion of effective presentation under the category of believability of evidence should be apparent. Effective presentation has little to do with the logical believability of the reporter. If the presentation reveals a reporter concerned with accurate and effective transmission of ideas, his disposition toward both the evidence and the group receiving the evidence is revealed, and the group is provided with strong clues concerning the reporter's ability and motives. If the effectiveness of the presentation is veneer thin, a group skilled in communication principles will soon expose the sham. If the presentation is shoddy, considerable doubt may be raised about the reporter's competence and motives, and the total believability of the evidence may suffer.

A well documented report is obviously valuable to the group when the members are assessing the quality of the minds through which the evidence has passed. The documentation of the report reveals the pains the reporter has taken to get as close as possible to the original sources of evidence and provides guides for the group that wishes to explore for itself. Like effective presentation, documentation lends credibility to the reporter.

A well qualified report is one which carefully separates statements of observation from inferences and claims no more and no less than is warranted.

Emotional Believability

The criteria in this category center around the social end of the reality continuum. Such criteria are based primarily upon our wish

---

[21] This includes most of the communication skills which will be discussed in Part V.

to believe rather than upon establishing a probability based upon logic or the personal characteristics of the reporter. These are the criteria we said that we did not endorse. When discussing the secure individual we said that beliefs should be grounded in social reality only if some measure of objective reality is not available, and that such beliefs should be held tentatively. That is our position here. The criteria of emotional believability are presented primarily to help the reader understand the grounds of much that is accepted by discussion groups. An understanding of the criteria may help group members reject, wherever possible, such means of inducing belief.

1. *Consistent With Our Beliefs.* "A foolish consistency," said Ralph Waldo Emerson, "is the hobgoblin of little minds." Too many little minds accept or reject evidence on the basis of whether or not it is consistent with what they already believe or want to believe. New evidence which corroborates old evidence and new evidence which tends to move the grounds of belief toward the objective reality end of the continuum are valuable additions to the store of evidence available to the group, but the fact of consistency does not, by itself, render the new evidence more logically sound. Copernicus' evidence about the relation of sun and earth was not consistent with existing beliefs; Newton's laws of motion were brilliantly inconsistent with existing belief; non-Euclidian geometry was obviously inconsistent with Euclidian geometry. In none of these cases were the inconsistencies detrimental to the logical quality of the new evidence.

The main value of new evidence that is inconsistent with what we already believe is that the inconsistency itself may spur investigation.[22]

2. *Consistent With Mass Belief.* This criterion is similar to the previous one except that the "Fifty million Frenchmen can't be wrong" notion is added to it. Advertisers, politicians, children, and university faculties are all guilty at times of using the claim, "Everybody else is doing it," to justify their actions. We can think of no better retort than the typical one used by most mothers—"but that doesn't make it right." Often such evidence looks deceptively like statements of observation that seem logically valid. We conduct hundreds of polls

[22] See Chapter 4, pp. 84-85.

and surveys annually to determine what people say they think about everything from sex to Schweitzer. The data are presented in statistical form and the report contains much statistical terminology such as probable error and significant shifts. They look very logical, and indeed many are, if they are trying to make accurate generalizations about what people think or believe. But when such surveys purport to prove what is *desirable* or *right,* they must be rejected. It is not easy to tell a reporter whose evidence shows a preponderance of opinion favoring a position that his evidence does not convince you of the desirability of that position. Remember the discussion about group pressure in Chapter 1.

3. *Emotional Relationship To Reporter.* A variety of interpersonal relationships lead people to believe or disbelieve evidence quite apart from the validity of the evidence. A person's evidence may be believed because he is an authority figure who holds power over us; another's evidence may be disbelieved because he is our subordinate. We may accept the evidence offered by a loved one and reject evidence offered by one whom we dislike. In short, our feelings about a reporter, though independent of his qualifications, bias, and reportorial skill, often form grounds of belief, the shakiness of which is obvious.

4. *Emotional State of Group Members.* It is certainly not a novel discovery that believability is influenced by the emotional state of the hearers of an argument. Aristotle put it precisely when he said, ". . . we give very different decisions under the sway of pain or joy, and liking or hatred."[23] The emotional state of group members is one of the criteria of believability although obviously it is not a sensible means of accepting or rejecting evidence.

These criteria are a list of various means, both good and bad, whereby groups may assess the believability of evidence.

STEPS IN SECURING EVIDENCE

The process of securing evidence on a given problem is no hit-or-miss affair if the group desires complete and sound evidence.

[23] Lane Cooper, *op. cit.,* p. 9.

Many groups seem to feel that announcing the topic for discussion to the members will be sufficient to start the research ball rolling, and many conscientious discussants feel that a quick trip to the library will be sufficient to fortify them for the discussion. Unfortunately, it is not that simple.

This section contains eight steps, four for the group as a whole and four for the individual member, that, if observed, should provide the group with plenty of good evidence efficiently procured. The steps should be followed in approximately the order listed when the group is faced with a new problem. When the problem is one of those recurrent varieties that the group understands quite well, some of the steps may well be eliminated altogether.

Group Responsibilities

Although he had the public speaker in mind when writing, the advice Brigance offers for preparing to speak is easily adaptable to the discussion group.[24] First, Brigance suggests, you should start on time so that you may cultivate your ideas. Second, think on the subject before beginning to gather evidence. Both novice speakers and novice discussants tend to reverse thinking and evidence gathering. "More than five hundred students were asked, 'How do you prepare your speeches?' Over half said the *first thing they did was to look for speech material in the library.*"[25]

This initial thinking stage should normally be carried out in a preliminary meeting of the discussion group. Normally it is unwise for a discussion group to attempt to deal with a significant problem in one meeting. Even if the individual members of the group have known about the discussion topic for some time, their individual preparation is likely to be inefficient, duplicating in some areas and lacking in others, indifferently researched by some members, if not most. Significant problems almost always require at least two meetings, and more complicated problems may require a considerable number of meetings during which these steps may have to be repeated several times if continued investigation reveals something lacking.

[24] William Norwood Brigance, *Speech: Its Techniques and Disciplines in a Free Society,* 2nd ed. (New York: Appleton-Century-Crofts, 1961), Chap. 9.
[25] *Ibid.,* p. 195.

1. *Insight Into the Problem.* The first step is for the group to begin discussing the problem as if it were intending to go all the way through the sequence. (The method to be followed here was discussed in detail in the previous chapter.) The purpose of this step is for the group members to begin to see the ramifications of the problem they have to solve. The difference between this preliminary examination and the one that will be followed when the group really tries to reach an agreement is that when disagreements or trouble spots are encountered, the group should spot these for further investigation rather than trying to thresh them out. In this initial problem examination the group should be especially careful to stress goals and should remember that at this stage it is not trying to solve the problem and should thus spend no more time on this step than necessary to give the members a good glimpse of the task confronting them.

2. *Canvass of Available Evidence.* In an amazing number of instances the members already possess much of the necessary evidence or know how to find it. Groups which meet regularly to solve problems are obviously most likely to have a ready supply of usable evidence. If, for example, the trustees of a college are meeting to determine what procedures ought to be followed to improve the financial support of the institution, it would indeed be surprising if they did not already possess most of the facts they need to know.

3. *Determination of Needed Evidence.* The gap between what is known and what is needed should become increasingly clear as the group moves along with its analysis and the members indicate what evidence they already possess. The members should be careful to note the kind of evidence needed, especially the kind that they might be most able to discover.

4. *Assignment of Individual Research Responsibilities.* This is an important step and one that is often neglected by discussion groups. In Chapter 2 we noted that the spread of responsibility was a limitation of discussion and that one way of reducing the limitation was to make specific assignments to group members. There are two obvious advantages to making specific research assignments. First,

it encourages individual responsibility and commitment to the group objective.[26] Second, it increases the likelihood that the group will have the evidence it needs when it next convenes.

In many groups this assignment of individual responsibilities is unnecessary since the composition of the group indicates pretty clearly who has the responsibility for what evidence. The people have been placed on the committee because of the special knowledge they possess.

When making the assignments, it is wise to let the members begin to volunteer for specific tasks while a recorder keeps note of who has undertaken which task. The more eager will volunteer first and the reluctant members will feel increasing pressure to carry their share of the load. By this time the enthusiasm of the members ought to be high if the other steps have been skillfully conducted. Coupling this motivation with the effects of volunteering makes it seldom necessary to cajole anyone into assuming at least some of the research burden. Anyone who has tried this method knows how much easier it is than having the chairman contact group members individually, asking them to throw their energies into the solution of a problem the nature of which they neither understand nor care about.[27]

Individual Responsibilities

The assignments have been made and now the individual must go to work. He must begin discovering needed evidence and creating ideas for problem analysis and solution. (The conditions and characteristics required for profitable discovery and creativity have already been discussed.) If the discussant is not already a competent researcher, he will find considerable information about potential sources of evidence in most good texts dealing with speaking or writing, not to mention texts that deal directly with the problems of research. The process of gathering and preparing the evidence so that it will be useful to the group has four steps:

1. *General Understanding.* Unless the member is already rather thoroughly acquainted with the nature of the problem to be solved,

[26] A recent study by Shaw provides experimental verification for this assertion. David M. Shaw, "Size of Share in Task and Motivation in Work Groups," *Sociometry*, Vol. 23 (1960), pp. 203-208.

[27] The public decision to undertake a specific job is particularly advantageous, as noted in Chapter 2.

he ought to spend some time investigating the nature of the overall problem before he begins looking for the specific evidence that is his assignment. The group's discussion of the overall problem will probably have been somewhat vague and incomplete since the members were approaching it with little previous preparation. Looking at the whole problem will help the individual in three ways. First, he will be better able to fit his specific assignment into the total picture. Second, he will be prepared to understand and evaluate the contributions made by others with different assignments. Third, he may discover some evidence or ideas that may have escaped the notice of those investigating the other aspects of the problem.

2. *Specific Research.* This is obviously the next step. The individual must hunt out the best evidence he can discover with his talents and resources. As he does his research, he should be constantly aware of the criteria of believability to which he must subject his evidence and to which the group will subject it. If he is uncertain of the value of a given piece of evidence, he should retain it, rather than discarding it, and let the rest of the group be the final judge of its value. Better to have the evidence in hand rather than to be forced to say, "Oh yes, I saw something about that, but I didn't think it was very good so I didn't copy it down."

3. *Assimilate the Evidence.* This is an important step. If the researcher does not thoroughly understand the meaning and implications of his evidence, it is unlikely that the rest of the group will. Assimilating the evidence means not only that the researcher must understand the use to which the evidence may be put; he must also be aware of the implications the evidence has for further investigation which might produce radical changes in the group's conception of the problem or means of solving it.

4. *Prepare the Report.* We discussed the importance of effective presentation of evidence in the previous section of this chapter.[28]

Although some texts recommend that the individual prepare a complete outline of the problem-solving sequence before coming to the discussion, the disadvantages of this practice outweigh the

[28] Part V will deal in detail with the communication principles necessary to prepare effective reports.

advantages. Such practice tends to rigidify each individual's thinking about how the problem should be analyzed and solved and results in each person tending to go his own way when the group discusses. Thus, collective thinking is rendered even more difficult.

SUMMARY

This chapter has attempted to look at the building blocks of belief: evidence. Specifically:

1. Evidence may be defined as those facts and statements used to induce belief. Evidence includes facts, statements of observation, and statements of inference.

2. The reporters of evidence may be either members of the group or people from outside the group.

3. Evidence is effectively discovered when the researcher:
    a. Is competent, both generally and specifically;
    b. Possesses the tools of research;
    c. Has access to potential evidence;
    d. Has the will to observe;
    e. Has flexibility in language and attitude necessary to observe effectively;
    f. Has the security to learn.

4. Criteria for measuring the believability of evidence may be grouped under the headings of logical, personal, and emotional believability. Evidence which meets the criteria of logical believability is to be preferred. Evidence which meets the personal believability criteria stands next in preference, and that evidence which must be accepted solely upon emotional bases should generally be rejected.

5. Securing evidence involves two fundamental phases. First, the group should meet to explore the problem, determine what evidence is already available and what is needed, and assign to individuals specific research tasks. Next, the individual must prepare generally and specifically, assimilate the evidence, and prepare his report.

EXERCISES

1. Observe a discussion group as it explores a problem requiring some research on the part of most members. Keep a running record of

(a) the things that are accepted as evidence, (b) the things that are rejected as not being appropriate evidence, (c) the types of evidence mentioned (whether accepted or rejected), (d) the manner in which the evidence was used, and (e) any methods used to verify or evaluate any of the evidence mentioned. Following the conclusion of the discussion, conduct a survey of the members in an effort to determine the extent to which they sought evidence and the sources to which they turned for it. The survey might range from informal inquiry to completion of questionnaires. What do you observe? What bearing do you feel the recognition and the handling of evidence may have had on the group's work?

2. Examine your likes and dislikes for several persons and also for several ideas or points of view. What are the bases for your feelings? Could you defend them logically? What types of evidence lead to your conclusions? How adequate is the evidence? To what degree are your reactions to ideas or things affected by your reactions to other persons who are identified with them? Does the influence sometimes operate in the reverse manner? What evidence would be required to bring about a change in one or more of your attitudes or feelings?

3. Select some current controversial issue being discussed and reported by the mass media. Analyze several reports from a variety of sources to determine the quantity, nature and quality of evidence being presented by both sides. To what degree are types of evidence confused? To what extent are the primary reporters of the evidence to be trusted? What are the qualifications of the primary sources or reporters of the evidence? How would you rate the believability of the evidence if you favor the major issue? If you oppose the major issue?

4. Continue your study of the issue selected for Exercise 3, compiling a list of persons who are reported to have taken stands, made statements, or expressed opinions on the merits of the problem. What positions do they hold? How are they regarded by the general public? By those most knowledgeable in the problem area? What weight do you believe should be given their opinions? What weight do you believe their opinions will carry in determining the final solution? Can you apply any of your observations to the committees and discussion groups in which you participate?

5. Plan a discussion to consider one or more of the following questions:

    a. How should we decide what constitutes evidence?

    b. What problems do we encounter when seeking to determine the competence of individuals as sources of opinion evidence?

    c. How shall we evaluate the current evidence available concerning the effects of cigarette smoking on the human organism? (Avoid attempting to analyze the lines of reasoning in which such evidence is used. That is reserved for the following chapter.)

     d. What evidence should be considered when seeking to determine the loyalty of an American citizen engaged in any nonsensitive work?

6. Much evidence that we use in group discussion is verbal, consisting of spoken words, written material, and mathematical representations. Consider other forms of evidence, noting their frequency and effect. Does this analysis suggest anything concerning our sensitivity to evidence and its impact? Deliberately attempt to inject nonverbal evidence into a conversation or discussion and note the effect.

7. It is true that no two individuals can ever perceive the same object, event, or process in exactly the same way. The significance of this varies with the individuals and the situation. Its potential may be illustrated by means of a simple experiment using the scene depicted in Figure 2 in this chapter. Select several individuals of similar ages and backgrounds who are unfamiliar with the picture. Allow each in turn to study the picture for a given period of time and then report immediately what they saw. Note the variations in the reports. A modification can be introduced by asking some subjects to report one or two days later, noting the variations within each set of reports as well as between the sets of reports. What does this suggest concerning observation, memory and reporting of evidence?

8. Review your beliefs and select two for examination, one which you hold deeply and another which you hold tentatively. In so far as introspection will permit, attempt to determine (*a*) whether they are founded in social or objective reality, (*b*) the processes by which you justify them, and (*c*) the degree to which each has a component of desire, habit, impulse, custom, or related type of response. Attempt the same analysis of two beliefs held by a friend, using your knowledge of his attitudes and behavior. Then attempt to check your conclusions by engaging him in conversation concerning the beliefs. Compare the two analyses you have made. What have you learned about the bases of belief? About the manner in which people think? What are the implications of your observations for the discovery and use of evidence in group problem solving?

9. Select two or three organizations of which you are a member or with which you are familiar and for each list the common beliefs of members that provide the foundation for policies and programs. Organize your analysis so that it falls into three parallel columns on a sheet of paper. First list the policies or programs; opposite each in the second column list the beliefs that you believe provide the bases for such poli-

cies; and finally, list what you believe to be the bases of the beliefs. What does your analysis indicate regarding objectivity? Regarding the forces that bring and hold people together? The effects of continuous association and communication with persons of similar orientation? The evidence and methods most likely to produce change in group policy or program?

10. Our consideration of evidence is conditioned by a variety of factors and forces. Read: "A Genetic Approach to Persuasion," by William Norwood Brigance, in the *Quarterly Journal of Speech*, Vol. 17 (June, 1931), pp. 329-339. Then do one or more of the following:

    a. Analyze the acceptance and use of evidence in a discussion in the light of the concepts which the article presents.

    b. Plan and carry out one of the discussions suggested in Exercise 5.

    c. Design and carry out with the help of your instructor an experiment based on the concepts developed in the article.

11. Read an article or case study which analyzes the abuse of evidence. Suggested sources might include: John A. Blatnik, "Making Cigarette Ads Tell The Truth," *Harper's*, Vol. 217 (August, 1958), pp. 45-49; Milton S. Mayer, "How to Read the Chicago Tribune," *Harper's*, Vol. 198 (April, 1949), pp. 24-35; D. Spitz, "Timken Edition of Lenin," *Harper's*, Vol. 222 (March, 1961), pp. 56-57. Then prepare a case study illustrating either the commendable use of evidence or the clear abuse of evidence.

SELECTED READINGS

Allport, Gordon W., and Postman, Lee, *The Psychology of Rumor*. New York, Holt, 1947.

Bois, J. Samuel, *Explorations in Awareness*. New York, Harper & Row, 1957.

Brigance, William Norwood, *Speech: Its Techniques and Disciplines in a Free Society*, 2nd ed. New York, Appleton-Century-Crofts, 1961, Chap. 10.

Haney, William V., *Communication Patterns and Incidents*. Homewood, Ill., Irwin, 1960.

Harvey, O. J., Hunt, David E., and Schroder, Harold M., *Conceptual Systems and Personality Organization*. New York, Wiley, 1961.

Hayakawa, S. I., *Language in Thought and Action*. New York, Harcourt, Brace, 1949.

The Language of Wisdom and Folly, Irving J. Lee, ed. New York, Harper, 1949.

Lee, Irving J., *Language Habits in Human Affairs*. New York, Harper & Row, 1941.

Rokeach, Milton, *The Open and Closed Mind*. New York, Basic Books, 1960.

Sherif, Muzafer, and Cantril, H., *The Psychology of Ego-Involvements*. New York, Wiley, 1947.

Weinberg, Harry L., *Levels of Knowing and Existence*. New York, Harper & Row, 1959.

CHAPTER 6

Reasoning:
The Process of Thought

To understand the theory of that which is the appropriate intellectual occupation of Man in general, and to learn to do that *well*, which every one will and *must* do, whether well or ill, may surely be considered as an essential part of a liberal education.

Richard Whately, D.D.*

An automobile is traveling down a street. There is snow on the road and more is falling. As he drives, a man is thinking: "This road is getting slippery; I better slow down. I wonder what that fellow up ahead is doing; he's been skidding around a bit. There's a hill ahead; I better shift down before I come to it. Good, I'll make the green light. Wait a minute! That car isn't going to stop for his red light! I can't slam on the brakes; I must pump them gently. Oh, no! Thank goodness, I got by him. That was too close."

The driver in this example was doing the kind of thing we must all do virtually every waking moment of our lives—observing and drawing inferences from observations. We draw inferences for two purposes, to *predict,* or to determine the existence of something that we cannot observe, or to *control* some future event. Our driver, for

* From the "Preface" to *Elements of Logic,* American edition, 1845.

example, was trying to predict road conditions and what other drivers were going to do. He was also trying to control his own car by slowing down, shifting down, and tapping his brakes. He could not be content with simply observing and describing what happened; he had to go beyond what he could observe.

The process of drawing inferences is the process of reasoning. To make reasonable decisions, one must first separate observation from inference or reasoning, as shown in the last chapter. Second, one must observe carefully and accurately. Third, one must reason carefully to predict and control what one does not observe. The aim of this chapter is effective reasoning.

FOUNDATIONS OF REASONING

The concepts of relationship and probability are two fundamentals that must be understood before examining the forms and rules of reasoning.

Reasoning and Relationships

Since reasoning goes beyond what is observed, the reasoner must discover some relationship between what he can observe and what he cannot observe. Thus, if a production manager, who has a reputation for accurate reporting, tells the group that several men have reported displeasure with the new payment plan, they may reason that he is probably telling the truth. What is done here will be repeated many times over during any normal discussion, and it is usually done without being conscious of the process. Let us describe the reasoning that led to the conclusion that the production manager's statement was accurate:

> All (or most) of Mr. X's statements have been accurate
>   in the past.
> This is one of Mr. X's statements.
> Therefore, this statement is quite likely to be true.

This is admittedly a rather simple type of reasoning, but it will suffice for the purpose at the moment. Note that a conclusion was reached concerning the accuracy of his statement without bothering to corroborate it by independent investigation. Instead, a *relation-*

ship was established between his past statements, that had been corroborated, and this present statement. This, then, is reasoning: the process of establishing useful relationships.

Three kinds of relationships are possible. They are *causal* relationships, *correlative* relationships, and *classificatory* relationships.

Causal Relationships. A causal relationship is an agent-reactor relationship. That is, one factor, agent, brings into existence or modifies another factor, reactor. Fire, under certain circumstances, causes water to boil; anger causes men to make statements they would normally not make; and authoritarian leadership often causes resentment.

We attempt to establish causal relationships whenever we wish to control one event by manipulating another. During World War II, for example, the federal government attempted to control inflation by placing ceilings upon prices and wages. It established the Office of Price Administration and the Wage Stabilization Board, acting upon the assumption that higher prices and wages *cause* inflation. Many argued that this was not a wise procedure because, they contended, prices and wages were not in themselves causes of inflation. The basis for the dispute is clear. If prices and wages *cause* inflation, then manipulating them will control inflation. But if prices and wages *do not* cause inflation, then manipulating them is futile.

In the previous example the reasoning process may be described as effect-to-cause reasoning. That is, the federal government began with the phenomenon of inflation, reasoned that the cause was higher prices and wages, and attempted to control the cause. The use of a causal relationship may quite easily proceed in the opposite direction. For example, college faculties and administrators are trying to predict the effect that will be brought about by the present and anticipated influx of students. Two questions are raised by this process of reasoning. First, what will be the consequences of increased enrollments? Second, what can be done to modify potentially undesirable effects? That is, how can the undesirable effects of increased enrollment be *controlled* by introducing new causes of desirable factors?

Correlative Relationships. This relationship, like the causal relationship, is "natural." That is, both are discovered rather than created. But a correlative relationship, rather than assuming that one factor influences another, is one in which the presence or degree of one factor allows the prediction of the presence or degree of another factor. In statistical terms this relationship is described by the coefficient of correlation, r, in which an r of $+1.0$ indicates a perfect positive covariance and an r of -1.0 indicates a perfect negative covariance.

This concept can best be illustrated by means of the following graph:

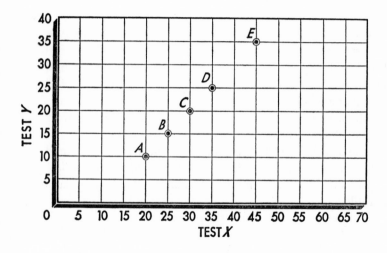

FIGURE 6.1

CONVARIANCE BETWEEN THE SCORES ON TEST X AND TEST Y

Each dot on the graph represents two scores for each of the individuals, A, B, C, D, and E. Thus, individual A scored 20 on Test X and 10 on Test Y; B scored 25 on Test X and 15 on Test Y, etc. Now, if individual F takes Test X and receives a score of 40, we can predict with fair accuracy that he will probably receive a score of 30 on Test Y. If these two tests are given to a sufficient number of individuals, and if there continues to be a comparable relationship between the scores obtained from the tests, then Test X correlates highly with Test Y. A knowledge of one score for an individual enables the prediction of the other because of this correlative relationship.

Sometimes we simply want to know the answer to this question: If we know whether or not one thing exists, can we predict whether or not another thing exists? Though the relationship between the two is frequently called a "sign" relationship, it is included under the heading of correlative relationship for purposes of convenience. When the birds return north, we say it is a sign of spring. That is, the *presence* of the bird leads us to conclude the *presence* or imminence of spring. This certainly does not imply that the return of the bird *causes* spring. Again, upon noting a school building, we customarily infer that there will be desks and chairs inside.

Let us note some further examples of correlative relationships. There tends to be a positive correlation among children between physical size and intelligence. There is a correlation between the speed that an automobile is traveling and the distance required to bring it to a stop. There seems to be a positive correlation between leadership and speed of making decisions.

One distinction between correlative and causal relationships is particularly important. Establishing a correlative relationship does not justify assuming a causal relationship. Physical size and intelligence *may* be causally related, as may leadership and decision-making speed. There is almost certainly a causal relationship between the speed of an automobile and the force necessary to bring it to a stop. The point is, however, that data showing only a correlative relationship do not allow us to make statements concerning cause and effect.

The establishment of a causal relationship makes possible an attempt to control one thing by controlling another. The correlative relationship, on the other hand, does not permit control since it is not established that one thing affects the other. We can, however, *predict* the existence or nature of one thing from a knowledge of the other when we have established a correlative relationship. For example, we can predict that after the driver applies the brakes, a normal automobile that is traveling at the speed of twenty miles per hour will cover forty-four feet before stopping. That is, there is a correlative relationship between the speed at which the automobile is traveling and the distance required to stop. The distance required to stop can be *controlled* by establishing a causal relationship between the size and nature of the brake shoes and the stopping potential of the automobile.

Classificatory Relationships. This last type of relationship is an arbitrary relationship created by the act of naming. Classifying according to some characteristic that things possess in common is essential to communication for it enables talk about many things at once. Any discussion of campus life, for example, would be halted at once if it were necessary to name each student on the campus whenever we wished to discuss matters relating to them. However, we may talk more meaningfully about college students in general, fraternity men, superior students, or resident students. That is, classification of college students in a variety of ways makes intelligent conversation about college students possible.

The reader may perceive for himself the way classificatory relationships operate if he will stop to think of all of the different ways that he, as a person, may be classified. He may be classified as an adult, as an American, as a citizen, and so on down a long line. None of these classifications tells all there is to know about the individual himself. But each, if the individual is properly a member of the class, tells about one or more characteristics he may have. The number of ways in which the individual may be classified is almost infinite.

Classifying is dangerous because of the tendency to believe that the classification tells more than is actually the case. The fact that a man may be classified as a war veteran, for example, is not necessarily evidence that the man is brave and courageous. The classification only tells that the man served in one of the armed services. He may have been drafted against his will; he may never have seen actual combat; and he may have avoided danger in many ways. If, however, it is known in addition that he may be classified as one who volunteered, served in combat, and was decorated for bravery, there is more evidence of his courage.

Classifying a group of things according to some common characteristic imposes a relationship between those things. Therefore the discovery that a given thing belongs to a certain classification, leads us to reason that the thing possesses the characteristic common to all members of that class.

The classificatory relationship is similar to the correlative relationship in that neither permits control from partial knowledge, only prediction. It differs in that the correlative relationship is a "natural" relationship while the classificatory relationship is imposed by the act of naming.

Let us summarize and contrast the three types relationships just examined. A causal relationship is a dynamic one wherein one factor actually affects another factor. This is called an agent-reactor relationship. A correlative relationship is one in which two or more things are related in such a fashion that we can predict the existence or degree of one from knowledge of the other. Finally, the classificatory relationship is the relationship created by grouping things together according to some common characteristic and giving a name to the grouping. The first two relationships are "natural" relationships since their existence must be *discovered*. The third relationship is one of convenience that enables us to talk about many things at once. Only the causal relationship allows us to attempt to control. The correlative and classificatory relationships only allow us to predict.[1]

Reasoning and Probability

Inasmuch as reasoning involves going from the observable to the unobservable, we are confronted with the problem of establishing the likelihood that our reasoning is correct. This means that reasoning is the process of establishing the *probability* or, if you wish, the *betting odds* that subsequent experience will confirm the truth of our inference. The business of modern statistics is to provide mathematical means of establishing these probabilities. The student of reasoning will do well to study one or more of the excellent texts

[1] We have already indicated that the process of naming *can* affect the thing named by virtue of the feelings engendered by names; that is, calling a program "socialized medicine" is likely to cause certain people to view the program with considerably more suspicion than they would were it called "health insurance." Calling a man brave has frequently been noted to "cause" him to become more brave. These are matters that we shall take up in greater detail in Part V. From a *logical* point of view, naming a thing does not alter it, although it may seem to from a *psychological* point of view.

on statistics in order to get a better understanding of the methods of establishing mathematical probabilities.[2]

Let us illustrate the way that mathematical probabilities may be employed in the reasoning process. Suppose the problem is to determine whether method X of training new workers in a factory is superior to method Y. We select forty new employees and assign twenty to receive each type of training. To the best of our ability, we keep all other factors that might affect the outcome equal for both groups of workers. After the training we find that those workers trained by method X are producing an average of two units per hour more than those workers trained by method Y. Our first inclination is to conclude that method X caused the difference, but when we apply the appropriate statistical techniques to the differences, we discover that this difference of two units per hour can occur by chance fifty per cent of the time. Thus, we will not be able to claim with any degree of assurance that method X *caused* the difference and is, consequently, a superior method of training.

Here is another example. A military commander must be able to assess the probabilities that the forces under his command can perform their assigned mission. A commander of a NIKE battalion can, in the following manner, predict the probability that a given missile will perform its mission. Counting only those missiles declared operationally ready, he will begin by determining the probability that a given missile can be successfully launched. Second, he can determine from repeated firings the probability that the missile will successfully fly and not "air abort." Third, he must calculate the probability that the missile can be guided toward its target. Fourth, he must calculate the probability that the missile can "lock on" to its target. And finally, he must determine the probability that the warhead will successfully detonate.

Each of the probability figures will obviously be something less than 1.0. That is, no one operation can be expected to function properly one hundred per cent of the time. Let us assume the probability figure for each of the five operations mentioned above as .90.[3] That is, we can expect that each individual operation will be successfully completed ninety times in every one hundred attempts.

---

[2] We have included some such references at the end of this chapter.
[3] None of the figures is accurate; they are hypothetical figures used to illustrate the method of calculating probabilities.

Each of these figures can be determined by a number of trials for the operation. By multiplying .9 x .9 x .9 x .9 x .9, we arrive at the figure of .59, which means that the missile will accomplish its objective fifty-nine times out of one hundred attempts.

A moment's reflection will reveal that even the simplest of statements is, of necessity, only a probable truth. Yes, even a statement of observation must be considered as a probability inasmuch as there exists the possibility that our senses have been deceived. To be sure, the degree of probability in many such statements is so high that we can operate as if the statement were certain truth, but we must keep in mind that for years people said that the earth was flat because it *looked* flat.

Seldom is it possible to calculate probability figures with the precision that the NIKE battalion commander can in determining the likelihood that a missile will perform as expected. Generally, such probabilities must be assessed in much less precise terms. Thus, instead of making an issue of whether an inference is true or false, we would make an issue of the degree of probability that we can attach to it. In the language of the courtroom, we say that the assertion does or does not have a "preponderance of evidence" supporting it, and we assess this preponderance of evidence to establish a kind of rough betting odds that would enable us to act upon the statement.

INDUCTIVE REASONING

The inductive form of reasoning is the first to be discussed here. It allows us to make generalizations possessing a degree of probability that can be applicable to specific instances. For example, we asserted in Chapter 2 that two heads were frequently better than one. This statement asserted a causal relationship between discussion and an improved product or solution. This statement was derived from an examination of a number of instances of discussion proving superior to individual effort in the solving of problems.

The essence of induction, then, lies in the use of a relationship to produce a generalization that will probably hold true for several instances. It is not reasoning at all if we assert, "We observed a discussion group which performed better than individuals working alone." Such a statement is nothing more than a statement of obser-

vation. It is reasoning if we conclude, "Upon the basis of this observation, and others, we conclude that discussion groups are superior
to individuals in the solving of problems."

Methods of Induction

The production of valid generalizations is an extremely important
task. It will not do to recommend simply that we should be careful
to accumulate sufficient data and explain away apparent exceptions
to the rule or generalization. We must examine more carefully this
inductive process to note the *methods* of assembling data and the
types of relationships that can be produced by these methods. John
Stuart Mill was the first to describe clearly the "canons of induction"
which we have appropriated, with modifications, for our use here.[4]

Method of Agreement. The method of agreement is the method of
induction whereby recurring similarities are noted in order to produce a generalization. It is illustrated by the following diagram:

Situation 1	$a \; b \; c \; d \; . \; . \; . \; e$
Situation 2	$a \; m \; n \; o \; . \; . \; . \; e$
Situation 3	$a \; x \; y \; z \; . \; . \; . \; e$
Situation 4	$a \; b \; n \; z \; . \; . \; . \; e$

In each situation two of the same factors are present, a and e.
Regardless of the other factors in the situations, these two seem
always to occur together. We can thus reason that there is some
possible relationship between factor a and factor e. But what kind
of relationship? In this case it is *only* a classificatory or correlative
relationship. Had the magnitude of factors a and e varied correspondingly, we could infer a correlative relationship, but it is clear
we are in no position to infer a causal relationship.

In a study of its alumni, Delta Sigma Rho, the oldest national
honorary debate fraternity, discovered that ten per cent of its alumni
from the years 1906 to 1931 were listed in *Who's Who*. In general
they discovered that successful debate experience and success in later
life seemed to go hand-in-hand. Can we conclude from this evidence
alone that debate training guarantees success? No, this data will not

---

[4] John Stuart Mill, *A System of Logic,* 8th ed., (New York: Longmans,
Green, 1900).

yield a causal relationship since it is an instance of the application of the method of agreement. There can be several reasons for the success of the debaters. Perhaps debate tends to attract the superior types of individuals; the qualities which make for success might simply have led people to participate in debate.

Sociologists and welfare workers noted that poor housing conditions and crime seemed to go together. They reasoned that poor housing conditions caused the crime and proceeded to tear down the slums and to build more attractive mass housing, only to find that the crime rate did not seem to abate. Again, we have an illustration of an erroneous application of the method of agreement.

On the other hand, meteorologists observed that barometric pressure tends to fall preceding a storm and concluded that this falling pressure could be used to predict a storm. Here was an accurate use of the method of agreement wherein a correlative relationship was used to predict.

Method of Difference. The method of difference is the method of induction whereby dissimilarities are noted in order to produce a generalization. Again, a diagram will illustrate this method:

Situation 1	$a\ b\ c\ d\ .\ .\ .\ e$
Situation 2	$-\ b\ c\ d\ .\ .\ .\ -$

In both of the situations the factors are constant except for the absence of factors a and e in Situation 2. Here again, we can infer a relationship between a and e, but we can conclude only a correlative or classificatory relationship. However, the method of difference *can* be used to demonstrate a causal relationship if we systematically introduce a into one situation, while holding other factors constant, and wait to see if e appears.

Many experiments are conducted using the method of difference. Antibiotics have been introduced into cultures of bacteria to see if the bacteria would be killed. Situation 1—antibiotics are present (a) and the bacteria die (e). Situation 2—no antibiotics are present and the bacteria do not die. In this type of experiment the factor a is called the independent variable, and e is called the dependent variable.

If we cannot control the introduction of the variable, we may find ourselves in the famous "chicken and egg" battles. For example, we may observe that city *A* has the city manager form of government and appears to be efficiently run, and city *B* has the mayoralty form of government and appears to be inefficiently run. Now, is there a relationship between the city manager form of government and efficiency? And if there is such a relationship, is efficiency the effect of the city manager form? It may well be that the attitudes and knowledge which led the city fathers to adopt the city manager form of government would produce efficient government quite as readily with the mayoralty form. If this were true, the city manager form would in itself be an effect of some other causes rather than being the cause of efficiency.

Now there is, of course, the *possibility* that a causal relationship exists between the city manager form and efficiency. At the moment, however, we have no data to convert this from a possibility to a probability. We can say nothing about the betting odds of the statement. But if we have no more evidence than is now before us, and if we are concerned about the efficiency of our present form of government, we may wish to act upon this possibility and experiment with the city manager form of government to see whether we can discover a causal relationship between the city manager form and efficiency.

Joint Method. The joint method is simply a combination of the methods of agreement and difference. Its virtue lies in that we have a little more assurance that the assumed relationship actually exists. We can diagram it as follows:

Situation 1	a b c d . . . e
Situation 2	a x y z . . . e
Situation 3	a b y d . . . e
Situation 4	$-$ b y d . . . $-$

The joint method is subject to the same cautions as urged for the method of differences. If we systematically introduce and remove *a*, we will have reason to believe that a causal relationship may exist. Simply observing these situations, without being able to control the factors in them, will allow us to infer only a correlative or classificatory relationship.

Much of our thinking employs the joint method. We observe a

number of similarities from one situation to another (method of agreement); we note occasions in which the absence of one factor is associated with the absence of another factor (method of differences); we experimentally test the phenomenon (another variation of the method of differences); and we put our observations together and conclude a certain type of relationship (joint method).

Let us apply the joint method to an actual situation. We observe in repeated instances that students who do well in course work almost invariably have a superior command of the English language. We observe further that students who do poorly almost invariably have little skill in the use of the language. Thus, factor a, skill in the use of the language, seems to be related to factor e, proficiency in course work. When we observe the students who have the command of the language and do well, we are using the method of agreement. When we add to this the observation that those students who do not have a command of the language (absence of factor a) do poorly (absence of factor e), we have demonstrated the joint method. If we systematically experiment by training students to improve their use of the language, and then observe to see whether their ability in course work is affected, we have utilized the joint method in such a fashion as to establish a causal relationship.

Method of Residues. The method of residues is the method of systematically eliminating the various factors that might be suspected of being related to the dependent variable until the critical factor is discovered. This is the basic method, for example, which the doctor uses in making a diagnosis of a patient's illness. The patient reports a high fever and general physical discomfort. Any number of things could be causing the illness, but the doctor proceeds to eliminate the vast majority of these possibilities by further questioning and routine checks until he comes to the factor, or group of factors, which seems to be critical. He may further test his hypothesis by laboratory experiments, the use of X-rays, and so forth, or he may act upon the basis of the hypothesis and prescribe some treatment for the diagnosed disease.

The method of residues is particularly valuable when it is difficult or impossible to manipulate the factor suspected of being the critical one. For example, a foreman may notice that a workman's production has begun to deteriorate quite rapidly. The foreman may eliminate various factors associated with the job, since he knows that they have remained relatively unchanged, and decide that there must be some factors outside the job situation causing the decreased production. Questioning of the workman may reveal that a member of his family has an illness which is worrying him, and the foreman may then be in a position to understand the man's problems.

The method of residues is frequently used in discussion as a means of establishing the area requiring more intensive examination. For example, if members of a sales force are discussing what might be done about an apparent decline in sales, the information which each individual brings may quickly eliminate a variety of the factors that might be causing the decline in sales. Nationwide prosperity, for example, has not been declining; unemployment is not rising. But if they are selling air-conditioning equipment and if the summer has been particularly cool, they may suspect the cool summer causes people to be less concerned with purchasing air-conditioning equipment. They may attempt to confirm this by the method of agreement and proceed to discover whether other air-conditioning companies are experiencing similar sales declines. If they are not, then the sales managers must return to examining the quality of their product, the effectiveness of their selling, and other possible reasons.

Method of Concomitant Variations. This method consists of observing the variation of one factor accompanied by a like variation of another factor. We can diagram this method as follows:

$$
\begin{array}{ll}
\text{Situation 1} & a^1\ b\ c\ d\ \ldots\ e^1 \\
\text{Situation 2} & a^2\ b\ c\ d\ \ldots\ e^2 \\
\text{Situation 3} & a^3\ b\ c\ d\ \ldots\ e^3
\end{array}
$$

Here we notice that the variation of a is accompanied by a "concomitant variation" of e. If we observe these situations without being able to systematically control a, we can postulate the presence of a correlative relationship, in this case a positive covariance between a and e. If, however, we have systematically manipulated the degree of a, while holding constant factors b, c, and d, then we can conclude with a reasonably high degree of probability that a causes e.

Agricultural experiments often utilize this method. If one is oncerned with measuring the effect of fertilizer upon crop yield, e may lay out fields of comparable soil composition, drainage, and xposure to sun and rain. Upon each of these fields he can systematically vary the amount and kind of fertilizer used. With the seed, planting times, and other factors thus held constant, he may observe the effect of variations in the amount and kind of fertilizer upon crop yield. This method results in a fairly accurate reading of the relationship between fertilizer and yield and may prove much more precise than any of the other methods described above.

The advantages of the method of concomitant variations are obvious, but it is equally obvious that we seldom have opportunity to utilize the method since it requires considerable effort to set up and control the necessary experimental circumstances. By the same token, more and more experiments of the sort described above are being conducted in many fields that once were governed by rule-of-thumb thinking. Professional organizations provide opportunities for people to exchange information gleaned from experience and experimentation. The Speech Association of America, for example, regularly publishes three journals in which may be found many articles attempting to produce generalizations of concern to students of communication. The growth of the popularity of the experimental approach to knowledge has been phenomenal in these past few years, and thus, we have unique opportunities to utilize the research of others in making decisions and conducting our own investigations.

Induction and Multiple Relationships

Thus far we have proceeded as if all relationships operated on a one-to-one basis: as if there are one cause and one effect, only two things correlated in a given situation, or only one characteristic of a class. Obviously, situations are seldom so simple. Usually several factors act as causal agents; usually several factors are correlated. Successful performance in school, for example, is usually caused by at least three things, native ability, previous training, and the ability of the individual to apply himself to the task of learning.

In handling multiple relationships, we must do what was suggested in handling any relationship. That is, we first must decide the purpose for ascertaining the relationship. Do we wish to predict, or do we wish to control? If we wish to predict, we may find a critical relationship that will enable us to make predictions with a high degree of probability. We need not worry about other possible relationships if we are satisfied with the quality of our predictions. If we wish to control, we generally seek to reduce the number of factors with which we have to work and confine our attention to the "key" causes and control them.

Practical aspects force us to another method of limiting the factors in a given situation. For example, if a teacher wishes to improve the performance of a student in his class, he will obviously be incapable of doing anything about the student's native ability. A knowledge of this, as gleaned from I.Q. tests, may prove helpful in predicting the student's performance, but, of course, will not help change the student's behavior. The teacher can affect or augment the student's previous training by suggesting supplementary readings to fill in gaps in his background. The teacher may be able to affect the student's performance by suggesting methods of study and application to the subject matter.

Still we must be very careful not to assume that we have exhausted the possibilities when we have discovered one relationship that seems to have some degree of validity. Perhaps the most dramatic illustration of this is found in industry where for years managers assumed that workers were motivated primarily by the amount of money they received and the threat of dismissal. *Time Magazine* had the following to say about this matter:

In dozens of plants, surveys of employees exploded the prize cliché of management's folklore—that workers wanted only more money. Actually higher pay rated far down the list of worker's desires. For example, 100 shop workers who were polled by Psychologist S. N. F. Chant on twelve alternatives rated "high pay" as sixth. The Twentieth Century Fund found that wage disputes, the ostensible cause of 80% of all industrial conflicts, are only secondary causes: "Some of the industries most plagued by strikes . . . are among those where the highest wages are being paid." After ten years of polling workers, Elmo Roper concluded that their four chief desires are (1) security ("the right to work continuously at reasonably good wages"), (2) a chance to advance, (3) treatment as human beings, and (4) dignity. [5]

[5] "Human Relations: A New Art Brings a Reevaluation To Industry," *Time Magazine.* Vol. 59 (April 14, 1952), p. 97. Courtesy *Time;* copyright Time, Inc. 1952.

Here the assumption of a single cause delayed improvement of relationships between management and labor for years.

Example and Analogy

Many texts discuss reasoning by example and reasoning by analogy as separate forms of reasoning. Actually, they are nothing of the sort. They may be classified under the heading of inductive reasoning. Let us examine each a bit more closely.

Examples may serve two functions. They may be used to illustrate a point, or they may be used to support a conclusion. The concern of this book is with the latter. If a discussant reports, "Peabody College uses the pass-fail plan of grading and finds it satisfactory," he has presented us with one situation using the method of agreement—a situation containing the pass-fail plan and satisfaction with the grading system. If, in a discussion of gardening problems, a person says that he finally got rid of the cutworms in his garden by the application of product X, he is presenting an instance of the use of the method of differences. That is, all the factors were, presumably, constant before and after the application of product X except that the cutworms disappeared after application. If an individual alleges that his example is typical of many that might be offered, he is simply presenting to us, in digested form, the results of his survey.

This discussion does not imply that the use of the example as a *rhetorical* form does not deserve separate treatment. The example has considerable value in making a point clear and understandable and in making it interesting and attention-getting. However, the use of the example as a *logical* form is a part of inductive reasoning. When we use an example to prove a point, we should not contend that it is a separate form of reasoning.

Likewise, the use of analogy or comparison can best be comprehended as a part of inductive reasoning. Like any generalization, the analogy depends upon a deductive rationale that says, in effect, if two situations are alike in all relevant aspects save one, they will be alike in that aspect also.[6] Thus, saying that worker participation in decision making will work in our factory since it worked in the Harwood Manufacturing Plant means we believe that all the rele-

[6] We will comment more upon this rationale in the next section of this chapter.

vant circumstances in the two factories are comparable except that the Harwood Plant uses worker participation in decision making. This is an illustration of the method of differences and has already been adequately discussed.

Contrary to the expressed opinion of many, analogy, the method of differences, is a valuable method of inductive reasoning. Actual testing is probably the best method of determining whether or not a given idea will work in a situation, but pertinent comparisons may be the best method short of actual testing to determine in advance whether we wish to try the new method. This reasoning should be sharply distinguished from the "everybody is doing it" reasoning. Comparisons should not be used to prove that it is good because others are doing it, but to prove that it might be good here because it apparently works in a comparable place.

DEDUCTIVE REASONING

Deductive reasoning is the other major form of reasoning. It is the process of relating two statements in such a way as to produce a third. Whereas inductive reasoning attempts to produce generalizations that hold true for a number of specifics, deductive reasoning attempts to make use of such generalizations in order to make application to a given case. Further, inductive reasoning is concerned with the probable truth of statements. That is, the inductive process is intended to relate the "fact world" to the world of symbols. Deductive reasoning, on the other hand, is concerned with the relation of symbols to each other independently of the degree of probable truth which each symbol or statement possesses.[7]

Earlier we attempted to demonstrate a correlative relationship by showing how the scores made on Test X tended to correlate with the scores made on Text Y. We then said that if individual F takes Test X and makes a score of forty, we can predict that he

[7] Of course, the ultimate objective of any reasoning is to establish statements that have a high degree of probable truth. In deductive reasoning alone, however, we proceed from statements to statements, and the validity of such reasoning depends upon the validity of the verbal relationships. For example, we can construct a perfectly valid deductive argument with an absurd set of statements such as, "All men are Chinese; Susie is a man; therefore, Susie is Chinese." Each statement may be patently false, but the deductive argument is completely valid.

probably will make a score of thirty on Test Y. Here we performed an act of deductive reasoning. That is, if we grant the probable truth of the generalization that scores on Text X are positively correlated with scores on Test Y, this application to the individual case surely follows.

The syllogism is normally regarded as the essence of deductive reasoning. The attention normally paid the syllogism and the complicated rules for its use are not as important to effective thinking as many other aspects of the reasoning process; therefore, the nature of the syllogism will be only briefly described, paying particular attention to the type most readily manageable by the discussant. It is important, however, that we grasp the essential concepts of the operation of the syllogism in order to examine with greater profit the essential values of the deductive form of reasoning.[8]

The Categorical Syllogism

The categorical syllogism generally receives the most attention. We will briefly describe it and point out its general characteristics, but save a discussion of its usefulness until we have discussed the other syllogistic forms. The following is a categorical syllogism:

> All cases of cancer are dangerous.
> This is a case of cancer.
> Therefore, it is dangerous.

1. *There are three statements in the syllogism*—two premises and a conclusion. The first statement is called the major premise; the second statement is called the minor premise; and the third is called the conclusion.

2. *There are three terms in the syllogism. Dangerous* is called the major term since it is the largest category dealt with. The term *dangerous* covers a multitude of specific instances. Pneumonia is dangerous; fire is dangerous; speeding automobiles are dangerous. *All cases of cancer* is called the middle term since it is the next largest category. It, too, includes a variety of specific instances since

---

[8] For those who are concerned with more detailed descriptions of the deductive form and the operations of the syllogism, we have listed suggested readings at the end of the chapter.

there are many types of cancer. *This* [*case*] is the minor term since it is the most specific of the three terms.

3. *The range of the middle term is specified.* This is frequently called distributing the middle term. In this instance, the middle term is specified to include all instances that can be classified as cancer. If the range of the middle term is restricted in some fashion, the range of the conclusion must be comparably restricted. For example:

> Sixty per cent of the male students at Central College are fraternity men.
> John Smith is a student at Central College.
>   ?

Now if this is the extent of the information we possess about John Smith, namely, that he has matriculated at Central College, we can offer betting odds of six to four that his name may be found upon the roles of some fraternity, and this will be the conclusion of the syllogism.

4. *No inference is necessary to move from the premises to the conclusion.* No new material is included in the conclusion, and, thus, the conclusion derives as axiomatically from the premises as the conclusion, four, derives from the premise, $2+2=$ —. As we have already pointed out, the inductive form requires an inferential leap from the assemblage of specific bits of data to the generalization which asserts that the pattern will hold for instances not included in the group studied. No such inferential leap is necessary between premises and conclusion, but do not conclude that no reasoning is done in the process of deduction. We will take up this point later.

5. *Each statement describes a relationship.* The major premise asserts a relationship between the middle term and the major term. In the first example, the relationship is a classificatory one between cases of cancer and dangerous things. It may be rewritten, "All cases of cancer *may be classified as* dangerous." The major premise may assert a causal or correlative relationship as well. Here is an example of a causal relationship in the major premise:

A decrease in consumer spending will cause prices to drop.
Consumers are spending less. (This is a case in which there is a decrease in consumer spending.)
Therefore, prices will drop. (This is a case in which prices will drop.)

The statements in parentheses are included so that the minor term may be readily identified. Normally, the reasoning will appear as in the statements not enclosed in parentheses. Here is an example of a correlative relationship in the major premise:

Darkness is accompanied by an increase in crime.
It is dark.
Therefore, crime will increase, or is increasing.

Acting upon these premises, we normally lock our doors and seek well-lighted streets when the sun goes down.

Both the minor premise and the conclusion normally describe classificatory relationships. In the minor premise, of course, the relationship is between the minor term and the middle term; in the conclusion, the relationship is between the minor term and the major term. Note these relationships in each of the previous examples.

There will not be a discussion of the rules of the categorical syllogism at this point for two reasons. First, there will be no profit unless the reader is willing to subject himself to a long and serious examination of the intricacies of this syllogistic form. There are five basic rules (some writers give seven, but the last two are deducible from the first five), and sixteen valid moods of the categorical syllogism. No cursory examination of these will help one use the categorical syllogism properly in the ebb and flow of a normal discussion.

The second reason for not examining the operation of the categorical syllogism is that another syllogistic form, the hypothetical syllogism, is capable of performing the functions of the categorical and is much easier to handle since there is, basically, only one form and only two rules for its operation.

The characteristics of the categorical syllogism show the essentials of the deductive process. It is necessary to understand these characteristics in order to properly utilize any form of deductive reasoning.

The Hypothetical Syllogism

The hypothetical syllogism is characterized by a conditional major premise and also by the fact that all three terms of the syllogism are included in the major premise. In the following examples, we have taken each of the syllogisms used to illustrate the categorical syllogism and converted it into a hypothetical syllogism.

> If this is a case of cancer, it is dangerous.
> This *is* a case of cancer.
> Therefore, it is dangerous.

> If John Smith is a student at Central College, the odds are six to four that he is a member of a fraternity.
> John Smith *is* a student at Central College.
> Therefore, the odds are six to four that he is a member of a fraternity.

> If there is a decrease in consumer spending, prices will drop.
> There *is* a decrease in consumer spending.
> Therefore, prices will drop.

> If it is dark, there will be an increase in crime.
> It *is* dark.
> Therefore, there will be an increase in crime.

The hypothetical syllogism possesses all the characteristics of the categorical syllogism with the exception of the location of the various terms. As mentioned, it adds the characteristic of the conditional form of the major premise.

The value of the hypothetical syllogism lies in the fact that there are only two rules for operating the syllogism once the major premise has been derived. In the minor premise one may either *affirm the antecedent,* the *if* or conditional clause of the major premise, or *deny the consequent* of the major premise. If one denies the antecedent or affirms the consequent, no valid conclusion may be drawn. In the examples given above, we have affirmed the antecedent in every case. Note what happens if we deny the consequent in each of the above examples. If we deny that this case is dangerous, we may conclude that it is not a case of cancer; if we deny that the odds are six to four that John Smith is a member of a fraternity, we may conclude that he is not a student at Central College.

Note what happens in these examples if we deny the antecedent or affirm the consequent. If we affirm that this case is dangerous, we cannot conclude that it is cancer. There are, obviously, many types of cases that are dangerous, and thus, no conclusion is possible. You can apply this same analysis to the remaining syllogisms to see what would happen if the rules are violated. Use one or more syllogisms such as the above as "touchstone" syllogisms to check your thinking when encountering examples of reasoning which seem to be confusing.

There is one important exception to the rules for handling the hypothetical syllogism. *If the two clauses of the major premise are reversible, it makes no difference whether one affirms the antecedent, denies the antecedent, affirms the consequent, or denies the consequent.* Let us look more closely at the circumstances that must prevail for this exception to the rule to be possible.

1. When the major premise asserts a causal relationship, we may reverse the antecedent and the consequent clause, if we can assume a high degree of probability that the cause is the only cause and that it invariably produces the effect. Thus, we can assume, at sea level and under normal conditions of pressure, that the only cause of boiling water is heat sufficient to raise the temperature of the water to 212 degrees. Thus, we may write our premise in either of the following two fashions:

> If the water is heated to 212°, it will boil.
>
> or
>
> If the water is boiling, it has been heated to 212°.

With either premise we may draw a valid conclusion by affirming or denying either part of the major premise.

2. When the major premise asserts a correlative relationship, we may reverse the antecedent and the consequent clause, if we can predict either factor from a knowledge of the other. Thus, in our example of the scores on Test X and Test Y, we concluded that we can predict an individual's score on Test X from a knowledge of his score on Test Y, and, with equal facility, we can predict his score on Test Y from a knowledge of his score on Test X. We can state

our premise: "If George scores high on Test X, he will score high on Test Y." The minor premise could affirm or deny either clause with equal validity, and, of course, we could reverse the clauses in the major premise and produce the same result.

3. When the major premise asserts a classificatory relationship, we may reverse the antecedent and the consequent clause, if the two elements in the relationship are synonymous. Thus, if we know that all students at Central College who have grade averages of C or better are members of fraternities, and if no students with grade averages of less than C are members of fraternities, then identifying a student as a member of either class—the class of C or better students, or the class of fraternity men—automatically identifies him as a member of the other class. Thus, the statement, "If John is a C or better student, he is a member of a fraternity," is equivalent to saying the reverse. Again, affirming or denying either clause will produce a valid conclusion.

The Disjunctive Syllogism

The last form of the syllogism discussed here is called the disjunctive syllogism. In it, the major premise is an *either-or* statement; the minor premise excludes one of the possibilities; and the conclusion affirms the remaining alternative. Thus, a man accused of a crime may allege that he was not at the scene of the crime during the period the crime was supposed to have been committed, but contend that he was at the home of a friend. The prosecution, of course, maintains that the accused was at the scene of the crime. Thus, by the contention of the prosecution and the defense, we establish only two alternatives: the accused was either at the scene of the crime or he was at the home of the friend. If the prosecution can disprove his contention that he was at the home of a friend, that is, if the prosecution can destroy the accused's alibi, the jury may reasonably conclude that he was at the scene of the crime.

The disjunctive syllogism bears a striking resemblance to the method of residues discussed earlier. The disjunctive syllogism is nothing more than the systematic elimination of possible alternatives and is used whenever it is difficult or impossible to prove the crucial factor directly.

The Values of Deduction

What is the value of deduction? Remember that deduction does not concern itself with the degree of truth of the statements; it concerns itself only with the symbolic relationship of terms in the syllogism. Thus, as we have stated, a syllogism may be perfectly valid even when the premises assert utter nonsense. We must also recall that no reasoning is necessary to move from the premises to the conclusion. Since the conclusion contains no new material, the result is dictated by the premises.

So far this is a rather discouraging view of the value of deductive reasoning. Were this to be the end of the argument, it would seem that much of this chapter is not worth the paper and ink necessary to print it.[9] However, the syllogism does have two fundamental values.

1. *A knowledge of syllogistic form and operation helps us to identify the factors necessary to form valid arguments.* First, it enables us to ". . . subject to inspection the crux of the controversy; that is to say, we perceive at once what identity is essential to the conclusion." [10] Second, it enables us to avoid a fallacious arrangement of our terms which would lead to an erroneous conclusion from premises that are materially sound.

Suppose a discussant offers the following argument:

> He is a Communist because he advocates the admission of Red China into the United Nations. Khrushchev and other Russian Communists have advocated this position, and all of the Communist countries have consistently insisted that Red China be admitted to the U. N.

[9] Alan Nichols summarizes the most inclusive attack on the value of syllogisms as follows:
"Thus . . . the syllogism is discovered to be almost useless. If the middle term is obviously the same, . . . then the conclusion is self-evident; and even Euclid did not think it necessary to reason about axioms. On the other hand, if the middle terms in both premises are not obviously identical, then we must compare them, and again the syllogism is futile. It cannot assure us of the identity of the middle term; hence, it cannot guarantee its conclusion; and the correct conclusion is after all the entire objective of reasoning. In the first instance the syllogism is puerile; in the second it is incompetent." Alan Nichols, *Discussion and Debate* (New York: Harcourt, Brace, 1941), p. 336.
[10] *Ibid.*, p. 337.

By putting this argument into the syllogistic form demanded by the argument, we arrive at the following:

> If he advocates the admission of Red China into the U. N., he is (may be classified as) a Communist.
> He does advocate this admission.
> Therefore, he is a Communist.

We see the difficulty at once. There is no trouble with the form of the syllogism as stated, but there is trouble with the inductive support of the major premise. The discussant has provided evidence to show that Communists may be classed among those who desire the admission of Red China into the U. N., *but he has not shown by means of some independent evidence that those who desire this admission may all, or even a sizable majority, be classed as Communists.* Thus, we discover that the term *Communist* and the term *those who advocate the admission of Red China into the U. N.* are not synonymous. To be sure, the difficulty in the reasoning was found in the inductive processes, but the syllogism helped to expose this difficulty.

To illustrate the second of the two aspects of this value of deduction, let us suppose that a witness to an accident reports: "She must have been driving too fast because she couldn't stop her car in time." This argument sounds reasonable enough until we cast it into proper syllogistic form, which will read:

> If she were driving too fast, she would not have been able to stop her car in time.
> She couldn't stop her car in time. (As evidenced by the accident.)
> Therefore, she must have been driving too fast.

Here the witness has violated one of the fundamental rules of the hypothetical syllogism and affirmed the consequent of the major premise. The antecedent and the consequent are clearly not reversible since any number of factors could have caused her to be unable to stop the car in time—faulty brakes; vision impaired by another automobile; immobility caused by fright. Thus, the conclusion simply does not follow.

2. *The deductive process enables us to create the questions, hypotheses, that we employ the inductive process to answer.* This is a very important advantage of the deductive form of reasoning. Induction rarely operates without some predirection of our thinking. We see what we are oriented to perceive and thus we seldom go about the laborious task of assembling data without some hypothesis to guide our research. The deductive form is uniquely equipped to enable us to form hypotheses since deduction proceeds upon a symbolic set of relationships without the necessity of having to relate each statement to the fact world. This enables us to interject unproved assumptions into the reasoning process until we arrive at an hypothesis which can be tested. For example, mathematicians and physicists had arrived at an impasse because they were operating under Euclidian assumptions concerning geometry. Einstein's great contribution was the now famous assumption that the speed of light be considered as a constant. Making this assumption, he was able to derive deductively a series of hypotheses that were later tested by others and found to be useful hypotheses. They enabled physicists to make better predictions and controls.

Deductive reasoning, therefore, has an important role to play in the solution of problems. We have shown a reasonably usable method of handling the deductive form that takes it out of the category of being a parlor game for logicians and mathematicians and returns it to its proper place in the world of sober deliberation.

STEPS TO LOGICAL CONCLUSIONS

In conclusion to both this chapter and the preceding chapter, here is an examination of the steps which a group must take if it is to come to logical conclusions.

1. Determine Whether the Objective Is to Predict or to Control

Failure to observe this first step has wasted uncounted hours for many groups. How often have you heard a group arguing about what might be the cause of a given problem when all they needed was sufficient evidence to predict what was going to happen? If the personnel staff of an industry is discussing means of screening prospective employees, they are faced with the job of prediction. They do not need to worry about *why* an individual scores high or low on a test that they are considering as an index of success on the job; they simply need to know whether his performance on the test can be expected to correlate with his performance on the job. If, however, they are discussing means of upgrading employees, they have the task of control and must be concerned with "why" questions.

2. Be Certain that the Argument Is Understood

Failure to observe this step has caused countless groups to be hopelessly split over semantic difficulties. We intend to discuss this matter in Part V, but for the present let us suggest that every group should adopt as its first operating rule the idea that no one has a right to agree, disagree, modify, or ignore another's argument until he can phrase that argument to the satisfaction of the originator. Scrupulous observation of this rule can save much grief.

3. Cast the Argument into Its Proper Form

On this enough has already been said.

4. Examine the Evidence

Determine both the general accuracy of the evidence of fact and opinion that is submitted and the relevance of the evidence to the case at hand.

5. Check the Inductive Method Employed

Determine whether the inductive method is capable of producing the relationship claimed in the argument and also determine the degree of probability that may be attached to the premises.

By following these steps we may be assured that we: (1) know where we are going; (2) know what we mean; (3) know whether we can draw a conclusion from the premises; (4) know how sound our data are; and (5) know whether our premises square with the world of fact. If we discover a flaw in steps (3), (4), or (5), we can then turn to step (6).

6. Present Counter Evidence and Reasoning

The unwary discussant is often tempted to present counter evidence and reasoning whenever he hears what appears to contradict his beliefs. However, presenting it *before* the other steps have been taken can only lead to trouble. Presenting it *after* the other steps have been taken *can* be a real contribution to group thinking.

EXERCISES

1. Experiment and experience indicate that most people believe their personal and public lives are governed by reason. During the next five days, observe the behavior of as many individuals as possible, noting three factors: (*a*) the frequency and intensity with which they state or imply that they are reasonable or that their actions and conclusions are based on reason; (*b*) the degree to which they appear to be governed by forces other than reason; and (*c*) their reactions when their reasoning is attacked or it is suggested that they are not reasonable. What conclusions do you reach? Compare your analysis with that of several other class members. To what extent do you feel any generalizations are warranted?

2. Observe a discussion for the purpose of analyzing the reasoning employed. Identify the major forms and the particular methods or subtypes being used. Evaluate the participants' choices of these forms and methods in the given situation. Evaluate the soundness of the reasoning. Note particularly whether or not the reasoning is sound in terms of the assumptions on which it rests. Note also whether or not the reasoning is sound in terms of the realities of the world and the relationships in which the group members must live.

3. Select an editorial or a short article which urges support for an organization, policy, or program. Analyze the reasoning following the first five of the steps to logical conclusions developed at the end of this chapter. In step three, reduce the argument(s) to simple structural forms such as agreement, residues, syllogisms. What do you conclude concerning the quality of the reasoning? What reasoning would you use to combat the editorial or article?

4. Arrange for another person to observe a discussion or committee meeting in which you participate. Agree that both of you will keep track of the generalizations drawn from examples, analogies, cases, and similar specific instances. (Include the generalizations which you make.) Compare your lists. How do you account for any differences which might appear? What do you note about your ability to recognize your own generalizations? How many of the generalizations do you judge to be logically sound?

5. One of the critical questions in American political life is the extent to which we should judge a man by his associates and organization memberships. Arrange for a discussion, or a series of discussions, to

explore this problem. (It might be interesting and profitable to make tape recordings of these discussions and analyze the reasoning processes at a later time.)

6. Examine the transcript of a discussion or interview which the public might observe, noting examples of both sound and unsound reasoning. Consider how the reasoning may be adapted to appeal to the general public. How would you strengthen the examples of sound reasoning? How would you refute or counter the examples of unsound reasoning?

7. One or more of the following often affect our reasoning as we proceed to conclusions: authority, custom, emotion, experience, or reflective thought. Select an actual problem-solution situation which you have observed a group consider from beginning to end and prepare a case study, pointing out (a) which of the potential influences entered, (b) the point(s) where they appeared, and (c) their effect on the final decision. It may be profitable to organize a discussion to consider ways of recognizing and dealing with these forces in group meetings.

8. The fact that people come together in groups creates conditions and forces which affect (both positively and negatively) the way in which they think. Some of the negative behavior tendencies are: increases in random thought, rationalization, and suggestibility; greater tendency to accept specious argument, give way to desire and ignore intellectual appeals; and also a tendency to accept the group's standards as well as give weight to prejudices.

　　　a. Observe a discussion group, noting the extent to which the members fall victim to these tendencies.

　　　b. Plan a discussion to consider means of anticipating and/or avoiding these tendencies.

　　　c. Review your own behavior and note the instances where your reasoning might have been influenced by one or more of these factors, the degrees of influence, and the effects on your decisions.

SELECTED READINGS

Barnlund, Dean C., and Haiman, Franklyn S., *The Dynamics of Discussion*. Boston, Houghton Mifflin, 1960.

*Beardsley, Monroe C., *Thinking Straight*, 2nd ed. Englewood Cliffs, N. J., Prentice-Hall, 1956.

Berlo, David K., *The Process of Communication*. New York, Holt, Rinehart and Winston, 1960, Chap. 10.

*Cohen, Morris R., and Nagel, Ernest, *An Introduction to Logic and Scientific Method*. New York, Harcourt, Brace, 1934.

*Copi, Irving M., *Introduction to Logic*. New York, Macmillan, 1953.

Edwards, Allen L., *Statistical Analysis*. New York, Holt, Rinehart and Winston, 1946.

Ewbank, Henry Lee, and Auer, J. Jeffry, *Discussion and Debate*, 2nd ed. New York, Appleton-Century-Crofts, 1951, Chaps. 8 and 9.

*Festinger, Leon, and Katz, Daniel, *Research Methods in the Behavorial Sciences*. New York, Holt, Rinehart and Winston, 1953.

Gulley, Halbert, *Discussion, Conference and Group Process*. New York, Holt, Rinehart and Winston, 1960, Chap. 8.

Handbook of Experimental Psychology, S. S. Stevens, ed. New York, Wiley, 1951.

Howell, William S., and Smith, Donald K., *Discussion*. New York, Macmillan, 1956, Part II.

Huff, Darrell, and Geis, Irving, *How to Lie with Statistics*. New York, Norton, 1954.

*Leonard, Henry S., *Principles of Right Reason*. New York, Holt, Rinehart and Winston, 1957.

*The starred readings are more sophisticated and advanced treatments of statistics and reasoning.

PART III

The Nature of Groups

CHAPTER 7

The Characteristics of Groups

... in order to form a more perfect union, establish
justice, insure domestic tranquility, provide for the common defense, promote the general welfare, and secure
the blessings of liberty to ourselves and our posterity ...

from the Preamble to the
Constitution of the United States

Part II examined the nature of the thinking that must take place in
effective discussion groups. Attention now turns to the nature of the
groups in which such thinking takes place. Part III includes the essential concepts necessary to enable the discussant to understand
what happens in a discussion group, while Part IV will help him
translate understanding into action. The material in Part III is intended to be theoretical, that in Part IV, practical.

Chapter 7 describes, with the exception of leadership, the essential characteristics of groups. Chapter 8 concentrates upon the
leadership structure and its consequent interpersonal influence.
Chapter 9 builds upon Chapters 7 and 8 to describe the dynamic
factors at work in a group. The characteristics taken separately mean
little until they are placed in dynamic relationship with one another.
These chapters are founded for the most part on social psychological
theory. The final chapter of this part, Chapter 10, sketches the philosophical groundwork which complements the preceding theory and

must preface advice concerning methods and techniques of effective group operation.

Discussion was defined as the process whereby two or more people exchange information or ideas in a face-to-face situation. The various kinds of discussion groups were classified as to purpose and formation. As indicated, the concern of this book is primarily with groups formed as a result of voluntary association or organizational requirement, and groups whose primary purposes are social, cathartic, or therapeutic will not be examined here. Thus, in this book, the characteristics of groups are limited to those discussion groups with task or learning as their primary purposes and to those groups with sufficient permanency and stability to acquire *group* characteristics.

The literature pertaining to group structure, characteristics, and operation is full of labels for and means of classifying groups. Perhaps, a better indication of the focus in Parts III and IV will result from underscoring distinguishing features of the kinds of groups considered rather than by further labeling. These distinguishing features are *size, interdependence,* and *continuity.*

Size. A size limitation of groups to be studied is essential since a whole new set of concepts must be introduced to study large organizations. Many people believe that small groups are merely prototypes of large groups. But while small and large groups are obviously similar, differences in the communication structures alone suffice to compel the distinction. There is no more warrant to attempt to equate small and large groups than there is to equate personality dynamics and group dynamics. Here the practice of Gardner and Thompson who define small groups as those ranging from two to fifty members will be followed.[1]

Interdependence. An essential feature of any group is that its members are dependent, to some extent at least, upon one another. This feature of interdependence is manifested in each of the group characteristics, in the group structure, and in the resultant forces operating upon the group members. It need only be underscored here. This feature does not distinguish one group from another since any

[1] Eric F. Gardner and George G. Thompson, *Social Relations and Morale in Small Groups* (New York: Appleton-Century-Crofts, 1956), p. 5.

form of collective behavior involves some degree of interdependence. It is stressed since the amount and kind of interdependence is the basis of all analyses of interpersonal behavior.[2]

The extent of interdependence may not be apparent until we examine a few examples. Talkers depend upon listeners; debaters depend upon opponents; and information seekers depend upon available sources of information. Considering *indirect* interdependence, it is apparent that we depend upon others for almost everything we want, but the concern here is only with the direct form of interdependence.

One way to further illustrate this feature of interdependence in groups is to use the "pathway" definition of groups. When individuals' paths toward their goals intersect, and when they become aware of this intersection, they possess the ingredients of a group. In the following diagram individuals A, B, and C find progress toward their goals—AG, BG, and CG—depending to some degree upon each other's behavior. Thus, X represents the place where the paths of the three intersect in their progress toward their goals, and the point at which they become a group, *even though individual goals may be different.*

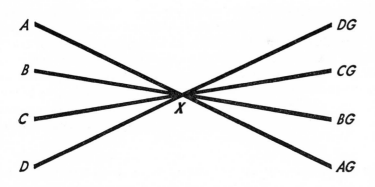

FIGURE 7.1

A "PATHWAY" DEFINITION OF A GROUP

[2] Recall that in Chapter 1 we pointed out that the small amount of interdependence was the primary reason for the individualism during the early period of our country's history.

Continuity. Newly-formed groups possess few characteristics that give them group identities. Groups that have existed for a time and expect continued existence present more complicated problems of analysis. This feature of groups is not an indispensable prerequisite of the kinds of groups that will be analyzed, but it is noted because the analyses presuppose a continuing group. The feature of continuity is especially important when considering leadership and group structure.

The remainder of this chapter examines in some detail four characteristics of the kinds of groups just discussed: group norms, group control, group climate, and group maturity. A fifth characteristic—group structure and power relationships—will be the subject of Chapter 8.

GROUP NORMS

Norms are standards or codes, explicit or implicit, which guide and regulate thinking and behavior. They are essentially criteria by which behavior is judged, and should thus be distinguished from means used to ensure compliance with the criteria.[3] Norms are not peculiar to small groups, of course. Such standards permeate the belief systems of each individual as well as of the society as a whole. To get a better idea of the nature and significance of norms, let us first examine the sources and then the values of norms.

Sources of Norms

Following Mead's concept of mind, all norms can ultimately be traced to interaction of some sort, but they may be most profitably considered as stemming from three sources.[4]

Laws or Regulations. Norms sometimes appear as laws or regulations that are either formed by the group itself, or dictated to the group by some outside agency. When a group adopts a set of by-

---

[3] See the distinction made by Kimball Young, *Social Psychology*, 3rd ed. (New York: Appleton-Century-Crofts, 1956), p. 242.

[4] See Chapter 4, pp. 58-59. We have not lost sight of the possibility that personal norms may be the product of solitary reflection. However, we believe that these norms are usually the product of choices between existing standards rather than the creations of the individual himself. In either event the net result is the same kind of norm.

laws to govern its operations, we note an instance of regulations formed by the group. When a group is created by a larger organization, the larger group almost inevitably sets certain rules and regulations to establish criteria for the smaller group. Although such laws and regulations are important characteristics of any group, we need not discuss them further since their nature is so obvious.

Cultural Products. Norms are sometimes generally agreed upon standards of the larger culture that includes each group member. The language we use, for example, and the connotations attached to the language are norms. Turning to the dictionary for the "right" definition of a word, we find a statement of the word's *normal* meaning. Even more important is the connotation of a term that gains currency in a culture. The term *free enterprise* is used to signify not only a type of economy but a praiseworthy idea to which all politicians must pay homage. Still more examples of this type of norm include the clothes we wear and the places we wear them. Talk about appropriate clothes and manners implies at times some law requiring certain types of clothing for certain events. In some groups, such as the military, laws *do* govern wearing of clothing, and, whether bound by law or not, few would wear jeans to a formal reception.

Religious standards and codes may be classed as products of the culture as well. Whether one argues that the Ten Commandments were handed down directly from God, or were a part of standards developed by attempts to regulate behavior of the Israelites, such norms became both laws and generally agreed-upon standards of conduct.[5] Today, standards such as honesty, fair play, neighborliness, and observance of Sunday as a holiday are norms that stemmed initially from religious standards.

It would be interesting and instructive to pursue further the norms that emerge from our general culture. The largest part of the process of "growing up" is the discovery of what is "expected of one" under given circumstances. Men may not weep; women may not smoke pipes (even the small jeweled pipe fad of a few years ago faded before this norm); boys may make only certain kinds of advances toward girls; girls may make only certain responses to these

[5] Read the rest of the book of *Exodus* to discover other laws that governed the people. Compare them with the laws of other primitive societies of which we have record.

advances; and so it goes. The existence of these norms is not news to any of us, but few of us realize the extent to which our lives are regulated by them. Since the products of the culture are not the prime concern here, however, let us turn to the third source of norms.

Products of Group Interaction. Norms sometimes emerge implicitly from the interaction of the group itself. These norms concern us most because they are peculiar to the particular discussion group. The group itself can do little about norms that are a part of the general culture, nor can the group do much about laws handed to the group from outside. The group *can* modify its own laws and regulations and norms that emerge implicitly from its interaction. In one sense laws and regulations are easier to deal with since they are open for all to observe. Implicit norms are often harder to modify since they are often not verbalized.

The implicit norms that give the most trouble are those based in social reality rather than objective reality.[6] The best demonstration of how such socially-based norms emerge is the research conducted by Muzafer Sherif almost thirty years ago.[7] He wanted to create experimentally norms based *entirely* in social reality. To accomplish this, Sherif utilized what is known as the *autokinetic effect.* A subject placed in a completely dark room and shown a stationary pin-point of light will perceive, after a time, that the light appears to move. Sherif first placed a number of subjects into the situation alone and asked them to judge how far the light "moved" on a series of trials. He observed that they tended to establish a range within which they made their judgments. This range may be called an individual norm. Next he placed them with one or two other subjects who had also previously undergone a series of individual trials. He found that individual norms tended to converge into a group norm even though many of the individuals denied that the presence of others announcing judgments had affected their own judgments.

Other variations of the experimental procedure included placing the individuals with one or two others before they were put through individual trials and placing a "naive" subject with a

---

[6] The reality continuum was discussed in Chapter 5.
[7] Muzafer Sherif, *The Psychology of Social Norms* (New York: Harper, 1936).

"planted" subject who had been privately instructed to make his estimates vary within a predetermined range. In every case Sherif found that interaction in this completely unstructured perceptual situation produced a norm or standard for making judgments and that this norm persisted even when the individual returned to making individual judgments.

Norms that arise from group interaction usually have an admixture of referents from both the objective reality and the social reality ends of the continuum. The significance of such norms is that the very process of interacting tends to produce norms. Further, as the group becomes more distinct and set apart from others, norms and standards that emerge will become increasingly peculiar to that group.

As societies become more highly differentiated, it has happened that groups of people voluntarily isolate themselves from the community at large to develop their own values and way of life. The history of the Protestant religions is full of such self-imposed formations. For example, the Shakers and Mormons "voluntarily isolated themselves from the larger community because their contacts with the community were unpleasant." The Shakers originally had no doctrine or creed, in fact protested against the rigidity of formal doctrine. However, as they became a group apart and carried on their activities, a *doctrine* arose. [8]

Values of Norms

The discussion of the nature and sources of norms has already indicated something of the values of norms for individuals and groups. *Norms provide psychologically meaningful shortcuts to decisions.* In situations in which judgments must be based primarily upon social reality, norms provide practically the only clue to appropriate behavior. In situations in which judgments can be based upon objective reality, norms save us the trouble of looking at the evidence each time we make a decision. Complete reliance upon norms or unwillingness to continually reexamine our norms is obviously an unhealthy way to make all of our decisions. But, lacking appropriate norms and standards, we would quickly dissipate our energies mak-

[8] Muzafer Sherif, *An Outline of Social Psychology* (New York: Harper & Row, Publishers, 1948), p. 180.

ing a multitude of relatively unimportant individual judgments. In fact, failure to establish generally universal social standards and norms could actually destroy sanity.[9]

GROUP CONTROL

The concern expressed in Chapter 1 would have no basis if groups did not control significant aspects of modern life. But groups *do* exercise control. To be examined here are the areas over which group control extends and the means groups use to maintain their control. Before launching the investigation, it is well to point out that control is not synonomous with evil. Groups must have appropriate control if they are to perform any useful function just as individuals must control a variety of things if the individuals are to be useful to themselves or others.

Areas of Control

1. *Task Control.* Decision making, action, appraisal, and advisory groups all control some area of investigation or decision making that has either been delegated to them by some outside agency or that they have arrogated unto themselves. Social, cathartic, therapeutic, and learning groups, since they exist largely to satisfy personal needs only, tend to have little task control.

Whenever we say that the proper function of a group is to perform such and such a task, we are indicating the task area which is, or should be, the province of that group. Identification of the proper area of task control is seldom easy for we observe groups struggling constantly to gain more and more control in order to improve their status. This is not surprising, of course, since the individuals composing those groups are often trying to do the same thing in their private lives. During the years of observing the operations of the North American Air Defense Command, it has been fascinating to see how different "shops" in the Command see their roles in dealing with the tasks facing the Command. Assignment of the ever changing tasks to be performed, as well as realignment of continuing tasks, results in a continual shuffling of the task areas of the existing groups, creation of new groups, and the occasional dropping of

[9] In Chapter 9 we shall see how norms operate as forces in the discussion situation, and in Chapter 13 we shall see how inappropriate norms may be changed or modified.

others. Add to this two more facts. Each group must constantly compete with other groups for a share of the available "defense dollars," and the personnel, with their differing talents and interests, are constantly changing. Thus, the struggle for control becomes understandable.

While there are obvious problems in the struggle for control in the military, such struggles are not necessarily bad, nor are military or government bureaus the only ones battling for control. One advantage of such struggles is that often the best way to secure control over some task area is to demonstrate that the group deserves the control because it is best equipped. This means positive accomplishment. The military makes an excellent illustration since it is a field with constantly changing developments and, consequently, little precedent for assignment of areas of control. This same sort of thing happens in every active organization we know. Let us cite an example that is familiar to everyone.

On most college campuses a constant struggle for control goes on between the student government on the one hand and the administration on the other. Not long ago the students at one major university were considerably upset because the dean of students unilaterally issued an order banning overnight fraternity functions. The students were not distressed because the "overnights" had been banned. Most of the student government representatives indicated that they would probably have banned the "overnights" anyway. They were incensed because they felt that the student government should have been consulted at least before action was taken. The issue—who should have control of the task area?

2. *Control of Individuals.* Without question groups exercise control over various aspects of the life of the individuals who comprise them. The kind and amount of control varies from group to group and from individual to individual. Groups ask members to devote time to group activities; groups seek loyalty; groups demand individual energy and talents; and, of course, groups expect members to abide by group norms. The evils that may result from group control arise from one or both of the following: the group may seek to exercise unreasonable control; or the individual may "make a bad bargain." That is, he may give up more than he receives from the group.

Chapter 1 presented a number of instances in which groups sought to exercise unreasonable control over their members. Such control expectations are the result of norms the group develops concerning standards of behavior and thinking that should be observed by the group members. Not long ago, for example, the Navy announced that the social competence of Naval officers' wives was to be taken into consideration when evaluating officers. This was done (the Navy said) because Naval officers and their families are unofficial ambassadors around the world, and social deportment as well as military competence should therefore be considered. When news of the promotion policy became public, many Congressmen and other officials expressed indignation. The reactions of Naval officers and their wives were generally more reserved. The merits of this Navy policy are beside the point, but the instance graphically demonstrates how groups extend control over lives of their members.

When groups attempt unwarranted controls over the members' lives, the norms that give rise to this attempted control should be changed.[10] The beginning of this chapter distinguished between small groups and large groups. This issue is one of the reasons. In a large group, such as a corporation or a military service, it is very difficult to get at the sources of the norms that may be detrimental to the lives of the individuals. When one begins to investigate a norm he wishes to change, he discovers that no one seems to know for sure just who thought up the idea or is responsible for promoting it. "I'm just doing what I'm told to do," protests the official. Thus, norms emerging from the interaction of large and complex organizations often achieve the stature of special cultural norms whose origins may be shrouded in bureaucratic obscurity.

Often the unfortunate results of group control are a function of the bargain made by the individual himself. (We use the word *bargain* advisedly since we hold firmly to the notion that human behavior can be understood and modified only in terms of concepts of economic exchange.) Siegel and Fouraker, cited earlier, have developed means of measuring this.[11] Another writer supporting this view is George Homans who contends that social behavior must be

[10] In Chapter 13 we intend to show how this may be done in *small groups.*
        [11] Sidney Siegel and Lawrence E. Fouraker, *Bargaining and Group Decision Making: Experiments in Bilateral Monopoly* (New York: McGraw-Hill, 1960).

viewed "as an exchange of activity, tangible or intangible, and more or less rewarding or costly, between at least two persons." [12]

An individual commits himself to a group because he perceives that the attainment of his goals depends upon others, as noted earlier in this chapter. He must pay something in order to secure these group benefits, and when the result of the bargain is that he sells his birthright for a mess of pottage, he has made a bad bargain. An insecure individual, for example, may be so concerned with belonging to a group that he exchanges his own integrity for social approbation. The numerous cases of social climbers will serve adequately to illustrate this kind of bargain.

Fraternities and sororities serve a very important function for many students, especially those in a large college or university. These groups provide the student with a sense of identity and enable him to be at least a moderately large frog in a reasonably small pond. Usually the area of control over individual life that fraternities and sororities maintain is reasonable. Occasionally the groups expect and the individuals allow more control than they should. The following are two illustrations of individual bargains with fraternities and sororities.

During the years immediately following World War II, at the University of Colorado, most of the debaters were veterans who were older and more mature than the average undergraduates of today. It happened that the debate coach asked one of his "veteran" debaters to participate in some debate project at the same time his fraternity was engaged in a project. The debater told his fraternity officers that he could not attend the fraternity function because of his commitments to the debate program. The fraternity officer threatened the debater with loss of fraternity membership if he did not attend the function; whereupon the debater took off his pin and handed it to the officer. In short, the strength of the area of control exercised by the fraternity was not equal to the strength of control exercised by the debate program.

The second example is more general. Several years of observing students and their fraternal affiliations has made evident the fact that the control exercised by fraternities and sororities over the lives

---

[12] George C. Homans, *Social Behavior: Its Elementary Forms* (New York: Harcourt, Brace & World, 1961), p. 13.

of members is strongest in the freshman and sophomore years. As the student grows older and finds more group associations outside of his fraternity, his attachment to the fraternity and the fraternity's control over him lessen.

Means of Control

To turn from examining the areas of group control to the means of enforcing their control, it is necessary to examine the resources that the group has to establish its bargaining position *vis-a-vis* the external world, when considering task control, and *vis-a-vis* individuals, when considering individual control. Our examination here will be brief since the majority of these matters are a function of leadership and power relationships.

Enforcement of control must take some form of reward, punishment, or both. These two terms have been used for a number of years in a variety of fields, and many people tend to view rewards and punishments as largely external things. A man is rewarded by payment for work; he is punished by dismissal or demotion.[13] In contrast let us cite two of the six assumptions developed by McGregor in his excellent treatment of management philosophy:

> 2. *External control and the threat of punishment are not the only means for bringing about effort toward organizational objectives. Man will exercise self-direction and self-control in the service of objectives to which he is committed.*
>
> 3. *Commitment to objectives is a function of the rewards associated with their achievement.* The most significant of such rewards, e.g., the satisfaction of ego and self-actualization needs, can be direct products of effort directed toward organizational objectives. [14]

The idea of bargaining leads us into the next section of this chapter—the problem of establishing effective interpersonal relationships within the group.

[13] In Chapters 12 and 14 we shall recommend kinds of rewards and punishments that are more meaningful than those that are largely extrinsic to the task to be accomplished.

[14] Douglas McGregor, *The Human Side of Enterprise* (New York: McGraw-Hill, 1960), pp. 47-48.

GROUP CLIMATE

A group may be characterized by the kind of relationship that exists among the several members. This relationship may be called the group climate. It is a function of the kind of interdependence that exists among the members of a group. As we have seen, becoming a part of a group means the individual is dependent to some degree upon other individuals for the accomplishment of his goals. The basic clue to interpersonal relationships is therefore found in the nature of the goals of the various individuals, so let us examine more closely the nature of goals and goal-setting behavior.

Goals: The Basis of Group Climate

Chapter 4 discussed the matter of goal setting in the pattern of reflective thinking and pointed out that it was important to assess correctly what goals would be adequate for the solution of the problem.[15] When we examine the behavior of any individual, we find that in a complex situation such as a group discussion he must solve a whole host of problems and, consequently, must select a whole host of goals. For example, when another member has just finished making a suggestion to the group, the discussant must solve at least these problems: Should I speak at all? If I speak, should I oppose, amend, expand, ignore the suggestion just made? That is, it cannot be assumed that there is only one main problem before a group at one time. Probably hundreds of small problems, some related to the main problem and some not, may confront the individuals in the group.

When we think of multiple problems, we must note further that a particular act may be intended to move an individual in the direction of *several* goals. For example, a contribution in a discussion may carry the discussant in the direction of the following goals: (1) the goal of helping the group solve the main problem; (2) the goal of being regarded as an indispensable member of the group; (3) the goal of discrediting another who did not have the information or whose reasoning was shaky; (4) the goal of manipulating the group. The individual is probably not directly conscious of much of his

[15] See pp. 71-73 above.

goal-selecting and goal-seeking activity. Doubtless he selects most goals habitually in response to certain stimuli. The group's norms, the individual's attitudes and personal security, and his prior state of well being all act to influence his selection and means of attaining goals. Certainly the individual seldom makes public most of the goals he seeks. Sometimes he is silent because he doesn't feel that announcing his goals is important; sometimes he is unwilling to announce them; sometimes he doesn't know how to announce them; and sometimes he doesn't know himself that he seeks them. Haiman calls this unannounced list of goals the individual's "hidden agenda." [16]

Some goal seeking behavior does not depend upon other individuals. Such goals are individual goals that do not require a group for satisfaction. However, if the attainment of the goal depends to some extent upon others' behavior, a group situation is involved.

Complementary and Antagonistic Goals

In his study of the effects of cooperation and competition, Morton Deutsch pointed out the essential distinction between the kinds of goals that give rise either to cooperation or competition.[17] In a cooperative situation the individuals in the situation can reach their respective goals *only if all the members in the situation can also reach their goals.* We will call such goals *complementary goals.* In a competitive situation the goals are such that an individual can reach his goals *only if the others do not reach their goals.* These goals we will call *antagonistic goals.*[18] For example, if a teacher tells his class in group discussion that they will be *ranked* on the basis of their contributions and that the best will receive a certain grade, the next best a lower grade, and so forth, a situation is created in which each individual can reach his own goal, a good grade, *only* if the others

---

[16] Franklyn S. Haiman, *Group Leadership and Democratic Action* (Boston: Houghton Mifflin, 1951).

[17] Morton Deutsch, "The Effects of Co-operation and Competition upon Group Process" (Unpublished Ph.D. dissertation, Dept. of Psychology, Massachusetts Institute of Technology, 1948). See also the article by Deutsch with the same title in Dorwin Cartwright and Alvin Zander, eds., *Group Dynamics: Research and Theory,* 2nd ed. (Evanston, Ill.: Row, Peterson, 1960), pp. 414-448. See also the articles by R. Victor Harnack cited in Chapter 13.

[18] Deutsch used the terms *promotively interdependent* and *contriently interdependent* for the terms *complementary* and *antagonistic* respectively.

in the group *do not* reach their goals. There exists an antagonistic set of goals. In order to accomplish this main goal, a discussant may have other goals such as discrediting others, disparaging their efforts, and blocking their attempts.

The other extreme might be a situation in which the teacher tells the members of the class that they will be judged as a group and the group will be ranked in comparison with other groups. In this situation the individual may reach his own goal, a good grade, only if the other members also reach their goals. There exist complementary goals. In order to achieve this main goal, an individual's other goals will probably include helping other members, actively encouraging them, and rewarding their efforts.

There are many examples of complementary and antagonistic goals. The goal of victory is a complementary goal for the members of one football team since none can achieve it unless all do. The same goal is antagonistic when the two teams are considered since if one team wins, the other must lose. The goal of speaking and holding the floor is a complementary goal if others wish to listen. It is antagonistic if another is trying to get the floor at the same time. In the football illustration the goal of victory is a shared goal; in the speaking illustration the goal of speaking is an individual goal. Yet either can be complementary or antagonistic *depending upon how the search for it affects others' goals*.

The terms *cooperation* and *competition* are frequently used to describe the climate of a group, and discussants are often given much advice about the virtues of cooperating with others. Some of the advice seems to make cooperation an end in itself. The hard-headed approach is to say that an individual will cooperate if he perceives his goals as complementary to those of others and he will compete if he perceives his goals as antagonistic to those of others.

An issue was made of the number of problems and goals that exist in the normal discussion because seldom are discussions completely dominated by one complementary or antagonistic goal. The situation is usually much more difficult to analyze. It is helpful to think of goal complexes or goal clusters which tend to dominate an individual's behavior. The relationships between goals and cooperation and competition are represented by the following diagram.

TABLE 7.1

Perceived Goals

Members perceive that the majority of their goals are complementary.	Members are not sure whether the majority of their goals are complementary or antagonistic.	Members perceive that the majority of their goals are antagonistic.

Member Behavior

Members cooperate.	Members are cautious and spar for position.	Members compete.

Effects of Cooperation and Competition

Before leaving this section on group climate the *effects* of co-operative and competitive climates upon group behavior must be compared. By now, it is already evident that cooperation means more than merely "getting along with one another." Morton Deutsch identified the following as fundamental differences between cooperative and competitive behavior.[19]

1. *More substitutability of action will be evidenced in cooperative situations than in competitive situations.* That is, individuals in a cooperative situation will not feel a compunction to perform the same acts that others have performed so long as the actions of the others are moving the group toward its goal(s).[20] We have all observed discussions go around and around until everyone had seemingly discovered the solution to the problem himself. Such discussions indicate fundamentally competitive relationships. Harnack and

[19] Morton Deutsch, *op. cit.* (either article).
[20] Many other studies have shown essentially the same thing. Note particularly Helen B. Lewis, "An Experimental Study of the Role of the Ego in Work: I. The Role of the Ego in Co-operative Work," *Journal of Experimental Psychology*, Vol. 34 (1944), pp. 113-126. Also H. Lewis and M. Franklin, "An Experimental Study of the Role of Ego in Work: II. The Significance of Task-Orientation in Work," *Journal of Experimental Psychology*, Vol. 34 (1944), pp. 195-215.

Goetzinger conducted an investigation a few years ago in which complete transcripts of discussions were kept. The suggestions advanced by the discussants were analyzed to determine what happened to the original suggestion. The researchers discovered that the majority of suggestions finally adopted, not counting routine procedural suggestions such as, "Let's arrange our chairs in a circle," were adopted after most of the discussants had made the same suggestion, usually in different words without giving credit to the originator.[21]

2. *Individuals will react more favorably toward the actions of others in cooperative situations than in competitive situations.* This effect is rather obvious. It simply means that cooperating individuals will evaluate their fellow cooperators more highly than their competitors.

3. *There will be greater positive inducibility in cooperative situations than in competitive situations.* That is, members of cooperating groups will be more inclined to adopt suggestions made by other members of the group. This type of acceptance should be distinguished from the acceptance that a submissive individual gives to actions initiated by a dominant individual. If the group is an optimum cooperating group, members will accept or reject suggestions made by others largely upon the merit of the suggestions. There will thus tend to be a greater degree of positive inducibility since members do not reject suggestions simply because their acceptance will help move a competitor closer to his goal and thereby preclude the rejecting members' attainment of their goals.

We have observed, nonetheless, a danger that a cooperating group may miss significant shortcomings in the suggestions offered by group members.[22] Another significant difference, however, between cooperating and competing groups is that cooperating individuals tend to openly criticize one another more readily than competitors. This seems contradictory at first glance, but a moment's reflection explains it. Constructive criticism of another is one way of helping that person. Withholding constructive criticism

[21] R. Victor Harnack and Charles Goetzinger, "Determining the Sources of Influence in Discussion Groups" (Paper presented at the national convention of the Speech Association of America, December, 1955).

[22] One way to avoid this is for some members to role play others whose goals are antagonistic. See Chapter 11, pp. 301-303.

of another allows that person the opportunity of making the same error again and again.

4. *More helpfulness will be exhibited in cooperative situations than in competitive situations.* This follows naturally from the fact that helping another attain his goals, if both sets of goals are complementary, is tantamount to moving toward one's own goals.

In addition to these differences, Deutsch noted that cooperating individuals communicated more readily and more clearly with one another. Further, it will come as no surprise that he also found that cooperative groups were more productive and produced a superior product.

Cooperative groups are obviously preferable to competitive groups, yet cooperation does *not* mean absence of conflict, as some believe. It does mean absence of conflict intended to *block individuals* and the vigorous presence of conflict intended to *explore ideas.* However, encouraging cooperative groups does not mean that cooperation is superior to competition in every situation. There is considerable reason to believe, for example, that a competitive economy is to be preferred over other economic forms. Competition on the political scene is also important. In short, preference for cooperation in discussion groups should not be considered as extending to all areas of human activity.

GROUP MATURITY

Like individuals, groups may be characterized by their capacity for growth and maturity, and, again as with individuals, chronological age does not automatically guarantee maturity.

Many people who read about the advantages expected from group activity are disappointed in the accomplishments of their groups. Students in discussion classes, for example, observe that their fellow discussants appear to be capable, skilled individuals, but the group does not seem to function effectively. Members of a newly-formed civic committee may be puzzled to discover that the group, composed of people who have experience in such groups, seems to take so long to get under way.

The answer to this bewilderment is that, despite the presence of able members, the groups in question had not yet matured.

We have referred to groups composed of otherwise able individuals. If the group is composed of individuals who lack the personal characteristics, skills, and insights requisite to effective discussion, the group will necessarily be immature.

Describing a mature group is describing an effective group. Thus, the remainder of this section, concentrates upon those factors necessary for a group to begin to mature and criteria whereby an observer may detect the degree of maturity of a group. Although these criteria are not exclusively related to maturity, they do indicate quite clearly the degree of group maturity.

Maturation Requirements

Our discussion of maturation requirements begins with the assumption that the group is composed of the able individuals whom we describe above. If the individuals have the capacity but lack the skills and understandings necessary to produce the mature group, the individuals can mature with the group. There are four additional requirements for group maturity.

1. *Justifiable Raison d'Etre.* The cause or reason for the existence of the group must be justifiable if the group is to mature. Recall the "pathway" definition of a group showing how a group provides a kind of gateway which mediates the goal striving of the group members. If either the individual goals, that the group is established to facilitate, or the group goal, that emerges after interaction, is significant, the first major requirement for maturity exists. If the group is one of the unrealistic groups described in Chapter 4, it has little chance of maturing.[23]

Sometimes the group objective is of such overriding importance that the group grows up in a hurry. War time emergencies are cases in point. Ernie Pyle has recorded hundreds of instances in which truly mature groups were formed almost instantly.[24] The international planning by the military leaders of the Allies in World War II was an instance of the importance of the group objectives in attaining maturity. It seems all the more remarkable that the United States and Canada have been able to work out such a mature approach to mutual defense through the North American Air De-

[23] See Chapter 4, pp. 77-78.
[24] Ernie Pyle, *Here Is Your War* (Chicago: Consolidated, 1944).

fense Command since the national objectives of both countries are not nearly so clear as they were during war.

2. *Realistic Opportunities for Progressive Successes.* The slogan, "Nothing succeeds like success," is a cliché, but it is nonetheless fundamentally sound. If a group is forced to tackle problems beyond its scope in the early stages of group development, the group may well fail and the members become dissatisfied with the group and pessimistic about its future. This point is especially important to remember in discussion classes. Early group tasks should be those that the group members can undertake with reasonable prospect of observable success. This does not mean that the group must meet with complete success on each task. Some failures are probably inevitable, but a measure of success must be present. Anyone familiar with amateur theatre groups realizes the importance of early success. When a mature group attempts a bizarre performance that fails, they can usually take the failure in their stride; if the same failure falls upon a newly-formed, immature group, the result may be fatal.

3. *Promise of Continuity.* This requisite needs no emphasis. If the members see no prospect of continuity, they cannot be expected to do more than attack the immediate problem as best they can without worry about the nonexistent tomorrow.

4. *Promise of Intergroup Status.* There is no need to cavil at the desire for status. If the group is to recruit and retain able members and keep their interest, the group must hold forth some promise of status in the world of which the group is a part. Second-rate schools, for example, have little prospect of attracting first-rate faculty members unless the school can provide evidence that it is "on the way" and the first-rate teacher can "get in on the ground floor."

Each of these requisites for group maturity is not necessarily an "either-or" condition. Seldom do we find a group, however, in which any of the requisites is entirely absent. The issue here is whether the requisite exists in sufficient degree to make further growth probable. Assuming that a group does possess the requisites in sufficient degree, how then do we distinguish the degree of maturity in that group?

Maturity Criteria

While the age of a group may be a clue to its maturity, the five criteria below are more reliable indices. Each of the criteria is related to criteria of group effectiveness, but focuses upon maturity.

1. *Degree of Reliance upon Rules and Regulations.* Generally speaking the more a group must be conscious of rules of procedure, the more immature the group, for the more mature group will have developed norms and traditions that enable it to operate without constant reliance upon constitutions or bylaws. A history of collective effort alone will not provide freedom from codified regulations unless that history is accompanied by a growth in the degree of interpersonal *confidence, respect,* and *affection.* Of dozens of examples of this criterion, here are a few:

International conferences today provide interesting examples of immature groups. The conferences must be preceded by exhaustive preliminary work to draw up agendas, and must follow rigidly prescribed rules.

When our country was formed, we found it necessary to draft a written constitution with a variety of built-in checks and balances because we lacked the traditions and the established confidence, respect, and affection that has enabled England to operate without a written constitution. Today, our interpretation of the Constitution is so broad and flexible that we appear to operate as much upon tradition as upon the written document.

Student governing groups, because they turn over membership so often, are plagued by considerations of rules and regulations. A good example is a student-faculty governing group consisting of nine students, three alumni members, and three faculty members. The faculty and alumni served for three-year terms, but the students served for one-year terms. Each year, therefore, new tables of organization, lists of responsibilities, and operating procedures had to be drawn up. Fully half the time was spent deciding upon the rules; only the time remaining was available for substantive discussion.

2. *Degree of Intragroup Competition for Status.* Until the group has begun to achieve a degree of intergroup status and until the members have committed themselves to attainment of the group

objective, there is likely to be considerable striving for status *vis-a-vis* the other members of the group. Moreover, the members of a mature group care less about intragroup status than accomplishing their main mission. Again, the amount of interpersonal confidence, respect, and affection are clues to this criterion. If these interpersonal relations exist positively, the rewards for successful action will ultimately be appropriately distributed among the members of the group. Successful athletic teams almost always display very little intragroup competition for status. Someone once said, "Nothing would be impossible if people didn't care who received the credit." It requires considerable individual and group maturity to accept the delayed and indirect rewards that attend a lessened concern for intragroup status.

3. *Degree of Operational Efficiency.* We distinguish here between *efficiency* and *effectiveness*. An efficient group is one which utilizes member resources optimally and one in which the members are readily able to pick up clues and ideas from one another.

Whenever a group is wasting member potential by assigning people tasks or roles to perform for which they are not particularly suited, this is evidence of an immature group. Sometimes haste, such as the emergency mobilization problems of wartime, forces the inappropriate division of labor; but in most instances, such inefficiency is born of immaturity.

The ability of members to pick up clues from other members is included under the heading of the efficiency criterion. Individuals not familiar with one another will often make many errors as they attempt to interpret one another's meaning and intentions. A familiar group serves as an illustration of this criterion. During the early stages of this group's development, one of the many roadblocks was the behavior of one of the members who spoke rather bluntly and forthrightly. Most of the group members interpreted his behavior as indicating antagonism toward the group objectives and methods. Once they learned to understand him better, the rest of the members discovered they had been reading too much into his behavior. He was an impulsive sort of person who spoke bluntly but could tolerate (and would, perhaps, expect) equally blunt rejection of his suggestions. Once this was clear, the group operations became much more efficient.

4. *Degree of Member Evaluation of Group.* The more highly the members of a group regard that group, assuming their evaluations are accurate, the more the members perceive that the group is capable of satisfying their needs, hence the more mature the group. Gardner and Thompson conducted an exhaustive study of fraternity members' evaluations of their fraternities in relation to the value they derived from membership and concluded that realistic member evaluation was a very usable criterion.[25]

5. *Degree of Permissiveness.* Sometimes this criterion is included under headings like involvement, freedom from apathy, or friendliness. The meaning here is simple. There is a degree in any group to which individuals feel free to speak their minds. Members of mature groups will speak their minds quite freely and frankly; they will be inhibited only by the normal restraints of tact, propriety, and common sense. Members of immature groups are often seen leaving meetings muttering ideas which they did not feel free to express during the meeting.

For example, here is the case of an experience an individual had when he believed that the group of which he was a part had matured sufficiently to allow free expression. After expressing some views about what he considered unwise administrative practices of the organization of which the group was a part, he found himself being called to account for a distorted version of what he had said. Another group member had apparently been telling tales out of school and there were even moves afoot to fire the frank member. By the time the smoke had cleared away, there was little love lost between the two. Both stayed, but because of this experience it was years before that group became mature enough to provide genuine permissiveness.

A number of reasons may create a lack of permissiveness. Authoritarian leadership, competitive wrangles, disorganized thought patterns all contribute to inhibit expression. The point is that the degree of permissiveness is an excellent criterion of maturity.

Though there are perhaps other criteria of maturity, if a group measures up to the five standards discussed here, the chances are strong that it is a mature group.

[25] Gardner and Thompson, *op. cit.*

SUMMARY

This chapter described some of the significant characteristics of groups. The list of characteristics does not exhaust the dimensions for measuring a group, nor will a knowledge of these group characteristics, alone, enable an individual to say that he understands groups. The characteristics are like parts of a motor. Taken singly they are instructive but incomplete; when understood and put back together in the dynamic unit that is the complete motor, their interaction begins to round out the picture of understanding.

Initially pointed out were features of the kind of groups to be studied; group size, interdependence, and continuity. The groups of concern are composed of from two to fifty members who are dependent to some extent upon one another for the accomplishment of their goals. The kinds of groups being analyzed, moreover, need the promise of continuity so that they have a chance to develop their own distinctive group characteristics.

Group *norms* occupied the first major portion of the chapter. Norms emerge in three forms: laws and regulations, products of culture, and products of group interaction. Norms may be grounded at any point along the reality continuum described in Chapter 5, though those grounded in the objective reality portion are given preference here. Norms serve as psychologically meaningful shortcuts to decisions; they are therefore essential to effective operation, but they must be examined from time to time to determine their appropriateness.

A group has some degree of *control* over task areas and over individuals. The task control area places groups in interdependent relationships with other groups. The group control over individuals is best expressed in economic terms of a bargain struck between the individual and the group. The discussion of means of control is brief since it involves group power structures, the subject of Chapter 8.

Group *climate* is best understood in terms of the degree of cooperation or competition existing among the group members. Goals are the basis of this relationship. When the goals are interdependent they can be divided into complementary and antagonistic goals: those that help another member reach his goals and those that make it difficult or impossible for another member to reach his goals. Cooperative groups tend to avoid duplication of effort; the members are more favorably disposed toward one another; and the members are more likely to support each other's ideas and help one another. In addition, cooperative groups are more productive than competitive groups.

Groups, like individuals, have the capacity for *maturity*. The conditions necessary for maturity include able members, a justifiable *raison d'etre*, realistic opportunities for success, a promise of continuity, and a promise of intergroup status. If these conditions are met, the group may be launched on the path to maturity. When attempting to discover the degree of maturity in a group, there are five standards to examine: the degree to which the group is dependent upon rules and regulations; the amount of intragroup competition for status; the group's efficiency; the level of member evaluation of the group; and the degree of permissiveness.

EXERCISES

1. Enumerate the norms for each of several groups, such as this class, one of your clubs, a church group to which you belong, or a family group.
    a. Note the common elements.
    b. Note the most important elements for each and their effects.
    c. Consider how you would take account of norms in attempting to gain group acceptance for an idea you might propose.
Try not to overlook significant norms because you assume "that is the only way it is done." Beware of being superficial.

2. A collection or association of persons does not immediately become or inevitably evolve into a group. Consider three to five associations in which you are involved and attempt to trace the development or disintegration to determine the critical events or points. Choose your cases so as to include one that has not yet clearly become a group and one that may be disintegrating. Do not hesitate to consider transitory associations such as seminars, review sessions, luncheon conferences, car pools, and child study clubs.

3. Using the cases chosen for Exercise 2, analyze the role of several individuals in changing the character of the association.
    a. Which ones were most receptive or helpful to the development of groups? Which ones were the least inclined to accept or aid group development? On what factors do you base your judgment?
    b. Which ones seem to be the first to disassociate themselves

from the group or allow it to disintegrate? Which ones seem most desirous of continuing the group relationship?

 c. Is there any relationship between individual inclination toward group development as compared to group disintegration?

 d. Where would you place yourself in the above analyses? Do you feel you are consistently in such a position with respect to group formation?

4. Invite several students or friends from other countries to join a discussion considering customs and practices in their homelands such as:

 a. the child's place in the family;

 b. making of acquaintances or establishing social interaction;

 c. the student-to-student and the student-to-teacher relationships;

 d. the citizen-policeman relationship;

 e. attitudes toward civic responsibility;

 f. attitudes toward charity.

Beware of discussing such obvious things as differences in dress or preferences in food.

5. Pair yourself with another individual with whom you are well acquainted and agree to exchange the following analyses.

 a. List 10 to 12 groups to which you belong and the same number to which your partner belongs.

 b. Rank each list in the order of importance you perceive it to have for yourself and for your partner.

 c. Rank each list in the order of control the groups would have over yourself and over your partner.

 d. Are there differences in degree of importance to you of the group and the degree of control the group exerts over you? Are there differences in such degrees for your personal lists and the lists you made for your partner?

 e. Exchange lists with your partner. What do you conclude?

6. Organize a discussion on a question such as:

 a. What are the causes of the large number of student organizations on college campuses? or,

 b. How may we account for the many committees, clubs and groups found in our society? or,

 c. What would be the result if the number of clubs and organizations on the campus, or in this community, was reduced by fifty per cent?

7. Plan a survey in which members of the class explore the specific means by which groups control members. Pool your findings and plan a discussion to analyze the implications.

8. Compile a list of 10 to 15 of the most important groups to which you belong, excluding your family. (You might find the list for Exercise

5 to be helpful.) For each group, attempt to make parallel lists of your personal goals and the group goals. Be fully honest with yourself since this will be a private exercise. Have you learned anything about your possible relationship to these groups? Have you learned anything about yourself and your goals? To what degree have you modified your goals in order to retain membership in any one of your groups? If you have modified your goals, how did the change come about? Were you aware of it? If you could turn the clock back, would you do as you have done?

9. Divide the class into three groups. Group A plans a role-playing discussion of some social problem such as juvenile delinquency, designing a sufficient number of roles for members of Group B, who will actually discuss the problems. In general, the roles planned by Group A should grow out of goals each discussant in Group B is to seek. It is essential to include a variety of antagonistic as well as complementary goals. Prepare a separate role description on a separate sheet of paper for each discussant, with directions to identify himself in general but not to reveal the details of his role or position. These should emerge "naturally" in the discussion. Allow Group B to discuss for approximately twenty minutes. During this discussion Group C should be observing and attempting to discover the causes of the group climate that emerges. They should analyze their individual impressions in a discussion before the class. Members of Group A can be called upon to corroborate role intent, and members of Group B can be called upon to corroborate impressions of effects of their individual goal seeking.

SELECTED READINGS

Barnlund, Dean C., and Haiman, Franklyn S., *The Dynamics of Discussion*. Boston, Houghton Mifflin, 1960, Chap. 9.

Group Dynamics: Research and Theory, 2nd ed., Dorwin Cartwright and Alvin Zander, eds. Evanston, Ill., Row, Peterson, 1960, Part 4.

Hare, A. Paul, Borgatta, Edgar F., and Bales, Robert F., *Small Groups*. New York, Knopf, 1955.

Homans, George C., *Social Behavior: Its Elementary Forms*. New York, Harcourt, Brace & World, 1961.

Sherif, Muzafer, *An Outline of Social Psychology*. New York, Harper & Row, 1948.

Siegel, Sidney, and Fouraker, Lawrence E., *Bargaining and Group Decision Making: Experiments in Bilateral Monopoly*. New York, McGraw-Hill, 1960.

Young, Kimball, *Social Psychology*, 3rd ed. New York, Appleton-Century-Crofts, 1956.

CHAPTER 8

The Theory of Leadership

> . . . I agree with you that there is a natural aristocracy
> among men. The grounds of this are virtue and talents.
>
> Thomas Jefferson*

Without doubt one of the most fascinating aspects of human relations is leadership. Hundreds of serious studies have focused
attention upon leaders in virtually every walk of life. Millions of
people have been exposed to what has been called "leadership
training," in circumstances ranging from traditional classrooms to
workshops and seminars designed to develop specific leadership
abilities. There is what amounts to a national mania for selecting
and publicizing leaders in all fields and representing all aspirations.
Leaders in business receive Junior Chamber of Commerce "Man of
the Year" awards, movie stars receive "Oscars," TV stars "Emmies,"
students receive scholarships, sports heroes receive "All-American"
designations. Such leaders are selected and publicized in cere-
monies ranging from the pomp of a presidential inaugural to the
hilarious "dunking" given a successful football coach.

Despite its excesses, our concern with leaders is well founded.
People know that leadership is an important ingredient of success
in any field. Religions must have their Mohammeds; governments
their Washingtons; businesses their Henry Fords; and every discus-

---

* From a letter to John Adams, October 28, 1813.

sion group its leader. But what kind of leaders? How do they rise; what methods do they use? Equally important, what standards can be best used to judge their effectiveness? And what roles, in all of this, do followers rather than leaders play?

LEADERSHIP[1] AND LEADERS

The first task is to arrive at an understanding of concepts and terms relating to leadership and leaders. What are these terms and what do they mean?

A Definition of Leadership

Surprising unanimity exists among writers concerning the basic definition of leadership. The statement offered by Tannenbaum, Weschler, and Massarik seems both sufficiently comprehensive in its scope and precise in its compactness: "We define leadership as *interpersonal influence, exercised in situation and directed, through the communication process, toward the attainment of a specified goal or goals.*" These authors go on to specify their definition's single common denominator: *influence.* "Leadership always involves attempts on the part of a *leader* (influencer) to affect (influence) the behavior of a *follower* (influencee) or followers in *situation.*" [2] Essentially, then, leadership is virtually synonymous with the act of influencing. And for this reason it involves persuasion, that is, the entire field of rhetoric, whether one uses a language in its

---

[1] This chapter is confined to the study of leadership in small groups. But the examination is more of a sketch than a complete portrait. If the entire book were devoted to a study of leadership, all of the relevant studies and observations about leadership in discussion groups could not be presented. As with virtually every other phase of the study of group discussion, we feel keenly the pains of incompleteness. Much of what we know is left out, and there is much more that we do not know. We state the fact of incompleteness—not as an apology or a confession of inadequacy—but to avoid being misleading. Were we to attempt completeness, this book would become a kind of encyclopedia of most of the social sciences and philosophies that would be out of date by the time it was read. What we present in this book can be helpful to one who wishes to understand groups and the manner in which they may be led. This chapter may provide some framework for continuing study, observation, and practice that are so essential to effective functioning of the individual within the discussion group.

[2] Robert Tannenbaum, Irving R. Weschler, and Fred Massarik, *Leadership and Organization: A Behavioral Science Approach* (New York: McGraw-Hill, 1961), p. 24.

spoken or written forms. The long tradition of studies in the field of persuasive speechmaking is thus relevant to any study of leadership.

Three other elements of the definition should be noted before attempting to define a leader. The first concerns the distinction between *attempts* to influence and *actual* influence of another person; the second, the followers' sanction of attempts to influence; the third, the concept of influence through communication.

Students of leadership have been plagued by the problem of distinguishing attempts to influence from actual influence. Clearly, if one is repeatedly unsuccessful in attempts to influence others, he can scarcely be called a leader. If we limit leadership acts only to those that are successful, however, our analysis of this aspect of the discussion process must await some evidence of success before we can even identify attempts at leadership.[3] Therefore, *attempted* influence shall be inserted into the definition.

Thomas Jefferson noted that governments derive "their just powers from the consent of the governed." Even in totalitarian states the government must seek approbation of the governed if it is to be effective. Hence, before calling an attempt at influence an act of leadership, it must be assumed the followers have sanctioned the attempted influence even though many forces may be brought to bear by the influencer to secure compliance. Therefore, an order, which the follower has no choice but to obey, is not an act of leadership.

The term *communication*, like the term *leadership*, is broad. It includes gesture and the use of nonverbal symbols as well as conventional language; but when the term is used here, it does not include the kind of communication involved in "pace setting." Certain women are known as fashion leaders because their preferences in clothing influence other women to copy them. Here, the term *leadership* excludes such influencing, which is largely emulation, since it is not accomplished by means of what is commonly called communication.

---

[3] The term *persuasion* is similarly difficult to interpret. Brembeck and Howell, for example, define persuasion as *"the conscious attempt to modify thought and action by manipulating the thought and action of men toward pre-determined ends."* Their difficulty with the word *attempt* is comparable to our own. See Winston L. Brembeck and William S. Howell, *Persuasion: A Means of Social Control* (New York: Prentice-Hall, 1952), Chap. II, p. 24.

Returning to the context of the discussion group, it is apparent that almost every assertion and many of the questions which a discussant makes and wishes to have the others believe are acts of leadership. Almost every discussant thus exercises some measure of leadership. To define leaders as simply those who do exercise leadership is thus pointless. What is significant, however, is that some people exercise *more* leadership than others; some are *more* successful than others in directing a group toward attainment of its goals. Let us look at such people more closely.

Leaders

Thus a leader is a focal person whose contribution to the accomplishment of the group's goals is significantly greater than the individual contributions of the majority of others in the group. This is a functional definition of a leader just as the definition of leadership is functional. Most definitions approximate this one though many ways to define a leader are available, and some overlap this definition while others name individuals excluded by this definition. To ask whether this is the only "right" definition is fruitless. It is a useful one, as the remainder of this chapter demonstrates, and it conforms to the bulk of the literature on the subject.[4]

Just as only one individual in a group can sometimes be called a leader so also sometimes no individual can be singled out in a group as contributing measurably more than any of the others. The first case is a single-leader group; the second, is what is known as a "leaderless" group. This latter notion has interested a number of researchers in the field, and raised considerable dispute concerning the relative merits of such a group "structure." Haiman, for example, contends that only the leaderless group can be a truly democratic group.[5]

Though one should be aware of the concern shown in much theoretical and practical literature to restructure traditional ways of looking at groups and their leaders, it is not necessary here to evaluate the bulk of this literature. Most of the time the leadership structure falls somewhere between these two extremes of a unique

[4] Alvin W. Gouldner, ed., *Studies in Leadership* (New York: Harper, 1950) is the best source of definitions and descriptions of leaders and leadership.
[5] Franklyn S. Haiman, "Concepts of Leadership," *Quarterly Journal of Speech,* Vol. 39 (October, 1953), pp. 317-322.

leader and no leader at all. That is, leaders may be singled out in a group—though this need not happen—yet seldom does one leader completely dominate a group. Typically, in most informally organized decision-making groups, about a third of the members can be called, at some point or other, leaders by our definition; and almost all people will, at least occasionally, perform certain acts of leadership.

THE RISE OF LEADERS

Why do leaders emerge? Why do groups normally see fit to select leaders? Why do larger organizations lay so much stress upon identifying and cultivating the leadership talent in the groups that compose the larger group? A better understanding of the rise of leaders will create a basis from which to talk about the character of leadership, or about the effects of different types of leadership.

Leaders Do Emerge

In a group that interacts long enough to begin to develop any distinctive characteristics as a group, leaders do emerge. Occasionally, as observed, situations do exist that can be called leaderless. Genuine leaderless groups seldom exist, except when the group is small or essentially temporary. The *leaderless* group, in which no leaders by our definition can be detected, and the *shared leadership* group, in which leaders can be identified but in which the leadership functions are widely spread, must be clearly distinguished. Groups that interact sufficiently to demonstrate characteristics above and beyond the characteristics of the individuals who compose them inevitably include a leadership structure.

Evidence for the emergence of leaders is abundant. No business organization of any size fails to make provision for filling, and refilling as necessary, its leadership positions. In the public sector also, in military organizations, educational institutions, government agencies, leaders are recruited, trained, placed, and promoted. Even in informal groups there is definite evidence of a leadership structure. Thrasher's study of gangs, which was conducted in the 1920's, found leadership structures in all groups.[6] And Whyte's famous

[6] Fred Thrasher, *The Gang* (Chicago: Univ. of Chicago, 1927).

"street corner society," which will be referred to often, is a gold mine of information about the emergence of leaders.[7]

For a number of years we have been gathering sociometric analyses of the leadership patterns in our discussion classes. When the semester is about two-thirds over, each student ranks privately the three individuals he thinks have exercised thus far the most leadership in class. Normally about half the members of a class of twenty receive one or more nominations, and, typically, three or four individuals dominate the voting.

Leaders, then, exist. Let us turn now to some explanation for their existence.

The Trait Theory

Early investigations of the phenomenon of leadership assumed it was possible to discover a profile of traits which would identify people as leaders or nonleaders. Such studies usually began by a study of acknowledged leaders in order to determine what traits they possessed in common, and dozens of such traits, ranging from those that are presumably inherited to those that are acquired, were described. Intelligence, energy, dominance, assertiveness, extroversion, judgment, physical size, and personality adjustment were among those cataloged.

The trait approach soon proved itself inadequate to explain *why* a particular leadership structure, or any at all, should exist. The best summary of the limitations of the trait approach is offered by Gouldner who lists five indictments.[8] (1) The lists of traits seldom distinguish between essential and less important traits. (2) Often they are not mutually exclusive. (3) Seldom do the studies distinguish between the traits necessary for a leader to emerge and those that enable him to keep his position. (4) Usually, the trait studies assume the leader possessed the traits *before* he became the leader. (5) And the studies frequently assume personality is simply the sum of various individual characteristics. Any concept of the dynamic relationship of characteristics or of personality structure is left out.

Clearly, the trait approach is as inadequate for understanding

[7] William F. Whyte, Jr., *Street Corner Society* (Chicago: Univ. of Chicago, 1943).

[8] Gouldner, *op. cit.*, pp. 23-25.

the psychology of leadership as the technique approach is for working successfully with groups. A good illustration of this is an account of what happened to a young assistant minister who attended a short training course during which he was exposed to a variety of new techniques for working with groups. He was particularly impressed with a training technique in which trainers provide no direction to trainees until the group has interacted and conceived its own sets of goals. He determined to try this technique with the large Sunday School class of college students for which he was responsible. The first Sunday they met no one stepped forward to guide the session. Everyone sat and whispered until someone suggested they sing some hymns. Good. The idea came from the group. They sang hymns for the rest of the period. The next Sunday much the same pattern was repeated. The third Sunday attendance was down almost to zero. The minister had failed to realize, of course, that the circumstances which made the "freeze-out" technique successful in his training course were not the same as the circumstances under which he conducted his Sunday School class. And his knowledge of the principles involved in the differences in motivation in the two groups was not sufficient to diagnose the problem.

Although the trait approach will not explain why leaders emerge, it does enable prediction of which people are most likely to emerge as leaders in a given organization. Many organizations have studied personality characteristics of their successful executives in order to discover which characteristics are keys to predicting the probable success of newcomers. While this procedure has a number of drawbacks, the potential advantage is obvious. The drawbacks consist primarily of the difficulty in finding meaningful ways to measure personality characteristics. The evidence suggests that perhaps personality structures rather than personality characteristics may be more meaningful.[9]

The Need Theory

In an attempt to understand why leaders emerge, researchers began to turn from studying the traits of leaders to studying the *situation* in which leadership operates.[10] As early as 1935, Pigors suggested

---

[9] See pp. 106-108 in Chapter 5 and pp. 207-210 below.

[10] One of the best statements of this concept is found in John K. Hemphill, *Situational Factors in Leadership* (Columbus, Ohio: Ohio State Univ., 1949).

the following variables must be considered when examining any leadership: (1) the goal or common cause; (2) the leader; (3) the followers; and (4) the situation.[11]

Leadership, according to this theory, arises out of the group's need to have given functions or roles performed in order to attain its objective. Leaders are those who emerge to perform successfully roles the group considers important. A group develops a hierarchy as it begins to accomplish something as a group and as functions within it are increasingly differentiated. This theory in outline includes all of the variables that Pigors listed. In order to better comprehend the implications of this theory, let us now consider the nature of a group's needs as well as the skills, resources, and desires necessary to perform its functions.

Group Needs. Every group may be said to have two sets of needs, both of which must be satisfied if the group is to operate successfully: *task needs* and *interpersonal needs*.[12] A group's task needs are those that relate to the substance of the discussion. They include thus the need to define and assess the task, to gather information, to study the problem, to find criteria for solutions, and the like.[13] Interpersonal needs are those relating to the problem of organizing and maintaining the group so that tasks may be handled effectively and members of the group may realize personal satisfaction in their collective efforts. Among such needs are achievement of harmony, release of tension, and enhancement of status.

Often task needs can scarcely be distinguished from interpersonal needs. This occurs when the group purposes are essentially personal, whether social, cathartic, therapeutic, or learning. However, in task groups, that is decision-making, action, advisory, and appraisal groups, the distinctions can and must be made if we are to diagnose accurately the circumstances affecting the group's deliberations.[14] Although the task group must deal with matters

---

[11] Paul Pigors, *Leadership or Domination* (Boston: Houghton Mifflin, 1935).

[12] Different investigators have used different terms for these areas. The chief difference is that Benne and Sheats add the concept of building and maintaining the group. We have included this concept in our description of interpersonal needs. See Kenneth D. Benne and Paul Sheats, "Functional Roles of Group Members," *Journal of Social Issues*, Vol. 4 (Spring, 1948), pp. 41-49.

[13] Part II presented material relating to the task needs of the group.

[14] See the distinctions between personal and task purposes in Chapter 3.

that go beyond the personal requirements of its members, the personal requirements remain.

Voluntary groups are subject to little pressure from outside the group while organizational groups feel considerable outside pressure.[15] Since all groups are under some outside pressures, the principal question is where does the main source of pressure lie for accomplishment of the group's tasks? Whether pressures for task accomplishment arise either largely within or without the group, task and personal pressures of the members create needs that the group, provided it is aware of them, will attempt to satisfy.

Objective existence of a group need is not the same as an individual's awareness of that need's existence. When discussing the problem of perception of group needs, we must consider the group itself, its leaders, and any outside agency or persons exerting pressure upon the group. Considerable evidence suggests that the formal leaders of a group are the most sensitive to the task needs of the group and outside agencies are almost always solely concerned with a group's task needs. Members of the group, however, are often not very sensitive to the group's task needs. Their sensitivity in this area is primarily a function of their understanding of group problems and of their motivation with respect to group tasks.[16] That is, the more the members understand how the group functions in general and in regard to a particular problem at hand, the more highly motivated they are with respect to the group's goal and the more likely they are to perceive accurately the task needs that confront the group.

Interpersonal needs, on the other hand, are more likely to be accurately perceived by the rank and file than by either those higher in status or those outside the group. For this reason so much of the literature on how to lead groups stresses the matter of interpersonal relations. Such authors as Gordon, McGregor, and the

---

[15] See Chapter 3 for distinctions between voluntary and organizational groups.

[16] Some interesting experimental support for the motivational part of this proposition is provided by Bernard M. Bass, Margaret W. Pryer, Eugene L. Gaier, and Austin W. Flint, "Interacting Effects of Control, Motivation, Group Practice, and Problem Difficulty on Attempted Leadership," *Journal of Abnormal and Social Psychology*, Vol. 56 (1958), pp. 352-358.

Lairds illustrate this concern.[17] Note the implications that may be drawn from the titles: *GROUP-CENTERED Leadership* and *The HUMAN Side of Enterprise.*

Leader Skills. The major problem in a group, once it has recognized and appraised its needs, is to match available abilities and essential functions.[18] The nature of the leader skills required for rating group needs may be inferred from the discussion of group needs, but again we must emphasize the concept of perception, of the group, the leader (existing or potential), and outside agencies. Although we dismiss the trait theory as an explanation for the rise of leadership, we do not contend that no relevant differences obtain among people. As Fiedler states, we can distinguish between traits that make for effective and for ineffective leadership.[19] Thus the questions are: Who distinguishes the differences, and what is the basis of distinction? The first question is easily answered. The leader holds his position either as a result of the preferences of the group members or by virtue of selection through some outside agency. The concern here is not with the "leader" who imposes his will upon a group by use of force or sanctions and compels unwilling obedience. The role of leader is seldom, however, assigned to unsuspecting candidates; it is usually sought. So let us note what the potential leader does to enhance the likelihood that he will be selected.

The aspiring leader must demonstrate he possesses the skills necessary to cope with the perceived group needs. He may do this by cultivating and publicizing the skills themselves, by manipulating the situation or the perception of the situation to create needs with which he is equipped to cope, or by doing both. Any political campaign will furnish illustrations of these practices. Are these perilous times that demand a candidate with courage? Our candi-

[17] Thomas Gordon, *Group-Centered Leadership* (Boston: Houghton Mifflin, 1955). Douglas McGregor, *The Human Side of Enterprise* (New York: McGraw-Hill, 1960). Donald A. Laird and Eleanor C. Laird, *The New Psychology for Leadership* (New York: McGraw-Hill, 1956).

[18] See pp. 288-300 for discussion of how group needs are recognized and appraised.

[19] Fred E. Fiedler, "Leadership and Leadership Effectiveness Traits: A Reconceptualization of the Leadership Trait Problem," in Luigi Petrullo and Bernard M. Bass, eds., *Leadership and Interpersonal Behavior* (New York: Holt, Rinehart and Winston, 1961).

date is a decorated veteran. Is knowledge of foreign affairs essential? Our candidate has such and such experience which qualifies him. Do the problems demand mature judgment? Our candidate is older and more experienced.

When the aspiring leader must look outside the group for assignment to a position of leadership, he will normally tend to emphasize those skills and traits related to task needs for the reasons pointed out earlier. When he must turn to the group for selection, he will tend to stress proportionately interpersonal needs. Hollander concludes that two things are particularly important for an individual to attain leadership. He must be seen "as competent in the group's central task . . ." and in a general way must be "perceived as a member of the group." That is, the potential leader must interact long enough with the others for them to first assess his ability and second, to accept, trust and appreciate him.[20]

Normally the leaders who are selected by a mature group will be most likely to possess the skills and attributes necessary to perform satisfactorily the functions that fulfill both task and interpersonal needs. A mature group thus does not minimize its task needs.[21] At the same time, its members are in a position to determine the capacity of any aspiring leader to satisfy its interpersonal needs.

Leader Resources. In addition to his skills the leader often possesses other resources essential to satisfy task or interpersonal needs. Command of these resources can be an important factor in selecting a leader, and certainly an important factor in perpetuating his position. He may possess, in any degree or combination, the resources of *information, money, prestige,* and *power.*[22]

Any member who has information needed to solve a problem or who can discover that information more readily than another has an inside track in the leadership race. In the classroom, for example, the student who has previously taken a class from the instructor has a certain advantage in the leadership struggle because of the real or fancied belief of others that his experience gives him a knowledge about the instructor's preferences and foibles

[20] E. P. Hollander, "Emergent Leadership and Social Influence," *Ibid.,* p. 38.

[21] See the discussion of group maturity, pp. 176-181 above.

[22] The nature of power in the leadership structure is discussed on pp. 203-207 below. Our description here focuses on the first three.

which will help the class make appropriate adaptations to the instructor's requirements. By the same token, once any member has attained the position of leader, he has greater access to this resource because of his position in the communication structure.[23]

Money is a particularly valuable resource in voluntary groups. At school, the student who owned a car used to be almost always a social leader, but automobile ownership today is too widespread to be, in itself, an index of leadership. In churches the heavy contributor is almost always a leader. A few years ago an annual income of $50,000 was cited as a minimum for anyone who wished to "move up in society." And individuals have held rather high positions in political parties largely because they could afford to spend their own money to attend various conventions and meetings.

Prestige may result from achieving a position of leadership in a group, but it may also be a resource that enables an individual to be selected as a leader. It is not surprising that B. M. O. C.'s (Big Men On Campus) [24] are often elected fraternity presidents, and vice versa. Major fund-raising organizations often utilize "honorary" offices in order to have prestige names upon their letterheads. The President of the United States is normally the honorary chairman of the March of Dimes, for example. Prestige operates as a resource because of the group's need to achieve status as a group, and one way to achieve status is to have leaders who already possess prestige.

Leader Desire. In addition to possessing skills and resources, the aspiring leader must be willing to use them to lead. Too often, unfortunately, willingness is the only qualification some leaders possess. While some leadership positions are essentially sinecures, especially in groups that have few task purposes, most leaders have to work at their jobs. Crockett thus observed that those who feel most keenly about the group's task tend to perform most of the leadership functions.[25]

In addition to being motivated by a desire to accomplish the group's goal because of exceptional interest in it, the leader is motivated by the promises of status and other rewards that befall

---

[23] See pp. 210-211 below.

[24] We hesitate to use the jargon because it is probably already out of date.

[25] Walter Crockett, "Emergent Leadership in Small, Decision-making Groups," *Journal of Abnormal and Social Psychology,* Vol. 51 (1955), pp. 378-383.

a group leader. As we indicated earlier, the group values certain roles, and the skills necessary to perform those roles, more highly than it does others. In our society, for example, both the sanitation engineer and the doctor perform functions designed to further the health and well-being of the members of our society. We regard the functions performed by the doctor as the more important, however, and he is correspondingly rewarded more highly in terms of both money and prestige. Similarly, in a discussion group we tend to reward more highly the functions of initiating and directing than the functions of critical listening with occasional feedback. Although the group may need both pairs of functions, performance of the former is likely to be rewarded far more conspicuously than performance of the latter.

Identifying Leaders

In the previous section we outlined the need theory of leadership, that is, we distinguished between task and interpersonal needs of a group and indicated how they arise in the course of interactions among the group's members. As specific needs become apparent, leaders are sought among persons who apparently possess the requisite skills, resources, and desires to satisfy those needs. More precisely, though, how does a group identify its leaders?

There are as many ways of identifying as there are of defining leaders. We see what we are oriented to see, and the scheme we use to identify leaders will necessarily reflect our conception of what we believe a leader to be. In the literature we have examined, we have encountered at least nine fundamental frameworks for studying leaders. Although these frameworks do overlap, even more of them may be useful as well as possible. The three methods presented here are consistent with the psychology of leadership thus far developed; each method also provides a slightly different dimension for analysis. If one is to translate theory into operational terms, he must understand some of the methodology that is applicable. Without the means to analyze the leadership structure of a given group, one can do little to modify the operation of that group.

1. *Job Analysis.* A job analysis is one in which the analyst studies the group needs and matches them with the skills and traits of

prospective or actual leaders. This is essentially the procedure used by military organizations as well as most business corporations. Whenever large number of jobs and people must be matched, some analysis of this type is probably mandatory. Some of the students in our discussion classes have studied fraternities and sororities in this fashion. One student made an intensive study of the requirements of the several elective positions in his fraternity. He then matched the qualifications of the candidates against his assessment of the requirements of the position. From the analysis he attempted to predict the outcome of the election and was remarkably successful. Other students have made similar studies using questionnaires to determine what fraternity and sorority members felt were the job requirements of the offices. Interestingly enough, the surveys showed that sororities tend to place somewhat more emphasis upon the "social" requirements of jobs and candidates to fill them than fraternities do.

The main disadvantage of this method of analysis, particularly in predicting appropriate leadership, is that the several needs and corresponding traits do not operate independently of each other. Even if the analyst is able to determine accurately the requirements, the combination of traits is not a simple additive process; it is an interactive process. Another disadvantage is that an outside analyst will probably tend to concentrate solely upon task needs and corresponding personality traits to the exclusion of interpersonal needs.

2. *Sociometric Analysis.* The foremost proponent of this method of analysis has been Helen Hall Jennings.[26] It consists of asking group members either to indicate their preferences for leaders or to indicate their judgment of those who have been most successful as leaders; sometimes it asks them to do both. Specific and typical questions are: "Rank the three people who have exercised the most leadership"; "Rank the three people whom you would most like to have as leaders"; "Rank the three people with whom you would most like to work in some future activity." In confronting these last two questions, the members are often given some specific activity

[26] Helen Hall Jennings, *Leadership and Isolation,* 2nd ed. (New York: Longmans, Green, 1950).

as the basis for their choosing. A three-two-one weighting scheme is conventionally employed to arrive at the leadership score of the chosen person. That is, a first-place choice is given a score of three, a second-place choice a two, and a third-place receives a score of one.[27]

The procedure above is descriptive only and neither permits the analyst to determine why given people were chosen nor to evaluate the quality of leader performance apart from the index of popularity. Gardner and Thompson have more recently developed a sociometric procedure that permits more precise evaluations even though it does not answer the "why" question. Although the scope of their scheme, which is most useful as a research tool, does not permit discussion of it here, the interested reader will find much of value in the original report.[28]

Sociometric analysis is a widely-used technique that is particularly valuable whenever one wishes to differentiate between a group's "formal" leadership structure, that is, the people who officially hold its leadership positions, and the group's "informal" leadership structure, that is, the people who are preferred by the group members. As often happens, the two structures are at variance.[29]

As indicated earlier, we have used the ranking system in our classes to measure the emergent leadership structure. Our students have also used the technique in a variety of research projects. Besides some of the main drawbacks already noted to this method, two more should be underscored. The accuracy of the rankings are seriously affected if the group members feel any compunction to be anything but frank in their ratings. Though this shortcoming is apparent, the second may be less so. The accuracy of the rankings is also seriously affected by the nature of the stresses upon and within the individual and the group and by the manner in which these interact to affect the group's internal relationships at the time of the ranking.[30]

[27] If you are a sports fan, you will recognize this as the same principle employed by the AP and UPI in ranking the country's top collegiate teams.
[28] Eric F. Gardner and George G. Thompson, *Social Relations and Morale in Small Groups* (New York: Appleton-Century-Crofts, 1956).
[29] See pp. 211-212, below.
[30] For a discussion and examples of this principle at work, see Chapter 9, pp. 245-252.

3. *Process Analysis.* A process analysis consists of examining the one who communicates, the persons with whom he interacts, and the nature of the communication or interaction. Perhaps the foremost proponent of this method is Robert F. Bales who developed a twelve-category interaction scheme whereby he could label each interaction and indicate the "who-to-whom" feature.[31] Such an analysis reveals not only the amount of participation, which correlates highly with other measures of leadership, but the nature and direction of communication. When studying a discussion group, it is possible to work out ratios by time periods for actions both initiated and accepted in a variety of the categories. This method enables the analyst to identify the source, nature, and direction of influence during the course of a group's progress through phases of problem solving.

The importance of this type of analysis is apparent upon noting a distinctive characteristic of leader communications in comparison with those of followers. Whyte, whose work has already been noted, was first to reveal this characteristic clearly by distinguishing between two kinds of events. A *pair* event is one in which an action originates between two people only. A *set* event is one in which one person originates action for two or more persons. Frequently a leader initiates action for his group without consulting any of his followers. Yet, in a pair event a follower may originate action for the leader and possibly himself as well. The follower does not, however, originate action at one and the same time for the leader and other followers, that is to say, create a set event. In the absence of a leader and his lieutenants, followers on lower levels may, on their own initiative, originate action in set events for other followers. By doing so, they establish for themselves quasi-leadership positions.[32]

This distinction between pair and set events has proved useful in many investigations. Often discussion groups flounder while some of the members, eager for a set event, search anxiously for a sign of approval from a leader. This desire for a set event can be a critical problem for the leader of an advisory group if he is also

---

[31] Robert F. Bales, *Interaction Process Analysis* (Reading, Mass.: Addison-Wesley, 1951).

[32] William F. Whyte, "Informal Leadership and Group Structure," in Gouldner, *op. cit.*, pp. 111-112.

one through whom the group's advice is to be directed. He must beware of unintentionally influencing direction and perhaps destroying the full value of the group's thinking. Sometimes his set event may consist of nothing more than a nod that indicates approval of an idea advanced by one of the members. Once members who are utterly dependent upon their leader have received what they perceive to be a go-ahead signal for a given proposal, they quickly line up behind it.

The method of process analysis has, however, two fundamental disadvantages. First, it is extremely difficult to score process interactions precisely enough to make accurate diagnoses. Any observer must be thoroughly trained both in discussion methods and observation techniques. Secondly, process analysis looks only at one segment of a group's life. To the extent that the discussions examined are representative of the group's interactions over longer periods of time, the process analysis will accurately portray the leadership structure. Seldom, however, does one find any given discussion or set of discussions representative enough to warrant extensive generalization.[33]

Although this presentation of methods for identifying leaders is too brief to permit much more than a glimpse of certain research techniques, it is extensive enough to reveal some of the ramifications of the problem of leadership. Once a pattern of leadership is established, we can examine some of the qualities that emerge.

DIMENSIONS OF LEADERSHIP

In the previous section elements of group operation and leadership were picked up, turned about and examined individually, but no effort was made to fit all their edges together and lock them into place like pieces of a picture puzzle. Indeed, the task of trying to perceive the nature of leadership is rather one of trying to find matching pieces in a pile of pieces from several puzzles, and with no assurance that all one will need are there. In fact, all the needed pieces clearly are not, at least thus far, available anywhere. But

[33] See R. Victor Harnack, "Problems in Measuring Discussion Process," *The Journal of Communication,* Vol. 3 (May, 1953), pp. 13-16.

let us reexamine in greater detail four pieces previously mentioned
—*power, personality, communication channels, structural rigidity.*

Power

Power means the capacity of one individual, or group, to induce
forces that affect the behavior of another person, or group.[34] In
terms of two-person relationships one person initiates an act (some
kind of communication) to induce certain forces that stimulate
another's compliance and thereby influences (leads) him. *At the
same time,* the act of leadership also induces certain forces to resist
and takes place in a context that includes both the goals of leader
and of follower as well as the strength of their motivations to reach
those goals. Take the "simple" example of a mother calling a child
to dinner. The child is hungry but he is interested in a TV program.
The mother is impatient and tired. The child is aware that obedience will bring praise and a pleasant atmosphere, but he is irritated
by the interruption and wishes to exercise his independence. The
mother calls again, this time inserting a threat of punishment. Resistance mounts higher in the child; now his pride is at stake. He
may continue to resist until he is dragged bodily to the table, or
he may decide to instigate a counter set of forces to test his own
power. He feels too sick or tired to eat, he says. With any kind of
skill he will soon have the mother, or more likely the father, paying attention to him and consoling him. In all probability he will
reward his parents in due course by coming to the dinner table
on his own terms.

   Several facets in the previous illustration of attempted leadership are important. First, the conception of power is a dynamic one
that includes the total situation. Second, resistance to influence is
distinguished from the use of countervailing power. Finally, regardless of the power introduced into a given act of leadership, there
usually remains a reservoir of power that may be tapped if the first
attempts fail.

   Before discussing each of these facets of power, let us clear
away one possible misconception of terms. Often the terms *power*
and *authority* are used interchangeably. Here, however, authority

   [34] Our position is essentially similar to Cartwright's. See Dorwin Cartwright, ed., *Studies in Social Power* (Ann Arbor: Univ. of Michigan, 1959).

means something very similar to the area of control discussed in the previous chapter. Power means the *capacity* for control, not the *scope* of control. One may, for example, have *authority* to decide a particular issue and *power* to enforce his decision.

The Dynamic Nature of Power. Most people make the mistake of talking about power as if it were something possessed by an individual which he can use or withhold. This is only partially accurate. It is more accurate to say, when A wishes to influence B, B can *receive* something as a consequence of his own reaction. This is why the term *induce* was used in our definition of power. Thus, to speak of the power of A over B, implies that, given a particular set of circumstances and considering the direction of the influence, A's act of leadership will, with a certain probability, stimulate B to act in certain ways in order to gain reward or avoid punishment, *either or both of which may be created by B himself.*

This distinction is not simply a matter of pedantry. If power is understood only as something possessed by an individual, then one perceives only those rewards and punishments that are largely extrinsic to the performance of the indicated act. An employer obviously has extrinsic power in that he may be able to pay well, poorly, or not at all for the performance of his employees. But to leave it at this is to overlook an employer's power to create circumstances in which his employees will work well *because they enjoy the very act of working.*[35]

Additional examples are easy to find. In voluntary speech programs in thousands of high schools and colleges, debate coaches have seen debaters by the thousands pour immense quantities of energy and effort into debate programs. True, there are extrinsic rewards. Some students receive trophies; the debater can win the coaches' approbation. But most debaters do not win trophies; a pat on the back can go only so far; and won-lost records are rather intangible. The answer must be that most debaters find profit and pleasure in debate.

Perhaps the saddest aspect of modern life is that so many people do not work because they find satisfaction in their vocations. They seem to work for extrinsic rewards. On the one hand we are

[35] This is the whole thesis of McGregor's *Human Side of Enterprise, op. cit.*

all subject to a cultural standard that approves continuous, organized productive effort even when it goes well beyond what is required for sustaining a reasonable standard of life. The person who does not "work" or has not "worked" is often suspect regardless of his demands on society or his economic self-sufficiency. Consequently, we work to avoid social censure. In other instances, many persons seek vocational rewards of money or prestige or both, which can be enjoyed mainly during "leisure" time away from the "job."

Reciprocal Power Relationships. Resistance to influence is often apparent; at the very least it may be a form of inertia, or it may be overt and very active.[36] It is a mistake to consider power only in terms of the power of a leader over his followers since the capacity of followers to shape the behavior of their leader can be great. This power may be expressed in terms of a series of pair events, of a revolt in the ranks, or of countervailing power used either to limit the authority, the extrinsic rewards dispensable by leaders, or both.

Let us first cite evidence of the extent to which a leader may be influenced by those under him or, to put it the other way around, the extent to which followers have power over the leader.

A study by O. J. Harvey dramatizes this process.[37] Members of an Army air-borne division are divided into groups of three men each; members of each group are studied and questioned so that the experimenters know which man is the formal leader, that is, the person officially designated as leader, and which is the informal leader, that is, the man the group members actually prefer. The men are then led into a completely darkened room and seated in such a fashion that an opaque panel separates the official leader from the members. They are all shown two flashes of light—one pair of lights is shown to the leader and another pair to the members—and *they all think they are seeing the same pair of lights.* For thirty trials both sets of lights are kept a constant twenty-four

[36] See Chapter 9 for discussion of the tendency to maintain the status quo, and Chapters 13 and 14 for a discussion of attempts to overcome resistance to change.

[37] O. J. Harvey, "Reciprocal Influence of the Group and Three Types of Leaders in an Unstructured Situation," *Sociometry*, Vol. 23 (March, 1960).

inches apart; but in the "influence session" the leader is shown flashes of light increased up to sixty inches while the members are still looking at flashes of light twenty-four inches apart. For some leaders this increase is *gradual* in steps of six, fifteen, and thirty-six inches, but for others the increase is *absolute,* that is, jumping immediately from twenty-four to sixty inches. During all of the trials, of course, all three men are reporting aloud their judgments of the distances between the lights and are allowed to discuss with one another. All of the leaders are distressed by the contradiction between what they think they see and what the other two are reporting; and all of them are influenced by the members' judgments. The one conforming most to the evaluations of the other members is the unpopular formal leader and particularly when his lights jump immediately from twenty-four to sixty inches apart.[38]

While there are obvious discrepancies between the experimental situation in the Harvey study and the normal discussion situation, the study bears out the principle that members of a group can exercise power over their leader. Additional support for this conclusion is not difficult to find. Collective action, as exemplified by labor unions, is an obvious attempt by employees to secure power that will counterbalance the power of employers. By using this power, the unions have sharply restricted both the scope of control and the exercise of power by employers. Various job security regulations, standard pay procedures, and hiring practices have been instituted to restrict the use of rewards and punishments by management. Indeed, while the ostensible objective of most labor disputes is securing tangible benefits for workers, securing greater power for labor unions and their leaders is often the main objective. Strikes have been called with no apparent intention of relieving a grievance; they seem rather to have been called simply to demonstrate power.[39]

The Power Reservoir. A leader usually does not actively use all of the power he possesses. Some of it almost always remains in a reserve that may be called the power reservoir. The very existence of this reserve can often condition the behavior of both leaders and

[38] *Ibid.,* pp. 66-67.
[39] We report this judgment on the basis of discussions with labor-management negotiators with whom we are familiar.

ollowers, as Kirk H. Porter demonstrates in his discussion of the
)roblems involved in administering university departments.

n so far as the chief officer has power officially to recommend salary in-
:reases, to recommend promotions, to recommend the appointment of
1ew staff members, to appoint student assistants, to sign or refuse to sign
·equisitions for this or that, to approve or disapprove teaching loads and
1ssignments, or the introduction of new courses, he possesses power
whether he misuses it or not. No measure of kindly and impartial behavior can dispel the fact. [40]

Because of the power reservoir, Porter contends that democracy
in university departments is impossible even though both the department head and his faculty try to be as fair-minded and decent
as possible. However, in view of reciprocal power relationships
department heads are just as dependent upon their department
members as they are dependent upon their chiefs. Usually an un-
tapped reservoir of power, which may not always be used, exists
on both sides. When a leader has to dip into his power reservoir,
and particularly when he has to employ coercive power, one may
well infer that the position of the leader is sustained by imposition
rather than by willing cooperation. On the other hand, if the leader
does not occasionally use some of the powers that he normally
keeps in reserve, the followers may come to believe that these
cannot or will not be used. As a result, one then sees numerous
instances of followers "seeing how far they can go" in order to test
the leader's strength. Something of this sort probably occurred in
the spring of 1962 when President Kennedy brought immense powers to bear upon the steel industry to compel a rollback of announced price increases. Although there were obvious indications
that not all of the President's available power had been used, the
effect of his actual display of power, and its later ramifications, was
a sobering lesson for both sides of the controversy.

Personality

In order to assess the dimension of personality, one must concern himself both with the leader and his followers since it is now

[40] Kirk H. Porter, "Department Head or Chairman?" *AAUP Bulletin*
(Washington, D.C.: National Publishing Co.), Vol. 67 (December, 1961), p.
341.

apparent that both of them condition the nature and success of attempts to exercise influence. Despite our earlier rejection of the trait theory of leadership, it is not denied that personality characteristics of different individuals contribute toward their effectiveness as leaders. Some characteristics like enthusiasm, insight, and ability in the task seem to be rather consistent from situation to situation, while other characteristics seem to be more dependent upon the situation in which they are employed. By the same token, it is not denied that personality characteristics of followers determine in large part both the nature and extent of the influence to which they are susceptible. In order to understand this variable, let us first examine different personality structures, then try to account for their distinguishing features, and finally, identify two sources of personal influence.

Personality Structures. The fundamental way in which individuals behave toward one another and toward the world outside them is more significant than a listing of specific traits or characteristics, which may themselves be results of behavior.[41] Rather than review the developments of theoretical constructs of personality, presented here is a well-conceived contemporary analysis of four fundamental personality structures that have been described by Harvey, Hunt, and Schroder.[42] Each type, identified by the simple labels 1, 2, 3, and 4, is viewed as a relative "stage" rather than a discrete one.

A stage 1 individual can be characterized as essentially an authoritarian individual. He looks to external sources for his determination of belief and behavior. It makes no difference whether he be dominant or submissive in a particular situation since the reasons are the same in either case. Initially such an individual is dependent upon authority figures; later he may transfer his dependence to concrete rules and regulations that serve the same function. Such an individual is oriented primarily in the social reality end of the continuum we developed in Chapter 5.

A stage 2 individual is essentially hostile to external authority whether personal or institutional. He tries to avoid any form of dependency on authority or control because he associates only neg-

---

[41] See, also, Chapter 5, p. 106.

[42] O. J. Harvey, David E. Hunt, and Harold M. Schroder, *Conceptual Systems and Personality Organization* (New York: Wiley, 1961).

ative consequences with attempts at control.[43] Such an individual tends to withhold commitment to others and to minimize the rewards or punishments that others can mediate.

A stage 3 individual is essentially dependent upon others in his social situation. He is similar to Riesman's "other-directed man" in that he depends upon other relevant individuals in his environment for clues to behavior and for acceptance and affection.[44] Stage 3 individuals are very much concerned with pleasing others and may, at first glance, seem to be ideal members of a discussion group because of their concern for harmonious relations. Individuals who may be characterized as stages 1, 2, or 3 are all oriented toward the social reality end of the continuum even though the basis of their orientation is different.

A stage 4 individual is information oriented and relatively independent of authority or peer approbation. At this stage individuals can become ego-involved in a belief or activity without closing their minds to alternative possibilities. They tend to be self-reliant and to look for objective reasons for their success or failure. They do not ignore others' beliefs, but they tend to have greater insight into the actual motives and experiences of others than any of the other types.

Personal Security. The critical difference among these personality structures is the extent to which an individual is personally secure.[45] A stage 1 individual derives his security from a concrete orientation to a predictable environment. A stage 2 individual derives his security by means of opposition to established authority. As a result, he tends to be relatively uninvolved in belief or activity. A stage 3 individual derives his security from his acceptance by other relevant groups or persons. For him rejection is tantamount to failure. A stage 4 individual finds security in the reasonably predictable consequences of his own and others' actions. Such security is based upon his understanding of experience.

Sources of Personal Power. Here we shall attempt to distinguish personal power from extrinsic powers and from the power that re-

[43] *Ibid.*, p. 178.
[44] David Riesman with Nathan Glazer and Reuel Denney, *The Lonely Crowd: A Study of the Changing American Character* (Garden City, N. Y.: Doubleday, 1953).
[45] See pp. 106-108 in Chapter 5.

sults from the rewards inherent in exhibiting the indicated behavior. A useful and important distinction is found in the terms "referent power" and "expert power." [46]

Referent power stems from the desire of the follower to be like the leader. This accounts for the power of the pace-setter. To the extent that a follower perceives himself as similar to the leader, or to the extent that a follower wishes to be like the leader, the probability that he will accept the influence attempt is increased. We have all said, or heard others say, "He is the kind of person I would follow." Stage 2 and stage 3 individuals are largely unaffected by this source of power. The reason the stage 2 individual is unaffected is obvious. The stage 3 individual is not likely to accept this source of power unless it is accompanied by the extrinsic reward of affection given in return for compliance. This latter is possibly the fundamental source of power that children have over their parents. Both stage 1 and stage 4 individuals react to this source of power, but for entirely different reasons. The stage 1 individual wishes to identify with an authority figure. The stage 4 individual reasons that acceptance of such influence is desirable to the extent that its net benefits seem desirable or the processes of arriving at a proposal seem essentially similar to those he would have employed.

Expert power is virtually self-explanatory. The basis for it was discussed in Chapter 5, and it need not detain us here. The predicted reactions of the several personality types toward it are also obvious.

Communication Channels

Information is one of the resources of leadership and to the extent an individual has access to relevant information his influence potential is thus increased.[47] In small discussion groups no difference exists among participants in regard to access to information *during a discussion*. However, in the intervals between discussions access to information is likely to differ widely. This is particularly true of persons in organizational groups; hence two channels of communication must be examined: formal and informal.

[46] John R. P. French, Jr. and Bertram Raven, "The Bases of Social Power," in Cartwright, *op. cit.*

[47] See pp. 196-197 above.

Formal Channels. The leader of a group is often the only member who has direct access to formal channels of communication with superiors in the organization of which his group is a part. The department or section head carries information from his group to the superiors and receives information from them. In many ways this channeling is the most powerful weapon in the leader's arsenal since the information he controls is often the most essential for group decisions.

Informal Channels. "Reliable sources" have been divulging information since the beginning of time. Visits, letters, telephone calls and office grapevines are among the informal channels of communication. By virtue of the group hierarchy, and often of physical placement, the leader of a group is often the hub of informal channels. The farther he becomes removed either physically or psychologically from the group, however, the less he has access to informal channels of communication. Since the leader's status is dependent in large measure upon the information he possesses, this access to information constitutes one of the most potent weapons in the arsenal of his followers.

This brief analysis of the communication channels and their effect upon leadership should be sufficient to make us cautious about attempts to generalize from studies of the interactions observed during the time the group was actually discussing. Though it is necessary to study many actual discussions, the group and its leadership structure must also be studied in the total environment in which the group exists.

Structural Rigidity

The leadership hierarchy that emerges in a given group may take a variety of forms. It may be a hierarchy with widely shared leadership functions, small status differences, and considerable viability. At the other extreme a hierarchy may be sharply pyramidical, that is, with rigorously assigned leadership functions, great status differences, and considerable rigidity. Let us examine here how the degree of structural rigidity affects leadership in two ways.

1. *Leadership Flexibility.* The more sharply defined the leadership functions and the more pyramidical the hierarchy, the less likely it

is that members low in the structure will be able to initiate set events. The leaders themselves will tend to have sharply defined areas in which they legitimately exercise their leadership. This means that attempts at leadership must travel up the hierarchy before they may be relayed back down. We have all observed discussions that tended to "polarize" around a central figure. Members of such groups direct all of their remarks to the leader, and when members and the leader interact between group sessions the behavior is similarly polarized. At the same time, members take little responsibility for initiating action. If they do show initiative, undoubtedly they have cleared their idea or proposal through the leadership hierarchy before the discussion session. And not infrequently the leader may voice the idea to the group directly without acknowledging its source even though it originated with a member.

2. *Member Attachment to the Group.* The psychological attachment of any member to such a group is largely personal—to the leader. Since a sharply defined hierarchy limits lateral interaction, a member is not likely to feel drawn to his peers in the group as a whole; consequently, he is not likely to feel responsible for maintaining a healthy group atmosphere. In such groups participation is likely to be quite formal and concerned primarily with task needs. If members do not highly esteem their leader, if they find him inaccessible, or both, the quantity and accuracy of the communication they send up through group channels will suffer.[48] During the years that we have taught speech to military officers, we have often observed officers, and sometimes fairly high ranking ones, refuse to propose ideas to their superiors. Such classroom episodes follow a usual pattern. The officer first gives a speech describing his idea to the speech class; the class members react favorably; someone next asks whether the officer has already presented this idea to his superiors or whether he intends to do so in the near future; the officer frequently responds he has no intention of presenting the idea officially, usually on the ground that his superior will "shoot it down." His feeling of responsibility to the group effort, in other words, is not sufficient to enable him to risk official disapproval.

The reasons for structural rigidity are complex, but at least some of the obvious reasons are the methods chosen by the leaders

[48] See pp. 210-211 above.

themselves. Let us examine the nature and effects of different types of leader performance.

LEADER PERFORMANCE

Leader Types

In what is now a classical study, Lewin, Lippitt, and White distinguished three different kinds of group climates produced by three types of leaders, autocratic (or authoritarian), democratic, and *laissez-faire*.[49] Although the literature of leadership contains dozens of names to describe leader types and behavior, the terms used by these researchers adequately characterize the main differences between leader types. The original experiments used ten-year-old boys as subjects and adults as leaders who operated in the fashion described below.

AUTOCRATIC (OR AUTHORITARIAN)	DEMOCRATIC	LAISSEZ-FAIRE
1. All determination of policy by the leader.	1. All policies a matter of group discussion and decision, encouraged and assisted by the leader.	1. Complete freedom for group or individual decision, with a minimum of leader participation.
2. Techniques and activity steps dictated by the authority, one at a time, so that future steps were always uncertain to a large degree.	2. Activity perspective gained during discussion period. General steps to group goal sketched, and where technical advice is needed the leader suggests two or more alternative procedures from which choice can be made.	2. Various materials supplied by the leader, who makes it clear that he will supply information when asked. He takes no other part in work discussion.

[49] This study is reported in almost every book dealing with leadership or group properties. Our source is Ralph K. White and Ronald Lippitt, *Autocracy and Democracy: An Experimental Inquiry* (New York: Harper & Row, Publishers, 1960).

AUTOCRATIC (OR AUTHORITARIAN) (Cont'd)	DEMOCRATIC (Cont'd)	LAISSEZ-FAIRE (Cont'd)
3. The leader usually dictates the particular work task and work companion of each member.	3. The members are free to work with whomever they choose, and the division of tasks is left up to the group.	3. Complete non-participation of the leader in determining tasks and companions.
4. The leader tends to be "personal" in his praise and criticism of the work of each member, but remains aloof from active group participation except when demonstrating.	4. The leader is "objective" or "fact-minded" in his praise and criticism, and tries to be a regular group member in spirit without doing too much of the work.	4. Infrequent spontaneous comments on member activities unless questioned, and no attempt to appraise or regulate the course of events. [50]

As can be seen from these descriptions, the *laissez-faire* leader was not a leader at all; for he did not exert enough influence to merit his designation. His role was included in order to distinguish the effects of free rein from the effects of democracy. The *laissez-faire* condition cannot be equated with the kind of leaderless discussion group mentioned earlier.[51] A *laissez-faire* condition results in what is a *leadershipless* group rather than a *leaderless* group. In the leaderless group, leadership functions are performed by no dominant person and no leaders can be singled out. In the *laissez-faire* condition described in this experiment, the leadership functions tended not to be performed by anyone. Perhaps because of the basic adult/child inequality or because of the boys' expectations for direction and guidance, they did not assume the responsibility of performing the leadership functions neglected by their ostensible leader. Hence only authoritarian, or autocratic, and democratic leader types need be distinguished.

Autocracy and democracy are distinguishable by one criterion, the extent of control over *content* and *process* decisions. Content decisions are conclusions in the group's task area. They are decisions

[50] *Ibid.*, pp. 26-27.
[51] See pp. 189-191 above.

about the substance of the discussion. Process decisions are primarily concerned with the interpersonal area. They relate to how the content decisions shall be made. The best illustration of this difference is the rather elaborate set of rules of parliamentary procedure and the responsibilities and prerogatives of the chairman. These rules are confined strictly to process matters. Who may make what kind of motion? When may motions be introduced? Who may speak? In what order? How long? These are the kinds of decisions that the chairman may make within the bounds of parliamentary procedure. The rules are set up to reduce as nearly as possible to the vanishing point the influence that a chairman may have over the content of the deliberations. When the chairman wishes to speak to the content of the motion, he must relinquish the chair. Thus, the chairman of a parliamentary group is a democratic leader *even though many of his process decisions are quite arbitrary*. Decisions about who may make motions, when they may be introduced, who may speak, in what order and for how long may be made by the chairman without seeking guidance from the group. That is, these decisions may be arbitrary, but they are not the same as autocratic decisions because they are restricted to process only.

Undoubtedly the manner in which process decisions are managed can influence content decisions. When a leader manages the process of deciding so that he restricts effective group control over the content of its decisions, we call that leader authoritarian. In the Soviet Union, for example, citizens regularly go to the polls in such large numbers they put our citizens to shame. It looks very democratic, but the *process* of selecting candidates for the ballot leaves the voter no choice. Voting thus becomes a kind of patriotic observance like pledging allegiance to the flag instead of a decision-making process.

Since the quantity of control a leader exercises varies inversely with the quantity his group exercises, we can talk meaningfully about directive and nondirective democracy as well as about absolute and partial autocracy. The critical difference between democracy and autocracy, of whatever varieties, does not lie in the *quantity* of control but in the *kind* of decisions over which control extends. The autocrat's control extends over content decisions; he may or may not control the process. The democrat's control is limited to process decisions; and he may or may not share that control.

Leader Methods

When discussing leadership care should be taken to separate leader *methods* from leader *types*. Leader types have been distinguished by the area of control; that is, the autocratic leader controls content while the democratic leader confines his efforts to control of process. But in neither case has the method of exercising the control been discussed.

A leader, either autocratic or democratic, may use, fundamentally, one of two methods to accomplish his objective. He may either *persuade* or *dictate*.

Selvin studied the differences between what he called "persuasive climate" and "arbitrary climate" in military settings.[52] The leaders studied were autocratic since they, as military leaders, had to control both the content and the process of group behavior. The differences were between the methods used to exercise control. Selvin concluded that the persuasive method came closest to what most would call "ideal." The men had confidence in their leaders and were supported by them. The leaders were fair and avoided coercive or punitive behavior. The leaders further managed to generate a lower level of tension than leaders operating in an arbitrary or dictatorial fashion. Since these arbitrary methods were essentially dictatorial, the term dictatorial will be used rather than arbitrary. With dictatorial methods the leaders did not have the confidence of the men and were perceived as unfair and untrustworthy. Since the men were in constant fear of punishment, their anxiety levels were high, "not so much because of what they have done or not done, but rather because of the essentially capricious nonrational behavior of the leaders."[53] Four combinations of leader methods and types can therefore be distinguished: the dictatorial autocrat, the persuasive autocrat, the dictatorial democrat, and the persuasive democrat. Presumably, of course, the method of any given leader could be placed on a continuum ranging from dictatorial at one extreme to persuasive at the other extreme; but being persuasive does not make a leader who controls content a democrat any more than being arbi-

---

[52] Hanan C. Selvin, *The Effects of Leadership* (Illinois: Free Press of Glencoe, 1960). He went on to distinguish a "weak" climate which we did not include because, as Selvin states, the leader in the "weak" climate "has virtually no effective leadership."

[53] *Ibid.*, p. 45.

trary or dictatorial converts one who controls only process into an autocrat.

Examples of dictatorial democracy are not difficult to find. In our society we establish laws regulating the *process* whereby individuals are to conduct their affairs and we use force, if necessary, to compel them to obey the laws. The law itself was conceived democratically but its application may be quite dictatorial. Similarly, examples of persuasive autocracy are easy to find. Many parents, for example, do not punish their children; yet the children do not have control over the rules that govern their behavior. Rather, the parents establish the rules and persuade the children to accept them. Doubtless this procedure is preferable to dictatorial autocracy and may well be preferable to any form of democracy, but it is not democracy.

Effects of Leadership

When considering the effects of leadership, one must examine both the effect upon the task needs and upon the interpersonal needs of both the leader types and the leader methods. The White and Lippitt study showed that democracy was superior to autocracy in getting both task and interpersonal needs solved. Autocratic groups did accomplish more *when the leader was present,* but their task accomplishment fell off sharply when the leader was absent. At the same time the authoritarian leaders produced among the boys considerable hostility and aggression that was sometimes directed at "scapegoats" in the group. Democracy, on the other hand, produced more originality, more individuality, and less leader dependence than did autocracy. When democratic leaders were absent, task accomplishment did, indeed, fall off somewhat but maintained a relatively high level contrasted with task accomplishment in autocratic groups when the leader was absent. Selvin's study of leader methods was primarily concerned with the kinds of tension produced. Personal needs were clearly better satisfied by persuasive methods than by arbitrary or dictatorial methods. And because of the personal climate, task efficiency was also enhanced.

A very interesting conclusion was discovered in some research done by Wischmeier. He compared "group-centered" and "leader-centered" leaders which, in our terminology, are comparable to persuasive democratic and dictatorial democratic respectively. While groups reported more satisfaction with the discussion process under a group-centered leader, they rated the leader-centered leader as the better leader.[54]

The best explanation of this result is that the members were less sensitive to the actual contribution made by the persuasive democrat than to the more overt contribution made by the dictatorial democrat. Unwittingly they gave highest praise to the persuasive democrat or group-centered leader when they indicated greater satisfaction with the process itself. The conclusions are obvious. In virtually every examination of the effects of leadership the persuasive democrat is more likely to be effective in meeting both task and interpersonal needs.[55]

SUMMARY

Leadership is virtually synonymous with attempts to influence others by means of communication under circumstances that concede the right of the influencer to influence. A leader is thus a focal person whose contribution to the accomplishment of the group's goal, of its task needs, is significantly greater than individual contributions by the majority of others in the group.

Leaders first emerge in groups that interact long enough to develop distinctive group characteristics. Although the trait theory is inadequate to explain the rise of leadership, it can identify, before the fact, which leaders are likely to emerge in a given situation. The need theory seems to be a better explanation of the rise of leadership. It involves distinguishing group needs, both task and interpersonal, the skills of the leader, the resources available to the leader, and the desire of the leader as well as the followers to perform needed functions. Leaders are identifiable by means of job, sociometric, or process analyses, or by a combination of all these methods even though each method operates from a different point of view and produces results consistent within that point of view.

Power is defined as the capacity of one individual, or group, to

[54] Richard R. Wischmeier, "Group-Centered and Leader-Centered Leadership: An Experimental Study," *Speech Monographs,* Vol. 22 (March, 1955), pp. 43-48.

[55] When the personality characteristics of the followers are basically authoritarian, persuasion is not accepted as readily as dictation. This conclusion follows from our discussion of personality types earlier in this chapter. See pp. 207-209.

induce forces that affect the behavior of another person, or group. The dynamic nature of power contradicts the notion of the leader giving something to the follower as a complete explanation of leadership. Rather must one consider intrinsic as well as extrinsic forces. Power does not flow only one way; it is reciprocal, and, in any given situation, the power reservoir must be considered as well as the actual power used. Two sources of personal power, the leader's referent power and his expert power, are also distinguished.

Individuals may be categorized into four basic personality structures: a stage 1 individual is authoritarian; a stage 2 individual is hostile to authority; a stage 3 individual is other-directed; and a stage 4 individual is information-oriented. Personal security is the distinguishing variable among these four.

Formal channels of communication are perhaps the greatest weapon of the leader while informal channels are potent weapons of the followers. In cases where a rigid hierarchic structure exists among groups, leaders are less flexible, less democratic, and followers show less attachment to the group and its purposes.

Under the heading of leader-types, authoritarian and democratic leaders were profiled. Their sharpest differences are in the kind and extent of their control over content and process areas in group deliberations. Under the heading of leader methods we distinguished between persuasive and dictatorial leadership. Persuasive democratic leaders tend to produce group behavior that can be broadly characterized as cooperative and mature.

EXERCISES

1. Examine several definitions of a "leader." Consider carefully the full implications of each. Observe several groups of which you are a member, seeking to determine the extent to which the definitions (theory) reflect group leadership (practice). Choose a wide range of groups so as to have variety in such factors as formality, maturity, goals, status, and frequency of meetings. Prepare a report or plan a discussion of your observations.

2. Select two or three of the groups observed in Exercise 1 and prepare a report which
    a. identifies the leaders;
    b. identifies the methods by which each leader exercises his leadership;

c. evaluates the appropriateness and the effectiveness of the leadership, including interaction among leaders within each group;

d. compares methods of leadership among the different groups;

e. reports your personal reaction(s) to the leadership;

f. reports your preceptions of your leadership role(s) in the groups.

3. Select some relatively stable group with which the class is well acquainted, for example, a student governing body. Attempt a comparative approach to identifying leaders by forming the class into three groups, each of which focuses on one method: job analysis, sociometric analysis, or process analysis. Each of the three committees should observe independently, formulate a short report and these may be used as a basis for discussions among the members of the class.

4. In consultation with the instructor, members of the class may plan an experimental discussion in which preoriented discussants (without other participants being aware) attempt to adopt given roles or use specific leadership approaches. A wide variety of possible plans for both the discussion and the observation-analysis will suggest themselves. Beware of introducing too many variables in any one discussion.

5. Arrange to have a group present a discussion before the class in which an expert on the problem chosen will be a participant. By prearrangement with this expert have him come about thirty minutes late so the group will have already begun. Meet the expert outside, inform him of the direction the discussion is taking and have him take an opposite view without regard to the fundamental merit of such a position. Provide opportunity for both the observers (class) and the discussants to analyze and discuss the effects.

6. Make a list of 10 to 15 leaders you have followed over a period of several years. Attempt to analyze the source and nature of the influence each exerted over you. Attempt to distinguish between the various types of power, i.e., extrinsic versus intrinsic.

7. Compile a list of 10 to 15 situations in which you found yourself to be a leader over the past several years. Apply to yourself the same analysis suggested in Exercise 6. What have you learned about yourself as a leader? If possible, check your perceptions against those of another person who observed you in one or more of your leadership roles.

8. Compare two voluntary groups of which you are a member in terms of need perception. How well do you feel the members recognize the needs? Did you become aware of needs to which you had previously been insensitive? Attempt to have one leader and one follower in each group prepare independent lists of goals and needs for his group. Beware that you do not suggest ideas to these people when explaining your pur-

pose. Compare leader and follower lists. What do you find? Compare your lists to each of theirs. What do you find? How would you account for the results?

9. Follow the procedure outlined in Exercise 8 using two organizational groups. (It may be useful for some class members to form teams and share the work of Exercises 8 and 9 so that comparisons between voluntary and organizational groups may be made.)

10. Develop a plan for observing leadership in operation that enables you to differentiate between informal and formal leaders or symbolic and functional leaders. What characterizes each? How do you determine each type? What contributions do each make? What limitations do each experience?

11. Leaders often influence groups by subtle and even subliminal reactions. Devise one or more experiments in which leaders deliberately attempt to exert influence in such ways. One possibility might be for the leader to first appear enthusiastic concerning a group's developing line of thought, followed by gradual withdrawal, silence or change in tone of voice. Other possibilities will suggest themselves. Plan also for careful observation and reporting of results.

SELECTED READINGS

Adorno, T. W., Frenkel-Brunswik, Else, Levinson, Daniel J., and Sanford, R. Nevitt, *The Authoritarian Personality*. New York, Harper & Row, 1950.

Group Dynamics: Research and Theory, 2nd ed., Dorwin Cartwright and Alvin Zander, eds. Evanston, Ill., Row, Peterson, 1960, Parts 5 and 6.

Harvey, O. J., Hunt, David E., and Schroder, Harold M., *Conceptual Systems and Personality Organization*. New York, Wiley, 1960.

Leadership and Interpersonal Behavior, Luigi Petrullo and Bernard M. Bass, eds. New York, McGraw-Hill, 1961.

McGregor, Douglas, *The Human Side of Enterprise*. New York, McGraw-Hill, 1960.

Studies in Leadership, Alvin W. Gouldner, ed. New York, Harper, 1960.

Studies in Social Power, Dorwin Cartwright, ed. Ann Arbor, Univ. of Michigan, 1959.

Tannenbaum, Robert, Weschler, Irving R., and Massarik, Fred, *Leadership and Organization: A Behavioral Science Approach*. New York, McGraw-Hill, 1961.

CHAPTER 9

Group Dynamics:
The Forces Operative within the Group

Thus conscience does make cowards of us all,
And enterprises of great pith and moment
Is sicklied o'er with the pale cast of thought,
And enterprises of great pith and moment
With this regard their currents turn awry,
And lose the name of action.

William Shakespeare*

Almost invariably some students in our discussion classes ask, "Are we going to use group dynamics in this course?" When we answer that we can scarcely avoid using group dynamics, the student is puzzled. The reason, of course, is that he thinks of group dynamics as a set of techniques including role playing, observer-feedback, and buzz groups. We hope to correct this common misconception. We use the term *group dynamics* in the sense that Lewin first used it and in the sense that it is used in such books as *Group Dynamics: Research and Theory*.[1]

Group dynamics is a field of inquiry which concentrates on forces operating upon an individual within a group. The idea of

---

* *Hamlet*, Act III, scene i.
[1] Dorwin Cartwright and Alvin Zander, eds., *Group Dynamics: Research and Theory*, 2nd ed. (Evanston, Illinois: Row, Peterson, 1960).

forces has already been explicitly introduced in our discussion of leader power, and implicitly introduced in the discussion of the "effects" of group norms and group climate. A norm, for example, can obviously have no mystical power to compel individuals to modify their behavior in the same fashion that a blow can affect that which is struck. Individuals in one social setting, however, behave differently from the same individuals in a different kind of social setting. The problem of determining the causes of differing behavior gave rise to the famous debate which culminated in the 1920's and 1930's between the "individual theorists" and the "group theorists." A review of that battle is pointless.[2] But the battle is not entirely over. From a research point of view there is still considerable controversy over whether the individual or the group should be the starting point for research.

It is useful to consider group properties and characteristics together with the properties and characteristics of the group's environment as forces which impel groups and individuals within the group in a fashion analogous to the forces in a magnetic field. These forces can be and have been measured in objective fashion, and the effects are similarly measurable. Thus, these forces can be considered as "real" as anything tangible which can affect behavior.

To take the position that the individual is helpless in the face of these forces leads to the same conclusion as that of the critics of group behavior examined in Chapter 1—that we should return to some form of individualism and abandon as much collective effort as possible. The individual, however, is not helpless as long as he understands something of the nature of these forces and has developed some skill in communicating and interacting with others so that he can modify the nature of the forces. Once man stood in awe of the forces of nature; today man has not only learned how to modify the effects of nature but is contemplating the control of nature itself. Similarly, man today need not stand in awe of the forces of groups. Through understanding and skill he may control both effects and causes of human interaction. This chapter, however, is concerned with description only. Both value judgments and techniques come later.

For the sake of convenience and also to conform with the dis-

[2] *Ibid.,* see Chapter 1 for a history.

tinctions already made, the forces operative upon the group are divided into those which are largely external to the group itself and those which originate within the group—its members and their inter-action. Many of the ingredients of this force field have already been examined, and so much of the discussion serves the function of putting these ingredients into perspective. Other ingredients are new. The last section of the chapter is a discussion of "resultant" forces.

EXTERNAL FORCES

In his book, *The Human Group*, Homans divided the factors affect-ing a group into what he called the "external system" and the "inter-nal system."[3] More recently Homans has abandoned the terms because of the implications of the word *system*.[4] This book simply talks about external and internal *forces*. External forces are discussed under the headings of those which arise out of task requirements, intergroup relationships, and multiple group membership.

Task Requirements

Task requirements of the group are grouped under the heading of external forces for the reasons developed in Chapter 3. If the group's goals are solely those of satisfying the goals of its individual members, it may be classified as a group with personal purposes. The members of such groups have little adaptation to make to the environment. However, when the group exists to decide, take action, advise, or appraise, it must adapt to the external world. Let us consider, therefore, both the nature of the task requirements and the manner in which they are levied upon the group. Then we will look at the consequences of task commitment.

Nature of Task Requirements. Four factors should be considered: the stability, complexity, intensity, and attractiveness of the task requirements.

[3] George C. Homans, *The Human Group* (New York: Harcourt, Brace, 1950).
[4] George C. Homans, *Social Behavior: Its Elementary Forms* (New York: Harcourt, Brace & World, 1961). He felt that the word *system* implied a degree of organization and structure which was not present.

The *stability* of the task requirement is a measure of the degree to which the task requirement is predictable by the members of the group. If a group is asked to come up with a decision on some matter and if that decision responsibility is taken away or changed to an advisory responsibility, there is bound to be considerable unrest among the members of the group. In complicated and diverse organizations such as the federal government, for example, often the groups low in the hierarchy fail to find much stability in the tasks they are assigned. Group members, therefore, tend to avoid individual involvement with the task since they do not know whether their group will be allowed to see the task through.

A specific example of this kind of discouragement occurred at another institution. A group of young faculty members enthusiastically began a project. When the project was beginning to bear fruit, it was taken from them by a group of senior faculty members. The younger members perceived that the older ones wanted the credit. The accuracy of their perceptions is beside the point. What is important is that those younger members hesitated thereafter to commit themselves to other group tasks.

The *complexity* of the task requirement includes both the difficulty of accomplishment and the diversity of skills required. If the group feels that success is unlikely, the members' achievement motivation will probably be less. Some support for this position is offered by Deutsch who studied the effects of: "(1) the objective probability of prize attainment; (2) the past experience of success or failure as a group; and (3) the perceived motivation of other group members toward participating in the group . . ." upon membership motivation and achievement motivation.[5]

When the complexity of the task requires sharply different skills, still other forces are engaged. Many examples of this force come to mind, but one is especially dramatic. A group was considering whether or not to embark upon a new set of responsibilities. A substantial minority of the group was objecting rather strenuously, and, at first, the rest of the members assumed that the objectors believed it would be unwise for the group to undertake the new task. The reason for the objection, however, turned out to be that the objectors feared the demands of the new task would go beyond their capacities and they would be shouldered aside if it were undertaken. Only when they were assured of a place in the new scheme of things were they willing, although still reluctant, to agree to the task.

Leaders of a group often hesitate to assume tasks that require different leader skills. If such tasks are assumed, and if the leaders' skills do not measure up, pressures will very likely emerge to change the group's leadership structure.[6]

The *intensity* of the task pressure can vary from a "mañana" level to a crisis level. Anyone who has gone to school knows that the first of February seems a long time away when the requirement for the term paper is levied by the teacher in September. But when Christmas vacation has come and gone, and the term paper has not yet been started, much sleep and other relaxation must go. Publishers' deadlines pose similar problems.

The effect upon the group of low pressure is, of course, negligible, but the effect of crisis can be revolutionary. Hamblin's experiment showed that during times of crisis the leader's influence rises sharply, and, if the leader has been unsuccessful, he will probably be replaced.[7] We have observed both results in the political arena where under the stress of war or depression Presidents have been given extraordinary powers. Equally obvious, many totalitarian leaders deliberately seek to create crises which they seem to feel they can manage in order to gain powers they may otherwise be denied.

The degree of intensity forms one of the most significant forces acting upon the group.[8] The degree of intensity is a function of the perception of the members. Often a group is faced with what is actually a crisis situation, but the members refuse to see, or are incapable of seeing, the gravity of the situation. (Recall our discussion of realistic groups.) Bringing the group face-to-face with the intensity of the task requirements is one of the leader's most important challenges.

Task *attractiveness* is such an obvious force that we need do little more than mention it here. The attractiveness of a task is a

[6] We will offer some experimental support for this assertion in the next portion. See pp. 250-252 below.

[7] Robert L. Hamblin, "Leadership and Crises," in Cartwright and Zander, *op. cit.*

[8] We shall return to this concept when we examine resultant forces. See pp. 245-252 below.

function of the rewards that individuals can expect during, and as a result of, successful task performance. (This has been discussed under the heading of leader power.) Dozens of studies and observations confirm the power of task attractiveness. But while the nature of the force is obvious, it is not, therefore, to be dismissed as being unimportant. Together with intensity, attractiveness is a potent force. Without the factor of intensity, it still remains potent.

Application of Task Requirements. The discussion to this point may suggest that tasks are always levied upon the group from sources outside the group. This is not true. Despite including task requirements under the heading of external forces, tasks may well be levied upon the group by the members of the group itself. In organizational groups the tasks are usually assigned to the groups by the larger organization. Most voluntary groups, however, levy requirements upon themselves, and many organizational groups seek to extend their area of control in such a fashion that they seem to be initiating their own task requirements.[9] The concern here is with how the group initially is confronted with the task requirement. The task may be levied upon, or created by, the group's leadership; the task may be levied upon, or created by, followers; or the task may be levied upon, or created by, the group as a whole. In each case the forces are somewhat different, so each is examined briefly.

When the task requirements originate outside the group, they usually are transmitted through the group's hierarchy. When the task requirements come from within the group, they are usually created by the group's hierarchy because of the reasons discussed in the previous chapter on the rise of leadership. Thus, the group's leadership is usually in the position of prodding the group into action. The effect of this upon the leadership structure forms the largest part of the discussion later in this chapter on the resultant forces. This problem is so significant that all of Chapter 14 is devoted to an examination of how leaders can move a group to some kind of action.

When the task requirements are created by followers, the impact upon the group as a whole is generally less than in the previous case. If the requirement is to be accepted by the group, the follower will probably have to initiate a pair event with the leader. If the

[9] This was pointed out in Chapter 7, pp. 166-167.

leader is unreceptive and if the task requirement is imperative, one of two things will happen. The leadership structure will be over-turned or undermined or the group's significance will diminish pro-portionately as the task significance rises.

An example of the different applications of task requirements is found in typical problems that come to the staff of a university department. The following tasks are cited as representative.

Such tasks as making budgets, recommendations for promotion, and curricular plans come directly from the administration and are levied upon the chairman who must assemble his department or its appropriate committees and make plans. Such tasks are not usually attractive, the guide lines for their execution not always stable. The complexity varies; the intensity is usually determined by deadlines set by the dean. On the other hand, tasks such as the creation of new courses or the expansion of programs which involves hiring new staff members are usually created within the department by people higher in the leadership hierarchy (not necessarily the chair-man). Often the intensity and attractiveness of such tasks are not immediately apparent to some of the department members whose areas of responsibility are directly involved. In such cases the forces for task achievement are weaker than when the leadership hierarchy is backed up by outside power. The accomplishment of such tasks requires the leaders to exercise either persuasion or coercion. By now it should be apparent that the former is preferable.

Members of the department who are lower in status are often in most direct contact with many students and thus are sensitive to task requirements involving organization and teaching of mass enroll-ment courses. The departmental leadership is usually less sensitive to such task requirements than to task requirements levied by the administration or involving departmental budgeting and control. Hence such followers have to be especially involved and persistent if they are to have much effect upon departmental policy.

Sometimes, as is particularly characteristic of groups that have been used for experimental purposes, the tasks are levied upon, or created by, the group as a whole. For this reason much of the litera-ture and experimental conclusions have not been widely appli-cable.[10] For example, if a group is told, when all are present, that

[10] Some of the more recent studies in the area of communication patterns and structures are remedying this deficiency.

they have twenty minutes to arrive at a solution to a problem and that the best group in the experimental series will receive such and such a prize, the appreciation of the intensity and attractiveness of the task requirement does not have to be mediated by some part of the group. The task pressure is applied upon each individual directly. The same kind of thing happens when the task requirements are set by the group as a whole. As we shall emphasize later, such procedures are most likely to generate effective task pressure with a minimum of interpersonal strain. (This is one of the reasons for the stress on goal-setting procedures.) Unfortunately, genuine creation of task requirements by the group as a whole is infrequent save in small mature groups.

Effects of Task Commitment. Once group members have accepted the task requirements and have committed themselves to the goal of task achievement, additional forces are created. These forces can be called the pressures for "closure." [11]

Task pressures are usually not, as pointed out earlier, accepted simultaneously by all members of the group. Some members of a group will have committed themselves to the task while other members are either not aware of task pressures or are resisting them. Thus a complicated set of forces is present during the stage when the group is formally or informally considering task commitment. Members who have committed themselves to the task face the immediate problem of securing the commitment of other members; those who are unaware of the task pressures do not yet feel any pressure; while those members who are resisting the task pressures will be contending that the task goals are unnecessary, undesirable, likely to be achieved without group activity, or some combination of the three. This is the point at which those who are committed may possibly succumb to the feeling that the end justifies the means and attempt to bludgeon recalcitrant members into task commitment.

Sometimes task activity is produced not by genuine commitment to the task itself but by acceptance of personal influence of others.

[11] In Chapter 4 we pointed out that the perception of an obstacle to goal achievement created in the person a state of disequilibrium which could be resolved only by solving the problem or by choosing another goal. Here we are restating this concept in terms of the forces acting upon the individual to complete the task requirement.

When this happens, we can distinguish between those who are task-oriented and those who are source-oriented.[12] The results of these two kinds of commitment were studied by McDavid who compared "message-oriented" with "source-oriented" subjects. He found that:

The message-oriented group differed from the source-oriented group in that members of this group (1) were generally less susceptible to group influence (2) were less affected by manipulations of task difficulty and (3) showed a tendency to compromise with discrepant group judgments rather than to agree completely with them when yielding did occur. In rating their own reactions to interpersonal communication events, the source-oriented individuals indicated significantly greater flexibility in modifying their perception of themselves following that event than the message-oriented individuals although the two groups did not differ in level of past-event self-evaluation.[13]

The effects of the pressures for closure can be dramatic when skillfully manipulated by group members. To test the extent of these pressures, one of the authors conducted a study to determine whether a minority could utilize these pressures to force the majority to shift its opinions and conform to the minority rather than follow the more usual direction of conformity.[14] Groups averaging six members each were given the task of making recommendations about a human relations problem and a strict time limit was given. (It could be assumed that all of the members had committed themselves to the task.) Although it was unknown to the four "naive" members, two of the members were "plants" operating under instructions by the experimenter. All members read the instructions and the problem. They then individually checked their reactions on a seven-point scale. The experimenter collected the individual reactions; read to the group as a whole the actual reactions of the four "naive" members; and reported that one of the two remaining had checked a score corresponding to the group mode and that the other had

[12] This distinction is comparable to the objective reality-social reality distinction in Chapter 5.
[13] John McDavid, Jr., "Personality and Situational Determinants of Conformity," *Journal of Abnormal and Social Psychology*, Vol. 58 (1959), pp. 241-246.
[14] R. Victor Harnack, "A Study of the Effect of an Organized Minority upon a Discussion Group," *The Journal of Communication*, Vol. 13 (March, 1963), pp. 12-24.

checked the most extreme position. The modal plant then began a personal attack upon the deviate who remained polite, unassuming, but firm. This was done to create group resentment toward the modal plant and thereby induce forces against a source representing the position taken by the group majority. At the same time sympathy was created for the deviate. About half way through the period the modal plant quit talking and pretended to consider his behavior. Then with only ten or fifteen minutes remaining the modal plant began the shift toward the position of the deviate by saying something like:

[hesitantly] "Wait a minute. You've been saying that . . . [repeats an argument that the deviate had offered]. Yes. I think I see what you're driving at, but seven is rather tough, don't you think? Would you be willing to come down to six?" (In the event that the deviate had been placed at position one, he would have been asked to retreat to position two.) The mode then continued the shift toward the deviate by turning to the naive Ss and asking them to do what he had apparently done—reconsider their first hasty impressions.[15]

The task had to be solved, and the solution consisted of getting group agreement upon one of the seven alternatives. The results showed a dramatic shift of the majority in sixteen of the twenty groups to the position taken by the minority of two. The forces for closure mounted as the deadline drew near. Most of the majority knew that something had happened to them, but they were not quite sure how to define it. The result, however, was what one normally would predict for the effect of the majority over the minority although in this case it was deliberately reversed.

The task to be performed, it appears, does induce considerable force upon the group members. The nature and extent of the forces are a function of the nature of the task requirement itself, including its stability, complexity, intensity, and attractiveness. The task forces are further modified by the manner in which they are applied to the group, whether through the hierarchy, individual members, or the group as a whole. Finally, pressures for closure are created when the group members have committed themselves to task accomplishment.

[15] *Ibid.*

Intergroup Relationships

An examination of some of the characteristics of *inter*group relationships will help in understanding how groups relate to one
another. In the study of *intra*group relationships, it was pointed out
that the individuals had to interact with one another in a situation
in which there was some degree of interdependence. The study of
intergroup relationships continues with the limitations of interaction
and interdependence, but does not limit the interaction to face-to-
face communication situations. While it is not introduced as a
further limitation, the concern is, for the most part, with groups
that have some formal or recognized relationship as, for example, a
group which is a part of a larger organization and is, therefore, formally related to other groups within the larger organization.

The examination of intergroup relationships is divided into brief
looks at intergroup climate, intergroup status, intergroup power,
and other institutional characteristics.

Intergroup Climate. The goal analysis of climate in Chapter 7 will
also serve for analysis of intergroup climate. Like the individuals
who compose them, groups can be described as having cooperative
or competitive relationships with other groups. The best way to
illustrate the nature of this intergroup climate is to describe briefly
some extensive experiments that were carried out by Muzafer Sherif
and his associates.[16] Sherif used twenty-four twelve-year-old boys as
subjects for his experiments. The boys were placed in a camp situation for several weeks during which time Sherif and his assistants
divided them into two groups and conducted a three-stage experiment. The first stage was the development of "in-group" feelings,
accomplished by presenting to each of the two groups goals which
could only be achieved by collaborative effort (complementary
goals). This action stressed the degree of interdependence within
the group and produced group solidarity. The second stage was the
development of intergroup hostility and competition, accomplished
by setting forth various goals which necessitated the failure of one
group in order for the other group to succeed (antagonistic goals).

---

[16] Muzafer Sherif, O. J. Harvey, B. Jack White, William R. Hood, and
Carolyn W. Sherif, *Intergroup Conflict and Cooperation: The Robbers Cave
Experiment* (Norman, Oklahoma: Univ. Book Exchange, 1961).

These goals consisted for the most part of a tournament between the two groups including a variety of athletic events. The final stage was the reduction of intergroup tensions, accomplished by means of imposing "superordinate" goals which could be reached only if both groups worked together. The results of this third stage produced considerable friendliness and other attributes of cooperation despite the rather bitter rivalry that had been engendered by the stage two activities.

Though the anecdotes about the boys' interactions make fascinating reading, it is necessary, here, to pass over them and point out some of the alternative approaches that Sherif rejected as means of reducing intergroup conflict and tension and the reasons that Sherif rejected them.

Personal contact between members of conflicting groups is often said to be the best method of reducing conflict and promoting cooperation. In the Sherif experiments, however, contact did not result in improved relations because of a lack of goals which required intergroup collaboration.

A *common enemy* is another way of bringing groups together. This has been, of course, the bond that has joined even strange bedfellows in times of war. Our alliance with Russia in the Second World War is a case in point. Schools have used the common enemy approach to produce harmony and solidarity by means of athletic and other contests with other schools. Business, military, and even church organizations have resorted to some form of the common enemy approach in order to weld diverse groups together within their organizations. The difficulty is that the common enemy approach still produces conflict which can often become bitter and wasteful. Superordinate goals need not be those of defeating some-*one;* they can be goals of defeating some common enemy like poverty, ignorance, and disease.

Individual competition and rivalry can reduce intergroup competition and rivalry, but group solidarity is destroyed in the process and the benefits of collaborative action are harder to attain.[17]

Leadership may be able to do much to reduce intergroup tensions, but leaders are often helpless in the face of the forces built up and sustained by their own followers.

The point should be clear. The forces engendered by the nature

[17] Remember this point in Chapter 1, pp. 9-10.

of intergroup climate can have a considerable effect upon the nature of group operation. The nature of *inter*group climate can be comprehended very much in the same way as the nature of *intra*group climate, and the effects upon *inter*group behavior are very much the same as they are upon *intra*group behavior.

Intergroup Status. As it is possible to discuss status as an attribute of individuals within the group, so is it possible to discuss it as an attribute of groups. A brief examination suffices for the elements of status have already been described. A group's status may be primarily a function of its area of control; the status may also be a function of the importance that others attach to the tasks performed by the group. A jury considering a murder case has a higher status, for example, than a jury considering traffic offenses. A group may gain status if its members possess status in their own rights. Finally, a group may be accorded high status by virtue of the requirements for membership. This is one of the main reasons for the high status of people on the social register and the prime source of status for members of honorary groups such as Delta Sigma Rho or Phi Beta Kappa.

The forces produced by the status of the group affect not only those individuals who seek to gain or maintain membership in the group; but also the power of the group in dealing with other groups.

Intergroup Power. This means the extent of the influence of the group over other groups or over individuals who are not members of the group. The concept of intergroup power contains precisely the same aspects of power as discussed in Chapter 8. The provision for intergroup power differs somewhat in that intergroup power is more often specified by laws, rules, and regulations. Thus, a legislative body has its power specified by law, and our system of judicial review operates to define the boundaries of that legal power. Within an organization both the scope of control and the authority of groups listed on the organization chart are specified.

This treatment of intergroup power is brief, not because it is an unimportant force upon group deliberations, but because power dimensions were described extensively in the previous chapter; the forces can be tremendous. This force can be especially great when it is applied by one group directly upon individuals in another. For example, manipulative application of promotion criteria is one way in which the larger organization can break up the power of groups within the organization by destroying their solidarity. If, for example, promotion is based upon behavior which requires intragroup competition, the solidarity of the smaller groups is almost impossible to maintain. Larger organizations can render small groups impotent by requiring multiple coordination between and among groups, limiting both the scope of control and the power of those groups. Classroom teachers are often mystified because student discussion groups, for which they have so carefully planned, do not seize their opportunities and assume significant responsibilities for their own learning. The reason may well be that the power of the teacher in the area of extrinsic rewards and punishments has never been relinquished. The students recognize their group's impotency and continue to resort to maintenance of personal relations with the teacher in order to derive satisfaction.

Other Institutional Characteristics. Large organizations, like the small groups which compose them, develop such things as norms, communication structures, and leadership hierarchies. These characteristics differ from those of the small group chiefly in that it is much more difficult for the individual to exercise influence over these norms and characteristics.[18] The effect of such characteristics upon intergroup relations and, consequently, upon group deliberations should be quite obvious by this time.

Multiple Membership

One aspect of the external forces that cannot be generalized from the previous examination of group characteristics is the set of forces generated by the multiple group memberships of the several group members. Each individual member of a discussion group is almost certainly a member of several other groups. These groups also have norms, structure, and status relationships, and the individual brings them with him into any other group. Sherif's autokinetic studies showed that when norms had been developed in one setting, they tended to persist when the individual was placed with another individual who had developed different norms.[19] True, a new norm was created, but when individuals had developed sharply

[18] See Chapter 7, p. 168 ff.
[19] Muzafer Sherif, *The Psychology of Social Norms* (New York: Harper, 1936). This experiment was described in Chapter 7, pp. 164-165.

different norms, their individual judgments of the movement of the light usually did not come completely together.

Problems of Representation. In Chapter 2 the limitation upon discussion imposed by the problems of representation was discussed. Individuals are often not free to act as they might wish when they have commitments as representatives of other groups. Whether this representation be formal or not, each individual usually feels to some extent the forces imposed by his other groups. The notion, "When in Rome, do as the Romans do," will free the individual only to the extent that his behavior can be unobserved by his fellow Carthaginians, or to the extent that the values and standards he has internalized can be quieted or harmonized, or both. One of the authors was a member of a student-faculty group in which a first name basis was a norm. One of the students had just taken a class from the author and simply could not bring himself to say "Vic." He evaded the issue by using no name at all and gained attention by other means such as a tap on the elbow.

Special Leader Problems. The leader, like the rest of the members, is also a member of other groups. The forces created by some of his memberships are somewhat distinctive, however. Because he is the leader of the group, he is usually a member of another group which stands higher in the intergroup hierarchy. In formal organizations this is worked into the recognized structure of the organization. A glance at the hypothetical segment of an organizational chart in Figure 9.1 will illustrate how this works. Person A is the leader and member of the group composed of himself and persons 1, 2, 3, 4, and 5. He is also a member of the group led by X and composed of B, C, D, E, himself, and X. He shares the values, sentiments, norms, and responsibilities of the alphabet group and the values, sentiments, norms, and responsibilities of the numerical group. If the attraction of the alphabet group becomes too strong and if the leader begins to transfer his primary allegiance to it, he becomes a poor member of the numerical group. If the reverse is true, he may become an isolate in the alphabet group.

Kurt Lewin discussed this matter at length in *Resolving Social Conflicts.*[20] He pointed out that although most members of the

[20] Kurt Lewin, *Resolving Social Conflicts* (New York: Harper & Row, 1948).

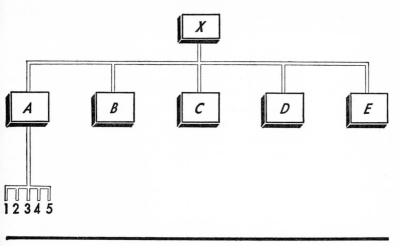

FIGURE 9.1

Jewish minority were not accepted by Gentiles, *the Jewish leaders were.* This produced forces which oftentimes tended to perpetuate unfortunate intergroup relationships because the leaders had been accepted under the *status quo.* Similarly, Louis Lomax believes that the Negroes' lunch counter sit-down-demonstrations are an expression of revolt against the leadership of the NAACP as well as a revolt against the Southern segregationists.[21] Despite the legal gains won by the organized Negro leadership, Lomax contends that the leadership have lost touch with mass sentiment. The Negro leaders, according to this analysis, find themselves accepted by the whites and therefore ". . . don't have the same fire in their stomachs that the students and the rallying Negro masses have."[22]

INTERNAL FORCES

The examination of external forces has included the forces levied by task requirements, those created by intergroup interaction, and those which arise as a result of multiple membership. But the group

[21] Louis E. Lomax, "The Negro Revolt Against 'The Negro Leaders,'" *Harpers Magazine,* Vol. 220 (June, 1960), pp. 41-48.
[22] *Ibid.,* p. 47.

does not react to these external forces as a unit. The analysis of the external forces must be countered, then, with an analysis of the forces within the group. Since Chapters 7 and 8 spelled out in detail the genesis of almost all of these forces, their further examination here is brief; they are summarized and put into perspective. The forces considered are: those produced as a result of the characteristics of the members; those that are a result of group characteristics including leadership structure; and those that arise from interpersonal attraction.

Membership Characteristics

Much has been said about individual differences and how they affect the individual's perception of and reaction to his environment. Let us see now how they induce forces affecting the operation of the group.

Personality. The personality types defined in the previous chapter create differences which affect the way in which a stage 1 individual reacts to his environment in contrast to the way in which a stage 2, 3, or 4 individual reacts. These differences also create demands upon group operation and structure. Here is an illustration:

A stage 1 individual demands a predictable structure and exhibits preferences for authoritarian control. He tends to be intolerant of compromise, equating that with defeat, or anything less than authoritatively stated perfection. Such absolutists can be extremely perverse when they fail to find the authority they seek in the group or when the group's authority is at variance with other authority. Recall the quotation from Elmer Davis with which Chapter 1 concluded and then read these words which precisely describe the stage 1 individual.

There must be a final truth and they must have it; experimental thinking is only a groping in the dark. And if its successes are written in the record of American history from Jefferson (yes, and Hamilton) through Lincoln down to Franklin Roosevelt, that fact can be obliterated by remembering that events happened in the desired manner—by knowing that press and radio and schools and colleges are all controlled by the Communists and that the Roosevelt administration had its critics shot.[23]

[23] Elmer Davis, *But We Were Born Free* (New York: Bobbs-Merrill, 1954), p. 190.

The force exerted by the stage 2 individual is obvious. He tends to resist any authority or influence.

The stage 3 individual exerts forces tending toward group harmony and interpersonal satisfaction. These forces are constructive. But he also exerts forces to resist task pressures since they tend to disrupt group harmony. These forces are particularly strong when the moment of decision arrives although they are not observed as the active opposition of the stage 2 individual.

The forces exerted by the stage 4 individual are more than likely to be task oriented. As contrasted with the stage 3 individual, these forces often ignore interpersonal solidarity and sentiment except as these are perceived as contributing to the effectiveness of the task.

Ability. Considered apart from personality structures, the relative ability of the members creates forces upon the group's operation and structure. It has already been pointed out how ability to perform needed roles affects a person's rise as a leader. In addition to the capacity to perform given roles, is the concept of role flexibility. Clearly, the more rigorously limited individuals are in the kinds of roles they can perform, the greater the forces tending to limit the group to certain kinds of tasks and to avoid further challenges. The other side of this coin was dealt with in the discussion of complexity earlier in this chapter. The forces created by member ability are reciprocal with the forces created by task complexity.

Stability. Finally, remember the forces created by the relative stability of the group's membership. If the membership is continually turning over, forces are created for integration and orientation which must be satisfied before genuine task accomplishment can be launched. A Federal Mediation and Conciliation Commissioner once told us that contract negotiations tended to improve over the years as pretty much the same faces appeared around the bargaining table and as the same commissioner tended to show up year after year.

Group Characteristics

Only a reminder is needed here of the forces produced by group norms, climate, control, maturity, and leadership. But three specific characteristics have been mentioned only indirectly and deserve some attention in this consideration of internal forces. These are the forces produced by group goals, group size, and group decision-making structure.

Common Goals. Goals and goal-setting have occupied much of the attention earlier in the book, and certainly when considering the forces that are operative in the group situation, the forces created by the common goal of the group must be considered. In Chapter 7 the importance of a justifiable *raison d'etre* was mentioned as a condition of maturity. Here it is time to talk about the group goals as exerting forces upon the members which result in goal-seeking activity. Earlier it was shown how task commitment exerted forces upon the members to achieve the goal of completing the task. In addition to the specific tasks a group confronts, it has those goals that involve the maintenance of the group itself and the long-range goals that are fundamental in the existence of the group.

To the extent that individual goals can be clearly merged with long-range group goals, the force exerted by group goals is increased. Merging of individual goals, coupled with facilitative task goals, results in the "image" of the group perceived by the individual member as well as outsiders. To separate the external forces from the internal forces in the complex structure of what emerges as the group goals is particularly difficult but at this point the distinction is largely semantic.

It is very interesting to observe several voluntary groups plagued by the problem of defining their fundamental group goals. A particular church group offers an interesting illustration. When first formed, it was intended to be primarily a learning group composed of young people from post-high school to middle age. As such, the group did not flourish. Attendance was sporadic and small. Later the group reorganized along social lines and more or less evolved into a young married couples group. Then the group flourished and, with the increase in interest and member resources, the group began to undertake a variety of tasks facilitating the maintenance of the church of which the group was a part. The forces induced by the first set of goals were simply not strong enough to develop the group. Once the group had generated member support for social objectives, the goals of enhancing the group as such allowed the group to do things, including learning experiences, it was not able to do under the first set of circumstances.[24]

Group Size. Size is a very important variable determining the nature of the forces operating upon the group. Genuine leaderless discussion, for example, seems unlikely to occur save in *small* mature groups. Before examining the forces produced by size, some way must be found of describing the variable of group size, and to do this the simple person-to-person relationships in a group must be defined. This can be done with the formula, $R = N\,(N -)/2$ where R equals the number of relationships, and N equals the number of people in the group. Thus, a group of two has only one relationship, *AB*. A group of three has three relationships, *AB, AC,* and *BC*. A group of five has ten relationships, *AB, AC, AD, AE, BC, BD, BE, CD, CE,* and *DE*. A group of ten has forty-five such relationships, and so on. The number of relationships increases geometrically as the group number increases arithmetically.

As Bass points out, the first consequent of increased group size is a reduction in the "interaction potential" of any given set of members.[25] That is, it makes it more difficult for individual members to gain satisfaction from one another by interacting. In his study of student learning discussion groups, Schellenberg found limited evidence that small groups showed slightly higher academic achievement, but he found a "surprisingly consistent inverse relationship between group size and student satisfaction. Students claimed greater satisfaction in the smaller groups." [26]

The second consequent of increased group size is multiplication of demand for specific structure. Hamblin discovered that, as group size increases, there is a tendency for one member of the group to become a substantive leader and another to become a procedural leader.[27] That is, as the group becomes larger, the leadership roles

[24] For an extended discussion of the relationship of both external and internal goals and the forces operative upon the group, see Cartwright and Zander, *op. cit.,* Part Four.

[25] Bernard M. Bass, *Leadership, Psychology, and Organizational Behavior* (New York: Harper & Row, 1960), Chapter 17.

[26] James A. Schellenberg, "Group Size as a Factor in Success of Academic Discussion Groups," *Journal of Educational Sociology,* Vol. 33 (1959), pp. 73-79.

[27] Robert L. Hamblin, "An Experimental Study of the Relationship of Communication, Power Relations, Specialization, and Social Atmospheres to Group Size," (Unpublished Ph.D. dissertation, Univ. of Michigan, 1955).

become more specialized. It follows that the greater the specialization, the greater the need for structure to regulate behavior.

Time and again discussion classes are frustrated by the complexities of increased group size. (Most of the early discussions in our classes, for example, are conducted in small groups of five to seven members each.) When the class as a whole is given a decision-making assignment *without instruction concerning group structure* they often flounder helplessly, trying to utilize the same leaderless or informal structure that had worked so well in the smaller groups. It usually takes a frustrating experience or two for them to accept emotionally the complexity introduced by increased group size.[28]

Group Decision-Making Structure. When the members are uncertain as to just *who* has the decision-making responsibility, or when they do not know *how* a matter is to be brought to a decision, forces tending toward disintegration and dissatisfaction are increased. Mulder found, for example, that the more centralized the decision structure of groups, the better will be the group's performance in regard to speed, quality, and efficiency.[29] He went further to distinguish centralized structures, as such, from centralized decision-making structures. A centralized structure with all member contributions polarized around a leader is not the same thing as a centralized decision-making structure. The former concerns interaction alone; the latter concerns the actual process of making decisions. Mulder found that centralized structures, without the centralized decision-making characteristic, were more "vulnerable" and resulted in negative performance.

The decision structure is not so important in the actual face-to-face discussion. It becomes an issue when subgroups of the larger group are faced with a variety of decisions and they do not possess the decision-making structure to enable them to cope successfully with the problem. Then questions such as these arise. Who is responsible for this matter? Should this matter come before the whole group? If I have an idea, to whom should I direct it? When

[28] Halbert E. Gulley has an excellent discussion of the effect of group size in *Discussion, Conference and Group Process* (New York: Holt, Rinehart and Winston, 1959), pp. 101-106.

[29] M. Mulder, "Communication Structure, Decision Structure, and Group Performance," *Sociometry*, Vol. 23 (1960), pp. 1-14.

the structure for initiating, processing, and solving problems is clear and appropriate, the forces tend toward efficiency and member satisfaction.

Interpersonal Attraction

The last of the internal forces is that of interpersonal attraction. Sentiment, affection, liking, or attraction are obviously important forces in group interaction. Many of the potential causes of interpersonal attraction having been examined, there is one fundamental cause to be examined in some detail, followed by a study of the nature of the forces produced by interpersonal attraction.

Contact. Interpersonal contact can do little to ease *intergroup* tensions. However, when the others are not seen as members of an outgroup and when the stereotypes attributed to the outgroup are not attributed to the individual with whom one comes into contact, the contact *does* tend to enhance interpersonal attraction. This principle has been well established by Festinger, Schachter and Back in their famous "Westgate" and "Westgate West" studies.[30]

When contact is buttressed by interdependent activity, homogenous background, and comparable values, interpersonal attraction is increased. Absence may make the heart grow fonder in legend, but in the world of reality there is little substitute for contact, as the wartime recipients of "Dear John" letters will testify. Clearly, the contact must be rewarding if it is to produce interpersonal attraction. This principle need not be spelled out except to remember that the rewards need not be extrinsic. The very act of establishing meaningful relationships with others is, according to the theory we have been developing, a highly rewarding act.

Balance Between Personal and Object Attraction. Attraction for, or liking of, an object or act is just as evident as interpersonal attraction. We like things as well as people. Heider develops, as the fundamental basis of his theory, the notion of maintaining a balance between one's liking for a person and for an object.[31] If *P*, for

[30] Leon Festinger, Stanley Schachter, and Kurt Back, *Social Pressures in Informal Groups* (New York: Harper, 1950).

[31] Fritz Heider, *The Psychology of Interpersonal Relations* (New York: Wiley, 1958).

example, likes O and if O likes X (some object or act), P will tend to like X. By the same token, if P likes O and O *dislikes* X, then P will tend to dislike X. The remaining two combinations are axiomatic. If P dislikes O and O likes X, P will tend to dislike X; and if P dislikes O and O dislikes X, then P will tend to like X.

This theory of balancing attractions is not new; Aristotle developed it rather extensively twenty-four centuries ago.[32] The novelty of the idea is not important, but the forces created by the balance or imbalance of attractions are significant. If the attractions are in balance, as in any of the four combinations above, forces are created to maintain this balance or equilibrium. P will tend to reject ideas that imply either O or X are anything but what he perceives them to be. Similarly, if the attractions are out of balance, forces are created which operate upon P to restore balance. Thus, if P likes O and *dislikes X*, and if O *likes X*, P is in trouble. He must find some way to reconcile this discrepancy.

There is evidence of these forces in the accusations that someone or some group is wittingly or unwittingly following the Communist line by supporting or attacking something that the Communists support or attack. If, for example, one attacks the John Birch Society, he is likely to be told that he should not do this because the Communists are also opposed to the John Birch Society and attacking it furthers Communist objectives. The logical fallacy of this kind of argument is apparent, but the emotional basis for insisting upon a balance of attractions is more difficult to perceive.[33]

If you are P, there are several ways you can restore the equilibrium created by an imbalance in your attractions for O and X. First, you can change your liking for either O or X. This is not easy unless you strongly like, or dislike, one and mildly dislike, or like, the other. Thus, the husband may give up playing bridge, which was never a passion with him anyway, when he discovers that his wife dislikes bridge, and the mother may become quite a student of baseball when she discovers her sons are excited about Little

---

[32] Lane Cooper, *The Rhetoric of Aristotle* (New York: Appleton-Century-Crofts, 1932).

[33] Balancing attractions is not solely emotional. Recall our discussion in Chapter 5 of the personal bases of belief. See also Chapter 6 for a discussion of the logical fallacies.

League ball. When both attractions are strong, however, such classical problems arise as the one created when persons of different faiths marry.

Another way to restore equilibrium is to change the other person's (O's) liking or disliking. The problems here are similar to those of changing your own feelings.

Of course, you can minimize the extent or importance of the discrepant feeling in some such fashion as, "She doesn't really dislike bridge; she simply prefers other forms of recreation." This minimizes, but does not resolve, the contradiction, and different individuals differ in the amount of contradiction they can tolerate. In debate, it is fascinating, and often distressing, to observe how some people simply cannot abide disagreement and controversy. If it is controversial, it is taboo.

If one can recognize differences and learn to accept them without a corresponding psychologically unhealthy compartmentalizing of oneself, one is probably a mature individual. Genuine tolerance and acceptance of individuals who hold different views demands this kind of recognition of disparity. Probably much of what passes for religious or political tolerance is simply the result of not caring very much about one's religion or politics. When people do care, and can still accept the discrepancy, this is the epitome of genuine interpersonal attraction.

RESULTANT FORCES

Rather than attempt to summarize the forces presented thus far, this section attempts to integrate them into the resultant forces that operate upon the group. These forces clearly act neither singly nor independently. Acting in concert, these forces tend to produce resultant forces. This concept of resultant forces was originally borrowed by Kurt Lewin from the concept of resultant forces in the physical sciences.[34] In Figure 9.2 we see that forces A and B are applied to object X. R is the resultant force. It is different from, and yet a part of, both A and B..

[34] Kurt Lewin, *Principles of Topological Psychology* (New York: McGraw-Hill, 1936).

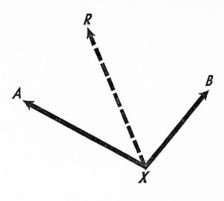

FIGURE 9.2

Quasi-Stationary Social Equilibrium

Again Lewin provides the theoretical construct. Lewin contended that the forces operating upon a group tended to result in what he called a state of "quasi-stationary social equilibrium." [35] That is, the forces *for* change tend to be counterbalanced by the forces *against* change resulting in a more or less stationary position. The group, or individual, will tend to go about operating in pretty much the same fashion in its day-to-day behavior unless one, or a combination, of two things happens. The forces for change can be heightened, or the forces against change can be lessened. If the forces for change are heightened without a corresponding lessening of the forces against change, the result will be increased tension. Obviously, the lessening of forces against change, particularly when coupled with heightened forces for change, will accomplish the change with the least amount of disturbance.

Let us further illustrate with the help of a diagram the concept of quasi-stationary equilibrium and the production of change—that is, resultant forces which are strong enough to produce perceptible movement. In Figure 9.3 the lines A, B, C, and D indicate both the direction and magnitude of the forces operating. The three lines labeled R_{AB}, R_{ABC}, and R_{ABCD} indicate force possibilities under cer-

[35] Kurt Lewin, *Field Theory in Social Science* (New York: Harper, 1951), Chapter 9.

tain circumstances. Let us first assume that only forces A and B are operating. These are complementary and produce a resultant force (R_{AB}) which is comparable to R in Figure 9.2. If we add the antagonistic force C, we produce a resultant force (R_{ABC}) which is essentially a state of quasi-stationary equilibrium. Now let us add still another force (D). The resultant force is R_{ABCD} which is almost identical with force D but is produced at the cost of considerable stress. If it is possible to identify the number, direction, and magnitude of forces operating, such an analysis may be conducted for any situation in which a number of forces are operating.

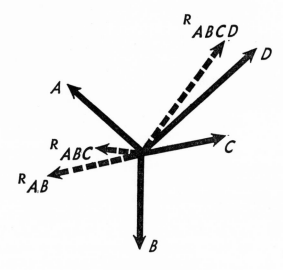

FIGURE 9.3

What are these counterbalancing forces? At the risk of oversimplification, we can say that the group has tasks to accomplish and at the same time the members wish to remain in harmony with themselves and with others. When the group has adaptation to make *as a group* to its external environment, forces are created to specialize role functions, streamline authority relations, create status differences, and generally disrupt harmony. Group harmony might be described as the socialist ideal—interaction which fulfills personal needs. Naturally status differences and other concomitants of role specialization would be obliterated. As the old saying goes, it's unfortunate but you can't have your cake and eat it too. Thus, the state of quasi-stationary social equilibrium is ambivalent at best. Bales states the issue technically but accurately:

Now, to sum up the argument to this point, we have an idea of two "chains of events" or "series of strains" starting from opposite poles and proceeding in opposite directions, tending to cancel each other out, and each in its terminal effects tending to set off the opposite chain of events. One chain of events has its starting point in the necessities of adaptation to the outer situation and proceeds in its series of strains through changes in the division of labor, changes in the distribution of property, authority, and status and has its malintegrative terminal effects in the disturbance of the existing state of solidarity. The other chain of events has its starting point in the necessities of integration or reintegration of the social system itself and proceeds in its series of strains through a reactive (or perhaps aboriginal) emphasis on solidarity which exerts a dissolving, undermining, equalizing or curbing effect on the differential distribution of status, on differences in authority, differences in distribution of property, and differences in functional roles in the division of labor, with an ultimate terminal effect that may be maladaptive. *The social system in its organization, we postulate, tends to swing or falter indeterminately back and forth between these two theoretical poles: optimum adaptation to the outer situation at the cost of internal malintegration, or optimum internal integration at the cost of maladaptation to the outer situation.*[36] (Italics ours.)

Examples of these ambivalent tendencies are easy to find. Following wars, nations almost always experience a period of reaction led by Hardings who cry, "Back to normalcy!" All have observed discussion groups proceeding efficiently toward a solution of a problem and suddenly, and apparently unaccountably, going off on some tangent marked by joking and expressions of tension release. Some of the tangents upon which groups embark are appropriate "fishing expeditions," but many are mild forms of revolt against the pressures of task accomplishment and represent efforts to reestablish group harmony and solidarity.

Are groups bound to be unhappy regardless of what they do?

[36] Robert F. Bales, *Interaction Process Analysis* (Reading, Mass.: Addison-Wesley, 1951), p. 157.

If they respond to external forces, they seem to disrupt internal harmony, and vice versa. This is only partially true. Successful interdependent action has already been shown to result in increased group solidarity and internal harmony. Torrence underscores the point that mild stress results in improved performance, but severe stress tends to be disruptive.[37] The ideal situation is one in which task pressures of appropriate levels of stability, complexity, intensity, and attractiveness can be tackled by a group that is mature enough to understand and accept the concomitant structure and role differentiations and can resist pressures to extend the structure beyond that necessary for successful task accomplishment. Stresses and ambivalent tendencies are inevitable in even such a group, but they are likely to be perceived more objectively and examined profitably by the group.

Often discussion groups, whose purposes are largely personal, attempt to impose some of the characteristics of task groups. In some learning groups, for example, a few of the members begin to act as if the group has some adaptation to make to the external environment. Such members seem to become impatient at the apparent aimlessness of the group and attempt to establish structure and role differentiation in order to improve efficiency. The reasons for this impatience vary, including such ones as the desire to obtain status, personality compulsions, and time pressures. Usually the rest of the group will quite properly resist such unwarranted extension of group structure. Barbara Schindler, who studied the effects of imposed leadership versus leaderless discussion in interscholastic festival discussion, concluded that under conditions in which the *training and development of the individual members* were the prime considerations, as opposed to conditions in which task accomplishment was primary, leaderless discussion was preferable.[38]

We recently observed an interesting instance of a group rejecting unwarranted controls imposed by its leader. The situation was a workshop discussing the educational implications of problems of

[37] E. Paul Torrance, "A Theory of Leadership and Interpersonal Behavior Under Stress," in Luigi Petrullo and Bernard M. Bass, eds., *Leadership and Interpersonal Behavior* (New York: Holt, Rinehart and Winston, 1961).

[38] Barbara Schindler, "An Experimental Study of the Relative Effectiveness of Leader-led and Leader-less Discussion Methods in Interscholastic Secondary School Speech Activities" (Unpublished M. A. Thesis, Univ. of Colorado, 1959).

intergroup relations. The participants were unknown to one another for the most part and were organized primarily for learning purposes. The group had spent the morning examining several aspects of the problem. In the afternoon session the leader was a woman who had not participated in the morning session. She had a background of working with decision-making and action groups dealing with this very subject. At the beginning of the afternoon session, she attempted to organize and structure the discussion in order to be efficient. The group resented such attempted control and for about an hour the discussion was unproductive. Fortunately, she was able to understand that her perceptions of what was required were not shared by the rest of the group. She stopped trying to impose unwarranted controls and the discussion then progressed more to the satisfaction of everyone concerned.

This ambivalence is reflected also in the literature about group discussion. Some writers clearly prefer the more nondirective, group-centered structure and lay more stress upon the personal development of the individuals. Other writers seem to be primarily concerned with procedures for controlling and structuring the group in order to improve production and efficiency. The battle between the advice-givers often seems philosophical entirely—one side favors democracy and the other side favors autocracy. Philosophical implications are present, of course, but a part of the reason for the difference is explained by the ambivalence between group cohesiveness and task accomplishment. That is, the experience and personal orientations of some writers lead them to focus primarily upon conditions that enhance group cohesiveness. The reverse is often true of writers who emphasize task accomplishment. It is not the point of this discussion to straddle the fence by saying that both camps are a little right and a little wrong, or by saying that, "It all depends upon the situation." Neither group-centered nor task-centered structures are endorsed as a *philosophical* preference.

The Leader Paradox

The focus of the forces is evidently upon the leaders of groups. Those people who seek, or have thrust upon them, the responsibilities of guiding the group occupy that proverbial "hot seat." Sometimes these responsibilities are enormous, such as those so effectively narrated by Alan Drury in *Advise and Consent*.[39] The responsibilities thrust upon such a person as the Commander in Chief of the North American Air Defense Command are not enviable. Sometimes the responsibilities are comparatively minuscule as when a group of children seeks to decide whether to play baseball or tag. But if the group has any justifiable *raison d'etre* and if the members feel genuine concern, the leader faces a paradox.

The *leader paradox* is simply this. The pressures of task accomplishment fall most heavily upon the leader, but he can't accomplish them without a cohesive cooperative group. The leader has the responsibility of maintaining a balance between what Berrien calls "group need satisfaction" and "formal achievement." Berrien's experiments showed that homeostasis (desirable equilibrium) broke down when stresses destroyed this balance.[40] What are the implications of this paradox?

If the leader succumbs to the internal forces for cohesiveness and ignores external forces, he may become another von Hindenberg whose "leadership" turned out to be impotent. If the leader owes his position to the group, if he is insecure in that position, or if he is still on the way up, the chances are increased that he will succumb to the internal forces. This condition is especially true of the second in command. An experiment by O. J. Harvey and Conrad Consalvi showed that pressures for conformity to the group were strongest upon the second in the leadership hierarchy as compared with the top leader or members toward the bottom of the scale.[41]

If the leader succumbs to the external forces, the members of his group may become impotent pawns, if they do not control his selection, or disgruntled rebels, if they have the power to replace the leader. No one who has been in such organizations as the military can have failed to experience that feeling of impotency. In such situations perhaps the most ennobling expression can well become, "Ours not to reason why. . . ." Perhaps the reports heard in the Navy about tyrannical officers "accidentally" being shoved over-

[39] Alan Drury, *Advise and Consent* (Garden City, N. Y.: Doubleday, 1959).

[40] F. Kenneth Berrien, "Homeostasis Theory of Groups: Implications for Leadership," in Petrullo and Bass, *op. cit.*

[41] O. J. Harvey and Conrad Consalvi, "Status and Conformity to Pressures in Informal Groups," *Journal of Abnormal and Social Psychology*, Vol. 60 (1960), pp. 182-187.

board are simply "scuttlebut," but read *The Caine Mutiny* again.

The idea of an individual striking a bargain with a group as the basis of membership has already been introduced. The leader must also strike a bargain, and the rewards, such as status, that he receives must be earned. The leader paradox exacts a price from the leader which is often more than many would-be leaders are willing to pay. Some leaders are rewarded more richly than their sinecures warrant. By the same token, the quickest way to "make a Christian" out of a foot dragger is to give him a specific leader responsibility and let him experience this paradox of leadership himself.

As mentioned before, we always conduct a sociometric poll in our discussion classes about two-thirds of the way through the semester. We ask the members to rank the three leaders who have exercised the most leadership in the past and to rank the three individuals whom they would most like to have as leaders in the future. Relatively few individuals receive votes on the "has-been" poll and relatively many receive votes on the "would-like-to-have" poll. The most striking result, however, is that the top "has beens" almost always take a beating on the "would-like-to-have" poll. The emphasis shifts in each individual case, but at least part of the cause stems both from the tendency of some "has beens" to succumb to task pressure and from the group's resentment of structure of any kind. Standing on a pedestal may be exhilarating, but it makes you a better target.

EXERCISES

1. Select several well established groups of which you are a member and analyze six to ten major forces to which each is subject at a given time. It may be helpful to chose groups that range from relatively immature to relatively mature ones. Using separate sheets for each group, list the external forces on the left side and the internal forces on the right. Did you discover any forces of which you had not been aware?

2. Using your analysis of groups from Exercise 1, attempt to determine how the forces relate in specific and observable ways. Check your conclusions with another member of each group studied. Prepare a report that could be the basis of discussion for either your class or one of your groups.

3. Attempt to examine your own reactions as a group member to the forces you have listed in Exercise 1. Does this introspection change

your conclusions as to the nature and effect of the forces? Does it change your understanding and attitudes toward the group and its work?

4. Plan a series of experiments with other members of your class in which you attempt to vary the conditions of the task requirement. Possible variables could be (a) presenting a new and complex task that had not been anticipated, (b) setting an immediate deadline for task completion, (c) bringing in information that the report is to be made by one person at a later time, or (d) shifting the task origin from outside to inside the group. Other possibilities will suggest themselves. Plan to use groups outside the class and develop a procedure for orderly observation and recording of data. Possibly discuss the experience and its results with those cooperating in your groups.

5. Draw up a list of tasks confronting a group of which you are a member. Give each member a copy and ask him to evaluate independently the complexity, intensity, and attractiveness of each task. Provide opportunity for each member to add and evaluate additional tasks you may have omitted. Summarize your findings including comparisons and contrasts that appear significant. Are there any correlations between these differences and member status in the group?

6. Review or discover a number of group discussions in which pressure for completion of the task affected significantly the solution or conclusion. How do you believe the group or individual members could have dealt with this force more effectively?

7. Select 5 to 10 groups on your campus or in your community and attempt to assess (a) the degree of multiple membership involved, (b) the relative status of the groups, (c) the intergroup climate, and (d) the degree of cooperation or hostility that might be possible on two or three issues or activities.

8. Select three or four persons you know well who are members of several of the groups analyzed in Exercise 7. Attempt to analyze their actual or potential relationships to these groups. Compare this analysis with your analysis of your own relationships. What do these analyses suggest about intergroup forces? What do they suggest about ways in which you should deal with such forces?

9. Observe and compare two groups, one which has considerable power and another which is much less powerful. How were the groups formed? What are their characteristics? How effective are they? What tasks do they undertake?

10. Organize a discussion on the problem of leadership as it relates to multigroup membership in your organization, college, or community.

11. Develop an experiment similar to that suggested in Exercise 4, except focus on internal forces that affect the group. Introduce such

variables as personality elements, divergent personal goals, size, hostility, and so on.

12. Explore the relationships among group size, group achievement, and member satisfaction by means of a survey of friends or coworkers. Ask questions that will determine the number of groups to which they belong, their preferences for these groups and their opinions as to the accomplishments of each group.

13. Consider the principal forces acting on a group of which you are a member. Attempt to estimate the forces and amount of change most likely to produce significant disequilibrium. Do you feel other members of the group would agree? Would these same forces produce the same effect in another group to which you belong? Organize a discussion on some aspect of this large problem.

14. Plan a discussion to consider the forces acting on your class or some comparable group. Evaluate the results in terms of achievement, satisfaction, and causes of member behavior. What are some basic problems you observe?

15. Observe a number of group leaders for a period of time to determine how each strives to meet or deal with the paradox of accomplishment versus group cohesion. Prepare a report of your conclusions including recommendations for general guidance of the potential leader.

16. Create in your class a role-playing situation in which those who are normally nonleaders must assume leadership positions. Following the experience, have those who acted as leaders report and discuss their feelings. (Children frequently engage in such activities when playing games where adult roles are involved.)

SELECTED READINGS

Bales, Robert F., *Interaction Process Analysis*. Reading, Mass., Addison-Wesley, 1951.

Bass, Bernard M., *Leadership, Psychology, and Organizational Behavior*. New York, Harper & Row, 1960.

Group Dynamics: Research and Theory, 2nd ed., Dorwin Cartwright and Alvin Zander, eds. Evanston, Ill., Row, Peterson, 1960, Parts 1, 2, and 3.

Heider, Fritz, *The Psychology of Interpersonal Relations*. New York, Wiley, 1958.

Lewin, Kurt, *Field Theory in Social Science*. New York, Harper & Row, 1951.

Lewin, Kurt, *Resolving Social Conflicts*. New York, Harper & Row, 1948.

CHAPTER 10

Bases of
a Philosophy of Leadership

The faith rests on the propositions that man is a political animal; that participation in political decisions is
necessary to his fulfillment and happiness; that all men
can and must be sufficiently educated and informed to
take part in making these decisions; that protection
against arbitrary power, though indispensable, is insufficient to make either free individuals or a free society,
and that such a society must make positive provisions
for its development into a community learning together.

Robert M. Hutchins*

One cannot escape the requirement of thinking deeply about our
fundamental assumptions concerning how man ought to influence
and lead his fellow man. He who leads is inevitably guided, consciously or more probably unconsciously, by a philosophy of leadership. The issue is not *whether* he holds to a philosophy of leadership;
it is *what* philosophy; and, more important, it is the basis of that

* "Is Democracy Possible?" *Saturday Review*, Vol. 42 (February 21,
1959), p. 16. In his article Robert Hutchins reported several events which
shook his faith in the democratic process. After considering them, however,
and considering what the alternatives would mean, he reaffirmed his faith in
democracy. Because we share that faith, we use his words to begin this chapter.

philosophy. A leader assumes an awesome responsibility because the heart of leadership is influence and control *of other human beings.*

Chapters 1 and 2 began the discussion of philosophy with the contention that the development of the individual was our prime concern. There the orientation was the relationship of individuals to others in collaborative action. Some of the questions whose answers have been attempted are: For what purposes should individuals engage in collaborative action? What are the relative advantages and disadvantages of discussion? Once the individual has committed himself to collaborative action, he finds himself in a situation in which some individuals exercise more influence than others. Whether he be a leader or a follower, he must come to grips with this question: What are the basic assumptions that underlie my attempts to influence others or to be influenced by them?

Clearly, one chapter is inadequate to examine all the ramifications of these philosophical considerations. It is clear by now that the more democratic concepts of leadership are preferred here. Persuasion rather than coercion is the better way of securing changed belief and action.

The brevity of this chapter is not to be lamented because it is conceived to be stimulative and suggestive rather than definitive. It has been demonstrated repeatedly and persuasively that there is simply no substitute for a liberal education, in the broadest sense of the term, as a foundation upon which to build a personal philosophy including concepts and attitudes regarding leadership. This chapter is entitled "Bases of a Philosophy of Leadership" advisedly. It sketches out those fundamental questions which provide the basis upon which others may wish to build. (Had we our preferences, we would like to join with the readers in literally discussing the essentials of such philosophies; the following pages will have to serve instead.)

Before going further, recall some conclusions about group functioning that have already been presented. In any thinking process, collective or individual, two functions must be performed—ideas must be created and ideas must be judged.[1] Another conclusion, perhaps not so apparent, is that two ends are always present in any discussion—the task goals and the goals of *training* the participants,

---

[1] We discussed these two functions in detail in Chapter 4.

as well as the goals of providing harmonious and meaningful relationships. The word *training* is used because we learn from our experiences, and experience in group processes is no exception.

With these conclusions in mind, this chapter first examines attitudes toward others as a basis of a philosophy of leadership, then looks again at that ever-present "ends-means dilemma," and finally, examines the "philosophical contradiction."

ATTITUDE TOWARD OTHERS

"What is man that Thou art mindful of him?" This question has troubled thinkers for centuries. Theologians, philosophers, artists, poets, businessmen, politicians, educators, all and more have raised the question. Is man basically good or basically evil? Is he created in the "image of God" just a little lower than the angels, or is he one of Jonathan Edwards' "Sinners in the hand of an angry God"? Is man naturally cooperative or competitive? Is man wise or foolish? Let us group together some of the positions that have been taken over the centuries on the capacity of man, in general, to create and judge between ideas.

Most Men Can Neither Create Ideas
Nor Judge Between Them

The fundamental position of authoritarians is that people in general are capable of neither creativity nor judgment. They must be told what to do and, if necessary, compelled to do it. Plato put the issue squarely when he contended that the wisest should rule; the philosophers should be kings.

One need not look far to find modern writers who have despaired of the ability of the average man to create and judge ideas. In our judgment the most responsible critic of the capacity of the masses is Walter Lippmann. Keep in mind that he is talking primarily about the capacity to make decisions affecting the national policy and not necessarily talking about capacity in small groups, but even so the indictment is severe.

The unhappy truth is that the prevailing public opinion has been destructively wrong at the critical junctures. The people have imposed a veto upon the judgments of informed and responsible officials. They have compelled the governments, which usually knew what would have been wiser, or was necessary or was more expedient, to be too late with too little, or too long with too much, too pacifist in peace and too bellicose in war, too neutralist or appeasing in negotiation or too intransigent. Mass opinion has acquired mounting power in this century. It has shown itself to be a dangerous master of decisions when the stakes are life and death.[2]

Most Men Can Create Ideas But Cannot Judge Between Them

When the responsibility for the decision is levied specifically upon an individual rather than upon a group, there is evidence for the philosophy that most men can create ideas but cannot judge between them. In any military organization, for example, the commander has the peculiar responsibility for the decisions that are made. However, his very position leaves him in a difficult position to create ideas since he does not work directly with the equipment, weapons, construction, and the like. Thus, he must depend upon subordinates to create ideas which he will judge.

Some organizations which adopt this philosophy go to great lengths to stimulate creativity within the ranks. Suggestion boxes and bonuses are used to encourage employees to create ideas. Many of the brainstorming projects discussed in Chapter 4 reflect this point of view. The brainstorming group creates but does not judge the ideas. Out of the dozens of ideas produced, those responsible for the decision may find one or more that they deem usable, but the brainstorming group is not entrusted with decisions.

Most Men Can Judge Between Ideas But Cannot Create Them

This position is, of course, the exact converse of the above. Those who hold this point of view contend that it is the responsibility of the leaders to supply the ideas and information and to communicate these effectively to the people who can then judge. Many public speaking texts adopt this viewpoint. It is particularly well stated by Brigance:

We thought that the multitude was not to be trusted, that it had no "popular intelligence." Now we have discovered the awful truth. The failure

---

[2] From *The Public Philosophy* by Walter Lippmann, Copyright 1955, by Walter Lippmann, by permission of Little, Brown and Company—Atlantic Monthly Press. p. 20.

was not with the multitude, but with the leaders. The multitude *is* capable of sound judgment *when the leaders are capable of supplying the ideas and capable of communicating them intelligently, effectively, and responsibly. . . .*

This, therefore is the point of departure for this book: *The system of speechmaking was born of man's early struggle for democracy. It is still inherent in a free society, and unless an adequate portion of leaders in all areas of human life can speak intelligently, effectively, and responsibly—among themselves and to the people at large—we must live in constant danger of internal breakdown. A course on speechmaking ought to be founded on this premise.*[3]

The argument for this particular stand is that most people have not the training or experience to enable them to create many ideas, but they do have the capacity for judging between the ideas of the experts. In any society that claims to be democratic, there must be this kind of confidence in the judgment of the people. From the distinction drawn in the previous chapter it is apparent that both the first and second point of view are usually associated with autocratic philosophies. The crucial matter is the control over decisions and this third point of view places that control in the hands of the people affected by the decision.

Most Men Can Both Create Ideas And Judge Between Them

In his very stimulating book, *Group-Centered Leadership*, Thomas Gordon comes directly to grips with these various concepts concerning the capacity of men.[4] He concludes that man's inadequacies stem not from his lack of capacity but from his lack of opportunity to exercise his capacities. Man is capable of both creativity and judgment, according to Gordon. He sums up the consequences of the leadership tendencies based upon a conceptualization of man as either incompetent or as competent.

Let us now summarize what it would mean if the social scientist should choose to follow a course of action that is based on little faith in the capacity of the individual. His approach to the problem of leadership would begin with attempts to select those few who possess certain quali-

[3] William Norwood Brigance, *Speech: Its Techniques and Disciplines in a Free Society*, 2nd ed. (New York: Appleton-Century-Crofts, 1961), pp. 6-7.
[4] Thomas Gordon, *Group-Centered Leadership* (Boston: Houghton Mifflin, 1955), Chapter 2.

ties judged as desirable for our leaders; to those few he would give special training, emphasizing the skills of diagnosing individuals and situations and the skills of influencing and changing others. The logic would be quite simple and straightforward: choose a select group of leaders; train them thoroughly in the most effective diagnostic and analytical methods upon which to base plans for their followers; and then equip them with the most effective skills for influencing others to accept and to carry out these plans.[5]

Thus this approach [group-centered leadership] would lead us toward the discovery of ways of developing the creative potentialities of groups, not just of leaders. Instead of concentrating on the diagnostic skills of leaders, it would open the doors to new methods of helping groups learn to diagnose their own needs and ills. It would help us discover more effective means by which group members could be freed of dependency on authority, so that they might develop their faculties for creative, critical, and independent thought and action.[6]

Gordon, of course, is not the only theorist who holds this position. We make no attempt to list numbers of writers who suggest the several points of view described. The readings at the end of this chapter include representatives of each point of view, and the reader will doubtless be acquainted with others.

Any of the four positions may be easily attacked by attempting to push an advocate into an "all-or-nothing" argument. Examples which seem to contradict each of these philosophies come readily to mind. Certainly one can find many people who, even with all the opportunity and training in the world, will not be able to create many worthwhile ideas or judge effectively between ideas. Certainly there are differences in the capacities of individuals, but such arguments miss the point. Let us examine these philosophies more closely in the framework of the "ends-means dilemma."

ENDS AND MEANS

We have all heard people say, "I approve of his objective, but I don't like his methods." Usually this is an attempt to apologize or rationalize a position. We heard this again and again in reference to the late Senator McCarthy, and the same refrain is repeated when

[5] *Ibid.*, p. 42.
[6] *Ibid.*, pp. 44-45.

people defend the John Birch Society or the Minute Men. When college athletic scandals come to light, the defense is usually couched in similar terms: "If you want us to win, we must engage in under-the-table practices."

Now it is very easy to theorize. The end does not justify the means. The end inheres in the means employed. We have the formula and the historical antecedents; Aristotle insisted upon the "right method"; Quintilian pointed out that the aim of the orator, a leader by our definition, was "to speak well, for his *art* . . . consists in the *act*, and not in the result." In modern times we see higher courts overturn convictions of patently guilty men because wrong methods were used to secure convictions. Yes, we have the theory. The only trouble is that it is very difficult to distinguish those ends and means.

The inner-directed man of an earlier day had an easier time of it. He knew what was right and what was wrong. His methods had the imprint of history; and who could doubt their validity? His code of honor was secure. But our world is no longer so neatly ordered. We need not review the evidence. The revolution which has shaken thinking in fields from anthropology to zoology has replaced our comfortably static world with a dynamic world in which ends and means become almost hopelessly entangled.

To illustrate, a cause of something is usually called the means, and the effect is usually called the end.[7] We are disturbed about juvenile delinquency. This is a bad end, we say, and we are determined to discover and eradicate the cause. Some shout, "There are no delinquent juveniles, only delinquent parents." The parents must be the cause! But reason makes us ponder. Those parents must have causes for their behavior. Is one not responsible for his behavior until he becomes a parent, and is parenthood an alchemy that transforms him into a responsible individual? Hardly. Let us look further, then. The movies, TV, and comics display violence and lust. Perhaps they are the cause and we should rigidly censor them. But then someone comes along and points out that it is impossible to shield children from violence and lust. Some people tend to react to and distort these stimuli while others are able to put them into proportion. Is the cause within the child? Can the geneticist help us? No.

---

[7] Remember that we did not define these concepts in this fashion in Chapter 6.

He has also compounded the problem by discovering a seemingly infinite number of genes and an astronomical number of combinations which interact dynamically. We could go on, but the point should be clear. Fortunately, we are a patient lot for the most part and we keep experimenting, trying, hoping, and working for we do not like to admit defeat. And we make gains even when we are not quite able to explain why.

Earlier it was stated that there were two ends present in every discussion—producing the result and training the participants. Now this seems rather oversimplified, and indeed it is. Let us see why.

Consequences of Experience

In our private dream worlds, most of us are like Walter Mitty and we believe that, given the chance, we can come up with brilliant performances even though we lack experiences as doctor, general, or trapeze artist. We know better, of course. We must learn; we must experience; or we are impotent. The squeaks from the violin are a necessary prelude to the proficient musician. We can be lectured at until that proverbial place freezes over so we can skate on it, but we won't be able to play that violin until we have practiced. Practice alone will not make us proficient for we can practice mistakes. We will probably need guidance, but we must practice. Capacity in discussion is no different.

To the Extent that People have No Opportunity to Create Ideas, They Become Incapable of Creativity. The requirements of creativity discussed in Chapter 4 emphasized opportunity. In many organizations this opportunity is reserved for the few. "Stay out of trouble" is usually the employee's way of describing the condition in which he may succeed. Even if an idea occurs to him, therefore, he will probably not consider it wise to express that idea. Even in groups that apparently encourage free expression of ideas, the prevailing norms may be such that ideas which deviate sharply from the accepted way of doing things may be "outside the pale." Thus, the full range of creativity may be denied the individual.

In our school systems are many pressures to restrict the creativity of students. Some of these pressures are well known. One example is manifest in the behavior of the child whose natural curiosity is discouraged by parents and teachers who tell him to stop asking questions. Another well known instance is the teacher who requires that his students regurgitate on the examinations his lectures—a process that someone once described as the transference of ideas from the teacher's notes to the students' notes and back to the teacher without having passed through the mind of anybody. Such practices can stifle creativity. (We are not terribly worried about them because we believe that these practices are diminishing.) Most teachers seem genuinely concerned about experimentation with methods that encourage thinking. There is, however, one other pressure over which the teachers have little control, and this pressure is of concern here.

Today the "College Boards," the National Merit Examinations, and other proficiency and personality tests are assuming an importance somewhat analogous to the famous "Eleven Plus" examinations in Britain. By scoring well on such standardized examinations, high school graduates receive scholarships, obtain advanced standing in college, and obtain special college courses designed for the superior student. By means of such standardized tests, many businesses hire, classify, and promote their employees.[8] Many students, who see these tests as their means of advancement, seemingly become professional test takers. The inability of such tests to measure creativity was pointed out in Chapter 4. Further, there is considerable doubt about the merit of such tests as measures of superior ability.[9] The point here is that learning to perform effectively on such tests may itself inhibit creative potential.

This problem has been brought close to home for us during the past several years that we have been teaching sections of a course in speechmaking designed for students who score high on the College Boards and high in the English Placement Test given by the University of Colorado. Such students are allowed to substitute a more advanced set of courses for the traditional freshman English courses. The course to which we refer is a part of that

[8] William H. Whyte, Jr., *The Organization Man* (Garden City, N. Y.: Doubleday, 1957) has an amusing and pathetic chapter on "How to Cheat on Personality Tests." It is amusing because of its style; pathetic because it may be all too true.

[9] See Paul B. Diederich, "Pitfalls in the Measurement of Gains in Achievement," *The School Review*, Vol. 64 (February, 1956), pp. 59-63. See also, Jacob W. Getzels and Philip W. Jackson, *Creativity and Intelligence* (New York: Wiley, 1962).

advanced sequence. Time and again we have seen some of these students do abysmal work on speeches or tests that required creativity. When given the more familiar types of tests, such students usually do quite well. This observation has been confirmed by others teaching this course. Our hypothesis is that such students may be bright enough, but their training in conventional test taking, whether accidental or designed, has rendered them uncertain and unskilled when creativity is required.

To the Extent that People have No Opportunity to Judge Ideas, They Become Incapable of Judgment. This conclusion is obviously analogous to the previous conclusion about creativity, and the arguments in defense of it are similar. Most people are familiar with the story of the old farm hand who had worked hard and loyally for many years. His employer, seeking to give him a job that would not tax his failing strength but which would allow him to maintain his income and self-respect, set him to work sorting potatoes. The bad potatoes were to be cast aside, and the good ones were to be sacked for shipment. Sometime later the farmer returned to check on the progress. He found his hired hand sitting exhausted and distraught with the work scarcely begun. What was the trouble? he asked. Surely the work was not too heavy? "No, boss," the employee replied. "The work is light enough, but these decisions are killing me!"

The story is a joke, but, like most jokes, it has a basis in fact. Those schooled solely in obedience usually make poor judges. Kurt Lewin put it well when discussing the effects of authoritarian, democratic, and laissez-faire leadership. "The change from autocracy to democracy seemed to take somewhat more time than from democracy to autocracy. Autocracy is imposed upon the individual. Democracy he has to learn." [10]

The problems many college students have in attempting to adjust to the greater freedom of the college environment is illustrative. A dorm counselor reported that many of the girls in her dorm had never so much as decided, before they came to college, what clothes they would wear in the morning let alone such matters as when, how, or if they should study. While this is somewhat of an

[10] Kurt Lewin, "The Consequences of an Authoritarian and Democratic Leadership," in Alvin W. Gouldner, ed., *Studies in Leadership* (New York: Harper, 1950), p. 417.

exception, it is true that most college students are faced with making many more decisions than they had to make, or were allowed to make, in high school. Thus we have the basis for the old dilemma facing the counselors, teachers, and administration. How much control over student behavior should be exercised? Should compulsory "study tables" be established? Many fraternities and sororities do this. What about dorm hours? Quiet hours? How much latitude should the student be given in choosing courses? Should teachers require daily or weekly checkups to insure that students are keeping up with their work? Should conferences with the student's academic advisor be compulsory? What attendance policy should the teacher establish? Some argue that the student should be put on his own as much as possible. "We must not spoon feed them," they insist. Others contend that we dare not risk so much freedom. Too many students are lost by failure or drop-out who might have succeeded had they been helped by being required to do certain things. All agree that much of the problem *for the college* would be solved if the students were more mature—if they had more experience in making responsible decisions before they came to college.

Expectations of Performance

It should come as no surprise that those who have observed only authoritarian structures, or people suddenly thrust into democratic structures, often believe that people in general are incapable of either creativity or judgment. When Alexander Hamilton uttered his famous statement, "The People, sir, are a great beast," he was not alone in his estimate of the capacity of the people. The men who framed our Constitution were generally chary of entrusting very much responsibility to the citizenry. Carl Van Doren records the issues concerning the capacity of the citizenry that beset these men.[11] The wonder is not that the vote was restricted to one adult in five; the wonder is that so much power was given to the citizens at all. Many argued for a monarchy, and the experiences in Europe seemed to support such claims. No one can say what kind of document might have resulted had our Constitution been drafted during the excesses of the French Revolution.

It further should come as no surprise that, even in democratic

[11] Carl Van Doren, *The Great Rehearsal* (New York: Viking, 1948).

groups, most ideas are created by the leaders. As pointed out earlier, leaders feel most keenly about tasks to be performed. They thus apply themselves to the task more vigorously than those less involved. When the leaders create the ideas and when the group holds the final decision-making power, the leaders must persuade. Here again, however, we face the dilemma. If the leaders spend their primary energies creating ideas and persuading others to accept them, the creative capacity of the rest of the group may diminish. If the leaders spend their primary energies helping the others release their creative potential, they run the risk of not coping with the task requirements. We are back to the ends-means dilemma.

THE PHILOSOPHICAL CONTRADICTION

Very well, we may say. Difficult as it may be to distinguish between ends and means, we shall try. We shall reject the notion that the end justifies the means, and we shall do all in our power to help those with whom we work to develop their creativity and judgment. You have shown us that this is difficult, but you have not shown that it is impossible. We are persuaded of the advantages of democracy and of the development of the individual, so here we take our stand. Let us get about the business of techniques of effective operation.

We sympathize with the impatience, but there are more questions to be raised. Let us develop the background for the philosophical contradiction.

Autocratic Circumstances

Doubtless some conditions demand autocracy. We do not allow small children to discover by themselves that it is dangerous to run into the streets. We do not expect drivers at a crowded intersection to discuss the problem and create their own answers to the flow of traffic. We do not expect a conductor to call for votes during a performance of Verdi's Aïda. Such circumstances, and dozens of others that any of us could name, are so obvious that we tend to eliminate them when we are thinking about a philosophy of leadership. These are not to be included, we say, in our thinking about group discussion. But we cannot dismiss the matter so lightly. Children grow up; traffic laws must be enacted by someone; and musicians are not mere automatons.

Drawing the Line

Someone has to draw the line. Someone has to decide when children are old enough to assume responsibilities, when nascent nations are capable of self-government, when new academic departments are to be created.

There is another issue. Someone has to draw the line between those who have the *right* to create and decide and those who do not. It may be true that "No man is an Iland," but we do not expect to have a vote in the faculty meetings of other universities.

Our ways of drawing these capacity lines are curious and contradictory. Most states establish twenty-one as the legal voting age. Most states allow a sixteen-year-old to have a driver's license. In some states girls can buy liquor when they are eighteen, but boys must wait until they are twenty-one. In some states youngsters can marry without their parents' consent before they can vote for the clerk who issues their marriage license.

Our ways of drawing the lines for those who have the right to decide are equally curious and contradictory. Corporations permit stockholders to vote in proportion to the amount of money they have invested, but employees who have invested their lives may have no vote. Membership in some organizations may be bought; in others it may be a right of family; in others simply attending a meeting and signifying intent may be sufficient; and in still others membership selection is complicated and rigorous.

When we ask *who* draws either kind of line, we come face-to-face with the philosophical contradiction. It is the colonial power, not the colony, that decides when the colony is ready for self-government; it is the parent, not the children, who decides when the children may assume responsibility; it is the school administration, not the students, who decide what control and power the student government is to have; it is the teacher, not the students, who decides the amount of "democracy" that shall prevail in the classroom. True, in all the cases a "revolution" may force the prevailing power to relinquish some or all of the control, but the concept that authority stems from the top is unaffected.

If we contend that the end does not justify the means, and if we believe that authoritarian means are undesirable, we face the philosophical contradiction in two ways. First, as we have pointed out, there are circumstances which seem to demand authoritarian behavior. This is not a terribly severe contradiction in itself, but the second seems to us to be more of a contradiction. *Securing the right to create and decide depends upon the benevolence of the authority— even in situations in which the leaders believe that they are behaving democratically.*

Let us be clear on one point. We are not necessarily dismayed by this contradiction. We believe in the concepts of democratic leadership, but we wish to recognize the fact that we, at least, are unable to piece together a single uniform philosophy out of one piece of cloth. We believe that a philosophy should be a dynamic thing growing as the holder grows in insight and understanding. Even though our own philosophy is not completely consistent, we hope that we are able to keep the aim of our behavior consistent. That aim is enhancing the dignity of the individual. We do not believe that it justifies our means, but it gives purpose to our struggle.

EXERCISES

1. Select two or three leaders you know and can observe over a period of thirty days. First engage each in a discussion designed to reveal his philosophy of leadership. Summarize the impressions you derive and check these for accuracy with the respective leaders. Then observe the leaders as they function. To what extent do the verbal statements agree with observed behavior? If there are significant differences do you feel they are justified? Do any of the leaders seem aware of the differences that you note? (What are your bases for assessing such awareness?)

2. Make two lists of 10 to 15 individuals whose performance as leaders you can recall. Place the successful ones in one column and the ineffectual ones in another group. Then attempt to review for each: (a) his approach to leadership as you perceived it; (b) the clarity and consistency of his application of his philosophy; and (c) the primary elements or factors contributing to his success or failures.

3. As our society becomes more complex, technical and overwhelming, can the philosophy which Gordon states be adequate to our needs? Can we expect the average man to be able to cope with the critical issues of our times?

4. Begin a systematic formulation and statement of your own philosophy of leadership by outlining on paper both its foundations and

superstructure. Next consider the extent to which you have been guided by this philosophy in the past (Have you been using more than one philosophy?). Consider how your philosophy would affect leader behavior if applied in situations you observe over the next two to three weeks.

5. Organize a discussion to explore the implications of one or more of the selected readings listed at the end of the chapter. Choose those of limited scope or consider a manageable portion of a more extensive source.

6. Plan a discussion that explores the moral implications of some means and ends problems of leadership.

7. In what ways has the leadership to which you have been subjected encouraged or retarded your personal growth and creativity? Consider relationships with parents, siblings, teachers, friends, and employers. Can you make the same analysis for several of your friends or acquaintances?

SELECTED READINGS

The Administrator: Cases on Human Relations in Business, 3rd ed., John D. Glover and Ralph M. Hower, eds. Homewood, Ill., Irwin, 1957.

Brigance, William Norwood, *Speech: Its Techniques and Disciplines in a Free Society,* 2nd ed. New York, Appleton-Century-Crofts, 1961, Forward and Chap. 24.

Carlyle, Thomas, (Several of his writings reveal his point of view. They may be found in a variety of sources. The most authoritative source is Scribners' 1897 edition. Among the more important titles are: *Heroes, Hero-Worship and the Heroic in History* and *Past and Present.*)

Gordon, Thomas, *Group-Centered Leadership.* Boston, Houghton Mifflin, 1955.

Haiman, Franklyn S., *Group Leadership and Democratic Action.* Boston, Houghton Mifflin, 1951.

Hutchins, Robert M., "Is Democracy Possible?" *Saturday Review,* Vol. 42 (February 21, 1959), pp. 15-17, 58.

Jefferson, Thomas, (Almost all of Jefferson's writings are pertinent. Perhaps the best single-volume collection is: *The Life and Selected Writings of Thomas Jefferson,* Adrienne Koch and William Peden, eds. New York, Modern Library, 1944.)

Lasker, Bruno, *Democracy through Discussion.* New York, Wilson, 1949.

Leadership in Action, Gordon L. Lippitt, ed. Washington, National Training Laboratories, 1961.

Lippmann, Walter, *The Public Philosophy.* Boston, Little, Brown, 1955.

Mill, John Stuart, *On Liberty*. (This essay may be found in literally dozens of collections.)

Plato, *The Republic*. (This dialogue may be found in several translations and in a variety of publications.)

de Tocqueville, Alexis, *Democracy in America*. New York, Knopf, 1945.

Toward the Liberally Educated Executive, Robert H. Goldwin, ed. White Plains, N. Y., The Fund For Adult Education, 1957.

Van Doren, Carl, *The Great Rehearsal*. New York, Viking, 1948.

Young, Kimball, *Source Book For Social Psychology*. New York, Knopf, 1927. (See Part 5: "Leadership and Prestige in Social Behavior," pp. 543-626, for some of the earlier concepts and studies of leadership.)

PART IV
Participant and Leader Behavior

CHAPTER 11

Becoming a Better Participant

... as the chief ends of conversation are to *inform* or to be *informed*, to *please* or to *persuade*, I wish well-meaning, sensible men would not lessen their power of doing good by a positive, assuming manner that seldom fails to disgust, tends to create opposition and to defeat every one of those purposes for which speech was given to us, to wit, giving or receiving information or pleasure.

Benjamin Franklin*

Whenever someone says, "He breaks all the rules, but he is very successful," the speaker is probably talking about techniques of one sort or another. We have already given a number of illustrations of techniques that worked under one set of circumstances but did not work under another set. Further, what works for one individual may not work for another. These discrepancies should not disturb anyone so long as techniques are regarded as tools that may be selected or rejected as insight and expediency dictate. When a carpenter wishes to cut a board, he has his choice of tools: rip, crosscut, hack, mitre box, dovetail, keyhole, and other saws. He may use an ax or a chisel. He may break the board over his knee, but no one will complain that he broke a rule if he uses a keyhole saw with rip teeth to cut a board against the grain because it was the only saw he had available to use in some tight corner.

* *Autobiography.*

Again some say, "You simply can't set up rules for this business [some particular area of discussion or group work]. It all depends upon the situation. You have to 'play it by ear,' and only the man who has had years of experience can know how to 'feel his way.'" Experience *is* important; effective discussion *is* an art as well as a science. But sound theory is not spun from the gossamers of idle speculation, and tested techniques are usually versatile. Those who disparage systematized theory and technique are often trying to draw a veil of mystery over their methods, thereby attempting to enhance their status by claiming that their activity can be neither described nor appreciated by anyone not a graduate of their own particular "school." They guard their techniques and insights as primitive medicine men guarded their potions and incantations.

A study of techniques grounded in sound theory may be a short-cut to help one eliminate much painful experience. Reading about theory and techniques and practicing these techniques in a class-room setting will not produce a polished discussant any more than a similar program will produce a polished public speaker, chemist, accountant, lawyer, preacher, or doctor. More experience is neces-sary, but when we come to think of it, few of us will trust our health to a "doctor" who has worked out some "cures" without any study of chemistry, biology, surgery, and clinical training.

The techniques described here have been tested in the class-room, the laboratory, or "real life." Most are old; a few are new. Not all the tools are in this chest. Some we do not know of; some are of questionable value; some are deceptive or immoral. We have tried to avoid the "gimmicks." Surely your experience has developed use-ful tools that you wish to keep in your own tool chest. You will find others here, that may make you a more versatile and competent builders of ideas in the company of other builders.

Though leaders are needed, it is true, a brief look at most dis-cussions proves that effective rank-and-file members are needed as well. Before we study means of modifying the behavior of others, therefore, we will study ways of making ourselves more effective participants.

The organization of these chapters in Part IV may seem debat-able. Grouping techniques for becoming a better participant into one chapter and techniques for leadership into another chapter suggests that followers have to master certain skills that are different from skills needed by leaders. Not so. Skills of becoming a better participant should be mastered by *all* discussants regardless of the leadership roles they may perform.

One point needs clarification before the discussion of techniques. While the group and its leaders have responsibilities for helping individuals within the group to become better participants, *the ultimate responsibility rests with the individual himself.* Time and again students complain that they do not seem to have a chance to perform well. "I can't make myself heard. The rest of the group just ignores people like me. They won't give me a chance." The rest of the group can doubtless make the work of learning to participate effectively easier for the individual; but no one can do it for him.[1]

"An audience will forgive a speaker almost any lack, if he is manifestly earnest," James Winans once said. So it is with the members of a discussion group. They also will forgive a novice almost any lack, if he is genuinely trying to make a contribution to the discussion. If all he seeks is sympathy or affection and makes no earnest attempt to contribute and help the group toward its goal, he usually receives short shrift. If the group is split into factions, his vote may be courted. But his membership is ephemeral unless it is based upon solid contribution. The rest of the group are usually more than willing to give him a chance—the limits of human patience are truly astounding. But he must earnestly try.

The remainder of this chapter discusses first, the participant's attitudes toward himself, the others in the group, and the subject matter of the discussion and then, adapting to the group's structure. The next two sections examine the functions that a group needs to have performed and the manner in which the participant can learn to discover and supply needed functions.

ATTITUDES

Need the importance of attitudes be underscored again? Attitudes affect perception of evidence; attitudes affect group climate, maturity, and norms; attitudes affect leadership; attitudes form the basis for choice of leadership methods.[2]

---

[1] See the next chapter for techniques for helping other individuals participate more effectively.

[2] See Chapter 5, pp. 103-106, almost the whole of Chapter 7, Chapter 8, pp. 207-210, Chapter 9, pp. 243-245, and Chapter 10, pp. 257-260.

Attitudes Toward Self

Psychologists tell us that of the many ways in which we differ, it is in our self-images that we differ most.[3] Our assessment of personal identity, potential, status, assets and limitations may be quite realistic or it may be as remote as the "Secret Life of Walter Mitty." While none of us can hope, or perhaps bear, to see ourselves with full clarity, or even approximate the perceptions others have of us, our contributions to a group are related to the way in which we see ourselves, find satisfaction for our needs and become active in the work of the group. In so far as the member increases his understanding and objectivity regarding self, he may be more effective and make better functioning of others possible.

We have stressed the concept of personal security that results from an appropriate assessment of ourselves. The issue here is: How can we learn to improve our assessment of ourselves? Some of us may need the help of psychiatrists, ministers, or other professionals; most of us can improve our attitudes toward self through more conventional channels. Here are four suggestions for taking stock of ourselves and doing something about those attitudes.

1. *Use Tests.* Our faith in standardized tests is not unbounded, but attitude, aptitude, achievement, and ability tests may be helpful if wisely used. Students in school will take many such tests as a matter of course. Others may take them with nominal or no fees from school guidance centers. Those not in school may usually obtain such tests easily by consulting the guidance directors of the school systems, who can either give the tests or refer the individual to a private agency. Many businesses make provision for testing as a part of their personnel programs.

If a student scores in the upper half of his class on an academic aptitude test, he has little excuse for protesting, "I just don't seem to be as capable as the others in the group. Everyone seems to be so much brighter than I." If a test reveals tendencies toward reticence and withdrawal, the individual can use one or more of the following techniques to modify such attitudes. Tests may *help* an individual

---

[3] Gardner Murphy, "Individuality in the Learning Process; A Symposium," *Notes and Essays on Education for Adults,* No. 12 (Chicago: Center for Study of Liberal Education for Adults, 1955), pp. 9-10.

assess his own attitudes and predispositions. There is no magic in such tests, but they can fill in part of the picture.

2. *Evaluate Your Own Work* BEFORE *a Professional Does.* Like most teachers, we encourage our students to come to our offices to discuss their performances in class. With distressing frequency students come in and ask, "How am I doing in class?" or "What was wrong with that last test?" When we try to turn the question around and ask, "How do *you* think you are doing?" or "What do *you* think was wrong with that last test?" the student is often nonplussed. "You are the expert," he says, "what do you think?" The student misses the point. He is the one who must ultimately set the value upon his work; he, not we, must live with himself. He cannot be helped until he begins to help himself.

The student may begin the discussion this way: "Last Monday when we were discussing . . . ., I did such and so. At the time I thought it was a pretty good idea, but it didn't go over. Was it poorly timed?" Now we can go to work! The student's diagnosis is probably sound, since he has gone to the trouble to think it out so well beforehand. But right, wrong, or indifferent, we have a basis for an effective analysis of the student's behavior and self-analysis. To begin, the recounting of specifics helps the teacher recall the incident, the circumstances surrounding it, and the student's role. Next, the teacher may give specific information to help the student understand group behavior and group reaction to his behavior.

Some people seem to shun self-analysis like the plague. Once we had assigned a paper to an upper division class in discussion group leadership. The papers were turned in; we handed them back without evaluation; and proceeded to hold a protracted discussion of the ideas in the several papers. Toward the close of the discussion one of the students kept insisting that we evaluate the papers. We replied that we would evaluate by the end of the semester but not then. We pointed out that we had discussed all of the papers and that she should have a reasonably good idea of what we thought of the papers, hers included. Finally, after much discussion of this sort, we handed her the paper and said, "Put a grade on it, and we'll count it as the grade for this paper." She refused the opportunity to set her own grade for the paper because she would not analyze herself.

3. *Use Learning and Therapeutic Discussions.* If you are taking a course in discussion, you probably know other students whose participation problems and self-attitudes are similar to your own. If you are not taking a course, you may know or be able to find others who have similar problems.[4] There is no particular mystery about learning and therapeutic discussion. Sharing experiences and feelings with others is a great help in self-understanding provided the sharing is both reciprocal and objective.

We often recommend this technique to students who seek assistance in improving their understanding of themselves. When they follow this advice, their participation often improves dramatically for at least two reasons. They have gained greater insight into their own problems by discussing them with others. Also, they feel more confident when they speak up in discussion because they know they have the sympathy and support of at least some of their colleagues.

Before such discussions can be valuable, however, individuals must admit that they have problems. If the discussion turns into a mutual sympathy session in which everyone blames the other people in the larger discussion group for the problems of the members of the therapy group, there will be little profit. If the discussants keep saying, "They won't let us get into the discussion; they dominate the discussion; they railroad ideas"; the only values of such avoidance responses may be cathartic. "They" may indeed be a problem, but you are a problem too, and you are the principal one who can do something about it.

4. *Talk to Yourself.* Some people need to get better acquainted with themselves. Some reflection, meditation, and private introspection may be necessary to introduce one to himself. Using information gleaned from tests, observations of professionals, and other experience, an individual can often do a good job of examining his own self-attitudes and their reasonableness. As one goes from group to group and adapts to first one norm and then another, it becomes very difficult to maintain one's sense of identity. Occasional reflection in privacy, therefore, may be the necessary answer.

---

[4] We have already examined the values of such discussions as a means of personal development. See Chapter 2, pp. 29-31.

Attitudes Toward Others

To separate our attitudes toward ourselves from our attitudes toward others is difficult. We tend to blame others, as shown above, when we are unable to face up to an understanding of our own feelings and desires. If we feel insecure, we tend to see the rest of the world as hostile. On the other hand, if we feel secure, we tend to see the rest of the world as friendly.

Understanding Others. After explaining the difficulties and hazards of understanding the personality of others, Allport concludes: *"A major task in life is to achieve increasing success in our perception of one another."* [5] We can scarcely disagree with this conclusion, but we caution against becoming preoccupied during a discussion with subtle analyses of one another. We make this caution not solely because the business of understanding others is difficult (and it *is* difficult) but primarily because preoccupation with the character, feelings, emotions, and attitudes of others can be positively damaging to interpersonal relationships. Let us illustrate.

If we tend to focus upon an analysis of the personality of others, we may find ourselves thinking something like this when we listen to someone else talk: "I'll bet he said that to bolster his own ego. Now I wonder. Is it good for him to have his ego bolstered, or should I give him his comeuppance?" What was the idea he expressed? Did we agree with it? How was it supported? No matter. Our minds are fixed upon his personality and our diagnosis of what is good for him.

"Judge not, lest ye be not judged," is a good motto for a number of reasons. The first reason is the old inability to see the mote in one's brother's eye because of the beam in one's own. The second is that for philosophical reasons we do not believe we have any right to determine what is right or good for another person and, thereby, manipulate or coerce him except when his actions are causing harm to others.[6] Finally, practical reasons indicate that interpersonal relations should rest upon a fundamental basis of respect for substantive accomplishment. Thus it is better to concentrate upon what other

---

[5] Gordon W. Allport, *Pattern and Growth in Personality* (New York: Holt, Rinehart and Winston, Inc., 1961), p. 522.

[6] John Stuart Mill in his famous essay, *On Liberty*, defined this position very well.

discussants *say* and the *goals* they seek rather than upon our *judgment* of their *motives*.

One more illustration may help clinch the point. Perhaps most beginning teachers have allowed themselves to be seduced by the image of the "popular young teacher who really understands students." Being popular and understanding seems reasonable enough, but the young teacher spends so much time being friendly, jovial, and understanding that he forgets to do much teaching. With unerring accuracy students mark him down when he passes out student-teacher evaluations at the end of the first semester. The next semester he resolves to build upon a foundation of respect for positive accomplishment. He prepares more thoroughly for lectures and class discussions; he grades papers more carefully. The next set of student-teacher evaluations show marked improvement. What is more important, he *knows* he has earned those evaluations!

The Charitable Assumptions. In place of attempting to become amateur psychiatrists each discussant should make, at least initially, the "charitable assumptions" about the motives of others. These assumptions are: *Your fellow participants want to reach a reasonable solution. Your fellow participants want to reach that solution in a reasonable fashion.* These assumptions are very much like the familiar "innocent until proven guilty" assumption of our courts. Until we have clear evidence to the contrary, we should assume the better motive.

Making the charitable assumptions does not mean that one abandons reasonable precautions. We assume that most people are not criminals, but still we lock the door at night. There are unscrupulous discussants too, and, despite our precautions, we may occasionally be injured by making the charitable assumptions. Still the advantages clearly outweigh the dangers.

There are two principal advantages. First, one can concentrate upon the substance of the others' discussion rather than becoming overly concerned about the motives. Second, people have a habit of behaving as others expect them to behave. We recall, from our student days, one professor's classes were rife with cheating on examinations. The popular student explanation was, "He expects us to be cheaters so we may as well oblige him." All have observed other classes, however, where cheating was rare; the professors had assumed honesty. If you assume that your fellow discussants are people of integrity, they will more often than not live up to the assumption.

I, You, and We. One of the most successful committees ever appointed was the atomic energy committee headed by David Lilienthal. Here is how one of the members pinpointed a major reason for the success of the committee:

Our first joint decision, then, was to liberate all our discussions from idea-possessiveness. No point would be argued down; we agreed that we would attack the problem inductively, working from the ground up, assembling all facts pertinent to the problem as a basis for conclusions, implied or explicit. We agreed that all questions coming up were to be considered as being brought up by the group as a whole rather than by any single member. If a member had an objection to any one point, it was to be regarded as something that troubled the group as a whole.[7]

How different is this approach from the "*I* thought up this idea and now *you* are opposing it," attitude toward others. Saying and *meaning* "we" is not easy. Some use *we* as a gimmick to conceal differences that matter, as a technique to fool people into believing that harmony prevails. The genuine use of *we* is based upon the foundations of respect and affection for others that come from placing task accomplishments above petty jealousies and rivalries. Was there conflict in the Lilienthal committee? Of course. Did the originator of an idea defend it? Sometimes, but, once the members learned how to think as *we*, the originator of an idea seldom defended it solely because it was his.

Attitudes Toward Task

Two fundamental attitudes toward the group's task make a difference in discussion. These are *objectivity* and *involvement*.

Objectivity. As indicated when discussing in Chapter 5 the problems of the researchers, objectivity does *not* mean that an individual has no convictions.[8] The way the terms *objectivity* and *open-mindedness* are used by some people may lead us to suspect that an open-

[7] Norman Cousins and Thomas K. Finletter, "A Beginning for Sanity," *Saturday Review of Literature*, Vol. 29 (June 15, 1946), p. 9.
[8] See pp. 102-108.

minded individual is empty-minded. Nothing could be further from the truth. We have our beliefs, sometimes based, as Allport has clearly shown, upon the scantiest evidence.[9] The issue is how we handle our beliefs concerning the group's task. Two criteria distinguish the individual's degree of objectivity.

Frankness with one's self and others is the first criterion. The frank individual will, within the limits of tact, propriety, and common sense, confess, rather than conceal, his beliefs. Recall that, when the experiment showing how a minority could coerce a majority was described in Chapter 9, this book did not endorse the tactics used by the minority.[10] One of the members of the minority concealed his "true" beliefs and pretended to shift during the discussion toward the position of the deviate.

When discussants conceal their beliefs from their fellow discussants, it is bad enough; when an individual manages to conceal his belief even from himself, it is worse. And this happens, probably to everyone at some time or another. All are familiar with the "liberal" who is loud in his denunciations of discrimination against minorities but who becomes upset when a Negro or a Jew wishes to move into his neighborhood. "I'm not prejudiced," he says. "I am just afraid that property values will fall."

Respect for evidence and reason is the second criterion. "My mind is made up; don't bother me with the facts," may be a humorous slogan to paste on our desks, but it is scarcely a motto to live by. Great men have always entertained a respect for evidence and reason. Albert Schweitzer placed "respect for truth" with "reverence for life" as the two cardinal points of his own philosophy of life. St. Paul wrote, "We can do nothing against the truth, but for the truth." The desirability of respect for evidence and reason is beyond question.

How do we acquire this objectivity? We must confess that we are not sure. The literature is rich with techniques for *distinguishing* the open from the closed mind and *predicting* the consequences of either.[11] Plenty of literature and experience deals with techniques of changing beliefs themselves. But how do we modify tendencies to-

[9] Allport, *op. cit.*
[10] See pp. 230-231.
[11] See particularly Milton Rokeach, *The Open and Closed Mind* (New York: Basic Books, 1960).

ward nonobjectivity in general? We doubt that daily repetitions of, "Every day in every way I am getting more and more objective," will help.

Just how difficult changing tendencies toward nonobjectivity can be was brought home forcibly once while preparing a discussion group to present a public program before a service club. The subject for discussion was "United States' relations with Cuba." When the students gathered to practice and polish their presentation, one of the student speakers presented nothing but a series of glittering generalities about friendliness, mutual respect, and similar abstractions, without including any evidence gleaned from any source that even pretended to know about the Cuban situation. After some examination, we discovered that he had taken a popularized non-university course in "personality development." He learned in that course, he said, that people do not want to listen to "dry facts"; they want speakers to present their own thoughts and feelings. He had done just that. We tried every technique we knew to convince him that mouthing personal prejudices was no substitute for sound evidence and reasoning. We failed. We excused him from participation and sometime later received a "Thank-you-gram" for our efforts. We were thanked for having further confirmed him in his beliefs!

This case is, of course, a little extreme, and, after all, at the moment we are concerned with improving our own objectivity, not that of others. The best methods to improve our own objectivity are to first surround ourselves with as rich, varied, and able a collection of people and ideas as possible. If we allow ourselves to be affected by this environment, it will not allow us to retain myopic beliefs that ignore evidence and reason. The stimulation afforded by the challenge of others may help us modify our basic belief systems. This is the very essence of a liberal education.

The second method of improving objectivity is to become as familiar as possible with the nature and use of evidence and reasoning. The causal connections are not as conclusive as might be hoped, but many reports from teachers contend that students trained in the use of evidence and reason seem capable of more objectivity than those not so trained. Whether such people are capable of compartmentalizing themselves so that they become objective in one or more areas of behavior while remaining rigidly closed in others, is uncertain. Further, it is not known whether a disproportionate number of objective people expose themselves to training in the use of evidence and reason while disproportionately fewer nonobjective people expose themselves to the same training. Nonetheless, these two methods still appear to offer the greatest promise for attaining that elusive goal, objectivity.

Involvement. It is easier to define involvement and to prescribe ways of cultivating it than was the case with objectivity.[12] Involvement in the task means simply that one cares about (is concerned with) task accomplishment, and further, that one is actively participating in task accomplishment. The participation may be vicarious. Some rabid baseball fans, for example, act as if they were members of their favorite team. But usually the participation should be direct.

Some people seem to go through life without ever allowing themselves to become involved, save peripherally, in anything except their own births and deaths. Yes, they participate. Most of us must participate in various tasks in order to exist. But their participation is bland because they have committed little of their personal concern to the task. While one is rightly critical of professional joiners whose frenetic activity involves them in every possible task, one feels pity for those whose main concern is whether the supply of beer is sufficient to sustain them through an evening of watching TV.

If you want to become involved in group task accomplishment, participate actively *and accept some personal responsibility for task accomplishment.* Simply attending meetings, sitting quietly, and speaking when spoken to won't do. Lightning is not likely to strike you. The task won't seize you; you must seize it. Do you lament your lack of involvement in politics? Attend a precinct caucus of your party and volunteer to distribute campaign literature or become a block worker. You will be warmly welcomed because there are never enough such workers to go around. Do the conferences at your place of employment leave you cold? You might try volunteering for something other than what you are told to do instead of sitting back and criticizing those who do undertake tasks. In short, if you wish to become involved, stick your neck out and *do* something.

---

[12] It is not so easy to learn how to secure the involvement of others. We turn to that in the next chapter.

STATUS SENSITIVITY

Many a discussion participant wastes potentially valuable contributions because he either is incapable of perceiving actual group structure or he refuses to accept the facts of life. This pertains primarily to the discussant who is relatively new to the group and who has not "grown up" with the group of which he is now a part. If he is to be effective, he will have to function within the established framework until he has proved himself and is capable of modifying that framework. In order to be effective, therefore, he must first correctly assess the group's structure, and second, he must, at least initially, accommodate himself to that structure.

Assess the Structure

To assess the structure seems simple. Ask who the designated leaders are. However, as was pointed out in Chapter 8, the formal leadership may differ from the informal leadership.[13] Moreover, some groups have no designated formal leadership structure, so the new member must determine the actual structure when the group may be pretending that it has no structure at all. Thus, whether the group has a *formal* structure or not, the individual member should seek to discover the *operating* structure.

In Chapter 8 three means of determining leaders were presented. Unfortunately, job analysis and sociometric analysis are often not available to the individual member as techniques, and he must rely upon an informal application of interaction analysis. Three criteria provide good clues to the power in the group and can be easily applied.

Communication Flow. One of the easiest ways to determine the source of power is to observe which individuals seem to be the focus of the contributions. If the discussion seems to polarize around a few individuals, it is a pretty safe bet that they are the group's real leaders.[14] Suppose that in a ten-person group three individuals seem

[13] See pp. 211-212.
[14] It will come as no surprise that many investigators have found talkativeness to be highly correlated with leadership. In a very interesting experiment, Riecken suggests that the greater influence of talkative members is

to receive most of the communications. Don't stop now. These three may be lieutenants and not leaders in their own right. Watch to see to whom these three talk. If they talk to each other and to the group as a whole, they are probably the leaders, whereas if they talk to someone else, he may be the real leader. Not infrequently powerful leaders do not themselves participate heavily in the discussion. Instead the lieutenants carry the ball much of the time and check their progress occasionally with the main leader. This pattern occurs most often in advisory groups when the main leader must also make the decision.

Authorization Source. Often a group may discuss a problem without any apparent leader in sight. Everyone seems to contribute, and the discussion flows in multidirectional patterns. "This is a true leaderless discussion," one is tempted to say. It may be, but watch a bit more. If one of the discussants says, "I think we have talked about this problem enough. Let us go on to the next issue," and if the discussion suddenly shifts to the next issue with little or no objection, one may suspect one has spotted a powerful leader. If he repeatedly concludes the "sense of the meeting," authorizes the group to continue discussing, authorizes a shift to a new topic, and the like, one may be reasonably certain that he is the real leader, *even though the group may deny that they have a leader.*

Expressions of Deference. Often one or more members receive more deference from the group than do others. These expressions of deference may be obvious such as standing when he enters the room, using his last name, or using his title when everyone else is on a first-name basis. Sometimes the expressions of deference may be more subtle. The discussion has been lively with much interruption, but then one person who has been rather quiet begins to speak. The discussion suddenly quiets down and the members give respectful attention to the speaker. Another subtle hint of deference is shown in the manner in which disagreement is expressed. When the rest of the members disagree with one another, they are direct. "John, I

---

primarily caused by their ability to win attention and support from the group rather than by their ability to reduce opposition. See H. W. Riecken, "The Effectiveness of Talkativeness on Ability to Influence Group Solutions of Problems," *Sociometry,* Vol. 21 (1958), pp. 309-321.

think you are mistaken because. . . ." But when they disagree with this leader, they tend to do so obliquely. "I'm sure we are in agreement, but there are some more circumstances we should note before we go on."

We recall one discussion in which expressions of deference were a giveaway to the leadership structure. (We both happened to be very peripheral members of this group and could, thus, spend most of our time sitting back and observing.) This group prided itself upon being very democratic. Everyone was almost vehemently on a first-name basis. The meeting was a planning meeting at which some fifteen or twenty people were gathered in a living room. The "leader" conceived of himself as a functionary performing the role of a host rather than exercising much direction. It soon became apparent that one of the members (let us call him "George") was very influential. We discovered after the meeting that many of the other members looked upon George as something of a hero. The main clues to George's leadership were the expressions of deference to his judgment. One instance was particularly revealing. Since the group was large, a number of side discussions broke out from time to time. George wanted to make a point to one of the members who was, at the moment, half listening to a side discussion. He began his statement, "Now Mary, you'll have to agree that. . . ." Hearing her name and the word *agree*, she turned abruptly and said, "Oh, yes!" Her deference was so great that she agreed with him even before she heard what he had to say! It was quite clear that her "Oh, yes," did not mean, "Oh, yes, I will listen to you." It meant, "Oh, yes, I agree!"

There are other ways of determining the leadership structure, but these three will suffice for most cases in which the informal leadership structure differs from the formal structure or those cases in which group members have deceived themselves into thinking that they have no leadership structure.

Accommodate to the Structure

Once he has detected the leadership structure, what should the new discussant do?

In Chapter 13 means of modifying the nature of the group will be discussed. In the meantime, the new discussant would be well advised to work within the structure, to accept a relatively subordinate role, and to initiate pair events with the leaders.[15] After all, there may be very good reasons for the emergence of these leaders. The communication may flow toward the leaders because they are particularly apt at coordinating and regulating participation; the leaders may be authorization sources because of their recognized sensitivity to group judgment and temper;[16] and deference may have been conspicuously earned. When the discussant has built a store of influence based upon respect for his solid contribution within the established structure, he will be in a position to start modifying the nature of the group if he believes that the existing structure is not desirable.

MEMBER FUNCTIONS [17]

This portion approaches the nature of participation by describing the functions a group needs to have performed. Recall in Chapter 8 the description of the need theory of leadership, that pointed out that emergent leaders were those who successfully performed the various functions. Although a number of functions and techniques for executing them have already been described, the functions have not yet been systematically grouped so that a participant

[15] See Chapter 8, pp. 201-202.

[16] An interesting case in point is the method the Quakers use for making decisions. No votes are taken, but someone states the "sense of the meeting" when he feels that the group is in unanimous accord. For a description of the method, see Stuart Chase, *Roads to Agreement* (New York: Harper, 1951).

[17] We have chosen to deal with member *functions* rather than member *roles*. Benne and Sheats, for example, identify a large number of roles including the initiator-contributor, the information seeker, the opinion seeker, and the like. Steinzor and Bales, however, concentrate upon the functions. Our reason for concentrating upon the functions is that we believe such an approach allows the discussant to concentrate more objectively upon group needs. When people describe functions in terms of roles, there is an inevitable tendency to attach personal characteristics to the functions. Further, there is a tendency to label people with the role name and thereby stereotype reactions to them and their performances. A person normally concentrates upon a group of functions which might be called his role. One of our purposes, however, is to make the individual more flexible in the number and kinds of roles he can perform. Labeling the role hinders rather than helps develop flexibility. For comparisons see: Kenneth D. Benne and Paul Sheats, "Functional Roles of Group Members," *Journal of Social Issues*, Vol. 4 (1948), pp. 41-49; Bernard Steinzor, "The Development and Evaluation of a Measure of Social Interaction," *Human Relations,* Vol. 2 (1949), pp. 103-121; and Robert F. Bales, *Interaction Process Analysis* (Reading, Mass.: Addison-Wesley, 1951).

can see at a glance the list of functions he may perform. There are also a number of functions not described in any other chapters. Techniques for performing these functions will be discussed as they are described.

Four qualifications must preface description of the functions. First, the functions are not discrete; they often overlap one another.[18] Second, the list is not inclusive. Negative functions such as blocking and status seeking are left out. Therefore, this list cannot be used as an instrument for classifying all behavior of group members, though it *can* be used to identify *productive* behavior. Third, the functions are not of equal importance either in an absolute sense or in the eyes of typical group members. Failure to perform some of the functions may scarcely be noticed while failure to perform others may be fatal to the group. Fourth, execution of the functions is not equally difficult; some may be performed by persons with little skill while others require considerable skill. Those that the novice might attempt are noted as such. Difficulty of performance is not always equated with importance of the function. Keep in mind that the differences in importance and difficulty are among the reasons for the rise of leaders.[19]

There are thirty-one functions grouped under nine headings. Where the functions are discussed elsewhere in this book, the chapter or chapters where descriptions may be found are noted in parentheses.

A. Managing Problems

1. *Discovering Problems.* (Chap. 4)

2. *Handling Agendas.* (Chaps. 4 and 12)

3. *Initiating Action.* (Chap. 14) Moving the group to action constitutes one of the most significant problems of the leader, therefore an entire chapter is devoted to the problems of initiating and terminating action.

[18] We chose to make many classifications and run the risk of overlap rather than make few classifications and run the risk of obscuring differences by all-inclusiveness.

[19] See Chapter 8, pp. 192-198.

4. *Maintaining Task Orientation.* In Chapter 9 the tendency of groups to vacillate between task accomplishment and interpersonal harmony was discussed. Pulling the group back from excursions away from the task is difficult for the leaders to manage by themselves. In many ways the veriest novice can be very helpful to the leaders at this point. All one has to do is to say something like, "I'm lost. Have we strayed from the issue? The last time I was tuned in we were talking about obstacles. Where are we now?" An alert leader with a sigh of relief and a nod of gratitude will reinforce the suggestion. He has been spared having to pull the group back all by himself since the suggestion came from the ranks.

5. *Following the Sequence.* (Chap. 4) Everyone can help at this point by keeping this question uppermost, "Is that a goal or a solution?" Don't leave it all up to the leaders.

6. *Terminating Action.* (Chap. 14)

B. Generating Ideas

1. *Diagnosing Need for Ideas.* (Chap. 4) This function requires someone who is alert and sensitive to the requirements of the problem. Often the person who performs this function may perform both of the next two, but not infrequently it works out that some people perform this and the next function while different persons perform the third. Let us mention the next two and then illustrate the point.

2. *Stimulating Thought.* (Chap. 4)

3. *Creating Hypotheses.* (Chap. 4) A chairman of an academic department in a college or university is, by virtue of his contact with administrative officials, continually brought face to face with the problems of dealing with increasing numbers of students. Where will we find the classrooms? Where will we find the teachers? How may we assess student needs more accurately in order to make our teaching most effective? These are the questions he encounters. Thus, he is in an excellent position to diagnose the need for ideas. By virtue of his contacts with other departmental chairmen in his institution and elsewhere, he is also in a good position to obtain in-

formation, anecdotes, and experiences which may stimulate thought. But it has been years since the chairman has taught some of the basic courses. He is out of touch with the needs and peculiarities of freshmen and he knows it. Thus, he must depend upon those who are actually teaching the freshmen to create hypotheses for improving the methods of handling larger numbers of students more efficiently.

Other examples show how these functions are often performed by different individuals. Thorstein Veblen, for example, offered few suggestions for improvement, but what a marvelous stimulus he provided with his *The Theory of the Leisure Class*.[20]

Diagnosing the need for ideas and stimulating thought are clearly as important as creating hypotheses, but one important caution: Unless your position in a group is very secure, or unless the reason for your failure to come up with plausible hypotheses is clearly understood, or both, you better be prepared to answer this question when you have finished diagnosing the need for ideas. What do you propose to do about it? Those who have been bearing the brunt of the battle can get irritated in a hurry by others who are continually pointing out the need for ideas but who have nothing better to suggest.

C. Testing Ideas

1. *Diagnosing Need for Evidence.* (Chap. 5)

2. *Stimulating Research.* (Chap. 5)

3. *Supplying Evidence.* (Chap. 5)

4. *Criticizing and Reasoning.* (Chap. 6) The same caution applies here as to the creation of hypotheses. Six steps were listed at the end of Chapter 6, not just *five*.[21] You must be willing to do some research of your own in order to be able to present counter evidence and reasoning. Your group will tolerate you only so long in the role of group logician. Some people in the academic world, for example, continually criticize others' research but have not produced any

[20] (New York: Modern Library, 1934.)
[21] See pp. 151-153.

research of their own in years. Their productive colleagues are not impressed.

D. Preserving Ideas

1. *Recording and Summarizing.* This can, but need not, be little more than a clerical function though these are not as easily performed as one might assume. As pointed out in Chapter 5, abstracting information from that which is potentially available requires making inferences about importance. What the recorder chooses to preserve can have a significant bearing upon the outcome of a discussion, particularly one prolonged over several meetings. We have all listened to minutes of meetings that contained little information other than who spoke and in what order. Contrast such reports with those that pinpoint crucial decisions and clearly identify significant issues yet to be resolved.

When groups designate recorders, they usually choose the newest member. This practice is evidence that most groups do not regard the role of recorder as very important.[22] Successful performance of this function and the one that follows is actually quite important for some of the reasons just given. Other reasons relate to the companion function of reporting progress.

2. *Reporting Progress.* This involves more than simply stating at periodic intervals the action taken. Sometimes the reporter is called upon by others. Often he must decide himself both *when* and *what* to report. Further, the report gives the reporter a marvelous springboard to present an analysis of *why* things have gone as they have or what might be done in order to make more progress. Also, the reporter can perform an invaluable service by bringing a helter-skelter discussion back to earth with some comment such as, "Wait a minute. I am trying to record our decisions but we seem to be going in all directions at once. What is the issue at the moment?" In making such a contribution the recorder is performing function A-4 and possibly A-5.

Successful performance of functions D-1 and D-2 requires good

---

[22] When the group has a choice, they usually choose a woman rather than a man. Perhaps this is evidence of a perpetuation of uncomplimentary stereotypes about women.

communication skills that will be suggested in Part V. However, even a beginner can do a good job of performing the functions if he is willing to discipline himself to study these skills, especially those of careful and critical listening. Performing these functions is an excellent way to build a sound foundation of respect for one's abilities and intentions in a group and may thus become an avenue for assuming increasing responsibilities in the group.

E. Mobilizing Human Resources

1. *Stimulating Involvement.* (Chap. 12) This function overlaps many of the others. Since this and the next function are most often performed by the group's leaders, their details are left to the next chapter. Again, however, remember that the group should not sit back and let the leaders assume all of the responsibility for stimulating involvement.

2. *Regulating Participation.* (Chap. 12)

F. Harmonizing

1. *Harmonizing Conflicts of Ideas.* (Chap. 6) The steps for accomplishing this function are listed at the end of Chapter 6, but at the risk of repetition, let us underscore one point again. *Conflict of ideas is good!* Do not become panicked when discussants disagree. Most of the time the group seeks to harmonize the conflict, to resolve the issue, but it is not always possible to resolve an issue. Reasonable men can and do differ. If action must be taken, the majority will have to prevail and those who differ will have to adjust while maintaining their right to dissent. Often, of course, the group does not have to resolve the conflict of ideas. If two members of a book study club, for example, do not agree on the best interpretation of a bit of literature, they usually need to do no more than thoroughly discuss their conflicting points of view.

2. *Harmonizing Interpersonal Conflict.* (Chap. 13) This function is discussed as part of the larger problem of building a better group climate. Harmonizing interpersonal conflict is a function that needs to be performed as the conflict arises and is, therefore, an immediate

problem rather than a long-range one. Nonetheless, the techniques necessary to accomplish the immediate problem are essentially similar to those used in making major improvements in group climate.

G. Building the Group

A harmonious group is both a means to an end and an end itself. Such a group not only facilitates task accomplishment but is a joy as such. In the first chapter the importance of maintaining meaningful relationships with others was stressed and has appeared in almost every subsequent chapter. One of the underlying themes of this book is that the doing of a task is quite as important as the result. Thus, we reject the notion, that might be inferred from our pragmatic orientation, that the group is only a means of task accomplishment.

1. *Diagnosing Process Needs.* (Chap. 13)

2. *Creating New Norms.* (Chap. 13)

3. *Improving Group Climate.* (Chap. 13)

4. *Developing Group Maturity.* (Chap. 13)

5. *Securing Intergroup Recognition.* Presumably a group that succeeds in coping with task problems and that may be characterized as a harmonious and effective group will be recognized. Unfortunately, however, excellence alone will not guarantee recognition. If excellence alone were sufficient, advertisers, salesmen, and public relations men would be out of work. Groups, like individuals, can labor long in obscurity if group members do not call to the attention of others outside the group the accomplishments of the group.

Leaders, obviously, do a great deal to communicate to others the group's progress. Their positions in organizational hierarchies make this communication almost inevitable. But even the lowliest group member can do his part, and often more effectively than the leaders, because the norms of society do not permit a leader to brag overmuch about his group anymore than an individual may brag about his own accomplishments. Popular school courses, for example, gain most of their student recognition from the testimony of students taking them. Time and again individuals grow in the esteem of their fellow group members when the reports filter back from others that the individual has been praising the group.

Successful performance of this function requires asking three questions. First, are there any tangible evidences of recognition which can be secured? Prizes and awards are often available to indicate effective groups. The group's leaders are usually expected to discover the possibilities of such group rewards or to help create circumstances in which their groups may secure tangible rewards. Second, who needs to know about the group's accomplishments? The answer may include prospective members, people of authority and influence or other groups in comparable fields. Finally, how can I best bring them the information? Most of the time a simple report will do; sometimes applications and forms have to be submitted; and sometimes mass communications are the answer.

The important thing to remember is that this is a function all can perform. See to it that your group's candle is not hid under a bushel.

H. Executing Group Decisions

1. *Routine Implementation.* (Chap. 12)

2. *Quasi-Legislative Implementation.* (Chap. 12)

I. Satisfying the Individual

Coming full circle back to the individual, the primary satisfaction of the individual will come in the successful performance of group task functions and in being a part of a cohesive, harmonious group. But there are a few more functions that are often overlooked by groups, even those that emphasize the essential worth of the individual.

1. *Maintaining Individual Dignity.* The objective of this function is to protect the individual from unwarranted control or abuse, and this objective cannot be achieved by an "every man for himself and the devil take the hindmost" attitude. Most adults are too sophisticated to engage in obvious cruelties toward others. Children may tease a blind man or abuse a speech-handicapped child, but their parents usually punish such behavior. We have come a long way from the

time when the mentally ill were put on display so that their ravings might amuse the bumpkins.

Nonetheless in many instances individual dignity is degraded, in manners which are sometimes almost unspeakable. The atrocities of the prison camps, the Nazis' attempts at genocide, forced labor camps and brainwashing are shocking evidence that all too many people countenance practiced cruelty.

The particular concern here is with those instances of cruelty which occur among "civilized" people in seemingly mature discussion groups. That cutting remark, that "perfect squelch," that ridicule of a suggestion—were they necessary? It is doubtful.[23] How many times have you seen a discussant, having won his point in a dispute, proceed to "rub it in"? "But," we say, "he is a pompous ass and deserves to be taken down a couple of pegs." Perhaps, but remember that adage about glass houses and stones. We are probably all guilty of degrading others, so we do not point an accusing finger. We simply insist that every individual, regardless of ability, sophistication, or experience, is entitled to human respect.

Performing this function requires first refraining from the sorts of cruelties just described. Listening patiently and courteously to what we feel is a silly suggestion is not easy. Finding some means of shutting off an attention-seeker without cruelty requires skill. But we should try.

Our next obligation is to stand staunchly beside those who experience cruelty from others. To stand up for the underdog may require courage, but it is not otherwise difficult. Simply remind the others that they ought to be able to refute a poor suggestion, get someone back on the track, or whatever, with the normal weapons of plain speaking. Poison gas is unnecessary.

2. *Providing Tension Release.* If not carried to extremes, this is a most important function. It is unnecessary to point out that the joke should not be cruel. You, yourself, or the group as a whole can serve as the butt of the joke. And, of course, tension release does not always require humor. A simple coffee break may do the job quite

---

[23] Let us be clear about the distinction between being curt or arbitrary and being cruel. In times of crisis someone often has to issue blunt orders or simply do things without explaining at the time what is happening. Some people regard this behavior as cruel; we do not unless the situation does not obviously demand arbitrary action.

adequately. Tabling a controversial item until more evidence is secured may also work. Any group needs a break from time to time to relieve tension. Successful performance of this function requires sensitivity, timing, and usually a sense of humor. Look for opportunities to relieve tension, but when you feel that tension release would be appropriate, pause a minute. Ask yourself whether providing this function is really needed or whether it is simply interrupting a profitable interchange. Beware of overdoing the function. You do not want to be labeled the court jester.

3. *Distributing Rewards.* (Chap. 12)

4. *Training Individuals.* (Chap. 13) In one sense training is a part of developing maturity and is discussed in that connection in Chapter 13. In another sense training permeates every act that influences another person, as pointed out in Chapter 10. In still another sense training may be regarded as any specific assistance that one person can give to another. Let us briefly consider training in this third sense for a moment.

Suppose that another member of the group says he doesn't know where to find some information he has been asked to discover. You do know and you tell him. You are performing a training function. If you go one step further and show him, perhaps after the discussion, how to find *any* information of this kind by using some standard reference such as the *Reader's Guide,* for example, you are doing an even better job of training because you are making him less dependent upon others.

Your opportunities for training others are probably far greater than you imagine. You don't have to be an expert in a field in order to train. You simply have to be able first to detect some area of behavior in which you can be of assistance, and second, to guide the other person to perceive what you have to offer. Beware of two things, however. As pointed out earlier in this chapter, it is not your business to manage other people's lives. Further, few people like to be criticized, but almost everyone likes to receive suggestions for improvement. Thus, couch your attempts at assistance in such terms as, "Have you seen that article in such and such a magazine?" or "I wonder if Jim would respond better if you gave him more warning before calling upon him for a report?" Remember what was said earlier about improving our own abilities. Learning discussions with others who are having similar problems will help. When you engage in such discussions, however, you must expect to help others as well as to receive help. Even in circumstances in which you are admittedly no better than the other fellow, therefore, you can train and be trained.

5. *Expressing Affection and Esteem.* Sometimes it seems that a person must leave town or retire before he is told by his fellow workers that they have enjoyed working with him. But a testimonial dinner in honor of a departing worker is a little late to tell him what he needed to hear years earlier. The affection and esteem of our fellows are among the most important rewards we can receive. One of the reasons that participation in team sports is so attractive to so many youngsters and adults as well is that one can receive praise immediately when one plays well. We can remember ourselves as high school athletes, wearing as a badge of honor every bruise received in a game. Any of our fellow-students who saw us would not only commiserate; they would also express affection and esteem because that bruise had been earned in a cause they considered important. This last function is the easiest of all to perform. Simply say, and mean, "Good job. Thanks," once in a while. Paradoxically enough, asking someone to do you a favor and genuinely expressing your gratitude will win friends at least as quickly as doing a favor for someone else and then leaving him beholden to you. If your expressions of affection and esteem are word deep, save your breath. You will soon be unmasked. If you really feel affection and esteem, speak up!

PERFORMING FUNCTIONS

Every participant must take two obvious steps if he is to make his understanding practical in the discussion group. First, he must study the group to determine what functions are being performed poorly or not at all. Second, he must arrange to provide the functions. Sometimes he, himself, can provide the functions, and sometimes he must work to find or train others to perform the functions. This chapter is confined to the participant's individual contributions.

Study Group Needs

Since most of the theory and much of the practical discussion in this book is intended to help the individual diagnose the nature of group needs, the treatment is brief here. Many of the exercises at the end of the chapters are intended to help the reader discover in "real" groups some of the concepts examined. The individual should keep his eyes and ears open, and, particularly, he should not allow himself to get so involved in the *substance* of the discussion that he becomes blind to the *process* needs of the group.

"This is all very well," you may say, "but my mind simply does not work that rapidly. I always think after the discussion of so many brilliant things I might have said during the discussion when my mind was a complete blank." You are not alone. Monday morning quarterbacks have always been more brilliant than Saturday afternoon quarterbacks. And why not? Intervals between discussions are excellent times to reflect upon what has happened and to construct methods for dealing with the problems that arose during the discussion.

If the group is continuing with the same problem, most of the functions needed today will probably be needed tomorrow. Did the group lack evidence today? That evidence will surely be needed tomorrow. Was the thinking stereotyped and routine today? It will be stereotyped and routine tomorrow unless someone does something about it.

Even if the group is moving to a different problem tomorrow, many of the process functions needed today will be needed then. Was the decision-making structure inadequate today? It will probably not improve unless someone does something. Did the group have difficulty staying with the topic? Tangents will almost certainly be as tempting tomorrow.

Finally, even if you will be joining a completely new group tomorrow, you can predict many of the needed functions by reasoning from your knowledge of comparable groups. If you are participating in an interscholastic discussion festival, for example, in which students from many schools will meet and work together on a problem for the first time, you should be able to anticipate many of the needed functions. Your teacher can help you and your experience in comparable groups can be studied.

As discussion teachers, we study each new class to try to predict what functions will be lacking or poorly performed when the class seeks to make decisions. We have become rather good at predicting, not because classes are alike, but because similarities are sufficient to enable us to notice the clues and assign weight to them.

Even though your diagnostic skills may be uncertain, you can profitably study your group's needs. Study them during the discussion and determine what is needed at that time, if possible. Always study the group between discussions or study comparable groups before discussions. As you grow in understanding and insight, you will be able to analyze group needs more completely and more accurately. When you conclude a need for one or more functions, you must ask, "What can I do about it?"

Supply Group Needs

1. *Examine Your Own Capabilities.* See the first part of this chapter for suggestions. Be liberal in your assessment. It is better to try to perform a function and fail than never to try.

2. *Prepare Yourself.* This may involve no more than reading and obtaining some evidence needed by the group. It may involve working out a proposal to present to the group; it may involve a serious re-examination of your own goals; it almost certainly will involve improving your communicative ability. The tools are here; use them.

It is a good idea to work with others to prepare yourselves for many of the functions the larger group needs. Often three or four individuals working together can do what any one of them could not do alone. When a rather large discussion class was put on its own to work out a plan for utilizing several weeks of class time, the members found it almost impossible to stick to a point long enough to see it through. About half-way through one meeting, for example, a member announced that he had a plan he thought would work. He never even had a chance to present his plan! The group badly needed someone to regulate participation, maintain individual dignity, and improve group climate, as well as satisfy many other needs. Three members got together between meetings, worked out a plan, and agreed to have one of their number present the plan while the other two fended off critics until the plan could receive a fair hearing.

When the class next met, the three announced exactly what they had in mind and proceeded to do it. Within minutes the plan, with modifications suggested by others, was adopted and the group began to make significant progress. Working alone, none of the three could have succeeded; working together, they made a significant contribution.

Role Playing

One of the best methods of training yourself to supply group needs is role playing, a technique already suggested in a number of the exercises listed at the end of chapters.[24]

The Nature of Role Playing. Hendry, Lippitt, and Zander present an excellent description of the use of role playing.[25] In this article they present a typical role playing exercise and then discuss the methods employed. Educational role playing, they observe, usually follows a definite series of steps. The first step sensitizes the group to the need for training. The second step is called the "warm-up, role-taking, and definition of situation." At this juncture, the role-players are helped to feel "at home" in their new characters. If an audience is involved, the third step is intended to help the audience observe intelligently. In a classroom, for example, one part of a class may play roles while the rest of the students observe. Such help may range from simply asking the audience to take notes on the procedure to providing them with extensive check lists or observation tools. Following the role-playing session, the audience must evaluate what happened. The final step in any role-playing sequence is the replay of the situation. Role-players often reverse roles, and sometimes audience members become players themselves.

Planning for role playing may be done in several ways. If group members discover a need to develop an insight into some problem, roles may be created spontaneously as a part of step two above. If the group wishes to learn how to cope with particular forces or circumstances, someone must usually create the roles beforehand. If

[24] Note particularly Chapter 7, Exercise 9; Chapter 8, Exercises 4 and 11; and Chapter 9, Exercise 16. Some other exercises involve role playing to some degree even though the term may not be used specifically.

[25] Charles E. Hendry, Ronald Lippitt, and Alvin Zander, "Reality Practice As Educational Method," *Psychodrama Monographs,* No. 9 (Beacon House, 1944), pp. 9-24.

the nature of the role playing demands that the role-players have incomplete knowledge of other's roles, someone other than the role players must create the roles.

Playing roles is not difficult, and most people enter enthusiastically into the spirit of the drama. We have used role playing as a training technique with such diverse groups as college students, Federal Mediation and Conciliation Commissioners, Chamber of Commerce Managers, Sunday School teachers, and business executives. Role playing is a widely used technique in therapeutic work. Psychodrama, a technique employing role playing, has been used with considerable success by J. L. Moreno, the originator, and many others.

Role playing is fairly simple, but you should nevertheless observe two cautions. First, when drawing up the roles, be careful to avoid caricaturing. Many people tend to draw roles in a black-or-white fashion. The dominator is drawn as a perfect tyrant, the submissive person as completely spineless, and so on. People are seldom like that, so roles should enable the participants to reflect, as much as possible, real people. Second, avoid overdoing the role when you are a role-player. Sometimes people begin having so much fun playing a role they forget why they are doing it in the first place. A teen-age girl need not try to make her voice quavery when portraying a grandmother, and an adult need not flounce around pretending to chew gum when portraying a teen-ager. Suggest the role rather than trying to impress everyone with your histrionic ability.

The Advantages of Role Playing. Considerable observational and experimental evidence point to a number of advantages of role playing.[26] These advantages will be summarized rather than discussing separately the findings of several researchers.

1. Role playing is an excellent way to "get into the other man's shoes" and see both how your normal behavior affects him and how his behavior is motivated. This double-barreled advantage tends to make individuals more understanding of the frustrations created by working with others.

[26] See Alex Bavelas, "Role Playing and Management Training," *Sociatry,* Vol. 1, No. 2 (June, 1947), pp. 183-190. David A. Rodgers, "Personality Correlates of Successful Role Behavior," *Journal of Social Psychology,* Vol. 46 (August, 1957), pp. 111-117.

2. Role playing enhances one's flexibility of self-perception—"the tendency not to be bound by one's basic personality, but to be able to see oneself in a way demanded by the situation even when that is contrary to one's basic personality."[27] Drama teachers have known this for years. They see actors by the score unshackle themselves from the crabbed limits of their basic personalities as they throw themselves into roles that demand more flexibility.

3. Role playing is a method of practicing skills under circumstances that approximate real life without the risks and repercussions of real life itself. Rehearsal for the real thing runs the gamut from war games to role-played interviews. Rather than just talking *about* it or being told *about* it, role-players can learn by doing, and no one has found a substitute for learning by doing! Actual doing is the acid test, of course, but what football coach has abandoned practice against enemy formations just because he cannot persuade next Saturday's opponent to send up a squad to run practice plays against his team?

Even when discussants do not intend to rehearse for some forthcoming event, role playing helps make the discussion more realistic. Mock United Nations Assemblies, for example, have become very popular around the country. Rather than discuss in a vacuum the problems facing the U. N., groups are able by role playing to levy some of the forces upon student delegates that delegates of the several nations actually feel. If nothing else, such experiences tend to make student delegates more tolerant of international problems. Boys' State and Girls' State programs sponsored by the American Legion are other examples of this use of role playing. Boys and girls learn about their government by doing!

Role playing is thus one of the finest means of training. We must constantly seek opportunities to translate theory into meaningful behavior using practice conditions that are as realistic as possible. Role playing allows us to do this, study our mistakes and relate theory to practice.

SUMMARY

The individual participant himself bears the prime responsibility for becoming a better participant. He cannot expect others to

[27] *Ibid.*, p. 113.

do his work for him. His first task is to examine and improve his attitudes. Attitudes toward self may be improved by taking tests, self-evaluation before professional evaluation, learning and therapeutic discussion, and solitary reflection. Improving our attitudes toward others requires first that we understand others; second, that we make the charitable assumptions that our fellow participants want to reach a reasonable solution in a reasonable fashion; and third, that we be able to say and mean "WE" rather than "I" and "YOU." Objectivity and involvement characterize desirable attitudes toward the task. Objectivity means becoming frank with ourselves and others and developing respect for evidence and reason. These are difficult objectives, but a liberal environment and thorough study of the nature of evidence and reasoning will help one reach objectivity. Involvement, which means caring and participating, is best achieved by accepting personal responsibility in a group.

To be effective a new member of a group must assess accurately the status structure of the group and then accommodate to it. Structure can be assessed by noting the communication flow, the authorization source, or the expressions of deference.

Thirty-one functions were identified in the next part. These functions are listed below. The chapters which describe techniques for executing the functions are in parentheses.

A-1. Discovering Problems (Chap. 4).

A-2. Handling Agendas (Chaps. 4 and 12).

A-3. Initiating Action (Chap. 14).

A-4. Maintaining Task Orientation (Chaps. 9 and 11).

A-5. Following the Sequence (Chap. 4).

A-6. Terminating Action (Chap. 14).

B-1. Diagnosing Need for Ideas (Chaps. 4 and 11).

B-2. Stimulating Thought (Chaps. 4 and 11).

B-3. Creating Hypotheses (Chaps. 4 and 11).

C-1. Diagnosing Need for Evidence (Chap. 5).

C-2. Stimulating Research (Chap. 5).

C-3. Supplying Evidence (Chap. 5).

C-4. Criticizing and Reasoning (Chap. 6).

D-1. Recording and Summarizing (Chap. 11).

D-2. Reporting Progress (Chap. 11).

E-1. Stimulating Involvement (Chap. 12).

E-2. Regulating Participation (Chap. 12).

F-1. Harmonizing Conflicts of Ideas (Chap. 6).

F-2. Harmonizing Interpersonal Conflict (Chap. 13).

G-1. Diagnosing Process Needs (Chap. 13).

G-2. Creating New Norms (Chap. 13).

G-3. Improving Group Climate (Chap. 13).

G-4. Developing Group Maturity (Chap. 13).

G-5. Securing Intergroup Recognition (Chap. 11).

H-1. Routine Implementation (Chap. 12).

H-2. Quasi-Legislative Implementation (Chap. 12).

I-1. Maintaining Individual Dignity (Chap. 11).

I-2. Providing Tension Release (Chap. 11).

I-3. Distributing Rewards (Chap. 12).

I-4. Training Individuals (Chaps. 11 and 13).

I-5. Expressing Affection and Esteem (Chap. 11).

Successful performance of these functions requires individuals to study their groups to determine group needs; and second, to supply group needs by examining their own capabilities and preparing themselves. A particularly good method of training is role playing. It permits an individual to "get into the other man's shoes"; it enhances his flexibility of self-perception; and it allows him to practice under conditions that simulate reality.

As a conclusion, here is a list of five simple questions an individual must ask and answer if he wishes to become a better participant. The techniques for performing each step have been discussed in this chapter, and several of the exercises at the end of the chapter will provide opportunities for development of the necessary skills.

1. What does the group need?

2. What have I done to meet those needs? Be honest. You may have to conclude that you have been a part of the problem instead of a part of the solution.

3. What can I do now? That is, what can you do with no more training, skill, or experience than you presently have? You might be surprised at how much you could do if you tried.

4. What can I train myself to do?

5. How do I intend to do the training? The time to start is now! Check the exercises that follow and those at the ends of other chapters. You will find more than enough means of training. Map out a program and go to work!

EXERCISES

1. Plan for each member of a discussion group to evaluate anonymously all the group members including himself. At the same time have one or more observers evaluate in the same manner using the same criteria. This may be handled well using half the group as discussants and the other half as observers. Whatever the arrangement, you should use some guide or check form to insure that each observer considers the same points. Each discussant should compare the anonymous evaluations he receives with his self-evaluation. It will be helpful to determine the mean and the median of the evaluations as well as studying the individual ratings. In some instances, a discussant may find it helpful to discuss the ratings with a friend or the instructor.

2. Undertake a thorough examination of a number of your beliefs that may be subject to challenge or that may differ from those held by some other individuals with whom you associate, i.e., your political, social, religious, moral, or similar beliefs as contrasted to beliefs in physical laws, necessity for an organized society, desirability of medical care, etc. Divide a sheet of paper into three parallel columns, heading these Public, Semipublic, and Private, respectively. In the first column list eight to ten beliefs that you hold and which you admit to and would discuss publicly without special emotional feeling or irrevocable commitment to a position. In the Semipublic column, list an equal number of beliefs that you would discuss publicly but with much greater reluctance and about which you feel much more keenly and perhaps emotionally. In the third column, list a number of beliefs that are essentially private and which you would reveal with great reluctance or not at all. Certainly you would not find it easy or possible to discuss these in public and if you were forced to, you believe you would find it difficult to change your position on them. Compare the matters or subjects to which the beliefs in each group are related. Why would you discuss the first group and not the second or third? Do these beliefs affect your consideration of certain problems or persons? If so, in what ways? Do you have any inclination to reexamine any of your beliefs? To what degree are you frank and honest about your beliefs, not only with yourself, but with others?

3. Arrange to duplicate the experiment reported in Chapter 5, pp. 104-105, illustrating the effect of attitudes and observation on the transfer of information. Use a group of individuals unfamiliar with the experiment. At the conclusion of the experiment, organize the subjects into one discussion group and the observers into another and ask each group to explore a question such as: What were the factors operating to produce the

results we observed? It may be helpful to have the two groups join and report their findings as well as to have the observers report the form each discussion seemed to follow.

4. Select some person that you know casually but not well and toward whom you have formed a definite attitude (positive or negative) in some area of human relations. Write down a 300 to 500 word summary of your feelings and file it in your desk. Next make a deliberate attempt to become better acquainted with this individual and learn more about his beliefs, reactions, etc. After two or three weeks of such effort, prepare a second summary of your feelings. Compare the two. How do you account for what you find?

5. Organize a discussion dealing with some question related to problems, procedures, or effects of participation. Use your imagination and initiative. This provides an excellent opportunity to explore and illustrate points by means of role playing.

6. Plan for several persons to cooperate in observing a discussion group that is well established. Keep charts of communication flow, authorization or control functions, and deference or status behavior. What do you conclude about the structure? About the potential roles different individuals in the group will play?

7. Plan a cooperative observation of a discussion group based on the thirty-one functions listed in this chapter, having each observer responsible for certain specific ones. Each person should organize his observation so that within his framework he notes (a) those functions that the group needed, (b) those needed functions that were supplied, (c) those functions needed but not supplied, and (d) those functions supplied but not needed. Pool your findings and prepare a summary that evaluates the group performance. Discuss your observations with the group observed if such an evaluation is desired and possible.

8. Select some group of which you are a continuing member and make a self-evaluation of your group and your participation. What do you perceive to be the group's needs? What functions have you been performing? What, if anything, can you do at once to improve group functioning? What can you train yourself to do that will help the group? (Indicate the means by which you propose to train yourself.) What can you encourage or train other group members to do that they are not doing and have the potential to do? By what means will you attempt to train them? To what degree would this evaluation differ for another group of which you are a member? Why?

9. Plan a role-playing demonstration of participation in which some of the particular problems or needs are illustrated and some of the positive potentials are also included. Provide only the general structure in a

realistic framework for all participants. Provide each discussant with more specific suggestions or descriptions of his goals and role. A number of possibilities will suggest themselves—a group where members have a wide variety of interests and levels of maturity; a situation where an appointed leader is to function while the group gets started on a problem of great importance to all; a young leader in a situation where established and high status individuals are members of the committee; or a group where several individuals are concerned with their personal hidden agendas.

SELECTED READINGS

Allport, Gordon W., *Pattern and Growth in Personality*. New York, Holt, Rinehart and Winston, 1961.

Chase, Stuart, *Roads to Agreement*. New York, Harper, 1951.

Gulley, Halbert E., *Discussion, Conference, and Group Process*. New York, Holt, Rinehart and Winston, 1960, Chap. 11.

Miles, Mathew B., *Learning to Work in Groups*. New York, Bureau of Publications, Teachers College, Columbia Univ., 1959.

Zelko, Harold P., *Successful Conference and Discussion Techniques*. New York, McGraw-Hill, 1957, Chap. 7.

CHAPTER 12

Becoming a Better Leader

So after he had washed their feet, and had taken his garments, and was set down again, he said unto them, Know ye what I have done to you?

John 13:12.

Virtually everyone will find himself, at some time or another in his life, in the position of group leader. Regardless of the importance of the group or its task, all of us owe it to our fellow discussants to perform the role of leader effectively. When we are followers, moreover, a knowledge of the techniques required of a leader can enable us to help the leaders perform their tasks better. Thus this chapter examines those functions normally performed by discussion group leaders.

It is not necessary to review the evidence of prior chapters to be reminded that the issue of leader skills cannot be evaded by claiming that everyone should bear equal responsibility for group success. Things just don't work that way, nor is there any reason why they should. Most of us are members of many groups but simply haven't the time or energy to keep abreast of the minutiae, regulations that circumscribe our groups' operations, changes in task requirements, changing membership, and changes in other group characteristics. We come rushing to a meeting, figuratively or literally, out of breath, desperately trying to purge our minds of a thousand and one other matters and trying to orient ourselves to the purpose of the meeting. If our "leaders" greet us with, "Well, what shall we take up today?" we are rightly irritated. Students who have as many as five different classes in a day feel harassed; many business men would be grateful if they could limit their daily conferences to a dozen. The point is simple. There is a job for the group's leader(s) to do, and it should be done well.[1]

One of the more popular clichés about leadership is: "The good leader should work himself out of a job." Like most such statements, this one says at once too much and too little. Fortified with the statement, some would-be leaders never go to work at all, and some others turn a perfectly respectable group into a shambles. It leads the inexperienced to conclude that a leader is really quite unnecessary in a truly mature group, that the most a leader has to do is announce the time and place of the next meeting. True, in *small* groups organized for *personal* purposes the leader should have little to do, but in *task* groups and in *most learning* groups a leader is much more than a necessary evil. In even the most mature group he can be a positive asset, as shown later, to the democratic process.

If "working himself out of a job" means that the group should become less dependent upon the leader for *content* and many process decisions, we agree. If it means that the skills and capacities of the several group members should be such that several or all of the members could perform the leader role *if ncessary,* we agree. If the statement means that irrelevant or unnecessary symbols of status or rank should be dismissed, we agree. And finally, if the statement means that *on occasion* a leaderless group is desirable, we agree.

One more point should be clear before moving on. *Discussion participation in general and leadership in particular are speech arts!* Make no mistake about it, oral communicative skill is essential. Occasionally communications are written, but the vast bulk are oral. Effective speaking should be listed first in the leader's repertoire of skills.[2]

---

[1] Whether there be one leader or several, we shall use the word *leader* in the singular to avoid confusion. We do not wish to imply by the use of the singular form that we believe every group must have but a single leader. See Chapter 8.

[2] In Part V we attempt to provide a foundation of understanding and skill in communication. Unfortunately, the scope of our treatment is all too re-

The remainder of the chapter is divided into three sections. The first discusses the basic orientation of the leader to his group—the leadership method selected and the relationship of the leader to others. The second section consists of a description of methods of stimulating involvement and regulating participation. The third section is an examination of the techniques of handling agendas, executing decisions and rewarding individuals.

LEADER-GROUP ORIENTATION

The leader's first task is to decide his fundamental approach to a given group. There is no need to repeat the distinctions between leader types and leader methods that were presented in Chapter 8 nor the philosophical issues examined in Chapter 10. But both the *quantity* and *kind of control* exercised by the leader are important. The assumption here is that the leader has decided to forego control over content as best he can, that he wishes some form of democratic procedure, and that he will resort to authoritarian control only when he feels he must.

This preface is an attempt to be fully realistic. All authoritarian behavior, as already indicated, is it necessarily bad. Much of the time it is bad, but even then it is sometimes the lesser of evils. Moralizing about leadership is easy; practicing what we preach is more difficult. The leader who feels a need to utilize authoritarian means should not, therefore, always feel guilty about his choice.

Again, the issue is the amount and kind of control over process. Some leaders will attempt too little control as often as others will attempt too much. When working with peers, leaders often attempt too little control, as evidenced by the practice of most student leaders in our discussion classes. When rank, status, or age put something of a gulf between leader and follower, leaders tend to exercise too much control. Each individual, of course, must determine his own proclivities. *Normally, it is wiser to err initially in the direction of exercising too much control.*

If the leader exercises too much control in the beginning he can relinquish it more easily and satisfactorily than he can institute

---

stricted. We heartily recommend some of the excellent texts on public speaking and, preferably, that the discussant take one or more good courses in public speaking.

it in place of chaos. The basis of leader-group orientation should be solid respect for accomplishment. When the leader relinquishes unnecessary control, therefore, he is subtly complimenting the group. But when leaders seek to impose order upon chaos, they often find themselves accused of tyranny. A wise counselor once urged: "First get the respect of your students and then it will be time enough to practice democracy." The advice is a little extreme, but the essence still seems sound.

Bases for Establishing Degree of Control

What, then, are some of the factors that condition the leader's choice of the degree of control?

Group Expectations of Structure. What the group expects of a leader is a function of the group's norms, climate, and degree of maturity. How does one gauge the group's expectancy? Berkowitz found that most people seem to feel the leader should assume strong control over process *when task pressures are not perceived to be urgent.*[3] With this qualification, group cohesiveness and satisfaction *decreased* as leadership sharing increased, although productivity remained about the same under both conditions. Apparently most people assume that the primary responsibility for group success rests with the designated leader.

In groups characterized by a competitive climate a strong leader must obviously control process. The leader becomes a kind of umpire or referee upon whom group members depend to insure that the other side does not gain some advantage.

Immature groups also expect leader control *even though they may deny their desire.* In books dealing with child rearing it has become commonplace to note that children actually desire clear, fair, and *rigorously enforced* rules. Immature groups of adults are similar. We recall an instance of a newly formed group that deliberated at length about whether to elevate one of its members to leader or to go outside the group's membership to seek a leader. This controversy occurred despite the fact that the group numbered, in its ranks, more than one leader of proven ability. Another imma-

[3] Leonard Berkowitz, "Sharing Leadership in Small, Decision-Making Groups," in A. Paul Hare, Edgar F. Borgatta, and Robert F. Bales, eds., *Small Groups: Studies in Social Interaction* (New York: Knopf, 1955), pp. 543-555.

ture group was desperately in need of some structure, but the members persisted in believing that they liked their relaxed and informal manner.[4] The leader came to us for guidance and we suggested that she begin extending control by carefully planning agendas, by securing in advance of the meeting individual commitments to provide evidence, and by physically arranging her living room to make herself the focus of attention. It worked. The group began to accomplish more with greater leader control, and this level of achievement led in turn to greater solidarity and group pride.

The point of the above analysis is that the leader should conform, at least initially, to group expectations of structure. Imposing extensive controls upon a mature group will almost certainly be resented. But allowing most groups to work out their own structure will generally prove disappointing unless members accept their task as urgent. As is pointed out in the next chapter, modifying the nature of the group cannot be done if the leader refuses to accept the group as he finds it.

Task Urgency. When group members perceive the task to be urgent, they worry less about how they think the leader should behave. Berkowitz concluded: "Not only does leadership sharing fail to lessen cohesiveness and member satisfaction in the more urgent conditions, but the leader's permissiveness and the proposing of solutions by the members tends to make for more attractive group situations." [5] The reason is obvious. If members are sufficiently concerned about the task, they do not care who does the job *as long as the job is done.* In Chapter 9 it was pointed out that in times of crisis, groups were willing to grant their leaders extraordinary powers. By the same token, a group will accede to sharing leadership as well.[6]

Implications of Berkowitz's observation are apparent. First, whenever possible, get members to perceive the task as urgent. Get them involved and concerned. Barnlund and Haiman feel so keenly about this point that they devote an entire chapter of their book

[4] The group's process was so chaotic that one member actually became violent with some others whose behavior struck him as irresponsible. He did what many frustrated discussants have often wanted to do. He got up and punched another member on the nose. He also resigned.

[5] Berkowitz, *op. cit.,* p. 554.

[6] See p. 226.

to "Apathy and the Problem of Involvement." [7] Second, when members perceive the task as urgent, resist the temptation to arrogate controls unto yourself. The group will allow you to do this, but they will also allow you to share your controls. Surely there is no need to repeat the philosophical and practical arguments for sharing control.

How does the leader get members to perceive task urgency? First, he must stimulate involvement so that members come prepared to work. Second, he must initiate the task so that its urgency becomes apparent.[8]

Group Purpose. Just a reminder. If the group's needs are personal, structure is less necessary than when the group is organized for task purposes.

Group Size. Again a reminder. The larger the group, the greater the need for structure.

Leader Skills. Your own skills as a leader will affect the amount and kind of control you attempt. To attempt limited control and to share leadership functions are unquestionably difficult. Sharing requires a degree of insight, timing, and skill not usually possessed by most beginning leaders. It is usually easier to do the job yourself than to get someone else to do it, but the easier way is seldom the best.

Leader-Group Relations

Designating an individual as a leader often does strange things to him. What was once a warm, natural human being sometimes becomes a cold, stuffy, aloof figure. Sometimes he bustles with the importance of his position, and sometimes he tries so desperately to be liked that he becomes another "Uriah Heep." Sometimes he becomes dogmatic and opinionated. Sometimes he becomes so convinced that a leader should be fair and impartial that he seems to have a "mirror mind." He thinks what he has most recently heard. The story is told of a certain president who was sitting in his study

---

[7] Dean C. Barnlund and Franklyn S. Haiman, *The Dynamics of Discussion* (Boston: Houghton Mifflin, 1960), Chap. 10.

[8] The techniques for stimulating involvement are found on pp. 318-322 of this chapter. Chapter 14, pp. 377-381, shows how task urgency is made apparent.

when a senator came to call. (You may substitute, when telling the story, the name of any president you do not like.)

The senator said, "Mr. President, we *must pass* this bill now before the Senate. The welfare of the country depends upon it."

"You're absolutely right, Senator," the president replied.

A bit later another senator came to call. "Mr. President, we *must defeat* this bill now before the Senate. The welfare of the country depends upon its defeat."

"You're absolutely right, Senator."

After the second visitor had left, the president's wife turned to him and said, "Dear, you simply can't tell one man that he's absolutely right and then tell another, who believes the exact opposite, that he's absolutely right."

"You're absolutely right, Senator."

Three suggestions may help the leader's relations with the rest of the group.

1. *Be Yourself*. Nothing very earthshaking has happened to you now that you bear the title of chairman or leader. Don't try to change your personality. You will have to change much of your behavior, but you were selected on the basis of the person you were *before* you became leader. You will naturally want to grow and develop as a person, and the role of leader may well hasten that growth and development, but growth is not characterized by metamorphosis —at least not in human beings.

2. *Participate*. Preston and Heintz found that participatory leaders were more effective than supervisory leaders in affecting attitudes and in creating a more desirable group atmosphere.[9] Paul Hare conducted a more recent study utilizing different subjects. His findings confirm what Preston and Heintz discovered.[10] These investigators reasoned that the group seems less consequential to the individual member when the leaders stand aloof from active participation.

There are two important qualifications, however. First, the

[9] Malcolm C. Preston and Roy K. Heintz, "Effects of Participatory vs. Supervisory Leadership on Group Judgement," in Dorwin Cartwright and Alvin Zander, eds., *Group Dynamics: Research and Theory* (Evanston, Ill.: Row, Peterson, 1953), pp. 573-584.

[10] A. Paul Hare, "Small Groups with Participatory and Supervisory Leadership," in Hare, Borgatta, and Bales, *op. cit.*, pp. 556-560.

leader's participation must not blind him to the process functions he is expected to perform. If his participation embroils him in the substance of the discussion, he may find it difficult to obtain the needed perspective to perform his process functions. Obviously, as the group becomes larger, the leader will be able to do less and less participating in the substance of the discussion because of the complications of increased numbers. Second, the leader must be careful not to consciously invest his substantive contributions with additional weight by virtue of his position as leader. Thus, the leader should be doubly careful about offering conclusions or solutions. He can instead offer evidence, suggest hypotheses, and stimulate thought and research.

3. *Maintain Proper Psychological Distance.* This advice needs some qualification and explanation. First, to define: *Psychological distance* means the tendency to be less dependent upon warm personal relations and correspondingly more dependent upon satisfactory job performance of others. One who is psychologically distant tends, therefore, to be relatively impersonal in his dealings with others.

In a very interesting series of experiments Fiedler found that psychologically distant leaders *who were accepted by followers* were more effective when working with *task* groups than were more personally oriented leaders.[11] Psychologically distant leaders were accepted by their followers, in the Fiedler experiments, as readily as psychologically close leaders. Task groups, as defined by Fiedler, most closely approximated our definitions of action groups.

However, when the leaders were working with policy and decision-making groups, Fiedler found that successful leaders ". . . would be relatively permissive and 'therapeutic' in relations with their coworkers."[12] Thus, psychologically *warm* leaders seem to be preferred in such groups.

Finally, Fiedler found successful *therapists* characterized as "warm" and as seeing themselves to be essentially similar to those with whom they worked.

These results may seem surprising or even contradictory, but

[11] Fred E. Fiedler, "The Leader's Psychological Distance and Group Effectiveness," in Dorwin Cartwright and Alvin Zander, eds., *Group Dynamics: Research and Theory,* 2nd ed. (Evanston, Ill.: Row, Peterson, 1960), pp. 586-606.
[12] *Ibid.,* p. 601.

a moment's reflection begins to suggest reasons. The more psychologically distant leader is in a better position to be fair and impartial with his followers. He can discipline or reward them with fewer charges of favoritism. His acceptance or rejection of an individual can be more readily based upon the effectiveness with which that individual performs his assigned role, rather than based upon criteria of liking or affection. Thus, in groups containing a large component of action purposes something of a gulf between successful leaders and their followers will almost certainly exist. We have long recognized this in the practices of separating military officers from their men, in the practices of business that draw a line between management and labor and between various levels of management, and in schools where teachers recognize that they must maintain some distance between themselves and their students if they are to evaluate their students with any degree of precision. Loneliness is the price that many leaders pay for their success. This was poignantly illustrated one noon in the senior officers' mess at NORAD. The Commander-in-Chief entered the mess, politely refused to join several parties of officers, and sat alone in a corner stealing a moment of quiet while he ate a bowl of soup. He could not join the relaxed camaraderie of the other senior officers. He looked, and indeed probably was, lonely.

To discover and maintain the proper psychological distance is not difficult when the group is clearly an action group or one where personal purposes dominate. The leader must simply focus his attention upon those aspects of the follower's role performances that are relevant—task roles or personal roles. The problem for the leader arises when his group has an admixture of several purposes. A group may often combine action, decision, advisory, appraisal, learning, and even social, cathartic, and therapeutic purposes. Some purposes will dominate, in all probability, but the result will still be enough heterogeneity of purpose to make it difficult for the leader to determine his proper psychological distance. The leader must remember, however, that his own personality forms part of the basis for making the judgment of the proper psychological distance.

STIMULATING AND REGULATING

Two of the most universally needed functions are *stimulating involvement* and *regulating participation*. Probably the single greatest difficulty of voluntary groups is generating interest and involvement. We've all attended meetings where the candidates for office outnumbered the voters. Door prizes, clever publicity, "name" attractions, fines for absence, and gold stars are among gimmicks used to get people to attend meetings. Sometimes they work; more often they are no substitute for more solid motivation. Techniques presented here are not those of the public relations specialist; they are techniques that ordinary leaders and group members may perform. Moreover, they are techniques that are, for the most part, conceived as intrinsic, rather than extrinsic, to the group's actual work.

Stimulating Involvement

The problem of stimulating involvement is self-evident to most of us. Sagging and sporadic attendance, bored or uninterested participants, and poor or no preparation for meetings are among the symptoms of lack of member involvement. Even in groups such as school classes where attendance, participation, and preparation can be required, the lack of genuine involvement is often very apparent. The problem is seen when students do as little as possible, speak when spoken to, and set their sights on a passing grade rather than on accomplishment. Yes, there is a problem.

The last chapter indicated how an individual might increase his own sense of involvement; here the problem is to learn how to involve others in the activities of our groups. This and the next function are listed under the heading of leader functions, but it should be quickly appended that these two functions are ideal areas for sharing leadership. Working alone, moreover, the leader can seldom do an adequate job of performing these functions. He usually needs help from others who are also concerned.

1. *Reason for Presence.* The *sine qua non* of the techniques is to guarantee that each member perceives a reason for his presence. He must have a job to do, else why come? It is assumed that the group as a group has an appropriate *raison d'etre*. It is not a group that "keeps minutes and wastes hours." But, nonetheless, the group may mistakenly try to involve certain individuals by having them come to admire what others are doing. Of dozens of examples of failure to provide individuals with something to do, two are presented here.

For a number of years we tried to secure involvement in meetings of a debate club. Our success was slight. We tried various techniques of publicizing and the like, but to no avail. We thought that getting to know one another and sharing experiences would help provide motivation. We should have known better even before Hetlinger and Hildreth showed experimentally that debaters have less need for affiliation than nondebaters.[13] Attendance at work sessions and practice debates was always better because in these meetings students had something to do. We finally gave up frequent general meetings and turned to smaller groups working on projects or decision-making activities.

A group that was alleged to be the major governing body of a sizable campus institution provides the second example. Actually, the group did little governing. Its chief tasks consisted of electing officers of the group itself and allocating to campus organizations a few office facilities. Fundamental decisions were made by others and occasionally explained to the group. When it was conceived, membership in the group was intended to be regarded as a "plum" for upper classmen. Ultimately most of the positions were manned by freshmen and sophomores pressed into service.

Listing all the kinds of jobs that individuals might be offered is pointless. The jobs depend upon the nature and purpose of the organization itself. Be careful not to substitute "make-work," however, instead of genuine individual jobs. Unless individuals can make a real contribution, they are unlikely ever to become involved in the group's work.

2. *Opportunity to Participate.* Part of the opportunity to participate may be secured by proper regulation of participation so that a few members do not dominate discussion. But if the group is too large and unwieldy, even the best attempts to regulate participation will be fruitless. For this reason large lecture sections in schools are broken down into smaller "quiz" sections to give all students an opportunity to participate. Buzz groups may also serve this function. Committees established to attack particular phases of a larger problem may accomplish this function.[14]

[13] Duane F. Hetlinger and Richard A. Hildreth, "Personality Characteristics of Debaters," *Quarterly Journal of Speech,* Vol. 47 (December, 1961), pp. 398-401.

[14] The evidence for the success of smaller groups was presented in Chapter 9 and need not be repeated here.

3. *Relate Individual Goals to Group Goals.* An individual may have a job to do and opportunity to participate, but his involvement will probably not be secured unless he perceives that his individual goals are somehow related to the goals of the group.

Many leaders mistakenly assume that individuals will discover this relationship for themselves. Since the nature and justification of the group's goals and the relationship of individual goals are so clear to them, leaders often assume that nothing need be said about goals. No assumption is less realistic. Individuals need to have group goals defined, defended, and related to their own.

One time we were conducting a training session for labor union leaders. We discovered that one of the main problems they confronted was to secure attendance and involvement in union meetings and activities. Thus, we assigned a series of speeches to be presented as if the leaders were talking to union members and trying to urge them to participate. With one or two exceptions the leaders stressed in their speeches what the union members could do for the union, but they skipped blithely over group and personal goals. The union member was given no basis for striking a bargain between himself and the union; he had to figure it out himself. He was not shown what he would receive, *in terms that were meaningful to him,* as a result of his involvement. Small wonder that he saw little reason to participate.

To perform this function, the leader and his group must spend considerable time examining group goals. Next, leaders must be aware of the goals of potential members. Finally, leaders must take the initiative in tying group and personal goals together.

4. *Listen Carefully and Understandingly.* The fundamental tenet of nondirective therapy demands that the therapist be a sympathetic and understanding listener. Listening is no less a requirement for the discussion group leader.[15]

Obviously, if the leader is to discover followers' goals, he must listen to them both during and between group meetings. Equally important, the very act of listening convincingly demonstrates to the member that someone else cares about him and his problems. Everyone needs sympathetic audiences. When we find someone

---

[15] The techniques of listening are presented in Chapter 16; a defense of listening as a technique for securing involvement should be presented here, however.

who cares enough to listen, we can scarcely escape involvement in the group he represents.

Like many techniques, listening is a two-edged sword. Not only does it present the advantages just mentioned, but careful listening may enable the leader to evaluate himself and his group. One of the reasons that many followers are not leaders is because they are not very articulate. Thus, many a grievance, resentment, or aspiration lies long buried for want of ability to command attention. Bottled up, such sentiments can become explosive, especially if an unscrupulous leader comes along and promises redress. If responsible leaders are unapproachable or "hard of hearing," they may find themselves the victims of revolutions.

5. *Accept Contributions Without Evaluation.* This is a necessary concomitant of the advice about listening. Sooner or later the contribution must be evaluated, of course, but leave this to the other group members. As leader, you must help every group member to feel that he has a right to make his contribution and have it accepted for serious consideration. Nothing will cool the eagerness of a discussant more rapidly than having his contribution ignored or summarily dismissed. If his contribution is accepted for consideration, *and if he participates in the evaluation of that contribution,* he will often be the one who rejects it when the idea cannot hold water. This behavior is ideal when attainable.

Of course, contributions are not all equally valuable. But if an individual has a right to be a member, he has a right to be heard. If he is to become involved, he must know that his contribution will be accepted.

6. *Be Stimulated Yourself.* Member involvement is so much easier to secure when the leaders are themselves involved and stimulated by what they are doing. Jacques Barzun, for example, contends that effective teachers dramatize the subject.[16] Such a teacher stimulates his students to learn because they can empathize, that is, feel along, with him. So, too, the effective discussion leader should convey his own enthusiasm for the group's activity. If the leader shows concern, his referent power is increased.[17]

[16] Jacques Barzun, *Teacher in America* (Garden City, N. Y.: Doubleday, 1955).
[17] See Chapter 8, pp. 209–210.

Evidencing your own involvement means more than just acting excited. You must learn to communicate feelings as well as understanding. Your words are a part of this communication, but, as you will discover in Part V, everything that you do is a part of your communication. Is your speech lazy and indifferent? Do you sit in a semisomnolent position? Your actions belie your words. You should be physically tired when you finish a good discussion because communicating enthusiasm requires energy—energy sufficient to stimulate yourself and a bit more to help stimulate others.

Regulating Participation

When a group of even moderately stimulated discussants begin exchanging ideas, someone usually needs to regulate participation. Small groups of up to five participants and even somewhat larger mature groups often have less need for a given individual to assume this function. The group as a whole can, in these circumstances, often do an adequate job. But even when everyone seems to be speaking, someone may still need to be particularly concerned with regulating participation. This is best illustrated by discussing first objectives of regulating participation and then techniques that are useful means of achieving the objectives.

Objectives of Regulating Participation. Some people seem to think that participation is effectively regulated if everyone speaks about equally. Unequivocally, balanced participation, as such, should *not* be the aim of regulating participation. Shelley, for example, found that spread of participation was negatively related to group cohesiveness.[18] Morton Deutsch used spread of participation as an index of the degree of competition in a group—the more balanced the participation, the more competitive the group.[19] Why should this be? Several reasons suggest themselves. First, potential contributions of group members are usually not equal. Democracy does not mean equal *ability;* but it does include equal *opportunity.* Second, as we pointed out in Chapter 7 when describing the characteristics

[18] Harry P. Shelley, "Focused Leadership and Cohesiveness in Small Groups," *Sociometry,* Vol. 23 (1960), pp. 209-215.

[19] Morton Deutsch, "The Effects of Co-operation and Competition upon Group Process," in Dorwin Cartwright and Alvin Zander, eds., *Group Dynamics: Research and Theory,* 2nd. ed. (Evanston, Ill.: Row, Peterson, 1960), pp. 414-448.

of a cooperative climate, one member need not duplicate the action of another, if the other member's action has moved both toward complementary goals. If they are competing, of course, one member cannot let another "get an edge." Finally, because of the status of some individuals or because of their involvement with a particular problem, others expect them to participate more heavily.

If balanced participation is not the aim, what is? There are three objectives.

1. *To bring out the total resources of the group.* If a sound contribution blushes unseen and wastes its sweetness on the deserts of silence, the group is the poorer. Often reticence results from shyness, inarticulateness, unfamiliarity, or deference. If the leader and the group have stimulated involvement and an individual wants to contribute, he may still need assistance to get the floor and speak. Probably all of us have had the experience of engaging in animated conversation *after* the main discussion with some person who spoke hardly at all during the discussion. When we discovered a number of interesting observations and ideas, we asked why he had not brought them up during the discussion. "I tried a couple of times, but the group was off on another track before I could get in," is often his reply. Or, "I wasn't sure the idea was appropriate at the time." When individuals fail to bring out good ideas, the individual and those responsible for regulating participation have both failed. The blame should probably be divided about equally, but the point is this—the leader might well have been able to elicit that contribution, *had he tried!*

2. *To enable everyone to feel psychologically a part of the group's activity.* An opportunity to participate, as just seen, is necessary to secure individual involvement. Simply knowing that someone cares to hear his opinion may be sufficient for an individual. He may have nothing to add to what others have said, but he should at least be given the opportunity.

3. *To ensure reasonable deliberation.* In many ways the tyranny of the majority is worse than the tyranny of an individual. If no one takes care to regulate participation, a majority may often brush aside or ignore the attempts of a minority. Maier and Solem found that leaders significantly improved the quality of group decisions by giving the minority a greater voice than was possible under lead-

erless conditions.[20] The size of the experimental groups was only five or six members. One might expect this advantage to be multiplied if group size is increased.

Techniques for Regulating Participation. Perhaps here more than at any other point, a leader must use tact and common sense. To a casual observer, one successful leader may appear almost brutal as he curbs a dominator while another equally successful leader may seem to be gentleness personified. The leader must be particularly sensitive to how the members of his group react to direction. The techniques listed here should, therefore, be regarded as suggestions only. If you have discovered other techniques that work with *your* groups, so much the better. Perhaps here you will find more.

One note before proceeding. Techniques of regulating participation must be preceded by, or accompanied by, techniques of securing involvement. After all, if a person does not want to participate, the leader has little opportunity to regulate.

1. *Encourage informal, multi-directional participation unless the group is large.* Members should not normally raise their hands and direct their comments to one leader unless the group is too unwieldy for any other procedure. Most of the time the participation will take care of itself if the members are involved. The leader need not feel that he must personally give the green light to each potential contributor. At first group members usually look to the leader for sanction to participate. As leader, you can simply acknowledge such requests as perfunctorily as possible. Others will soon learn that they need not secure leader approval every time they wish to speak.

2. *Be hypersensitive to attempts to enter the discussion.* An alert leader will spot the individual leaning forward starting to make a contribution. If the individual is a bit shy or hesitant, he may never get a chance to enter the discussion without some help from the leader. We have observed dozens of groups in which one or more members made several unsuccessful attempts to enter the discussion. Sometimes we keep simple tallies of the number of contributions made by each individual. After the discussion we ask some of the

[20] Norman R. F. Maier and Allen R. Solem, "The Contribution of a Discussion Leader to the Quality of Group Thinking: The Effective Use of Minority Opinions," in Dorwin Cartwright and Alvin Zander, eds., *Group Dynamics: Research and Theory* (Evanston, Ill.: Row, Peterson, 1953), pp. 561-572.

more vocal members why others did not participate. "I guess they had nothing to say," is the usual reply. When we point out that some tried, but could not "get a word in edgewise," the talkative ones confess that they had not noticed the attempts. A good leader *should* notice these attempts and help the member elbow his way into the discussion.

3. *Warn the shy before directing questions to them.* If a member has been participating seldom, but appears to be otherwise interested, you may be able to secure his participation by asking his opinion. However, if you bluntly ask, "John, what do you think of this point?" you will probably receive nothing more than a non-committal reply for your efforts because you caught him off guard. It may work, however, if you bring the discussion up short with some comment like this: "Before we go on, I want to make sure that we have heard all of the ideas that people may have. Some of us haven't had a chance to say much, and may have some ideas that haven't occurred to others. Let's summarize the ground we've been over and then see if anyone has anything to add." You have now warned everyone that you are going to solicit opinions, and you have given them time to arrange their thoughts by the simple expedient of requesting a summary. Now when you turn to the non-participant and ask if he has anything to add, you stand a better chance of securing a worthwhile contribution.

4. *"Slap wrists" cautiously, if at all.* Often one or two discussants monopolize the discussion, and leaders are sorely tempted to put them in their places.[21] Think twice before you put them down, however. A person dominates discussion for several reasons. Almost certainly two of the reasons will be genuine involvement and need for attention. Such persons often seem to have leather skins, but they may often be extremely sensitive. Rudely curbing such dominators may lose valuable contributors or create vengeful enemies; it is much better if you use a little tact in some such manner as: "George, you have been pulling the bulk of the load so far. I wonder if others have some ideas to add." If you have been talking a bit yourself, you might say, "George, if we're not careful, you and I will have started a two-person group. What do you say that you and I sit back for a bit and let the others express themselves?" In

[21] Contrary to popular clichés, our experience is that men, as often as women, suffer from a lack of terminal facilities.

the first case you complimented George for his contribution; in the second, you made yourself as well as him the butt of your humor. If these somewhat subtle means do not work, you may wish to try the next technique.

5. *Use private, between-discussion conversations.* Such conferences may often be used to sound out nonparticipants and to speak directly to dominators. By striking up a conversation with one of the quiet members, you can often discover many things about them that furnish valuable clues to points in the discussion or topics likely to stimulate them to participate. Further, such conversations enable the nonparticipant to get to know you better and thus make him feel more at home in your group. Some people simply take longer to warm up than others, and these conversations may hasten the process. With the dominator, such conversations may help you find ways to let him obtain the attention he needs without talking all the time. Occasionally, you must come directly to the point and tell him that his actions cause resentment. Couple this observation with the suggestion that he help you curb other excessively vocal members. If he sees the need, he may be the ideal one to help.

6. *Occasionally turn the whole problem of regulating participation over to the group.* The time may come for the group as a whole to give its undivided attention to the problem of regulating participation. If you believe that participation problems warrant drastic action, simply call a halt to the proceedings and announce, "I believe we have some serious problems of participation. What do you think?" And then, keep still. If the participation problems are real, someone will surely pick up the discussion. However, there may be a long painful silence before anyone musters up enough courage to say what is troubling him. For this technique to work, you must resist the temptation to step in and begin explaining what you believe to be wrong. If you do step in, the other members are relieved of the responsibility of coming to grips with the problem. Once you pose the question, what had been a process matter, that is, regulating participation, now becomes the substance of discussion. You have confessed that normal means of regulating participation have failed, and, if other members agree that a problem exists, the group must seek the answer in their own emotions and actions.

One last word before moving to the next section. Sometimes leaders who succeed in drawing out Silent Sue embarrass everyone by calling unwarranted attention to the contribution. You may heave an inward sigh of relief, but have the decency to evaluate the contribution by the same standards you would use to evaluate the contribution of a more talkative member. To overpraise the contribution is to patronize the contributor. Accord the contribution no more nor no less than its due regardless of its maker.

SPECIAL LEADER FUNCTIONS

The three functions examined here—handling agendas, executing decisions, and distributing rewards—are rather arbitrarily grouped under the heading of special leader functions. They are significant functions that usually fall to the lot of the leader.

Handling Agendas

Perhaps the most widespread complaint about meetings concerns the advance planning. Berkowitz, for example, reports a survey of the opinions of business executives.[22] Of the factors they considered important, 86 per cent were those normally handled by the leader in advance of the conference. Our own experiences with military officers, as well as business executives, confirm this observation. Most people expect a leader to plan carefully for a conference, and the agenda is a large part of that planning.

Despite people's normal expectations concerning agenda planning, students of discussion methods disagree about methods of preparing agendas. The reason is that the items on the agenda constitute the goals to be achieved by the group. Thus, if the leader puts down items *he* thinks should be discussed, he *may* be controlling the content of the discussion and thus be depriving the group of their democratic rights. If the leader lists what he thinks the *group* wants to discuss, he may be reducing the involvement created by participating in the decision.[23] At the other extreme, if the leader leaves agenda planning up to the group, the group may spend all its time creating agendas. This dilemma is in many ways reminiscent of the "traditional-progressive" controversy in education: Should the teacher plan the learning experiences or should the students decide what they want to learn?

Earlier in this chapter factors were listed that condition the amount of control the leader should exercise. Most of the issues

[22] Berkowitz, *op. cit.*
[23] Recall the evidence on this point in Chapter 2.

relative to agenda planning can be resolved by recourse to these standards. In a large group that meets infrequently, for example, failure to plan carefully worked-out agendas can be disastrous, while in a small cohesive group that meets often, agenda planning is probably one of the least of the leader's worries. Thus, in the suggestions that follow the bulk of situations fall between these extremes. Specifically, the assumptions are: (1) The group needs some sort of agenda to be prepared in advance of the meeting. (2) The leader assumes responsibility to see that an agenda is prepared. Sometimes a subgroup such as the Rules Committee of the House of Representatives has this responsibility. (3) The leader wants the agenda to reflect genuine group concerns.

1. *Start Early.* The time to be thinking about next month's agenda is during this month's meeting. When issues come up in the discussion, when problems are uncovered, when hints of new directions are thrown out, note them immediately. Equally important, check with the group at the time. Toward the end of the meeting point out the items that seem to constitute the grist for next month's mill. Ask the group if they agree to these matters for the agenda. Also, ask if there are other items that you have overlooked. A minute or two stolen from one meeting to plan for the next may save much grief later.

2. *Keep Communication Lines Open.* Of course, issues will come up between meetings. Your agenda for the next meeting will seldom be neatly packaged at the adjournment of the previous meeting. In Chapters 8 and 9 the problems of communication flow and the source of task requirements were discussed. We stressed the point that effective leaders need to be in constant touch with group members as well as with those over them in the organizational hierarchy. If group members feel they can talk to you between meetings, you have opportunity to discover problems that they have discovered and you may communicate to them issues that have come to your attention since the last meeting.

3. *Publicize Agendas.* Let group members know as soon as possible what you believe should be covered during the meeting. If possible,

put the agenda on paper and get copies into the hands of members before the meeting. Most certainly you should present the whole agenda to the group at the very beginning of the meeting. Do not disclose the agenda item by item as the group moves along. This practice is wrong for at least two reasons. First, group members have no basis for judging the relative importance of the several items. How much time should be spent on the first? Must we decide the matter now? These questions cannot be answered if the rest of the agenda is a mystery. Second, group members do not have opportunity to pass judgment on your agenda and suggest revisions if they feel it necessary.

4. *Consider* your *Agenda As A Starting Point Only.* As just pointed out, the group should be the final judge of the agenda. The first order of business should be acceptance of the agenda, whether done by formal vote taking or by informal concensus. If others have revisions to suggest, the group may need to discuss these before it can go farther. In any event, *your* agenda must be transformed into the group's agenda.

One example that illustrates all of the above techniques for managing agendas is a case history of a large women's organization that met monthly. In the past the group's leaders were quite casual about agenda planning. Meetings dragged on with little purpose or direction. Many of the women became increasingly irritated, especially those with small children or other responsibilities that required them to be elsewhere by the stated time of adjournment. At one particular meeting, one of the ladies who did not know the overall plan, asked if she could present some information that interested her very much. She did, at length. Partly as a result of this, many of the women had to leave the meeting before it was two-thirds over because they had to meet their children coming home from school. Later this woman was embarrassed at the difficulties she had caused, but the blame was only partly hers. The leader had not publicized the agenda and had let the woman add to it without consulting the group's planning committee. The next leader made it a point to plan agendas carefully and to stick to the agendas unless her planning committee approved a *substitution,* not an addition! As a result, the meetings had direction and members could count on the adjournment time. The only members who were not more pleased were those who had nothing else to do but attend the meeting.

Executing Decisions

One of the most persistent sources of group frustration and one of the easiest to remedy is the frustration stemming from a confusion of legislative and executive functions. In Chapter 2 it was noted that several of the limitations upon discussion as a method could be mitigated by attention to the separation of these functions. The intention here is to show how both routine and quasi-legislative implementation can be managed in order to preserve advantages of democratic collaboration without crippling busywork.

Many people equate democracy with collective action; unless the group does it, they feel that the action is authoritarian. A student did an extensive research project in which he studied in detail the leadership behavior of two ministers serving two different small churches. One of the ministers, he reported, was very interested in applying democratic principles to the management of church affairs, but he was becoming discouraged with the process. Questioning revealed why, and one instance was especially illuminating. The church's governing body had authorized the purchase of screens for the windows of the parsonage, but summer had come and gone and the screens were not yet installed. Why? The minister had not been able to get the group together to go downtown, purchase the screens, and install them! Apparently it had not occurred to anybody that, once the group had decided to purchase the screens, they could give somebody the money and authorize him to buy and install them. No wonder the minister was discouraged!

An effective group continually examines its behavior and asks this question: Does the activity involve formation of basic policy that requires group action or can the task be delegated to an individual or subgroup? Many groups will be amazed to discover how many man hours may be saved by attention to this distinction. Once the group decides to delegate responsibility, attention to the following techniques will enable the leader, or whoever is designated to execute decisions, to discharge the function in keeping with democratic principles.

1. *Anticipate Scope of Authority.* In so far as possible get the group to set in advance the limits of the leader's authority. Is there a maxi-

mum that can be spent? Are certain features essential? Can possible alternatives be ranked in order of desirability? These questions the group can anticipate and thus provide needed direction to their representative.

Get group members to observe two important cautions, however. First, they should not spend time conjuring up improbable circumstances that might possibly affect the implementation of the decision. The group may just as well forget about delegation as to try to plug every single loophole. Second, they should not tie the hands of their representative(s). The group must have some confidence in the judgment and integrity of the individual. If he sees an opportunity to strike a better bargain or pursue a different route that seems to him to be consistent with the group's basic intent, he should have the opportunity. One of the basic problems of bureaucracy is that individuals go by the book in order to avoid any blame for exceeding their authority, and while going by the book, they miss one opportunity after another to take more effective action. No one can anticipate everything, and the group that tries is simply penalizing itself.

2. *Consult With Others When Interpretation Borders Upon Policy Making.* If you are the representative, and if you face a decision that seems to involve basic policy, you will usually have opportunity to make a few telephone calls to key members of the group to check your assessment of the situation. Some representatives do this at the drop of a hat because they are afraid to take responsibility for their decisions. Writing in *Nation's Business,* Charles Cerami offered this illustration:

Not long ago . . . a colleague came into my office and began: "You know, I have quite a problem with Arnold Smith. He's not really doing a job for us, but I'm wondering whether he shouldn't be given a chance in the shipping department, rather than letting him go entirely."

We spent 45 minutes discussing the pros and cons of such a transfer. This may seem to be a worthwhile subject for consideration. Unfortunately, though, neither Mr. Smith's present department nor the shipping department came under my control. My colleague was just seeking moral support before proposing the change.[24]

[24] Charles A. Cerami, "You Can Cancel Most Meetings," *Nation's Business,* Vol. 45 (November, 1957), pp. 40-41.

Clearly, this sort of practice is not recommended. You have no business undertaking executive responsibilities if you have no confidence
in your judgment. The consulting we recommend is for the purpose
of getting opinions from those who have some real insight into the
kinds of decisions that you confront and is valuable if you are genuinely unsure of the groups mandate.

3. *Report to the Group Both Your Final Action and the Basis of
Your Decision.* The report to the group is obviously necessary; the
group must know what was done. Reporting the *basis* of the decision
is as necessary as the report of the action itself, not so much to
praise or censure you for your interpretation but to form the basis
for further implementation. If your interpretation coincides with
the intention of the group at the time they drew up the policy, well
and good, but if your interpretation departed from the group's intent or if you exceeded the bounds of your authority, the group has
three alternatives. (1) They may decide that your action is an
improvement over their previous intent and may, thus, establish
policy after the fact. (2) They may prohibit such interpretation for
future action. (3) They may decide that you are not competent to
execute group policy. The last alternative will be seldom used, of
course, if you and the rest of the group are conscientious about the
previous steps in handling responsibility.

Either of the first two alternatives may be accomplished without
acrimony or bitterness if these conditions prevail: (1) You have
done your job competently; (2) You have not tried to usurp group
prerogative; (3) You have reported fairly and not defensively; and
(4) The group is mature enough to understand what constructive
criticism means. Only the third condition needs further comment
here.

A committee member told us that his committee was deliberat-
ing whether or not to accept a thesis presented by a graduate student as part of the requirements for an advanced degree. All of
the members of the committee, except the thesis director, were
convinced that the thesis did not measure up to acceptable standards; they felt it should be thoroughly reworked before they approved it. The thesis director, in this case the person entrusted with
implementing the group's research standards, finally announced he
would regard a vote against the thesis as a vote against him. He,
after all, had approved the thesis. The committee chose what

seemed the lesser of two evils. They decided to approve the thesis. No one was happy with the action, and, needless to say, personal relations among committee members were strained for some time after. The thesis director's big mistake was not in agreeing to submit to the committee what proved to be an inadequate thesis. It was in not being willing to admit that he had erred. Had he accepted the judgment of the committee, taken the thesis back to the student, and explained what needed to be done to bring it up to standard, both the product, that is, the thesis, and group relations would have been improved. A word of advice: Don't undertake to perform executive functions if you are too insecure to admit an error.[25]

Distributing Rewards

Most leaders must distribute rewards.[26] Parents must reward children; teachers must grade students; organizational leaders must recommend promotion, dismissal, and merit recognition. In Chapter 8 the discussion of the nature of leader power pointed out that the rewards mediated by the leader constitute a considerable part of his power.[27] The distinction was made between *intrinsic* rewards, those inherent in the task the individual performs, and *extrinsic* rewards, those things that the leader can give or withhold from the follower. Here only the latter are considered because most of this book seeks to help individuals to gain satisfaction *directly* from the discussion activity.

Though evidence shows the most significant rewards are those intrinsic to the discussion activity itself, extrinsic rewards are also meaningful, and their poor management may undo much of the best efforts of leaders. To prove this you need only recall what happened the last time someone's name was inadvertently omitted from a newspaper account of some group activity.

Distributing rewards is probably at once the most gratifying and the most onerous task that leaders perform. Few teachers enjoy grading students; most regard grading as distinctly unpleasant. From all the literature and discussion on the subject one must conclude that properly rewarding children is one of the parents' most difficult tasks. Certainly no decisions cause supervisors in business or

[25] The implications of varying group standards are discussed in the next chapter.
[26] When we use the term *reward,* we include the concept of *punishment.*
[27] See pp. 203-204.

military organizations more headaches, and heartaches, than the periodic evaluations of their subordinates. There is good reason for regarding the task as difficult and unpleasant; the means of measuring competence are crude at best. Teachers may use tests and student papers as means of measuring competence, but we know that these are far from precise. The means of measuring competence in most activities that include discussion are usually even less precise than classroom tests. If you performed those exercises dealing with group evaluation at the end of the previous chapter, you have experienced the problem.[28] Also, we know that results of our rewards can markedly affect those people we evaluate and reward. If one individual is promoted, for example, while others whom group members regard as better qualified are not promoted, the effect upon group morale may be devastating. Distributing rewards is thus difficult and thankless—no job for the incompetent or the weak-willed.

For one basic reason, no attempt is made here to list or rank the various rewards the leader may distribute. Aside from the broadest categories, rewards, and the importance attached to them, vary so much from one situation to another that ranking becomes impossible. You will discover the rewards available to you and the rewards you may create. You should also discover the meaning of the rewards *in the eyes of those who receive them.* Let us examine, therefore, some basic principles in the *management* of rewards.

1. *Rewarding Should Be Realistic.* That is, the evaluation should be as accurate as possible; evaluation and reward should be impersonal; and the reward should not purport to differentiate more closely than the evaluation scheme used. Each of these three characteristics of realism needs comment.

Evaluation should obviously be accurate, but more is implied by this criterion. Some leaders seem to feel that if they over evaluate followers, morale and consequent performance will improve. Thus, teachers may give higher grades than they think students deserve because they believe that the student will feel less threatened and will do better work. The evidence, however, does not bear out this position. A very interesting experiment by Howard and Berkowitz concludes that: "the present results show that people do not necessarily accept a very favorable evaluation in preference to a less favorable one. . . . The desire for reliable and accurate evaluations

[28] See particularly Exercises 1, 7, and 8, pp. 306-307.

at times did outweigh the desire for self-enhancement." [29] Other observation supports this conclusion. If the individual cannot accept reasonably accurate evaluation of his performance, he has problems that will not be solved by receiving distorted evaluations from the leader.

The second criterion may seem confusing at first glance. Why should evaluation and reward be *impersonal* since many rewards such as praise and appropriate publicity seem so *personal?* Impersonal means that the evaluation and reward should, within limits of ability, be objectively determined and personal factors, such as affection, should be minimized. Recall what happens to the "teacher's pet." Maintaining proper psychological distance, discussed earlier in this chapter, is the best way to achieve the perspective needed to be impersonal when evaluating and rewarding. At best, however, to eliminate personal factors is difficult. Tannenbaum, Weschler, and Massarik offer convincing evidence that supervisors tend to give far too much weight to ". . . those characteristics of performance which are related to their [the supervisors'] personal needs." Further: "The quality of the relationship between the superior and the subordinate is a determinant of the superior's perception of that subordinate's performance." [30]

The reward may not purport to differentiate more closely than the evaluation scheme used. This third criterion means that, if the evaluation methods are crude and likely to reflect the personal needs of the evaluator, only relatively gross differences in performance can be noted with any degree of certainty. Rewards should usually not, therefore, attempt to reflect small, precise differences. Speaking of economic rewards in business, McGregor concludes that only four categories of rewards above base salaries are realistic:

a. Those that can be directly tied to objective criteria of accomplishment such as profit and loss. . . .

b. Those that are administered as "time-service" increments, received automatically at intervals so long as performance is not unsatisfactory. . . .

[29] Robert C. Howard and Leonard Berkowitz, "Reactions to the Evaluators of One's Performance," *Journal of Personality,* Vol. 26 (December, 1958), pp. 494-507.

[30] Robert Tannenbaum, Irving R. Weschler, and Fred Massarik, *Leadership and Organization: A Behavioral Science Approach* (New York: McGraw-Hill, 1961), Chapter 20.

> c. Merit increases to the small proportion of individuals in a given salary classification whose performance is clearly *outstanding*. . . .
>
> d. Group rewards for departmental, or divisional, or company-wide achievement of objectively measurable economic results.[31]

For reasons of this sort many people oppose all but the simplest merit pay plans. Also, for the same reasons, most schools have abandoned numerical grades in favor of *A, B, C, D*, and *F*. Some schools have gone even further and use only two or three grades such as superior, adequate, inadequate.

From economic rewards and school grades, the principles may be extended into any kind of extrinsic reward that depends upon the evaluation of a superior—a leader.[32] Realistic rewarding, then, means that the leader must try to be as accurate, objective, and impersonal as possible. He must remember, however, that even though he may try, he will probably fall far short of these ideals. Thus, his rewarding must indicate only those differences which he can clearly demonstrate.

2. *Standards Should Be Common Knowledge.* If the rewards are to be meaningful to the recipient, and if individuals are to have any security in the group, the standards of both evaluation and reward should be known *and accepted* by all. If there is mystery about evaluation techniques or if members do not accept the evaluation standards, rewards are likely to produce tension and antagonism rather than satisfaction. Differential rewards are likely to produce tension in any event.[33] However, this can be alleviated by the satisfactions of successful task achievement. That is, if differential rewards are given but are not perceived by the individual as related to task accomplishment, the result in morale may be catastrophic.

To have the group participate in determining standards that form the basis of rewarding will help remedy the problem.[34] If the larger organization does not permit the group to determine its own

---

[31] Douglas McGregor, *The Human Side of Enterprise* (New York: McGraw-Hill, 1960), p. 97.

[32] These extrinsic rewards may, of course, be symbols as well as rewards that have tangible value. Plaques, medals, and citations are examples of potential extrinsic rewards.

[33] See Chapter 9, pp. 247-250.

[34] We described this practice in the evidence for the advantages of group discussion in Chapter 2.

standards of administering rewards, the leader should at least discuss standards with his group so that members may accurately predict consequences of their own behavior.

3. *The Right People Should Be Told.* One of the most effective rewards is simple recognition of individual accomplishment. When the leader gives recognition, he must make certain that the right people learn about these individual accomplishments. Sometimes letters of recommendation, personnel evaluations, and the like tell the right people. Another method is a short letter or memo to those concerned with the individual's accomplishment and whose opinion is important *in the eyes of the individual himself.* For this reason house organs have become valuable as means of publicizing achievements of individuals within an organization. The leader may often believe that *his* superiors are the only ones who need know. They do need to know, of course, but an individual's peers may be at least as important in his eyes as leaders two or three levels removed from him.

4. *Promote Your Group Members.* When leaders find a valuable and productive group member, they are tempted to keep him in the group and maintain the relationship so satisfying to the leader. But people grow and must have head room. Often they cannot remain in the group because they can and should be allowed to go on to more significant and more demanding roles. It is probably no easier for a leader who has developed affection for a productive associate or subordinate to let him go than it is for a mother to cut the apron strings. But, difficult as it may be, we must let go. Not infrequently, leaders find themselves working for those who were once their subordinates. This is as it should be. In the beginning of this book its objective was stated—the development of the individual. When he leaves his group for other fields, the group will be the poorer. But if it has any reason for existence, it will somehow stumble along until others come along to take his place. In any event, that individual's welfare is the only thing that finally matters.

SUMMARY

The leader's first obligation is to work out the fundamental leader-group orientation. The bases for establishing the degree of control over the process include group expectations of structure, task urgency, group purpose, group size, and leader skills. More mature and able groups that perceive the task as urgent allow the leader more latitude to share leadership functions. Leaders may achieve effective leader-group relations by being natural, participating, and maintaining proper psychological distance.

Techniques of stimulating involvement include: providing a reason for the individual's presence, providing an opportunity to participate, relating individual goals to group goals, listening carefully and understandingly, accepting contributions without evaluation, and being stimulated yourself. Regulating participation is necessary, but balanced participation is not the objective. Participation objectives should be: to bring out the total resources of the group, to enable everyone to feel psychologically a part of the group's activity, and to ensure reasonable deliberation. Techniques of regulating participation include: encouraging informal, multidirectional participation unless the group is large, being hypersensitive to attempts to enter the discussion, warning the shy before directing questions to them, "slapping wrists" cautiously if at all, using private, between-discussion sessions, and occasionally turning the whole problem of regulating participation over to the group.

Agenda planning is essential for most groups, and the leader may accomplish the task without either robbing the group of their democratic rights or wasting time if he starts early, keeps communication lines open, publicizes agendas, and transforms his agenda into the group's agenda. Separating executive from policy actions is an excellent means of circumventing the limitations of discussion. Effective executive implementation requires leader and group to anticipate the scope of his authority, that he consult with others when he feels he is creating policy instead of simply implementing, and that he report fairly both his action and the basis of his decisions. Distributing extrinsic rewards is a difficult but essential task. If the function is to be effective, rewarding should be realistic, standards should be common knowledge, the right people should learn of individual accomplishment, and the leader must learn to let individuals go if they need opportunities the group cannot provide.

EXERCISES

1. Have several members of the class form a committee to develop two or three leadership situations in which role playing by other class members is possible. Select one of the situations and present a discussion with a third group acting as observer-evaluators.

2. Select a group leader that you can observe for several meetings. Attempt to analyze his work as a leader in terms of the concepts of this chapter. Arrange for an interview or conference where you discuss his concepts of leadership and his evaluation of his group's operation. To what degree do his perceptions agree with yours? What suggestions would you have for his improvement?

3. Pair yourself with another class member to observe and analyze two different situations:

    a. A situation in which a leader has emerged from a group, owes his selection to the group, and has continued in such a position;

    b. A leader who has been designated as leader by some authority outside the group.

What, if any, changes occurred in each leader's relationship to the group? How did the group perceive him after he became the leader? Why? Was this good or bad, or did it make any difference? What advice would you give each leader? Would the leader be able to accept and act on it? Compare and contrast the results of the observations.

4. Organize a discussion considering the question, "How can we secure better involvement on the part of our group members?" Plan to have two or three persons present three to four minute case studies of groups that have had problems of inadequate involvement. Use these as the bases of a discussion aimed at recommending both principles and procedures.

5. Pair yourself with another class member. Have one person make a tape recording of a committee meeting or similar group. Observe the leader's work while the discussion is in progress. The second person should attempt to analyze the leadership from hearing only the tape recording. How do your analyses compare? What seems to come out in each analysis that was not evident in the counterpart?

6. Organize two comparable discussion groups, each to consider a problem that has potential for both creativity and evaluation. Arrange for one to be led by a person with an authoritarian philosophy and the other to be led by a person with a democratic philosophy. Compare the products and also the member satisfactions.

7. Looking around you, evaluate leadership in a variety of groups

and situations on the bases of both appropriate and desirable behavior. List first a number of cases where either authoritarian or democratic approaches were used and where you felt these were proper. List next some situations where you feel the leader should have used or applied different methods than he used. Review both lists and possible effects of leader behavior opposite to that which you observed. What might have been the effects?

8. Keep a list of all the decisions you make as an individual, or in which you participate as a member of a group, for a period of one week. Were there alternative ways of arriving at the decision? (That is, could some of the individual decisions have been shared, or could some of the group decisions have been made by an individual—yourself or another?) Would the alternative have been wise in terms of either or both efficiency of process or quality of decision?

9. Observe a group in which one or more individuals gives some evidence of wishing to participate but finds it difficult or impossible to enter the discussion. Arrange for private interviews with such persons to explore as fully as possible their perceptions and feelings concerning their relationship to the group as a whole and to the leader. Attempt to determine how they feel about their experiences and their attitudes toward participation in the future. What, if anything, do you believe the leader failed to do? Or, what did he do that should not have been done?

10. Review your role as leader of one or more groups. What rewards are available to you for use in stimulating group production? How might these be used? What accounts for the variation in both availability and use from group to group?

11. Review your role as a participant or member of several groups. What rewards were available to the leaders of these groups, and how were they used? To what extent were the rewards used effectively or ineffectively? Compare your perception of and reaction to such rewards when you are a leader and when you are a participant.

SELECTED READINGS

Barnlund, Dean C., and Haiman, Franklyn S., *The Dynamics of Discussion.* Boston, Houghton Mifflin, 1960, Chaps. 10, 13, and 14.

Haire, Mason, *Psychology in Management.* New York, McGraw-Hill, 1956, Chaps. 3 and 6.

Keltner, John W., *Group Discussion Processes.* New York, Longmans, Green, 1957, Chaps. 15, 19, 20, and 21.

Laird, Donald A. and Eleanor C., *The New Psychology for Leadership.* New York, McGraw-Hill, 1956.

McGregor, Douglas, *The Human Side of Enterprise.* New York, McGraw-Hill, 1960.

Petrullo, Luigo, and Bass, Bernard M., *Leadership and Interpersonal Behavior.* New York, Holt, Rinehart, and Winston, 1961.

Tannenbaum, Robert Weschler, Irving R., and Massarik, Fred, *Leadership and Organization: A Behavioral Science Approach,* New York, McGraw-Hill, 1961, Chaps. 4, 5, and 20.

CHAPTER 13

Modifying the
Nature of the Group

Ah, Love! could you and I with Him conspire
To grasp this sorry Scheme of Things entire,
    Would not we shatter it to bits—and then
Re-mould it nearer to the Heart's Desire!
                    Rubáiyát of Omar Khayyám

Up to this point methods by which individuals can improve their participation in general and their leadership in particular have been discussed. Surely group operations will improve if one can improve his skills. But this may not be enough. The finest leader may be frustrated if his group is inadequate—if group norms are unrealistic, if the group climate is competitive, if the group is immature, if the other members have not begun to reach their potential.

What can you do, then, to improve the nature of your group? That is the subject of this chapter.

The first question is, can the individual affect the nature of his group? The answer is *yes*. Throughout this book there has been evidence that the individual is not helpless. For additional evidence look at the results of an interesting experiment conducted by William Haythorn.[1] He found that *able* discussants could significantly affect the characteristics of small groups. The word *able* is under-

[1] William Haythorn, "The Influence of Individual Members on the Characteristics of Small Groups," in A. Paul Hare, Edgar F. Borgatta, and Robert F. Bales, eds., *Small Groups: Studies in Social Interaction* (New York: Knopf, 1955), pp. 330-341.

scored because Haythorn found that successful individuals were described as cooperative, efficient, and possessed of insight. They were also mature and accepting individuals. These findings support the point made here from the beginning: that the dull and inarticulate can expect little success, but groups feel the impact of the *able* person.

Those who initiate change will probably be among the group's leaders, and members who have little influence will not be likely to accomplish very much directly. Nonetheless, the term *leader* is not used to designate the person who initiates or creates the change; rather such a person is called a *change agent*.[2] This term may identify one who produces the change directly or one whose limited power compels him to operate indirectly. Still another reason for using the term is that it connotes more accurately the functions to be performed. No one can literally change another's belief or behavior. A change agent can, however, create circumstances that may induce another to change.

Much of the literature and discussion of means of producing, or engineering, change causes considerable resentment because many people feel that engineering change means manipulating others. The dignity of the individual is at stake, some feel. The change agent seems to array the forces in the group in such a fashion that individuals are changed without being aware of the fact, that individuals are pawns in the game of group discussion.

This book is written from the beginning with a keen awareness of this charge. The techniques in this chapter, therefore, are all "cards on the table" practices. Sometimes such techniques take a bit more time than undercover manipulation, but consequences for both the group and the change agent are worth the added effort. The leader who is suspected of manipulation will confront an increasingly hostile and suspicious group; change produced by trickery can boomerang. But the line between facilitative leadership and domination is difficult to draw.[3] We must trust that the reader will not read into our techniques an intent to manipulate individuals contrary to their will.

[2] Lippitt, Watson, and Westley use this term. Much of their theoretical and practical analyses is reflected in this chapter. See Ronald Lippitt, Jeanne Watson, and Bruce Westley, *The Dynamics of Planned Change* (New York: Harcourt, Brace & World, 1958).

[3] See Chapter 10, pp. 366-368.

This chapter examines techniques for performing six functions —creating new norms, improving group climate, developing group maturity, diagnosing process needs, harmonizing interpersonal conflict, and training individual members. Since there is considerable overlapping among these functions, this chapter is developed around norms, climate, and maturity. Diagnosing process needs is a necessary first step of each of these three tasks and is treated thus. Harmonizing interpersonal conflict is considered as part of improving group climate. Training group members is introduced in connection with developing group maturity.

CREATING NEW NORMS

When group operations are ineffective, inadequate norms are often to blame. Norms that emerge implicitly from group interaction and especially those based largely in social reality tend to cause groups the most trouble.[4] The trouble arises because, first, we are often unaware of either the existence or effect of such norms; second, changing inappropriate norms based in social reality is more difficult than changing inappropriate norms based in objective reality.

Thus, this section examines only those techniques for creating new norms to replace those based primarily in social reality, including both explicit and implicit norms. Little can be done about norms that are a part of the larger culture, and tools were already presented for dealing with norms based in objective reality. Ordinary problem-solving procedure should suffice for the latter. First some norms that often need to be changed are identified.

Inappropriate Norms

The norms identified here are representative of those that often cause trouble. The list is suggestive, certainly not exhaustive. Every individual must examine his own group to identify those norms that facilitate profitable discussion and those that hinder it.

Time-Wasting Norms. Many accepted norms may only waste time, but this charge alone justifies their examination. Simple lack of skill in discussion may perpetuate the norm—"It seems to be the way we've always done things"—but often the cause is at least partly

[4] See Chapter 7, pp. 164-165.

rooted in personal insecurity. This reason may become more apparent in the examination of a few typical time-wasters.

1. *Using meeting time to report activities.* "Everyone should be informed of what others have been doing during between-discussion intervals," is often the defense for spending hours of group time listening to recitals of details. Of course, they should! But is the group meeting the time to do it? It may be, but in many cases written reports that are distributed and individually filed will serve the purpose more accurately and consume less valuable time. When the group was new, small, and when it met often, written reports probably seemed unnecessary and possibly pretentious. Now that the group is larger, the practice of oral reports persists simply because "We've always done it that way." The norm is fairly easily changed, however. In one group the chairman and other members recognized the problem and literally "kidded" themselves out of the practice by referring to routine reports as "housekeeping" functions. Occasionally the whole group had to engage in housekeeping, but the group was able to agree to avoid oral reports unless they were intended to form the basis for group action.

2. *Using the group to spread responsibility.* This is a troublesome norm because it is difficult to decide when a particular problem is or should be an individual responsibility, a subgroup responsibility, or a whole group responsibility. In the preceding chapter the concept of delegation of responsibility was examined. The norm that everyone ought always to bear the responsibility for decisions may well need to be changed. If the norm exists because people are too insecure to cope with personal responsibility, the issue may be individual or collective maturity and the norm is a symptom of the problem. But if people have been simply distorting the "two heads are better than one" concept, norm changes may serve the purpose.

Time-wasting norms are legion, but these two will suffice to point up the problem. In general, whenever you feel that the group is taking too much of the time of too many people, ask yourself this question: "Must we go through all of these steps with all of these people?" In examining your own groups you may find several norms that serve no purpose other than delaying action.[5]

[5] Sometimes, of course, the practice was established for precisely the purpose of delay in order to prevent hasty or ill-considered action. Our bicameral legislative structure has this as one of its avowed objectives.

Talk-Action Imbalance. If we are to believe popular stereotypes, "men of action" in the business community scorn talk and make decisions at the drop of a hat. College professors, on the other hand, are supposed to seldom make decisions but will cheerfully talk an idea to death. Probably neither stereotype is very useful, though not always unreal. If it seems as though undue stress is put upon securing action, it is probably because we have been so often frustrated by nonproductive talk. However, the objective is not to categorize either businessmen or college professors; it is simply to point out that prevailing group norms may favor one extreme or the other of the talk-action balance. If they do, the norms may need to be changed.

Unrealistic Standards. The standards by which the worth of our actions are measured are often unrealistic. Sometimes they are too high. Some students feel they have failed if they do not get an *A*; some teachers expect too much of students; some managers in business drive subordinates toward impossible levels. However, most groups typically tend to set standards that are below their potential abilities. A number of years ago Roethlisberger and Dickson clearly identified the effects of standards that tended to sharply define the upper limits of factory workers' production.[6] The workers argued that these standards represented maximum safe levels of production, but experimentation belied that contention. Dozens of other studies of factory workers have confirmed the tendency to set restrictive production norms.

Restrictive norms are not confined to factory workers. The "gentleman's C" has plagued more institutions than Harvard; for years the military has had to contend with restrictive norms; voluntary organizations often fail to reach their potentials because everyone believes that there are strict limits to what they can accomplish.

The nature of the forces that restrain standards is much too complicated to explain in general terms. Each case must be examined to understand why standards are not higher, or lower, as the case might be. The framework for this analysis is discussed along with the procedures for producing change.

[6] For a complete description of the famous Western Electric studies, see Fritz J. Roethlisberger and William J. Dickson, *Management and the Worker* (Cambridge, Mass.: Harvard Univ., 1941).

Opposition to Change Itself. This norm is widespread and pernicious. Browne puts the problem clearly and identifies an interesting antidote.

It seems to be almost the nature of human beings to develop plans and anticipations along with established or habitual behavior to use in various situations. A change becomes terrifying when it is not expected and when it has not been taken into account in planning. Therefore, people don't want things to be different because no established plan of action will fit into the conditions which arise when differences are introduced into a situation. The development of "a set to be set for that which we are not set for" would take the terror and the dread out of change.[7]

Browne's advice that groups develop a "set to be set for that which we are not set for," suggests that some groups do develop a tolerance for change and may even welcome it. From Heraclitus to Korzybski great thinkers have insisted that the only constant is change itself; but far too many individuals and groups seek to freeze the present.

Genuine conservatism that insists upon basing change upon tested principles is, naturally, not out of date; nor are all who advocate change doing the group a favor. Any given change may be good or bad. It is just that he who proposes the change has the burden of proof, the responsibility for proving that the change is an improvement over the status quo. But change is inevitable and even the status quo must be considered dynamic.[8] Thus, a group whose norms include resistance to change, come what may, is headed for trouble.

This list of inappropriate norms may help you perform the first step—discovering the norm(s) that may be causing trouble. Once you have done this, you are ready to begin the change process.

Changing Inappropriate Norms

Before you rush forth, determined to rid your group of its vanities, shibboleths, and crippling beliefs, remember that your task will be difficult and slow. Norms based in social reality are not easily

[7] C. G. Browne, "Leadership and Change," in C. G. Browne and Thomas S. Cohn, eds., *The Study of Leadership* (Danville, Illinois: Interstate Printers & Publishers, 1958), pp. 419-420.

[8] Recall the discussion of this point in Chapter 4, pp. 65-66.

changed. Moreover, a *direct attack* upon such norms will probably
have two consequences—the norm will become more firmly en-
trenched than ever, and you may find yourself a group outcast.
Remember from Chapter 7 that norms form a part of our very sanity,
*particularly in the absence of clearly perceived objective frames of
reference.* You do no one a favor if you determine by yourself that
a norm is inappropriate and then proceed to lay about yourself with
a broadsword. Thus, take care to note both the techniques that follow and the sequence in which they appear. And remember that
patience and persistence may well be your most important weapons.

Accept the Norm. This advice has been given before. Accepting
a norm involves at least these three actions: (1) acknowledging the
reality of the norm; (2) understanding the meaning and implications of the norm; and (3) subjecting one's self to the influence of
the norm. There are two reasons for accepting the norm. First, it is
tactically necessary. In what is still a classical study of the process
of norm changing, Ferenc Merei demonstrated that would-be leaders who failed to accept the group's norms proved to be ineffectual
and did not become true leaders.[9] Merei's experiments used children
as subjects, but many other experiments and case studies, particularly those of therapists, confirm the point. He who would change
another's belief must first accept that belief.

The second reason for accepting the norm is that it subjects you
to its influence! Once you have accepted the norm, you may be less
inclined to change it because you may discover that it is much more
appropriate than it seemed before. However, if you accept the norm
and still find it wanting, you will have experienced the total impact
of the norm and will be in a better position to assess the scope of
your task of changing it. You will be ready to take the next step.

Analyze the Norm. This step contains three parts. First, you must
analyze the nature of the norm itself. Second, you must identify the
actual effects of the norm upon group process. (You probably began
both of these steps when you first determined that you had spotted
an inappropriate norm.) Third, you should try to discover why the
norm came into existence in the first place.

[9] Ferenc Merei, "Group Leadership and Institutionalization," *Human Relations,* Vol. 2 (1949), pp. 23-40.

When you analyze the nature of the norm you should ask several questions. Is the norm broad and general, capable of infinite interpretations, or is it rigid and specific? If it is the former, you may not need to change the norm at all. Altering the interpretation may serve the purpose. You should also ask whether the norm is clearly perceived or whether it is distorted. In an intriguing set of experiments Tuddenham found that distorted norms produced less conformity than unambiguous norms, but they still affected the group.[10] For illustrations of the use of distorted norms you may read some of the speeches that Mussolini and Hitler gave during their rise to power. These speeches are full of fascinating and horrifying examples of norms distorted to serve their purposes. Some of the finest norms of Christianity, national feeling, and pride became distorted into norms that apparently justified some of the most inhuman behavior the world has seen.

When you seek to examine the effect of the norm, you must be careful to establish whether the norm actually causes the effect you wish to change or whether something else is involved.[11] For example, many people become disturbed about the norms that govern the clothing worn today by unmarried young women. "Bathing suits are too revealing," they contend. "Girls should wear something more conservative." This may be, but another norm will probably negate the effect of more conservative bathing suits. Courtship procedures require that girls attract boys indirectly, and girls will probably go right on doing that as best they can.

Knowing the cause of the norm is important. The discussion here is about the forces that perpetuate a norm; not about the reason for bringing the norm into existence in the first place. The practice of oath-taking, for example, originated during a time when people believed that supernatural powers were invoked when certain words were uttered. If a man broke an oath, therefore, these supernatural powers would punish his transgression. Today, however, there is no reason to hold such belief in the magic of words. Requiring loyalty oaths of college professors and of certain students, for example,

[10] See Read D. Tuddenham, "The Influence of a Distorted Norm upon Individual Judgment," and "The Influence of an Avowedly Distorted Norm upon Individual Judgment," *Journal of Psychology*, Vol. 46 (October, 1958), pp. 227-241, and pp. 329-338.

[11] The techniques for this analysis are discussed in Chapter 6.

cannot be expected to keep Communists or any other presumably undesirable individuals out of schools. Most people are aware of this today, even if a decade ago they acted as if they were not.

The very process of tracking down the cause of an undesirable norm may sometimes be sufficient to modify or change it. Usually you have to begin by asking other group members if they know why a particular norm was adopted. Often the others do not know either, and your question may stimulate their curiosity and evaluation of the practice. For example, many organizations that insist upon sharply limiting the tenure of chairmen and prohibiting them from succeeding themselves had at one time some unfortunate experiences with chairmen who could not be controlled. Rules limiting tenure and succession were created to prevent anyone in the future from obtaining a stranglehold on the office. But these rules may also have the effect of turning a chairman out of office just about the time he begins to get the feeling of the job. Others may begin to suspect what you have begun to suspect—that the circumstances whereby a chairman may be reviewed and appraised are different now from the time when the rules were adopted. If so, the process of change has begun.

Analyze the Forces For and Against Change. There is no need for repetition here of the forces and their interrelations set out in Chapter 9. That information should serve as a framework for determining the reasons for the state of quasi-stationary equilibrium of any given norm.[12]

Condition the Group to Change. If you are in a position of leadership, you may make a variety of minor changes in the norm structure without causing resentment for having altered the basic norms themselves. Such minor changes serve the function of preparing the group to accept change itself.

But be careful. This step in the change process is most susceptible of abuse. Every dictator whose techniques we have had opportunity to observe has made extensive use of this technique. Every decline in standards that comes to our minds began with a series of "insignificant" changes. Change for the sake of change is not desirable. Arbitrary tinkering with procedures produces a

---

[12] See pp. 246-250.

confused situation that makes it impossible for members to predict what is happening and renders them increasingly dependent upon the leader. As Merei demonstrated, you can change the basic norms this way,[13] but you may also subvert the democratic process. The group's energies will be spent attempting to counteract the various changes until out of the confusion one of two things happens. Either a revolution will oust you as leader or the group will capitulate from exhaustion and frustration. Neither outcome is desirable!

Thus, when you make changes, remember that you hold the burden of proof for showing that you have a right to make the change and that the change is an improvement, and when called upon to account for your actions, remember what the previous chapter said about reporting the results of executive behavior.

Improve Perception of Forces. As has been pointed out again and again, the forces that operate upon the group are conditioned by the perceptions of the members. If a person believes that something exists, that something is real *for him* whether or not it has any basis in fact. Thus, regardless of your "objective" determination of the forces that may be operating, you must consider how the members of the group may be perceiving the forces, and work toward improving the communication that determines perception.

Lippitt, Watson, and Westley report a study by Lau which showed that:

. . . a preponderance of fraternity boys tended to believe that their fellow fraternity members were more "conservative" than they were themselves. When they were shown the results of a survey which revealed the real attitudes of the members of their own and other fraternity houses, the resulting discussions served as a stimulus toward change. That is to say, the distribution of correct information about the willingness of members to admit Negroes, Orientals, or Jews often led members to re-examine their opinion of what the official house membership practices should be.[14]

This particular perceptual shortcoming, the belief that others might not be ready to accept a change, is often seen. Not only does

---

[13] Merei, *op. cit.*
[14] Lippitt, Watson, and Westley, *op. cit.*, p. 41.

it make members less willing to express their true feelings, but it makes them resist attempts of others to effect the change because they believe that such pressures would disrupt group harmony. Turning back to the fraternity illustration, it is obvious that, *if* other members were as conservative as each individual suspected, there would be little point in a member or leader attempting to change the norms about group membership. The force against change might be too strong.

Of course, there are dozens of other perceptual distortions of the norms themselves or the forces operating for or against change. University freshmen, for example, "hear" that their professors are unapproachable and will ridicule attempts to seek assistance and that other students will regard attempts to talk with professors as apple-polishing. Thus, forces are created to keep the student from seeking faculty assistance when he is having academic difficulty. Perhaps the largest single objective of new student orientation at the University of Colorado is to convince the new student that these perceptions are almost completely inaccurate.

It will be helpful to recall here the discussion in Chapter 5 of the reasons for perceptual distortions and in both Chapters 5 and 11 of some means of improving objectivity. Fundamentally the reasons for perceptual distortions are one or more of the following: communicative failure of the source of information, failure to receive accurately sound information, or incapacity to evaluate properly conflicting or contradictory information. (Part V contains techniques for improving the communicative process.) When you suspect faulty perception is creating barriers to change, you must do two things: (1) find some means of discovering the correct information, (2) find some means of communicating this information to the others so that their perceptions become more realistic. Usually these steps will facilitate the change process.

Weaken or Eliminate Forces Against Change. One of the reasons that college professors are given tenure (continuous contracts) is to remove the fear of dismissal that may act as a force to keep them from discovering or advocating new knowledge or insights. In the Lewin food experiments, discussed in Chapter 2, making a public decision removed a force against change—the fear of innovating alone.[15] Both the tenure practice and the food experiment are examples of weakening or eliminating forces against change.

As pointed out in Chapter 9, increasing the forces *for* change tends to produce greater tension; decreasing the forces *against* change tends to reduce tension.[16] Thus, it is wise to first seek methods of decreasing forces against change. Unfortunately, most of us, when we are change agents, become so obsessed with the changed circumstances that seem to us to dictate the need for new norms that we fail to understand why others do not immediately adopt the change. If employees can get more money by working harder, why do they refuse to step up production? They may fear social ostracism. If restrictive management practices have been demonstrated as ineffective, why do many managers refuse to discard those practices? They perhaps feel personally inadequate in the new role. Since speeding is so obviously a cause of accidents, why cannot teenagers be easily persuaded to drive more conservatively? They may need opportunities to demonstrate courage and skill. In each of these instances experimentation has shown that norms can be changed when these forces against change have been eliminated.

Sometimes you personally will have the power to work directly on the force. Sometimes you will have to use the total resources of the group to make changes in forces that tend to restrict change. Sometimes you will find it desirable to go outside the limits of the group to find people who have either the power, the perceptions, or the skill to effect changes. Sometimes you may have to relinquish power in order to remove some of the restraining forces. But whatever the means, remember that your task of changing norms will be much easier if you can remove or reduce forces against change.

Strengthen or Add Forces for Change. Too often the change agent who perceives the need for changing norms skips all the previous steps and begins to push his group into the change. It should now be clear that this step should be the last one. If possible, you should avoid it altogether since group members who are conscientious about their task should be themselves producing forces for change.

[15] Kurt Lewin, "Group Decision and Social Change," in T. M. Newcomb and E. L. Hartley, eds., *Readings in Social Psychology* (New York: Holt, 1947), pp. 330-344. See the discussion of this experiment on pp. 27-28.

[16] See pp. 246-247.

If group standards are too low, for example, the more able members will surely become concerned. If you have been able to clear up inadequate perceptions of existing forces and have been able to remove some of the forces against change, the group may adopt higher standards and be almost unaware of the fact that they have changed.

Having properly managed the other steps, however, the change agent should not feel guilty if he finds it necessary to strengthen or add forces for change. The group may well need prodding to overcome the inertia of established habit.

Strengthening or adding forces for change means simply that the change agent must utilize whatever powers[17] he possesses that seem appropriate to the occasion. If the change agent does not possess the powers directly, he must persuade those who do hold power to utilize it. In either case beware of extremes—one does not use a cannon to shoot a rabbit. The dangers of overdoing are at least as great as the dangers of leaving the situation alone.

Punitive powers should obviously be avoided if at all possible. Positive rewards should be used. People will usually work much harder to get something than to avoid some kind of punishment. And the consequences for group harmony are much better if the change agent does not have to use threats or actual punishment.[18]

Be patient! Long established norms are extremely difficult to change, and even relatively newly established norms may be difficult. Often the best that the change agent can hope for is a little less or a little more of a particular kind of behavior. Often we become impatient at what seems grossly inappropriate behavior, and, as mentioned earlier, most people should become more capable of change. But when we think about it for a moment, we should be glad that people are not capable of being swayed by every breeze

[17] We discussed the nature of these powers in Chapter 8 and in Chapter 12 we dealt specifically with the matter of the proper use of reward and punishment. See pp. 203-207 and pp. 333-337 respectively.

[18] We have discussed with insurance agents the application of these concepts to selling insurance. A number of years ago the prevailing practice was to "back the hearse up to the door" when selling insurance. Today the basic practice is estate planning. The threat approach, they found, worked only with low income, unsophisticated families. The practice changed when insurance agents discovered that they were much more successful using an approach that helped the buyer obtain a balanced program to effectively manage his estate. The emphasis shifted to positive rewards, and this worked with the more sophisticated buyer.

that blows. If they were, predictability would become only a dream. What was settled today would be discarded tomorrow. As it is, change is difficult but not impossible. The skilled and conscientious change agent *can* do much to improve his group's norms.

IMPROVING GROUP CLIMATE

As shown in Chapter 7, if the group wishes to obtain the maximum benefit from collaboration, the group climate must be cooperative. The advantages of cooperation seem unequivocal, yet we have all observed groups whose climate is characterized by suspicion and competition rather than cooperation. Members have to "be on their toes" all the time lest another gain some advantage. When the discussion is over, everyone is exhausted and the only gains appear to be some shifting of the relative interpersonal standings.

The theory presented in Chapter 7 suggests that in most groups there are opportunities for both competition and cooperation. When the group goal is of overriding importance, the opportunities for competition may be sharply limited. But usually groups do not confront task demands of such magnitude that cooperation is virtually dictated. Thus, in most groups the climate will warrant attention and often correction, *and the climate can be improved!* Specific experimental evidence shows that groups may be trained to make significant improvements in their group's climate.[19]

Let us first look at some common problems that may result in an unfortunate group climate and next examine a series of steps designed to harmonize interpersonal conflict in particular and improve group climate in general.

Common Problems

The objective here is the same as that of identifying some inappropriate norms. Some of the most significant problems that give rise to competitive behavior are identified.

[19] The basis for most of the advice given here is research done by Harnack and reported in R. Victor Harnack, "An Experimental Study of the Effects of Training in the Recognition and Formulation of Goals upon Intra-Group Cooperation," *Speech Monographs,* Vol. 22 (March, 1955), pp. 31-38. See Chapter 7, pp. 171-176 for the discussion of theory referred to above.

Competition for Reward. This is an excellent method of stimulating *individual* effort, and our society makes considerable use of it. Prizes of one sort or another are eagerly sought in hundreds of contests. But when *collaborative* behavior is required, competition for reward must be discarded. This point should be obvious from the discussion in Chapter 7 of the nature of competition and cooperation. The group should be careful to see that rewards are determined upon the basis of attaining standards of excellence, not upon the basis of worsting another.[20]

Competition for Limited Resources. According to nineteenth century Darwinism, this was supposed to account for intraspecies' competition with the result being the "survival of the fittest." Certainly, limited resources can give rise to competition, especially intergroup competition, but it need not. Margaret Mead reports studies of primitive people living on the edge of starvation who do not resort to competition.[21] Rather cooperation of the highest sort is often called for since they dare not waste their energies or the resources themselves in struggle for possession. In the past score of years the world has seen examples of prisoners of war cooperating completely in the allocation of food and clothing. We have also witnessed degrading breakdowns of this cooperation in some of the prison camps in Korea. The fundamental fact is this: resources are almost always limited, compared with an ideal at least; individuals or groups may either compete for these resources or set up rules for equitable management of them. Thus, when competition for limited resources becomes troublesome, groups should establish rules to render wasteful competition unnecessary.

Failure to Distinguish Appropriate Areas of Competition. Competition, as already seen, may often be very good, but sometimes individuals find it difficult to judge where and when competition should be the order of the day. One of the chief functions of the United States Chamber of Commerce, for example, is to help businessmen *cooperate* to promote the health of business in their communities. At the same time these businessmen *compete* for customers. Dozens

[20] See the discussion in Chapter 12 of the problems of rewarding.
[21] Margaret Mead, ed., *Cooperation and Competition among Primitive Peoples* (New York: McGraw-Hill, 1937).

of other organizations are established for similar purposes—to help people identify areas in which their goals are complementary and should thus stimulate cooperation. Often, however, individuals become so blinded by the pursuit of antagonistic goals that they miss opportunities to cooperate and thereby make substantial improvements in their lot. In adult training classes both businessmen and labor representatives, asked whether they thought that the goals of labor were more complementary or antagonistic to those of business, were divided in their answers. It is obvious, however, that there are large areas in which cooperation makes more sense than competition.

Confusion of Competition and Controversy. It has already been noted that some people seem incapable of handling controversy. When someone differs with them, they seem to assume that he is the embodiment of everything they do not like. Thus, his personal defeat becomes mandatory. There is little that can be done about such people, so the real concern is with those who, when engaging in controversy, forget the prime goal, an examination of the problem, and substitute the goal of having their position adopted by the rest of the group. The line is difficult to draw. If we feel keenly about a matter, it is easy to begin to attribute personal malice to those who differ with us. The discussion becomes more heated, and soon any semblance of cooperation is gone. "Winning" such debates may be catastrophic, and particularly so for the "victor."

Confusion of Rivalry and Competition. Margaret Mead makes a useful distinction between rivalry and competition.

. . . whereas competition was behavior oriented toward a goal in which the other competitors for that goal were secondary, rivalry was behavior oriented toward another human being, whose worsting was the primary goal, and object or position for which they competed was secondary.[22]

Kept within appropriate bounds, rivalry is often a stimulating and effective incentive *within highly cooperative groups*. Often associates, who are close personal friends and who exhibit every evidence of cooperation, nevertheless stimulate each other by outstanding work. Probably all of us recall some instances of productive activity

[22] *Ibid.*, p. 17.

that would have been less satisfying without the stimulus of friendly rivalry.

For rivalry to be effective, the rivals must be rather evenly matched, and each party must take care that the rivalry does not get out of hand for when it does, energy and resources are wasted.

Again, more problems could be described, but this suggestive list should be adequate for a basic analysis. Though some remedies have already been suggested, let us look at some more.

Restructuring Goals

Whenever possible, we must restructure the situation itself in order to improve the group climate. If we can modify the bases of reward or establish rules for managing limited resources, we can do much to improve climate. However, when the competition is the result of pursuing antagonistic goals *set by members themselves and not dictated by the situation,* we must start helping members restructure their own goals in order to create and emphasize complementary goals. As pointed out in Chapter 7, the multiplicity of problems and consequent goals present in any discussion allows opportunity for discussants to emphasize "goal clusters" that may be either complementary or antagonistic. What can we do about it?

The basic principle is to concentrate upon *goals* and not upon *motives* that may be impelling individuals toward those goals. We cannot deal directly with motives; they are complicated, personal, and usually a mystery to the people driven by them. But we can identify and evaluate the goals for which people are striving. There may be dozens of reasons why a man wants to be promoted to a particular job, for example. Even if we were professional psychiatrists we would be hard put to identify them. But we can talk meaningfully about the nature of that job, its obligations and opportunities, its present and its future. Academic advisors do this all the time when they help a student choose what he wants for a major field. Thus, each individual should wrestle with his own motives while other individuals should confine themselves to examining the goals that he seeks. This examination of goals has three aspects.

Sensitize to the Effects of Goals. This brings us back to one of the basic considerations of problem solving discussed in Chapter 4.

Many people are simply unaware of the goals they seek.[23] This lack of awareness hampers solving problems of interpersonal relations just as much as it hampers solving any problem.

First, you must become sensitized to your own goals; you must put yourself under the microscope and discover exactly what you are trying to accomplish. If you discover that some of your goals are antagonistic to the goals of others, you have at least three courses of action open to you. You may disregard the consequences and plunge blindly ahead; you may bring the matter out into the open and indicate your desire to compete; or you may attempt to restructure your own goals so that they become predominantly complementary. If you choose the third alternative, you must abandon or suppress those goals that are antagonistic. In their stead you may emphasize existing complementary goals, substitute new complementary goals, or both.

Suppose that you want to be designated chairman of a subgroup. Another member wants the same office. Your choice is clear. If you want the chairmanship badly enough, you may decide to compete even though you are likely to create animosities. For any of a number of reasons this may be your wisest choice. If, however, you decide that your reasons for selecting this goal are largely to obtain personal gratification, you may decide to give it up. You will then concentrate upon doing a good job as a member. Some time later you may decide that a similar goal is important enough to warrant fighting for. Then your previous action may be very helpful in avoiding unfortunate repercussions.

Helping others to become sensitive to their own goals is not so simple. Asking leading questions is about the only way you can focus another's attention upon the consequences of his behavior. Sometimes you may do this in the context of a discussion, and sometimes in between-meeting conversations. Often such sensitizing may be handled in the same manner as that recommended in the last chapter for improving participation. If things have gotten out of hand, you may need to bring the group up short and turn their attention, as a group, to the problem of examining the goals that have generated the trouble.

Discuss Some Goals Openly. When an antagonistic situation has either developed or is developing, it is often wise to call a halt to the

[23] See pp. 71-73.

wrangling, summarize the positions, and describe what seem to you to be some of the goals of the competing individuals. This serves both to sensitize others to goals and to start an examination of at least some of them. Of course, when you are identifying goals, you will be careful to mention only those that are quite obvious and will not embarrass anyone involved. You may discuss goals as an integral part of your summary of what has been said. By beginning to consider content problem goals, you may suggest the existence of personal goals that may be causing trouble. Possibly by this means you may stimulate others to discuss openly their goals; almost certainly you may start others thinking privately about their own goals and their effects upon group climate.

Search for Substitute Goals. You cannot ask another, directly or indirectly, to give up some goals without helping him find some substitute goals. For example, if one member has been critical of some group projects, perhaps contending that action has been hasty and ill-considered, you may suggest that he head a committee to study means of developing efficient operating methods. See what has happened. The member's goal, whatever his motive, has been to block further action. Now he has an opportunity to set as a goal the streamlining of operating methods. This was essentially the technique that President Truman employed when he appointed former President Hoover to head a group charged with studying means of improving the operations of the executive department of the federal government. Mr. Hoover remained, of course, a critic of the policies of the Truman administration. But he was able to pursue a complementary goal of improving government operations. Mr. Truman himself estimated that Mr. Hoover's work saved the government billions of dollars.

Sometimes the individual will be able to see for himself the wisdom of exchanging some antagonistic goals for complementary goals, but sometimes, he will need some help if he is to strike a reasonable bargain with the rest of the group.

Allow Opportunity to Change Without Losing Face

Often when an antagonistic member becomes convinced of the desirability of restructuring some of his goals, he finds that he is not in a position to change. The group has been badgering him and ganging up on him. In short, the rest of the members have adopted the goal of defeating him. Now, if he changes, he may appear foolish or weak-willed. He doesn't want to appear as either and thus he may continue his antagonistic behavior for reasons other than those that launched him on the behavior. But whatever the reasons, the result is the same. He is balking, rather than helping, the group. And you and the rest of the group are to blame!

The remedy is simple. Leave him alone for a while. Let him change his behavior as unobtrusively as possible. Don't force him to admit publicly that he was wrong and intends to mend his ways. If some notice of the change must be made, continue to make the charitable assumptions discussed in Chapter 11.[24] Allow that he may have misunderstood or been misunderstood and that no dramatic change has taken place. Often skillful leaders get a group to drop an issue directly and proceed on the tacit assumption that the differences have been resolved. When the issue finally comes up for a vote, the whole matter is quietly settled.

There is evidence that the above procedure is often used in labor-management negotiations. When certain concessions are made, the other side prudently refrains from making any issue of the concession in order not to embarrass the negotiators in the eyes of those whom they represent.

Always remember that, unless the circumstances have changed dramatically, it is asking a great deal of an individual to admit that he was wrong. Count as your triumph not his changed behavior, but the positive task accomplishment itself.

DEVELOPING GROUP MATURITY

Developing group maturity, like developing personal maturity, takes time, and, in both cases, much maturation will take place without conscious effort on the part of anyone. But, just as a parent or teacher does not take the child's maturity for granted, neither do good leaders assume that groups will mature without paying attention to the process. What leaders do may hasten or retard development of group maturity. Many parents actually attempt to retard the maturation of their children, wishing to keep their children dependent upon them. So too, many leaders deliberately retard the matura-

[24] See pp. 280-281.

tion of their groups for similar reasons. After all, maturity implies greater independence, and the leader of a mature group is much more the servant than the master of it.

One of the quickest methods of developing group maturity is to weed out those clearly incompetent members and replace them with exceptionally able individuals. Whenever the leader has an opportunity to do this, he usually does so as a matter of course. Employers either fire or refuse to take up contract options of inferior employees, then attempt to hire superior individuals. But even with able members, as was pointed out in Chapter 7, maturity is not automatic.[25] Much work still remains.

Provide Maturation Requirements

Chapter 7 listed four maturation requirements. They were: a justifiable *raison d'etre,* realistic opportunities for progressive success, promise of continuity, and promise of intergroup status. Here are some techniques for approaching each requirement:

Justifiable Raison d'Etre. Every group should periodically reexamine its reason for existence. This activity is closely related to extending and defining the group's area of control and to the process of creating involvement by relating individual goals to group goals.[26] The circumstances that originally called a group into being have a habit of changing and the group must change too, or go out of business. Further, new members may not be aware of some of the objectives that originally constituted the group's task. A whole new collection of members may have replaced the founders, and the new group may remain forever infantile if the members do not examine and accept as their own the *raison d'etre* of the group.

There is no better illustration of changing *raison d'etre* and the consequent need for periodic reexamination than the role that fraternities and sororities play in most colleges. At one time such organizations provided the bulk of social opportunities on a campus. Further, they controlled campus politics in such a way that anyone

---

[25] See Chapter 7, pp. 176-181 for a discussion of the theory of group maturity.

[26] See Chapter 7, pp. 166-170, for a discussion of area of control and Chapter 12, p. 320, for a discussion of the process of relating individual goals to group goals.

who wished to be somebody simply had to belong, and often to a certain select group of houses, or be cast aside. Not infrequently job opportunities after college were enhanced by the individual's fraternal affiliations during college. Today, however, this preeminent position has largely disappeared. At the University of Colorado, for example, fewer than thirty per cent of the students are "Greek." Highly organized programs in residence halls and university-wide organizations make it possible for independents as well as Greeks to obtain many social and political opportunities. Fraternal affiliations are not needed to obtain jobs. Fraternities and sororities have had to make noticeable changes. Libraries are replacing recreation rooms as these groups are placing more emphasis upon scholarship. "Help Week" is replacing "Hell Week" all over the country.[27] And in many additional ways fraternal organizations are seeking to adapt themselves to changing conditions. Today there is much evidence of more mature groups than a few years ago.

Realistic Opportunities for Progressive Successes. Success is meaningless, of course, unless there is some opportunity for failure. Cooperative groups, moreover, are much less likely to be crippled by early failures than individuals working alone, as Lichtenberg discovered.[28] Thus, leaders should not set up "straw men" for their groups to conquer for this will defeat the objectives of involvement and creation of a justifiable *raison d'etre*. But by the same token, the leader should not confront the group with the toughest task at the outset.

Enhancing success probability is partly a problem of both long-range and short-range agenda planning. Long-range planning suggests that the leader set not only simpler tasks in early meetings but tasks that may be completed and the effects observed rather quickly. With a history of demonstrable successes behind it, a group may approach more complicated and drawn-out tasks with more assurance.

[27] This may not be an unmixed blessing. Aronson and Mills found a positive correlation between severity of initiation and liking for a group. Within bounds, the more severe the initiation, the greater the initiate's liking for the group. Thus, fraternal cohesiveness may well suffer as initiation becomes more bland. See Elliot Aronson and Judson Mills, "The Effect of Severity of Initiation on Liking for a Group," *Journal of Abnormal and Social Psychology,* Vol. 59 (September, 1959), pp. 177-181.

[28] Philip Lichtenberg, "Reactions to Success and Failure During Individual and Cooperative Effort," *Journal of Social Psychology,* Vol. 46 (August, 1957), pp. 31-34.

Short-range planning concerns the order of the items on the agenda for a given meeting. Place on the agenda for early consideration those items that are least likely to arouse controversy and may be handled with dispatch. Leave the longer, not necessarily the more difficult or important, items further down the line.

The time-wasting practice of using group meetings to make routine reports was mentioned earlier. One way to modify this norm, and to hasten maturity at the same time, is to place such routine reporting as seems necessary toward the *end* rather than the beginning of an agenda. If the group runs out of time, such reports may be either abbreviated or circulated in written form after the meeting. This is an example of a minor change that may lead to major changes. It also enhances the possibilities of success by the simple expedient of allowing more time for group deliberation on those items that merit group action. Nothing is more frustrating than spending half a meeting with routine matters and then having to stop some significant task just short of accomplishment because time has run out.

Finally, groups should not expect to solve some problems at one sitting. Make sure that the rest of the members understand when you believe that the task will require more than one meeting. Then set specific goals to be accomplished during the meeting, such as preliminary examination of the problem, assignment of research responsibilities and brainstorming potential solutions. Recognize that, though the group needs to feel a sense of accomplishment, that need not necessarily mean the completion of an entire problem-solving task.

Promise of Continuity. You can do nothing on this score if the group is to disband when a particular task is completed. However, if there is honest justification for continuing the group and if there is possibility of its making additional positive contributions, you should do everything in your power to obtain assurances of continuity from those responsible for creating the group. Nonetheless, the continuity of a group is a situational factor that you may or may not be able to affect.

Promise of Intergroup Status. In addition to emphasizing to the members the significance of their work, you must keep reminding the group of its potential intergroup status. You should also point out evidences of success and recognition. Discovering that others are taking note of the group's accomplishments is a strong force for producing a cohesive and cooperative climate. Whether accomplishments receive favorable notice from outsiders or not, it is wise to review periodically the group's accomplishments. When the group is embroiled in a particularly difficult task, members are likely to become discouraged. Reminding them of some of their past accomplishments may be just the spur needed to overcome discouragement.

These are some techniques for providing maturation requirements. Two additional suggestions may also hasten group maturity.

Share Leadership

If you do not share leadership, you keep members overly dependent on you.[29] The group in which leadership potential is limited to one or two individuals will remain immature, and if other members never have opportunity to exercise leadership, they are not likely to develop their leadership potential.

For leadership to be shared, the members must see the task as urgent and they must have opportunity to perform functions in keeping with their ability. The next chapter shows how the task can be presented as urgent. Here are offered some suggestions for giving members leadership opportunities.

Appoint Others Chairmen of Subgroups. Many times parts of tasks can be "farmed out" to subgroups, and leadership of such groups is an excellent proving ground for more significant responsibilities in the main group.

Let the Group Meet Without You. When you must be absent at the stated time for the group meeting, do not always postpone the meeting. Get in touch with one or more promising members, brief them about your agenda and other plans, and let them serve for you in your absence. Sometimes good leaders deliberately contrive to be absent from meetings in order to give others opportunities.

Obviously Restrict the Scope of Your Functions. Though it has already been suggested that a leader should avoid controlling the

[29] See Chapter 10, pp. 262-266.

content decisions, you can go one step further and make it apparent that you are not controlling them. Another way to restrict the scope of your functions is to call attention to the need for having someone perform some of the functions listed in Chapter 11 and indicate that you believe some member, other than you, should perform them.

Occasionally Sit Back and Wait. For this technique to work, the group must be strongly motivated to accomplish the task. If they are, others will step forward to assume leadership tasks. Be warned, however, that others are likely to become impatient and irritated with you, *particularly if your behavior is patronizing,* or if you are simply shirking the performance of some routine tasks.

Encourage Reasoned Controversy

We have repeatedly emphasized the value of controversy. We do not wish to belabor the point, but we do wish to make one suggestion for developing the group's capacity for controversy and thus hastening maturity.

In the early stages of a group's development it often discusses a matter, discovers no apparent disagreement, and proceeds rather blandly to a conclusion. Before the group accepts the conclusion, however, you might try something like this: "We all seem to be in accord on this matter, but I know that some others outside this group do not share this view. Just to make sure that we haven't overlooked some important matters, why don't I play the role of 'devil's advocate' and raise all the arguments I can think of *against* the proposal. Maybe some of the rest want to share my role." Then you may role-play someone who feels differently from prevailing group sentiment. As a result the group may witness a demonstration of the use of controversy as a means of *illuminating* an issue rather than as a means of *defeating* an opponent. All of the benefits of role playing are apparent here. Further, the group may discover that its previous examination was superficial and that the conclusion must be reexamined. And still further, you may discover that not everyone was in as complete accord as it seemed at first. Some may not have liked the conclusion but did not know quite why or did not know how to make their feelings known. Of course you must restrict your use of this technique to issues wherein genuine controversy is possible, but if it is, this can be a potent means of hastening group maturity.

SUMMARY

Able individuals *can* affect the nature of their groups, but they should be careful to avoid trickery or manipulation as they attempt to change others.

In discussing the creation of new norms a number of typically inappropriate norms were pointed out: time-wasters, including use of meeting time for routine reports and use of meetings to spread responsibility; talk-action imbalance; unrealistic standards; and opposition to change itself. Producing change requires patience and attention to a step-by-step procedure. First, the change agent must accept the norm; second, he must analyze the norm to determine its nature, its effects, and the reasons for its existence in the beginning; third, he must analyze the forces for and against change; fourth, he must condition the group to change in general; fifth, he must improve the members' perception of existing forces; sixth, he should work to weaken or eliminate forces against change; and, finally, he should strengthen or add forces for change if necessary.

Several common problems often give rise to poor group climate. Competition for reward, competition for limited resources, failure to distinguish appropriate areas of competition, confusion of competition and controversy, and confusion of rivalry and competition are often reasons for poor interpersonal relations. The basic procedure for improving group climate is restructuring goals rather than becoming overly concerned about motives. This requires sensitizing others to the effects of goals, discussing some goals openly, and searching for substitute goals. Asking people to change behavior should be done in a fashion that allows them to save face.

We cannot simply hope that groups will "grow up" by themselves. Secure leaders should hasten the process. The leader should first see to it that the maturation requirements (Chapter 7) are present. That is, the group must continually examine and adopt a justifiable *raison d'etre;* the leader should take care that the group can experience success; he should do what he can to increase the possibilities of continuity; and he should help the group feel pride in their accomplishments. In addition, leadership should be shared by appointing others chairmen of subgroups, letting the group meet without the leader, restricting the scope of the leader's functions, and occasionally sitting back and waiting for the group to move ahead. Finally, the leader should encourage reasoned controversy by using the technique of the "devil's advocate."

In affecting any of the changes discussed in this chapter, some outside consultant is often helpful. A prophet is not without honor, save in his own country. And sometimes a person who is somewhat removed from the issues may be in a better position to notice the need for change and to suggest procedures for making it than the members of the group. For these reasons management consulting has recently become a big business in this country. Schools engage curriculum consultants. The United States sends military consultants to aid the armed forces of many other countries. Some wit once defined a consultant as a man with a briefcase who is away from home. In a few cases he may be little more than that, but often the fresh perspective is just what the group needs to jar itself out of a rut. Of course, you will usually want to seek a trained specialist. If the consultant is one who has specialized in the problems of group discussion, he may often be able to make significant contributions to the improvement of the operations of a group *even when he is not trained in the matters that the group discusses.* Don't hesitate to admit that you may need help. And when you ask for help, get well informed substantive experts and get equally well trained discussion specialists!

EXERCISES

1. The differences in and sources of group norms can be illustrated well by a simple experiment based on preferences for art. Secure three or four pictures ranging from realism to extreme abstractionism (Grant Wood to Jackson Pollock), and of sufficient size to be readily seen by the class. Exhibit each in turn and then ask the class to vote as to which picture is preferred. Then proceed to a discussion of the bases for choice, the changes in preference the class members have experienced over the past four to six years, and the forces producing the change. Repeat the experiment with other groups of significantly different economic, social, or educational backgrounds.

2. Analyze the stated or implied norms of two or three groups to which you belong. Which norms do you judge to be inappropriate? Why? How could you proceed to effect a change? Discuss your observations with another member of each group. On the bases of these analyses,

select one or two changes you feel to be most desirable and possible and attempt to put your theory into practice.

3. Analyze some group's standard that you feel to be unrealistic. Attempt to determine the degree to which members are aware of the relative level of the standard, the source of the standard, and the possibility for change. What suggestions would you have for producing positive change?

4. Compare two or more groups of widely different age levels in their resistance to change. What factors do you feel contribute to rigidity or flexibility? How would you suggest group leaders or members proceed in each case? To what degree are we justified in generalizing concerning the relationship between age and change?

5. In this chapter we suggested that the change agent accept the group's norm as a first step to producing change. How can this action be consistent with advice given elsewhere to retain one's personal integrity and the emphasis placed on the value of concepts and controversy? Prepare a statement of distinctions to guide the group member.

6. Plan an experiment to condition a group to change. This can be a a class project or it can be developed by a small number of individuals. Keep a careful record of techniques employed, group reaction and estimated long-range potentials. Employing observers may be helpful to increase objectivity. Finally, organize a discussion among the experimenters (and some subjects too if appropriate and possible) to consider the effects and the ethics of the conditioning.

7. Plan an analytical survey of opinions of group members concerning the change of some recognized and accepted norm. The norm need not be the same for each group. For each group surveyed, ask one-third of the members what they think about a change. Ask another third what forces they feel tend to suggest change. Ask the final third what forces they feel tend to prevent change. Compare the replies *within* each group. What do you note as to number, specificity, intensity and related characteristics of the responses? Is it possible to compare responses *between* groups? What do you observe? What have you learned with respect to producing changes in these norms for these groups? For groups in general?

8. Plan a role-playing situation that presents the potentials of one or more of the following group situations:
   a. Competition for limited resources, or
   b. Confusion of appropriate areas of competition, or
   c. Confusion of controversy and competition
   d. Need for substitute goals.
   e. Need to save face while accepting change.

Following the presentation, conduct a discussion to analyze what occurred and how the situation might be handled more constructively.

9. Join with one or two class members to explore and analyze the climate existing in some group that is available for observation. What are its strengths and weaknesses in this area? What forces produced and sustained the situation? To what degree has the group succeeded in resolving the problem of individual and group goals? Are the group's goals clear and reasonable? To what degree do you believe change is required? What do you estimate are the possibilities of productive adjustment?

10. Conduct a survey of representative members of three to four groups to determine their (a) understanding of the group objectives, and (b) their judgments of the group's value or contribution. If possible, compare member perception of purposes with known, written, or stated group objectives. Also attempt to observe one or more meetings of the group surveyed. What do you conclude as to group maturity, function and needs? If you were the group leader, what would you do?

11. Analyze your behavior in a group (leader or member) as it enhances or hinders the development of group maturity. Formulate a specific program that you feel will be productive. Consistently evaluate the results as you attempt to put the program into effect.

SELECTED READINGS

Benne, Kenneth D., and Muntyan, Bozidar, eds., *Human Relations in Curriculum Change.* Circular Series A, No. 51, Illinois Secondary School Curriculum Program Bulletin, No. 7, 1949.

Group Dynamics: Research and Theory, 2nd ed., Dorwin Cartwright and Alvin Zander, eds. Evanston, Ill., Row, Peterson, 1960, Parts III and IV.

Lippitt, Ronald, Watson, Jeanne, and Westley, Bruce, *The Dynamics of Planned Change.* New York, Harcourt, Brace & World, 1958.

Merei, Ferenc, "Group Leadership and Institutionalization." *Human Relations,* Vol. 2 (1949), pp. 23-40.

The Study of Leadership, C. G. Browne and Thomas S. Cohn, eds. Danville, Ill., The Interstate Printers & Publishers, 1958, Part IV.

CHAPTER **14**

Moving the Group to Action

And indeed there will be time
For the yellow smoke that slides along the street,
Rubbing its back upon the window-panes;
There will be time, there will be time
To prepare a face to meet the faces that you meet;
There will be time to murder and create,
And time for all works and days of hands
That lift and drop a question on your plate;
Time for you and time for me,
And time yet for a hundred indecisions,
And for a hundred visions and revisions,
Before the taking of a toast and tea.

T. S. Eliot*

Surely one of the most persistent criticisms of committees in particular and group discussion in general is that groups take so much time to accomplish anything. "If you want something accomplished," some say, "give it to an individual."

The reasons why groups are reluctant to accept task requirements and to come to some conclusion are spelled out in Chapter 9.[1] Groups tend to vacillate between the goals of task accomplishment

---

* From *The Love Song of J. Alfred Prufrock*, in *T. S. Eliot: The Complete Poems and Plays* (New York: Harcourt, Brace & World, Inc., 1952), p. 4 and in *Collected Poems* (London: Faber & Faber Ltd.).

[1] See pp. 246-250.

and internal harmony. The leader paradox is directly traceable to this vacillation. Moreover, many individuals fear to accept genuine problems and thus subject themselves to task pressures. Insulated and witch-hunting groups manage to create bogus tasks rather than genuine tasks.[2] Yes, for many reasons groups often fail to come to grips with a task and accomplish it with reasonable dispatch.

This chapter is in one sense a culmination of all previous chapters. Mature, cooperative, and realistic groups are able to undertake and complete significant tasks. Groups whose norms include high standards and willingness to accept change will rather easily face up to task challenges. When groups contain able members who are personally involved in group activities, initiating and terminating action are seldom difficult. Certainly, a group whose members think together effectively should be able to conclude a task with dispatch. In short, almost every virtue we seek in a group will contribute directly to task acceptance and completion.

This chapter is in another sense a foundation upon which all the rest of the advice must build. Group member commitment to task objectives energizes the group, stimulates research, permits leadership sharing, and builds cooperation and maturity. Task accomplishment is focal in our analysis of the relation of the individual to his group. It is the basis for the distinctions made in Chapter 3 between groups with personal purposes and groups with task purposes.[3]

Thus, those who wish to improve the character of their groups must be concerned at every stage with the effective and satisfying management of tasks. We cannot first build a well rounded group and then set it to work. Neither can we cajole an immature group into acepting a task and expect that all other problems will take care of themselves.

This chapter is relatively brief because the theoretical advantages of task commitment have already been discussed, as have the consequences of failure to cope satisfactorily with tasks. The techniques presented have stood the trial of use, and their support is primarily anecdotal rather than experimental, because to create, experimentally, task pressures that approximate those found in "real life" discussion situations is difficult. While many experiments utilize

[2] See Chapter 4, pp. 77-78.
[3] See pp. 41-47. There we indicate our primary concern with task purposes and learning purposes rather than personal purposes.

"task relevance" or "task intensity" as experimental variables, the techniques of creating relevance, intensity, and similar forces in the experimental situation can seldom be adapted to most normal discussion situations. Hence, the experience and testimony of successful practitioners of discussion arts must be relied upon.[4]

INITIATING ACTION

Some assumptions must be made clear before proceeding. It is assumed that the task requirements have not been levied upon, or created by, the group as a whole.[5] That is, whether the task requirement originated outside the group or within it, relatively few members have come to appreciate fully the significance of the task and the desirability of having the group undertake the task. It is assumed that the group's leaders are among those who appreciate the significance and intensity of the task requirements. It follows with a high probability that the task is indeed significant and not simply a personal "pet" of one of the leaders. The advice here is directed toward the group's leaders, since they normally have sufficient influence capacity to affect the behavior of the other group members. However, the advice may be adapted rather easily to individuals standing lower in the leadership hierarchy, even though they have less influence. Their "group" will consist of the main group's leaders rather than the group as a whole.[6]

The fundamental premise underlying this advice is that group members must adopt for themselves the goal of accomplishing the task. If they simply go through the motions of complying with a task requirement, the values of group participation will be sharply limited. If the goal of task accomplishment becomes every member's goal, quality of participation will be improved and problems of successfully terminating action will be greatly reduced. Thus, simply getting the group to start work on a task is not sufficient. Failure to secure commitment often causes drawn-out argument and watered-down compromises.

[4] See, for example, Ronald Lippitt, Jeanne Watson, and Bruce Westley, *The Dynamics of Planned Change* (New York: Harcourt, Brace & World, 1958), particularly Chapter 7, "Initiating Planned Change."

[5] Almost the whole of Chapter 9 is relevant at this point. Note particularly the sections entitled "Task Requirements" and "Resultant Forces."

[6] Recall the discussion in Chapter 8, pp. 201-202, of pair and set events.

Chapter 9 showed that a task may be characterized by its stability, complexity, intensity, and attractiveness.[7] These characteristics form the framework for the discussion of techniques in the pages that follow. These techniques are not arranged in a time sequence; nor must leaders use each technique. Each leader must judge for himself in each situation which techniques are needed and which will have the fewest unfortunate repercussions. He must always keep in mind the nature and potential consequences of the "leader paradox."

Stabilize Task Requirements

Little need be said about this technique. The leader must be careful to avoid jumping from one task to another. When he feels beset by many tasks to accomplish, he is tempted to confront the group with too many and too varied tasks. The same leader also is tempted to push a task onto a group before clearly determining that the group's area of control extends over that task. Giving groups tasks and then pulling those tasks away before they are half completed is a sure way to create tension. A wiser practice is to be more selective and to confront the group with only those tasks that are clearly significant and within the province of the group's control.

Emphasize Success Potential

Two issues are important here. First, the group must perceive their abilities and skills to be equal to the task. Second, the group must perceive that they have, or can obtain, the necessary resources to accomplish the task. Recall from the previous chapter how early successes can be used to hasten group maturity. Here the concern is with helping groups to perceive accurately their chances of success.

Before attempting to convince others of the success potential of the group, however, the leader should check the accuracy of his own perceptions. Evidence suggests that leaders tend to overestimate their own capacity while those lower in status tend also to overestimate the leaders' capacities but *underestimate* their own.[8] Typically, then, leaders will tend to be overambitious for themselves and

---

[7] See pp. 224-227.

[8] O. J. Harvey, "An Experimental Approach to the Study of Status Relations in Informal Groups," *American Sociological Review*, Vol. 18 (1953), pp. 357-367.

their groups while followers will tend to be overcautious. With this warning in mind, the leader should seek to help others perceive accurately the group's success potential. This perception may be accomplished in at least two ways.

Praise Individual Abilities. You can kill two birds with this stone. Few people are not pleased to be praised, if it be genuine praise and not mere flattery, and such praise can help others raise their sights. Of course, you will assess and praise those skills that are relevant to the task to be accomplished.

When do you praise? You will naturally praise individual abilities when the task is introduced and when the group is considering whether they have the skills necessary to undertake that task. You may also use praise during individual conferences before the task is formally presented to the group as a whole. More about this technique later.

Assess Existing and Potential Resources. What is needed to accomplish the task? Information? Special facilities? Special equipment? Money? Cooperation from other groups, institutions, or individuals? Your group must know that these and other needed resources are available or can be secured before they can feel confident about the group's success potential. You can assess these existing and potential resources in at least three ways. Obviously, you can look them up yourself. You can ask other group members (not necessarily the whole group) to assess the resource possibilities. Or you can bring in an outside resource person to present the resources himself, or direct the group to those resources, or both. Usually, for reasons that should be apparent, one or both of the last two are wiser choices.

Again, a reminder: Because of the leader's position in the group and his access to communication channels, he may be aware of the existence of needed resources and assume that everyone else knows about them. If the others do not know, or have forgotten, the leader's assumption that they do know may be deadly. He becomes frustrated because the group balks at undertaking what appears to him to be a reasonable assignment, while the rest of the group becomes increasingly frustrated as they conclude that they are being handed an impossible task. Soon the leader and the rest of the group begin attributing unfortunate motives to one another with disastrous results. Unless you are completely certain that others know all that you know, take a minute to review the information about resources. Even if most of the members know of the existence of the resources, the review will often serve to reinforce confidence in the group's success potential.

Spread Task Pressures

Don't present a group with a major, unanticipated task requirement unless you have no opportunity to spread the task pressures among people and over a period of time.

Spread Task Pressures Among People. The more members you are able to fire up before the task is presented to the group as a whole, the more likely are your chances of success. Thus, talk to as many members as possible before the group formally convenes. Sometimes you can talk with members individually, and sometimes you talk with small groups of members. First, you have an opportunity to check your perceptions of the desirability of undertaking the task. You may find your perceptions are totally unrealistic, and these premeeting conferences may therefore help you to avoid taking up group time fruitlessly. Second, you will, at the very least, reduce resistance caused by novelty; more likely, you will gain some supporters for your task proposal.

With whom do you talk? Each situation must be analyzed. Sometimes mere chance will dictate with whom you talk—you talk with those whom you happen to meet before the group convenes. Sometimes a "steering committee" has been created by the larger group for this very purpose—to appraise and winnow potential tasks. Sometimes you will make deliberate attempts to prime the slow-to-catch-on types in the group. If the task falls within the particular bailiwick of one or more members, you will certainly want to confer with them before presenting the task to the main group. Failure to confer with them is a gratuitous insult, and you are certain to create resentment even if (in such cases, a very big *if*) the rest of the group agrees to the task commitment.

When possible, have someone other than yourself present the task to the group. Then you can support others rather than being the prime mover. Sometimes the presentation can be collectively handled by several members. Regardless of the mode of presentation, the principle is the same—the broader the base of presentation, the more likely the acceptance by the rest of the group.

In your efforts to spread task pressures among group members, beware of creating special subgroups or cliques and be equally cautious of leaving the *impression* that you have done so.

Spread Task Pressures Over Time. Remember the virtues of carefully planned and publicized agendas. If members know in advance what tasks are going to be undertaken, they will have time to do some thinking about them. One reason behind the "notice-of-motion" practice is to guarantee that groups will not be surprised by action they have not had time to consider. Whether or not your group adopts some formal procedure of giving notice of motion is not the issue. The issue is the amount of time that you allow between the first application of task pressure and the point that you hope the group will begin actual work on the task.

Sometimes it is desirable to set aside an entire meeting, or at least a part of a meeting, to describe tasks you intend to urge upon the group at a later time. As an example, the President's "State of the Union" address serves primarily the purpose of alerting the Congress to what the President considers "must" legislation. You may use such opportunities to bring to bear most of the techniques of initiating action. To be most effective arrange to present the tasks *without discussion at that time.* Let people think about the tasks for a while before they discuss the propriety of actually undertaking them.

Intensify Task Pressures

Observe the same caution here as when intensifying pressures to change norms. If you must increase pressures beyond the levels already perceived by group members, you are certain to increase tension and may create resentment. Don't be panicked by an initial lack of enthusiasm on the part of the other members. They may just be evidencing normal inertia that will be overcome as they perceive the significance of task commitment. Unnecessary intensification of task pressures may cause members to feel that they are being "railroaded" into something against their better judgment, thereby having the opposite effect from the one intended. Members may refuse the task because they do not want to be pushed around. However, just as there are reasons for increasing pressures to change norms, there will often be reasons for intensifying task pressures. Tactful and judicial use of the following techniques may be an essential part of securing task commitment.

Pressure from Authority. Organizational groups are forever sub- jected to pressure from individuals or groups standing above them in the organizational structure. Deans exert pressure upon academic departments in universities and vice presidents exert pressure upon divisional managers in businesses. Examples of the whole host of priorities, demands, and deadlines are not necessary as all are acquainted with at least some of them.

This pressure from above may be a boon to harassed group leaders because they may shift the "blame" for the pressure from themselves to their superiors. "The boss says we must do this by next week. There isn't anything that I can do about it." But while placing the responsibility elsewhere is tempting, use caution. If the boss learns that you are unwilling to face up to your own responsi- bilities, you may be welcomed with something less than enthusiasm the next time you are in his office.

For the pressure from authority to be effective at least two conditions must prevail within your group. First, the group must believe that the superior has the *right* to levy such pressures. If they perceive that he is trying to extend his area of control in an unwarranted fashion, the consequences will be what one may expect from any kind of authoritarian leadership.[9] Second, the group must perceive that he actually levied the pressures *as you have reported*. The importance of keeping others aware of your sources of information has been mentioned before. Nowhere is that injunc- tion more in order than when reporting pressures from others for task accomplishment. If any number of group members believe you have exaggerated or distorted pressures from superiors, you are headed for trouble. If you suspect your report may be unconvincing to some of the members, use one or more of the following means: ask your superior to present his demands personally to the group; ask your superior to put his demands in writing; take others with you when you talk to your superior. You may often wish to employ

[9] See Chapter 8, pp. 217-218.

such techniques even when no one is likely to question your reporting. If the task is critical, pressures from authority are intensified
when at least some others receive, along with you, the story
"straight from the horse's mouth." [10]

Pressure to Cooperate With Other Groups or Individuals. Both
organizational and voluntary groups are subject to this pressure.
Whenever your group members perceive that their group goals
complement another group's goals, pressures are created for your
group to undertake tasks that help the other group attain its goals.
For example, college and university departments of English have
undertaken a variety of tasks in diagnosing and analyzing the
English background of entering freshmen. Such activities help the
departments to handle problems of training their freshmen, of
course, but these activities also help high school English teachers
to assess the methods they use in training students for college work.[11]

Intergroup Comparisons. A group need not be engaged in a competitive struggle with another group for relevant comparisons to be
an effective pressure for task commitment. What other groups are
doing is a legitimate question to raise whether or not one group
wishes to emulate another. If a bit of healthy rivalry exists between
the groups, so much the better. One can easily think of worse
motives for raising sights.

Desire to Obtain Extrinsic Rewards. Just as individuals can be stimulated to work for rewards, or to avoid punishment, so groups can
be stimulated by the promise of recognition, improved intergroup
status or extended area of control. You will probably not be in the
position to mediate the group rewards, but you should be in a
position to know what rewards are available and the procedures

[10] Need we add that a consistent history of your accurate reporting will
do much to eliminate the need for such precautions?
[11] The techniques suggested in Chapter 9, pp. 232-235, for improving intergroup climate and the techniques discussed in Chapter 13 for improving intragroup climate will suffice here for creating those intergroup relations necessary
for this pressure to be effective. A more complete treatment of the problems of
intergroup relations is well beyond the scope of this book. For a comprehensive
coverage of research in this area we recommend the *Research Bulletin on
Intergroup Relations,* ed. by Peter I. Rose, Smith College. The *Bulletin* is published periodically, and copies may be secured by writing Mr. Rose.

necessary for placing your group in line to receive such rewards. During the Second World War, for example, factories were given "E" awards for effort when their production rose to significant levels. Groups as well as individuals receive letters of commendation. Sometimes these rewards are won in competition with other groups, but, like individual rewards, group rewards may also be earned by attaining given standards of excellence.

Personal Influence. Assuming that you are indeed a real group leader, and not simply a figurehead, your own personal influence may well be the second most potent force for task commitment. (The most potent is task attractiveness discussed next.) The leader's control of both extrinsic and intrinsic rewards coupled with the sources of personal power combine to make his personal influence quite potent. People will do any number of things to please their leaders, and undertaking tasks recommended by their leaders is a common way of pleasing them. Thus, you can often significantly intensify task pressures by simply indicating, *without giving further reasons for your assertion,* that you personally believe the group should accept the task. You are relying upon personal influence whenever you say or imply, "Take my word for it; we should attack this problem." You may hint at pressures, information, insights, and the like. But unless your group members have reasonably complete access to the same bases for deciding as you, they will have to judge your assertion by standards of personal believability, and the pressures to act upon your suggestion will stem largely from your own personal influence.

You will seldom be able to completely eliminate personal influence from the task pressures that are levied upon the group. However, use it as sparingly as possible. You can use it like money in the bank—trading upon it for a variety of things that you want done. But you can deplete that store of influence and at the same time create more and more resentment stemming from others' dependency upon you. To a greater or lesser extent every leader who gets his group to make significant accomplishments creates some resentment and often some enemies during his tenure. You must accept such consequences as the price of being a dynamic leader. Leaders can neither avoid using personal influence nor escape, completely, the consequences of its use. But the leader's productive tenure can be prolonged if he uses his personal influence with discretion.

The consequence of the use of personal influence is one reason why many organizations make a practice of changing their leaders periodically. Military organizations do this as a matter of course; many businesses and churches also engage in the practice. When the organization does not compel turnover of leaders, the leader himself must usually decide when it is time to step aside and turn over the reins to someone else, as shown by the case of one leader of a large voluntary organization: He led his group through a series of significant and demanding tasks for a period of five years. When election time came around, many of his associates urged him to make himself available for still another term. He would almost certainly have been reelected, but he was sensitive to many indications that his personal influence had begun to wane sharply. He decided, wisely, that the time had come to quit. He was loudly lauded for his work, but there were also many sighs of relief when his decision not to run again was made public.

Emphasize Task Attractiveness

Without the joy that comes from doing and making, from having a creative purpose, from working with others toward a common goal, he [man] is less and less satisfied with having more and more.[12]

Magda Arnold reached this conclusion in her book, *Emotion and Personality,* and we agree completely. Task attractiveness is the most potent force for initiating action.

On the surface emphasizing task attractiveness seems easy—point out the pleasure in doing the task. Unfortunately, however, it is not that simple. Some tasks are difficult to enjoy; they are monotonous, repetitious, or otherwise beneath the dignity of the doer. Dozens of external pressures such as need for haste may rob the doer of much of the pleasure. Many people have never learned to enjoy work; their lives are measured by clocks and compulsions; for one reason or another their creative capacity has been stultified. Though these are some of the reasons, there are doubtless many

[12] Magda B. Arnold, *Emotion and Personality: Vol. II, Neurological and Physiological Aspects* (New York: Columbia Univ., 1960), pp. 306-307.

more. But there is one more that should be mentioned. Many leaders have never discovered the need or the means of communicating to others the rewards inherent in the doing.

Learning, for its own sake, is perhaps the most exciting and rewarding activity we know. Yet far too many students at all levels of education regard learning, as it takes place in schools at any rate, as a distinctly unpleasant chore. Part of the blame must rest upon the teachers of those students. The teachers either never discovered for themselves the joy of learning or were incapable of communicating this joy to students. For such students the task of learning often becomes solely a means to an end, rather than, to some extent at least, an end in itself. If they pass their courses, they can obtain a degree, stay eligible for sports, and "go active" in a fraternity or sorority. The teacher, like any other leader, has the responsibility of helping students discover rewards in the learning activity.

Almost all of the techniques of stimulating involvement discussed in Chapter 12 are applicable for emphasizing task attractiveness. The leader must be certain that the task is worthwhile; he must see that the follower has an opportunity to participate; he must relate individual goals to group goals; he must listen carefully and understandingly; he must accept contributions without evaluation; and he must be stimulated himself. In short, he must motivate the follower.

Motivation is not, as Smith and Scott have so ably pointed out, a kind of "push button" activity.[13] One does not select some "emotional appeals" or a few "drives" or "needs" such as the need for status, or power, or prestige, and then say in effect, "Do this task and you will obtain status, power, or prestige." Rather, the problem-solving framework introduced in Chapter 4 is a more appropriate framework for communicating task attractiveness. Doing the task becomes the solution to problems facing each participant. The goals may be different for each individual, and the tensions that are relieved as a result of performing the task may vary. But each one may discover pleasure in the task.

Suppose that a group of students has been appointed to study registration procedures and recommend a plan for improving the

[13] Donald K. Smith and Robert L. Scott, "Motivation Theory in Teaching Persuasion: Statement and Schema," *Quarterly Journal of Speech*, Vol. 47 (December, 1961), pp. 378-383.

process. The confusion and chaos in registration may upset some students; their goals may be achieved by bringing order out of chaos. Others may be stimulated by the opportunity to learn about the inner workings of university administration. Still others may be stimulated by the difficulties to be overcome. Of course, there will be long range rewards. Student members will receive some status and the experience gained will be invaluable in later years. But at least some of the motivation for accepting the task may be found in the task activities themselves.

The conclusion? To motivate others effectively, the leader must study both the task and the members. He must study the task to learn what excitement may be found in it; he must study the members to learn what goals will attract them. Having studied, he will be in a position to demonstrate task attractiveness.

TERMINATING ACTION

Our worries do not end once the group is committed to action. Getting the group to terminate action with some reasonable conclusion is often at least as difficult as getting them to begin in the first place. As individuals we are prone to procrastinate and we hate to commit ourselves to any course of action until we are forced to do so. We don't improve when we get into groups. In fact, as we have already shown, forces are created which aggravate rather than improve the situation. We all know about the existence of the problem. We know that reasonable people can become quickly disillusioned about the values of group discussion when their groups talk endlessly and come up with watered-down compromises instead of effective plans of action. What can we do about it?

Before suggestions for terminating action, some assumptions must be stated. One is that you have done a good job of initiating action. If members are concerned about the task and have undertaken their work cheerfully, you have set in motion a powerful force for concluding the task with dispatch. Of course, another assumption is that the group has been progressing with all of the characteristics of first-rate groups. A very important assumption is that the group does indeed have some requirement to arrive at a *group* decision. Social, cathartic, and therapeutic groups seldom have to reach group consensus; learning, advisory, and appraisal groups can often "agree to disagree" and present a divided report or simply terminate action when the problem has been adequately explored; but decision-making and action groups must reach a group decision. The final assumption is that you are not trying to "railroad" some preconceived project through the group. If these assumptions are in order, the following techniques may help in terminating action.

Set Deadlines

Once the group has committed itself to the task and has surveyed the requirements of solving the problem, the *group as a whole* should begin to set deadlines. If the task is large, it should be broken down into subproblem areas with a deadline set for each. All deadlines must be flexible, of course, since it is impossible to foresee exactly what must be done to accomplish any given task. But being flexible is different from being spineless. Deadlines serve no purpose if they can be abolished by complaints of the lazy.

The procedures for setting deadlines parallel those for initiating action. Often deadlines are set by authorities outside the group. But in any event the group members must make the deadlines their own if deadlines are to serve any purpose. If members agree that the deadlines are reasonable and if they agree publicly to attempt to meet them, the first step toward terminating action has been taken. Take some time to get the group to make deadline decisions; you will save time in the long run.

Provide Resources

The procedures in Chapter 5 for how the group can see that necessary evidence and other resources can be made available should suffice; but some people will still protest, "We can't make any decisions until we have *all* the facts." The plain truth is that we can never have *all* the facts. We must abstract information that seems important; we can't get it all. To say that we should not do anything until we can be *certain* that it will work is a contradiction in terms. All inferences are necessarily probability statements, as we show in Chapter 5.[14]

The best way to cope with the caution of those who want to be certain is to urge the group to consider the probable consequences

[14] See Chapter 5, pp. 93-95.

of their action, or lack of action. If the group does take a particular course of action, what does it stand to gain and what does it stand to lose and what are the probabilities of each? In some situations the possible loss is so great that prudent people will refuse the hazard. Most of us refuse to drive automobiles unless we are covered by liability insurance. We are not insuring ourselves against probable loss; we are trying to protect ourselves against that *improbable* instance when a judgment of several thousand dollars may be returned against us. At the other extreme the present situation may be so bad that almost any action will be an improvement. During Roosevelt's famous "hundred days," Congress passed all kinds of legislation with little caution. Many acts, such as the NRA, were later declared unconstitutional, and many others proved to be hasty and ill-considered measures. But the economy was in a critical condition, and potentially constructive change was imperative.

Most of the time, however, the choices are not so clear-cut. We must decide whether or not we have sufficient information to predict reasonably well the consequences of proposed action. If we have taken the necessary steps to insure that pertinent resources are available, and if we urge the group to consider the possible gains and losses, we increase the probability that the group can take positive action.

Maintain Objectivity

We should seek to maintain objectivity for a number of reasons, but two apply particularly to the problem of terminating action. First, objective discussion helps avoid emotional commitments that can prove embarrassing. If a discussant lets himself get carried away in espousing a position that others will not accept, he may be unable to accept gracefully an alternative action. Second, frankness, an essential part of objectivity, helps clear away confusion about where people stand. After many unduly prolonged discussions, a substantial majority of the group members admit they were ready to take action long before the group finally stopped discussing, but because they felt that others were not ready, they said nothing. Frankness would have shortened the decision-making time.

Means of developing and encouraging objectivity have been examined already. Here is just one more suggestion: After the problem has been thoroughly explored, some members may still offer

reasons against a proposal for action or against taking action at the
time suggested. Simply ask them whether they are expressing their
own feelings or whether they are offering arguments they think
others hold.

In one instance that comes to mind an individual kept reopening
the question for more discussion every time the group seemed ready
to decide. When pinned down, he admitted that he was ready to act,
but he was afraid that *others* might still have reservations. This kind
of behavior is typical of the stage 3 individual. He is so worried that
everyone may not be in perfect accord that he invents every possible
excuse to prolong the discussion.[15]

In Chapter 13 it was suggested that it was wise to raise arguments against the group's conclusion when the group seemed to have
come rather casually to a conclusion. That advice is not contradicted
here, but when the discussion has been thorough and complete, why
prolong it because some people hesitate to be frank about their own
feelings. If some members have genuine reservations, they should,
naturally, be encouraged to voice them. But people should not be
voicing objections that they do not share *after* the point where
reasoned controversy can be productive.

Summarize and Review

In a typical discussion members reach a point where they begin to
repeat arguments over and over again. Often they are not aware of
what they are doing, but sometimes they are very much aware and
are employing delaying tactics. Surely little can be accomplished by
going over the same ground, but sometimes people act as if an
argument can be proved by repetition. Effective summaries and
reviews can help minimize the problem of sterile repetition.

To help hasten action, summary and review must go a bit
beyond what was suggested in Chapter 11. Conflicting lines of argument must be stated with scrupulous fairness; points of agreement
must be clearly identified; and logical consequences of unresolved
lines of argument must be stated. Then, two more important steps
must be taken. First, *get the proponents of the conflicting positions
to agree that your summary is accurate.* If necessary, you must keep
rephrasing until everyone can agree that the arguments have been

[15] See Chapter 8, p. 209.

fairly stated. Don't forget that fair statement includes appropriate *emphasis* upon crucial arguments. Next, ask the members if they have anything to *add*, and underscore the word *add* when you make the request. If some members persist in going back to old arguments, the rest of the group may now help you keep reminding them that the ground has been covered. If members have nothing more to add, further talk is unnecessary. *You are not now necessarily ready to vote;* you are ready to move to something else.

Provide Time to Think

Several times we have cautioned against attempting to cram everything into one meeting. Most problems of any consequence require at least three meetings. Other matters may well be discussed during each meeting, of course. The first meeting should be concerned with preliminary analysis of the problem; the second should allow the group to work through the problem; and the third should allow the group to recapitulate and decide.[16]

Providing this time to think is advantageous for several reasons. As pointed out in Chapter 5 the time between the first and second meeting can be used for individual thinking and research. The time between the second and third meetings is equally valuable. During this time passions may cool and members may reflect. If legitimate arguments have been overlooked, they may be discovered during this time and brought to the group's attention at the next meeting. The procedure also provides a face-saving device for those whose positions are not accepted. Somehow it seems much easier for people to concede a point after some time has elapsed. Most important, the time to think alleviates many of the unfortunate pressures for conformity.[17]

Some may contend that this additional time simply provides those who wish to block action with the opportunities to think up additional stratagems. For the most part, experience proves differently. This technique allows many groups to make decisions calmly and rationally when, in an earlier meeting, the members had been at each other's throats. But when groups press for decision hard on the heels of vigorous debate, there are charges of railroading, bitter-

[16] Cf. Chapter 5, pp. 116-118.
[17] See Chapter 9, pp. 229-231.

ness, failure to carry out decisions, and even later, rejection of the whole plan or policy. And, of course, the total group time required to come to the decision is *longer* when the group does not wait until another meeting to make the decision.

Decide

When a group has had opportunity for full and free discussion of an issue, and when sufficient time has been given to think about the problem, it is time to decide. Occasionally all members agree by this time, and the decision represents group consensus. On minor matters most members will agree to a kind of group consensus even when they do not agree completely with the solution. Often, however, group members are not of one mind. What should be done? Three courses of action are open.[18]

First, we may have to give up. Sometimes a group is hopelessly and bitterly split; the members see no way to resolve differences and produce a decision that comes close to representing a reasonable majority point of view. The group may have to resort to arbitration (having a "disinterested" third party make the decision) as often happens in labor-management disputes, or the group may have to abandon the project altogether, at least for the time.

Second, the group may press forward and attempt to integrate the various points of view and reach a consensus. If such consensus be a genuine meeting of minds, it is valuable because member satisfaction and commitment to action are likely to be stronger than when sharp differences remain. But if consensus entails unduly prolonged discussion, the price paid may be more than the value of the consensus.

Third, the group may decide by majority vote. This method of making decisions is perfectly valid and should be used with no feelings of guilt for having failed to obtain consensus. It is not meant to be implied that voting must always follow some formal parliamentary procedure. If they reach consensus, well and good. If not, a reasonable majority will have to suffice.

This point of view is not shared by all who have written about discussion methods. Following are some representative positions for and against voting, taken from four recent textbooks.

[18] We exclude as reasonable alternatives watered-down compromises or platitudes with which no one can disagree. Such means of resolving differences are beneath the dignity of reasonable groups.

Finally, and most important of all, the decision rests on a quantitative rather than a qualitative basis—the number of votes that can be marshaled by either side. A decision means that a powerful majority has brought a minority to its knees, or that a compromise between competing factions has been arranged. Settling disputes through voting does permit a group to act (and this is often important), but it does not really resolve the differences nor change people's minds about the nature of the problem. A vote seldom produces greater unity of thought or feeling within a group. Often the defeated members of an organization work, thereafter, not to execute the policy, but to bring about a realignment in the balance of power so that the matter can be brought up again and the decision changed. A compromise may be nothing more than an uneasy truce with the losing side working, consciously or unconsciously, to sabotage the decision and vindicate itself.[19]

A good discussion group needs to arrive as nearly as possible at *real* agreement and consensus, real in the sense that it represents an actual coming together of the minds and attitudes of the people in the group after extended study and personal soul searching.[20]

Majority Vote. If modification fails to result in general approval or near consensus, the group may be forced to reach agreement by counting noses. In small-group discussion, a vote should be taken only when the possibilities of reaching consensus or compromise have been thoroughly exhausted, and when members of the group are almost literally exhausted![21]

The ideal outcome of discussion, theoretically, may be consensus, the common high ground of unanimous agreement. This, however, is never to be sought at the price of the slightest coercion of even one member. When discussion does not lead to unanimity within the time limits which are practical, the democratic process calls for decision or action by majority rule. Discussion ought not to become an instrument of endless delay foisted upon a majority by a willful minority.[22]

The issue seems to be: Will a majority vote so split a group that consensus should be sought even though it may require considerably more time and effort than voting? All agree that consensus is to be preferred; none regards voting as distinctly bad; and none

[19] Dean C. Barnlund and Franklyn S. Haiman, *The Dynamics of Discussion* (Boston: Houghton Mifflin, 1960), p. 159.

[20] John W. Keltner, *Group Discussion Processes* (New York: Longmans, Green, 1957), p. 192.

[21] Halbert E. Gulley, *Discussion, Conference, and Group Process* (New York: Holt, Rinehart and Winston, 1960), p. 282.

[22] Rupert L. Cortright and George L. Hinds, *Creative Discussion* (New York: Macmillan, 1959), p. 14.

is talking about groups that are hopelessly split. Let us restate *the* position of *this* book so that it is completely clear: *Groups should expect to vote. If they have reached consensus, they will have a unanimous vote which is ideal. The more tenuous the majority, however, the less confident the group should be of its decision.*

This position is advocated for several reasons. First, observation does not indicate that groups whose members expected to vote, and did, experienced such divisiveness that they could not function properly in carrying out their decisions. Of course, immature people in immature groups may have trouble accepting a majority decision; rigid and close-minded people may refuse to believe that they could be wrong. But it is doubtful that prolonged attempts to secure consensus would help such people very much.[23] The beginning of this book proposed to speak of "discussion as employed by reasonable able, mature, sensitive, and objective people." [24] That is still the position here, and most people of this sort seem to be able to accept a majority decision that goes against their arguments.

Second, the majority vote offers the finest face-saving device known. Members may say, "I do not agree with the decision, but I will do all I can to support it." Now, whatever the outcome of experience with the decision, they are protected. If the decision proves to be wise, they can always say, or imply, "I was wrong to oppose the plan but right to agree to help carry it out." If the decision proves to be unwise, they can be pardoned for a tactful, "I told you so."

Third, in few groups do votes always split along the same lines. Usually an individual finds himself aligned with different members on different issues. The most predictable divisions are between action-minded and more conservative members. Some people seem to be ready to vote when the problem for discussion is stated, while others seem to be never quite ready to decide. These two extremes must always compromise on the issue of defining what they mean by "full and complete discussion" and, consequently, deciding *when* to vote.

[23] It may be of some interest to note that Canning and Baker have discovered that authoritarian persons seem to be more susceptible to group pressure than non-authoritarian persons. See Ray R. Canning and James M. Baker, "Effect of the Group on Authoritarian and Non-Authoritarian Persons," *American Journal of Sociology*, Vol. 64 (May, 1959), pp. 579-581.

[24] See Chapter 2, p. 21.

Finally, consensus is often too expensive. Unless the stakes are very high, most people prefer to have a decision go against them and get on to something more productive than to almost literally exhaust themselves in the pursuit of consensus. Further, when one or two members are still holding out, the temptation for coercion is too great for most people to resist. The minority has no right to block majority action indefinitely, and the majority has no right to bludgeon "hold-outs" into consensus. Voting avoids both evils.

SUMMARY

In this chapter techniques have been examined for performing the functions of initiating and terminating action. Task accomplishment is more easily achieved with mature groups, but it is an essential ingredient in building groups. Thus, it is exceptionally significant.

Initiating action may be accomplished by paying attention to several techniques. Stabilizing task requirements will help. Emphasizing the group's success potential is necessary and can be achieved by praising individual abilities and by assessing existing and potential evidence. By spreading task pressures among people and over time, the leader can minimize barriers to task acceptance. Task pressures must often be intensified. Five ways were suggested to intensify task pressures: (1) pressure from authority, (2) pressure to cooperate with other groups or individuals, (3) intergroup comparisons, (4) desire to obtain extrinsic rewards, and (5) the personal influence of the leader. The last should be used with discretion. The most potent force for initiating tasks is the attractiveness of the task itself. The leader should help others find meaningful goals in the doing of the task.

If the group is not to talk itself to death, the leader must be concerned about terminating action effectively. Collectively setting deadlines will help. Securing relevant information and assessing the consequences of action are important. Maintaining objectivity helps to avoid unfortunate commitments and enables everyone to know where others stand. Make certain that people are expressing their own views rather than those they think others may hold. Summarize and review often to avoid unnecessary repetition. Provide enough time to think so that members do not feel pressured into decisions. Finally, after thorough discussion of the problem, groups should expect to vote. If a unanimous vote can be secured, so much the better, but groups should not regard a vote as the second best method of deciding.

EXERCISES

1. Select two groups of which you are a member and that differ markedly in willingness to reach decisions and take action. Analyze and compare these groups on the bases of (a) nature and importance of objectives and specific tasks; (b) group maturity and commitment to common interests; and (c) the potential for utilizing suggestions offered in this chapter for moving the group to action.

2. At the first opportunity when you find yourself a member of a group that seems reluctant or unable to move to a decision, attempt to apply those principles, outlined in this chapter, that seem possible and appropriate. Analyze your efforts in a short report that points out the results and also the particular strengths and limitations of your efforts.

3. Prepare one or more case studies of groups as they attempt to reach decisions or take action. Student governing groups and executive committees provide good material. Identify the forces or elements that seem to block action. Point out the forces or conditions that appear to move the group to action. Suggest the activities, procedures, or roles that you feel would be both helpful and appropriate in facilitating action. (Each case study should be a clear and concise statement of approximately 600 words in length.)

4. Prepare one or more case studies of individual group members (these may or may not be formal leaders) as you observe their efforts to help groups reach decisions. If possible, consider the individual's efforts over a period of time and in relation to several groups. How well does the individual diagnose group needs in this regard? To what degree is he aware of the principles and techniques that may be used? How effective are his efforts? What suggestions would you make for his future guidance?

5. The instructor will pair you with another class member whose name you will know but who will not know yours. First you will write an analysis of your own efforts at moving groups to action. Then you will write a similar analysis of the other individual's efforts. The latter will be turned in to your instructor, your name deleted, and then the comments passed on to the other individual along with the instructor's comments. In turn you will receive an anonymous analysis of your efforts. Compare this with your own self-analysis. Are the differences in perception significant? What accounts for the agreement or disagreement? Do the instructor's comments give weight to any special points? What, if any, action do you contemplate as a result of the comparison?

6. Think back over a number of groups of which you have been a member. Analyze the manner in which each reacted when faced with the need for a decision. Make one list of those decisions where all seemed to proceed effectively and constructively (not necessarily harmoniously or to full consensus). Make another list of those situations where decision was difficult, led to unhappy results, or was avoided. Is it possible to identify "success" or "failure" with the presence or absence of any of the factors discussed in this chapter? Consider how the final result might have been affected by such presence or absence.

SELECTED READINGS

Barnlund, Dean C., and Haiman, Franklyn S., *The Dynamics of Discussion*. Boston, Houghton Mifflin, 1960, Chap. 8.
Lippitt, Ronald, Watson, Jeanne, and Westley, Bruce, *The Dynamics of Planned Change*. New York, Harcourt, Brace & World, 1958.

PART V
Communication

CHAPTER 15

Communication Principles

> Those societies which cannot combine reverence to their symbols with freedom of revision, must ultimately decay either from anarchy, or from the slow atrophy of a life stifled by useless shadows.
>
> Alfred North Whitehead*

The title of the first chapter was, "The Individual vs. the Group: A Conflict in Communications." From that page to this the concern has been in one way or another with the process which we call communication. In the discussion of thinking together, for example, the concern was with how people observed and how their language affected what they saw and heard; with "statements" of observation and "statements" of inference; with how words could be related to the world of facts and how those words could be related to each other. In the discussion of the nature of groups and the consequent relations of individuals to one another, the assumption was that somehow the creation, perpetuation, and modification of group characteristics were dependent upon what people said to one another. All of the techniques presented involve either saying something or noticing something, or both. Even the suggestion in Chapter 12 that a leader should notice attempts to enter a discussion

* *Symbolism: Its Meaning and Effect* (New York: Macmillan, 1958), p. 88.

and should help the member get into it, really pertained to communication. In effect, by leaning forward in his chair, exhibiting a general tension, opening his mouth, and so forth, the member was communicating, "I have something to say and I want to say it, but I can't seem to get in."

The whole book has inescapably dealt with communication, and all of us know how to talk and listen. But these facts do not allow us to dispense with further consideration of communication. Effective communication in discussion involves considerably more than an understanding of the concepts covered so far, important as those concepts are, and it obviously involves more than a good vocabulary, clear articulation, and acute hearing.

To assume two chapters on communication can accomplish what is normally difficult to accomplish in at least three books is fatuous. Several books have been written about the nature of communication in general; dozens of books, many of them rather bulky, exist to give advice to the speaker; and there are several texts on listening alone. Then add the material in linguistics, semantics, voice and articulation, and organizational communication, the task of "boiling down" the essential material becomes preposterous. To repeat advice given earlier—the wise discussant will seek additional training in speechmaking, listening, communication theory, and interpersonal relations. At the ends of these chapters helpful books are suggested. The reader will be acquainted with formal courses that he might take.

What, then, is proposed here? Those factors in the group discussion situation that have a marked effect upon communication are identified and then techniques of dealing with those factors are suggested. Rather than upon communication theory, speech principles and techniques, and listening, as such, the focus is upon the *situation* in which people exchange ideas. This approach will enable the individual who studies communication more extensively to apply his knowledge to the discussion situation. It will also suggest to the novice in communication, directions which may prove useful in refining his communication understanding and skill. Finally, this approach will help both the skilled communicator and the novice to make immediate improvements in their ability to communicate effectively in discussion groups.

The rest of this chapter first attempts to produce a clear understanding of just what we mean by the term *communication*. Also this section examines characteristics of desirable communication in the group discussion situation. Thirdly, the theory of communication is examined as it bears upon small groups. Finally, a few of the variables involved in intergroup communication are mentioned.

CHARACTERISTICS OF COMMUNICATION

Communication Defined

Defining communication is no simple task.[1] Here the term is intended to apply to a special situation, however, and thus some of the limitations of its use should be identified before an attempt is made to define it.

The consideration of *communication* here is restricted to *interpersonal* communication. The term as used here, therefore does not include communication between man and his environment, man and machines, machines and machines, or even between man and society. Much interesting research has been done in many of these areas. Studies in the Bell Telephone and IBM laboratories have emphasized machine communication, for example. And though much can be learned from such research about means of studying and measuring human communication, we need not extend our thinking here to cover communication which includes nonhuman components.

For the most part, our use of communication is also restricted to nonwritten communication that usually takes place in a face-to-face situation. (Note that we did not say *verbal* communication because much of the communication in a typical discussion is gestural and otherwise uses nonverbal means.)

With these two restrictions in mind communication is here defined as *the process by which people interact for the purpose of interpersonal and intrapersonal integration.*[2] Some key concepts in this definition need to be spelled out in greater detail.

[1] If this statement still seems too strong after you have finished reading this chapter, we suggest that you read Newman's excellent discussion of the problem of defining communication. John B. Newman, "A Rationale for a Definition of Communication," *The Journal of Communication*, Vol. 10 (September, 1960), pp. 115-124.

[2] This definition is very similar to the concepts advanced by Jo F. Richmond and Roy E. Buehler, "Interpersonal Communication: A Theoretical Formulation," *The Journal of Communication*, Vol. 12 (March, 1962), pp. 3-10.

First, communication is identified as a process, not as an act or the result of an act. This process characteristic is one of the complicating aspects of communication because it is impossible to completely isolate and study an "act of communication." We can look at a building, for example, as an entity, if we ignore the submicroscopic processes which physicists tell us are going on constantly. We can measure and describe that building in many ways —size, color, structural properties, location, and others.[3] But we cannot approach an "act of communication" in the same way. True, we can record the words used and examine them in many useful ways, but we lose a great deal of meaning when these words are taken from the process situation in which they were uttered. This process problem is further discussed when the theory of communication in the discussion situation is examined.

The term *interact* is probably clear. It includes the sum total of everything that people do and say. It also includes their appearance, dress, surroundings, and everything else that could conceivably affect another person.

The concepts of interpersonal and intrapersonal integration are not confusing after a moment's thought. When you talk to a friend, for example, you may attempt to convey some information to him, change his mind, or cheer him up. You may also attempt to learn something, modify your own beliefs, and strengthen your friendship or enmity. In any event the communication is purposive. Whether the purpose is conscious or unconscious is beside the point. You seek a response from your friend, which response provokes another response from you, which response—and we are back to our process.

This concept of communication is in keeping with the approach throughout this book. Oversimplifying the concept has been avoided. The concept has been tied to our main goal—an understanding of how individuals may best relate themselves to others in small groups. It will become clearer with progress through this and the following chapter. As a step toward that clarity let us examine some acts of communication. Hopefully, this will help us to avoid the pitfall that John Haney suggests may result from preoccupation with communi-

---

[3] When we begin to talk (as some artists, architects, and other students of the visual arts, talk) about what the building "communicates" to people, we are right back to our process problems.

cation as such—asking questions like "What do we mean by 'What do we mean by *communication?*'" [4]

Characteristics of Desirable Communications

Despite the hazards already indicated, a *communication* will be described as a contribution made by a discussant during the discussion. This contribution may be a question, a statement, an imperative, or an exclamation; it may be long or short; it may have several purposes or just one. Here the intent is simply to describe what characterizes a good contribution—a good communication. Ideally, most contributions should measure up to each of the ten criteria which follow.

1. *Relevant.* A contribution should be relevant to the group's task and personal needs. Naturally, there will be quite a number of irrelevant contributions in most discussions just as any individual finds his mind wandering into irrelevant channels when he is engaged in solitary thought. Before any contribution is classified as irrelevant, however, more should be known than whether it was specifically concerned with the topic the group was considering when the contribution was made. It is necessary to know whether the intention of the contribution may have been to suggest a more profitable line of thought, whether it was intended as tension release, or reflected some similar objective. Relevance, in short, does not mean "on the topic"; it does mean "centered on significant task and personal needs."

2. *Related.* Often a contribution is relevant—it is directed to some significant task or personal needs—but it is not related to what has preceded and what is likely to follow. Often in discussions each person "has something to say" and he says it when it is his turn to speak! Such contributions are like parts of a machine dumped on the floor. Each one is relevant, but useless until the parts are put together by a competent engineer. The discussant might relate a relevant contribution by some statement like: "John suggested a moment ago a cause for our present difficulties. Here is another bit

[4] John B. Haney, "Commentary on 'Some Characteristics of the Study of Communication in 1960,'" *The Journal of Communication*, Vol. 10 (December, 1960), p. 173.

of evidence that supports (or contradicts) his conclusion. . . ." If the contribution is to be used, someone must, sooner or later, relate it to other contributions. If the maker of the contribution cannot relate it himself, he should at least ask someone else for help.

3. *Well-Timed.* This criterion is especially difficult to meet because the idea may not occur to the discussant at the appropriate time, or because he may not be table to get the floor when it is timely, or both. Appropriate timing is difficult for another reason, however. Individuals differ in their speed of comprehension and capacity for "leaping to conclusions." One individual will occasionally see the perfect way out of a difficulty, present his suggestion triumphantly, and then be dismayed when his more pedestrian companions ignore the contribution. The fault may be the timing or it may be failure to measure up on one or more of the following criteria. Of course, the fault can lie with the hearers. But let us not anticipate our development.

4. *Sufficient Length.* A contribution should be long enough to make its point. Most contributions that fail to measure up on this criterion are too short rather than too long. Over-talkativeness is more often a function of frequency than length. Obviously, the contribution is of little value if too little was said to make the point clear and related.

5. *Clear.* Both the maker and his hearers must impute substantially the same meaning to the contribution. This criterion could occupy us for some time. Some years ago, Ogden and Richards produced a massive volume in which they struggled with the "meaning of meaning." [5] There is no intention of retracing their steps or, for that matter, the steps of hundreds of other researchers who have sought to define and prescribe for meaning. Here it must be enough to indicate just a few of the reasons why meaning is so elusive.

Words do not contain meaning, as semanticists are quick to point out. Words are symbols that are rather arbitrarily assigned to designate objects, creatures, acts, feelings, action, being, state of being, and so on. The meaning is to be found in the minds of the users of the words. Add the fact that inflection, gesture, verbal con-

[5] C. K. Ogden and I. A. Richards, *The Meaning of Meaning* (New York: Harcourt, Brace, 1925).

text, and the like can all be used to signify the meaning of the communicator, and the problem of identifying meaning is further complicated. Walter Coutu, a sociologist, describes the problem of meaning very well: "Since meaning is not an entity, it has no locus; it is something that occurs rather than exists. Meanings do not inhere in things or words, but in sign behavior." [6] Coutu goes on to point out that nothing actually "has" meaning, but anything can become a stimulus to evoke meaning in the mind of one who perceives the stimulus. Dictionaries, of course, do not tell us what a word means; they tell us how our society expects us to react to a given communication in a given set of circumstances. "Languages and their dictionaries are socially prescribed blueprints about how to treat something. . . . Language thus appears to be a blueprint of a sign-system—a set of instructions about how and when to give what meaning to what referent." [7]

6. *Information-Oriented.* This criterion stems naturally from our point of view throughout the book that the basis of effective discussion should be the genuine contributions that people can make to each other's understanding. As indicated in Chapter 5, contributions should be rooted in objective rather than social reality.[8] This criterion will be underscored again in the next chapter in the consideration of techniques for improving communication.

7. *Permit Evaluation.* An effective contribution is not only information-oriented but also indicates to the hearers *how* the contribution may be evaluated and suggests the *willingness* of the contributor to have that evaluation made.

In order to indicate how the contribution is to be evaluated, the contributor must describe or suggest the thought processes that the hearers must follow to reach the conclusion. Assume, for example, that a group is discussing the future developments of our economy, and one member offers this contribution: "The price of gold stock is *rising* on the international stock market. This shows that our economy is headed for troubles." He has presented his evidence and his conclusion, but he has not shown the reasoning

[6] Walter Coutu, "An Operational Definition of Meaning," *Quarterly Journal of Speech,* Vol. 48 (February, 1962), p. 64.
[7] *Ibid.,* p. 64.
[8] See Chapter 5, pp. 106-108.

process by which he reached the conclusion. That is, economists point out that the rising price of gold stock indicates a lack of confidence in other stocks and is, therefore, a predictor that investors will become increasingly chary of investing money in other businesses. Of course, we often do not bother to spell out the thought processes because our hearers will perceive them by themselves. If we look up at the sky and say, "It's clouding up. I believe it will rain," we do not describe the thought process that leads us from the evidence to the conclusion, and we do not need to. Often, however, we erroneously assume that these thought processes are understood by the other persons. Our failure to suggest or describe them denies to all concerned the potential evaluation.

Evidencing a willingness to have the contribution evaluated is a virtue difficult to master as shown repeatedly in our discussions of personality characteristics. Jack Gibb's studies of what he terms "defensive behavior" demonstrate that such reactions reduce communicative efficiency.[9] His experiments indicate that one of the major causes of "defensive behavior" is evaluation, while description tends to produce what he calls "supportive behavior." His implied conclusion that description should replace evaluation is clearly valid when groups are organized for social, cathartic, and therapeutic purposes. However, the conclusion can apply to few learning groups and almost no task groups, because evaluation of contributions is a must if the groups are to reach conclusions. Thus the problem seems to be learning how to make and accept evaluations rather than how to avoid them. This issue has already been dealt with and in the next chapter more techniques are offered.

8. *Internally Consistent.* If the ideas within the contribution are not consistent with each other, the value of the contribution is obviously diminished. Since the chapters in Part II dealt with this criterion and techniques for meeting it, further discussion here is unnecessary.

9. *Provocative.* So often contributions, particularly those made by high status persons, say or imply, "This is it. Two plus two equals four and no more need be said." Such contributions cut off controversy and dampen the desire to think further. All are familiar with

---

[9] Jack R. Gibb, "Defensive Communication," *The Journal of Communication,* Vol. 11 (September, 1961), pp. 141-148.

such conversation stoppers. Here are a few typical ones. "But that's socialism!" "We've tried it before, and it won't work." "It's just as simple as that." Becoming provocative involves much more than simply avoiding these conversation stoppers. It is an art that good teachers, for example, have mastered. Hopefully this entire book has been an example of provocative discussion.

10. *Considerate.* Any contribution should be considerate of the feelings of others. Sometimes it is difficult to be considerate; sometimes it is best to keep still.

Having looked briefly at some characteristics of good communication, let us return to theoretical problems and discover those factors in the discussion situation that influence both the nature and the quality of communication.

GROUP COMMUNICATION THEORY

The purpose of this section is to clarify the nature of the communication process. First a communication model is described in order to identify points or junctures in the process. Then two alternative ways of using the model are discussed. Third, we see how our thinking about communication must be modified as a result of the interaction within a discussion group. Finally, three problems that are inherent in the discussion situation and that tend to reduce the effectiveness of communication are discussed.

A Communication Model

The first step in making sense of the communication process is an examination of its ingredients. This will make it possible to talk more meaningfully about the parts that need attention to improve communication in any given situation.

The model used here is taken largely from Berlo, *The Process of Communication.*[10] This model is a useful tool for examining the

[10] David K. Berlo, *The Process of Communication* (New York: Holt, Rinehart and Winston, 1960). The first contemporary model was developed in the Bell Telephone Laboratory by Shannon and Weaver. Other researchers have developed similar models. For some of the relevant comparisons, see: Claude Shannon and Warren Weaver, *The Mathematical Theory of Communication* (Urbana: Univ. of Illinois, 1949); Wilbur Schramm, "How Communication Works," in Wilbur Schramm, ed., *The Process and Effects of Mass Communica-*

communication process, and there is no advantage to inventing new labels where perfectly satisfactory descriptions already exist. Four essential parts comprise this model—a source-encoder, a message, channels of transmission, and a decoder-receiver.

Source-Encoder. Somewhere the communication process must begin. Someone must have an idea—a feeling, a thought, a reaction—he wishes to communicate. Further, that idea must be coded into some symbol system since brain waves cannot be transmitted directly to another person. So a source-encoder is a part of the communication model.[11] It is tempting to substitute the word *speaker* for the term *source-encoder,* but this temptation should be resisted, because the "listener" is communicating at the same time as the "speaker" even though the listener may not be actually using audible words. In addition, the speaker may be talking in whole or in part to himself. Often the speaker talks in order to discover what is proper or desirable to think. Later it will be shown how this curious process operates.

Upon examining the source-encoder, we can discuss meaningfully his attitudes toward himself, others, the idea, and the discussion situation itself. We also can talk meaningfully about his knowledge, the forces that operate upon him, and his discussion or communication skills. Throughout, this book has talked about all of these aspects of the source-encoder. The primary concern in these two chapters is with his communication skills: *what* he chooses to communicate, *how* he encodes that idea, *when* he communicates, and *to whom* he talks.

Message. The message is the product of the coding process. It consists of the words, vocal inflections, gestures, and other perceivable elements that can be used as symbols. These elements are placed

tion (Urbana: Univ. of Illinois, 1954), pp. 3-26; Bruce Westley and Malcolm MacLean, Jr., "A Conceptual Model for Communication Research," *Journalism Quarterly,* Vol. 34 (1957), pp. 31-38; Franklin Fearing, "Toward a Psychological Theory of Human Communication," *Journal of Personality,* Vol. 22 (1953), pp. 71-78; Wendell Johnson, "The Fateful Process of Mister A Talking to Mister B," *Harvard Business Review,* Vol. 31 (January-February, 1953), p. 50.

[11] For some purposes it is desirable to separate source and encoder. In machine communication and in much human communication that utilizes machines, these two functions may be performed by different entities. For our purposes, however, the source and the encoder are one person.

in some structure. The message, then, is the combination of symbols in some structure.

Recall that meaning should not be sought in the message; it should be sought in the users of the message: the source-encoder and the decoder-receiver. Let us illustrate by using some "meaningless" symbols for a message. Suppose we say $a + b = 12$. Conventionally agreed upon meanings exist for the structural elements, $+$ and $=$. There is also a conventionally agreed upon meaning for a portion of what may be denoted by the figure 12, only a portion because we do not know what the symbol refers to. We may assume that it is a number in our decimal system, and that the number designates twelve units of something. But we do not yet have any agreed upon meanings for a and b. If we agree that a shall equal five units in our decimal system, we can reason that b must equal seven. We can continue adding to the meaning in the equation by specifying what the figures refer to. We can change the meaning we have given by changing the structure. For example, $a - b = 12$ must mean something different from our original equation.

Words and others symbols must be handled in much the same way. True, we have conventionally agreed upon definitions of words, but the difficulties of using a dictionary to find meanings have already been shown. We can, however, talk about the probability that different people will impute the same meaning to a given message. We can advise a speaker to use words that he believes will be within the vocabularies of his listeners. We can talk about the ways in which structure is likely to affect meaning as in this old classic: "The teacher said the student was lazy." Add commas after *teacher* and *student* and see what happens to the meaning.

Channel. The channel is simply the means whereby the message is sent and received. When we talk, we set in action our phonating and articulating organs to create sound waves that are carried through the air to the ear of a listener. Visual channels operate in a similar fashion. The operation of the channel is not of concern here since neither defective speech or hearing nor machine communication are included in our communication study. The next chapter speaks briefly about the relative advantages of oral versus visual communication, and beyond this consideration, it would be belaboring the obvious to make an issue of speaking audibly, using a pleasant speaking voice, and articulating sounds carefully.

Decoder-Receiver. Once the message has reached the decoder-receiver, he enters into the communication model. He must decode the sounds and sights that were sent and interpret the message. The decoder-receiver's role is not passive, but active. He must decide which of many possible meanings the source-encoder intended; he must relate the message to all of the other stimuli impinging upon him; and he must evaluate the message. We normally do all of these things so rapidly and habitually that we sometimes lose sight of the complexity of the process. The tendency to underrate the importance and complexity of the decoder-receiver's task constitutes one of the main problems of securing effective communication. Most people habitually tend to put all the responsibility upon the source-encoder. If communication has broken down, most of us are likely to say: "He should have chosen his words more carefully. He should have arranged his thoughts more appropriately. He should have anticipated the others' desires," and so on. Actually, there is little to choose when deciding whether the source-encoder or the decoder-receiver has the greater responsibility. In studying the decoder-receiver, we can use the same form of analysis that is used for the source-encoder and we can talk quite as meaningfully about the communication skills required.

These are the parts of the communication model. Let us examine two alternative ways of using the model.

Approaches to Communication Analysis

There are many ways of studying communication and prescribing for its improvement; here are just two fundamental approaches. The first is the information theory approach and the second is the field theory approach.

Information Theory Approach. This approach starts with a given —some information to be transmitted by a source-encoder to a decoder-receiver. What happens to that information as it is encoded, transmitted, decoded, interpreted, and finally fed back to the original source? If we are considering human beings, we try to investigate the thought processes that take place as the information is coded and as the potential means of transmission are selected and utilized. We analyze in detail the message itself, and, of course, the situation or circumstances in which the message is conceived, transmitted, and received. We are concerned with analyzing which aspects of the message were actually detected by the decoder-receiver and what happened to that information in the process of interpretation. Finally, we check the process by securing some kind of acknowledgment of receipt from the decoder-receiver; we ask a human to report what he heard or answer a test of comprehension; we "ask" a machine to print out the information or play back a tape.

When the information does not go through the model as we wish, we ask where and what are the "barriers to communication?" We may look for these barriers in any part of the model. Once we have discovered what seems to be a barrier, we may wish to experiment with changes to see if we can minimize the barrier or otherwise facilitate information transmission. Here are some examples of actual questions that researchers have asked: Does it make any difference whether the audience perceives a speaker as tall or short? Does it make any difference whether or not a speaker documents the source of his evidence? What is the effect of the order of arguments in a speech? Should the strongest be placed first, in the middle, or last? Does it make any difference whether or not listeners take notes during a lecture? In each of these investigations, the researcher tried to hold constant all parts of the model while he systematically varied the one part whose effect he wished to study.

The examples of research cited pertained to the area of human communication and particularly to the speaker-audience communication situation. Information theory was originally developed in machine communication—electronic "brains," telephone, radio. In these areas the term *information* has a much more specific meaning than the one we conventionally give it. For that matter, despite the applicability of information theory to much human communication, it is not pursued here further because it is less suited to our purposes than the field theory approach.

Field Theory Approach. The best rationale for studying communication in the discussion group is the one offered by Richmond and Buehler, cited earlier when communication was defined.

Research on communication to date has emphasized "message" and "barriers" to message. It has tended to generalize from the mathematical to the human. It has not clarified the function of interpersonal communication and why the replication of this function is technologically improbable. The function of interpersonal communication is to integrate the organism, intrapersonally and interpersonally; the function of technology is to send messages through time and space. The technology of communication is outside the face-to-face interpersonal context and the information conveyed is not accompanied by the full range of communicative behaviors which are necessary to complete the transactional process. The human organism, opposed as it is to disintegration, utilizes the full range of communication in the maintenance of its integration. Thus, while man is the bio-social model and the facilitator of communications, he is also the bio-chemical barrier to communication attempts to span the gap between biology and technology. A communication model of man based on his neurological system alone does not take into account the other physiological sub-systems which also participate in the total communication process.[12]

Simply stated, the essence of the field theory approach is that the "given" with which we start is man's desire to maintain integration (the equilibrium spoken of before). Proceeding from that given, we examine the way he discovers what he wishes to communicate and attempts to interact with others in the communication process. We ask such questions as: Why did the group start talking about "irrelevant" issues? Why did some members fail to present information they had with them? What happened to change attitudes *when no direct attempt was made to change them?* To whom do people talk, and does it make any difference?

Let us be as clear as possible on one point: The field theory approach is not necessarily superior in general to the information theory approach. For many purposes of research and improving communication ability, the information theory approach is preferable. The speaker-audience situation, mass media communication, and all kinds of machine communication will use information theory in one way or another with profit. But, to understand and improve communication in the small discussion group, the field theory approach enables us to answer the kinds of questions that are most important in that context. This approach to the study of communication is, of course, consistent with the approach taken throughout

[12] Reprinted by permission: "Interpersonal Communication: A Theoretical Formulation." Jo F. Richmond and Roy E. Buehler, *The Journal of Communication,* Vol. 12, No. 1, March, 1962.

this book. Thus, most of the rationale for the position has already been provided. Let us develop this field theory of communication further by examining some additional characteristics of communication in the discussion situation.

Interactive Communication

The fundamental characteristic to be reckoned with is that each discussant is both source-encoder and decoder-receiver at virtually one and the same time. Of course, that does not mean that everyone talks at the same time. They do on occasion, but no one endorses the practice! While one person is speaking, however, the others are transmitting messages by gesture or facial expression. Further, many of the "listeners" are beginning to encode messages which they will shortly transmit orally. Let us look more closely at what happens during this extremely complicated interaction.

Feedforward Communication.[13] The interaction must begin at some point; someone must initiate a thought or idea. This is called feed-forward communication. The distinguishing characteristic of this activity is, however, that feedforward communication typically suggests the direction and content of further communication. These preliminary messages included in feedforward communication may serve one or both of two functions. The first, and most apparent, function is to alert others to what is to come. This is the "road sign" function. Often feedforward communication makes road signs explicit as when a chapter begins with a sketch of what is to be included. But often the road sign function is only implied or suggested as when a frown and a tense manner suggest that a discussant is intending to register a complaint.

A speaker, however, may use preliminary messages for quite another function. He may be including these messages in his feed-forward communication in order to "get a reading" as to whether or not he should continue in a given direction. These may be called the "trial balloon" function of preliminary messages. A job seeker who is being interviewed by a formidable-appearing employer, for ex-

[13] This concept was developed by Bess Sondel using a term coined earlier by I. A. Richards. For further explanation, see Gardner Murphy, "Toward a Field Theory of Communication," *The Journal of Communication,* Vol. 11 (December, 1961), pp. 196-201.

ample, may begin talking rather vaguely and noncommittally about a variety of subjects until he discovers a line that seems to be acceptable to the employer. Once he has discovered the "party line," our job seeker may suddenly become much more confident and may express all kinds of positive opinions that he hesitated to express earlier.

The importance of preliminary messages in feedforward communication becomes apparent when we remember that the main goal of communication is intra- and interpersonal integration. For many reasons an individual may feel hesitant or unsure of his position. Sometimes the reasons may stem from unfortunate personality characteristics, such as the insecure discussant shows. Sometimes one who is seeking to learn may evidence "reasonable" insecurity. In any event the individual is unsure of himself; does not wish to appear foolish or incompetent; hence, he sends out trial balloon preliminary messages in order to find out what is proper to say later.

To decode and interpret an extended message is difficult enough. Consider, therefore, how much more difficult it is to decode and interpret an abbreviated message like many trial balloon and road sign messages. Thus, others in the group may well misinterpret the preliminary message feature of feedforward messages and discourage or inhibit a potentially valuable contribution. Further, many others in the group will be sending out their own feedforward messages. They will, of course, be preoccupied with their own messages and may devote less energy to decoding and interpreting others' messages.

The preliminary message feature of feedforward messages is naturally most prevalent during the beginning stages of any discussion. Many matters must be settled, at least tentatively, before the group can actually begin stating and examining serious content ideas. One mark of a mature group, as indicated, is the ability to keep "sparring for position" down to a minimum.

Whether wisely used or not, preliminary messages in feedforward communication deserve our attention. Road signs used to indicate clearly to others the direction of further communication are potentially very valuable. Both the source-encoder and the decoder-receiver have a responsibility for careful consideration of messages intended to "set the stage." The more complete, specific, and stable such messages and their interpretations become, the more useful they are to the group. When trial balloons are used to discover what

is proper to think and say, however, both the individual and the rest of the group are obliged to help reduce anxiety motivations. If the individual is unsure of the ideas he wishes to express, the group atmosphere should be permissive enough, and he should be secure enough, to allow him to confess his uncertainty and thus produce preliminary messages that are sufficiently specific for him to receive meaningful assistance from the rest of the group.

Reactive Communication. Reactive communications, of course, are those called forth by another's communication. In psychological terminology, feedforward communication may be called the stimulus and reactive communication the response. If an individual attends at all to the communications of others, he will react. His reactive communication may be private internal reactions without outward signs or public reactions that can be detected and interpreted by others. Let us consider two forms of reactive communication—*feedback* and *jamming.*

Feedback serves the function of acknowledging receipt of a message and checking the accuracy of the transmission. Public feedback may range from a nod of approval or a frown of puzzlement, on the one hand, to a detailed rephrasing and evaluation of the communication, on the other hand. Private feedback operates in many curious ways, some of which we can only speculate about since it involves the individual "talking to himself." For example, a discussant who is speaking may say something like this to himself. "He did not give any sign that he liked what I was talking about. I bet I'm on the wrong track. Maybe I should hold back for a while."

Feedback is one of the most important kinds of interactive communication. Extensive and nonevaluative feedback has become almost an article of faith with therapists. By feeding back to the client his thoughts and feelings, the therapist helps the client discover for himself the accuracy and significance of his own communications. In the discussion group intelligent, spontaneous feedback helps both the original communicator and the others in the group. The original communicator receives a check on the accuracy of his communication, and the rest of the group (remember, everyone is feeding back to some extent) can check the accuracy of their reception of the message. More will be said on feedback in the next chapter.

Jamming is a form of communication that disrupts or obscures other communication attempts. Essentially, jamming consists of transmitting messages that seemingly complement, but actually violate, the intent of other messages. Like feedback, jamming may be either public or private. Let us illustrate.

One time a middle-aged woman was talking to a group of junior high youngsters. In order to illustrate her point, she made repeated references to baseball. Unfortunately, she knew little about the game and many of her references were erroneous. In the discussion that followed her speech it became apparent that the youngsters missed her point altogether because their minds were occupied with straightening out her understanding of baseball. In this instance the inaccurate illustrations triggered a series of private reactive communications—jamming—which interfered with the rest of her message. These private reactions became public after the speech, but by then the main objective of communication had been lost.

Jamming has many causes. Inappropriate humor can trigger jamming if the listeners are either overly amused or offended by something that is said. If the source-encoder fails to organize his message appropriately, the decoder-receiver may impose an inappropriate organization upon the message and, consequently, jam the communication. For any of dozens of reasons, a decoder-receiver may misinterpret a message or follow some tangent. When he begins to become source-encoder and starts transmitting messages, first to himself while another is speaking and later to others in the group, he will be jamming the message that triggered his reactive communication.

Both the source-encoder and the decoder-receiver have responsibilities to avoid the unfortunate effects of jamming. The sensitive sender will think of many techniques to minimize jamming by others, but receivers should be even more concerned, for a large part of the responsibility must rest upon listeners. They are the ones who do the actual jamming.

The Communication Structure. Some interesting and significant work has been done studying various communication "networks" and the resultant structures.[14] The basic method of creating these com-

[14] Many researchers have investigated communication structure. Among the more significant studies are: Alex Bavelas, "Communication Patterns in Task-Oriented Groups," *Journal of the Acoustical Society of America,* Vol. 22

munications nets is to separate the subjects by partitions and allow them to communicate with others by use of written messages pushed through slots in the partitions. This procedure also allows the experimenter to intercept messages and substitute others when he wishes to control the content of the communication as well as the direction. Some of the most frequently used communication nets are reproduced in Figure 15.1. In these diagrams the circles represent individuals and the lines show communication linkages.

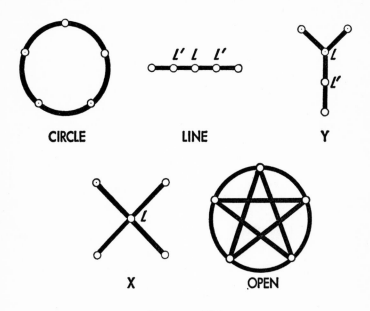

FIGURE 15.1

The symbol *L* in the various diagrams indicates individuals who, because of their "centrality," tend to become leaders. There are no *L*'s in the *circle* and *open* networks because no one's position in the

(November, 1950), pp. 725-730; Marvin E. Shaw and J. C. Gilchrist, "Intra-Group Communication and Leader Choice," *Journal of Social Psychology*, Vol. 43 (February, 1956), pp. 133-138; Harold J. Leavitt, "Some Effects of Certain Communications Patterns on Group Performance," *Journal of Abnormal and Social Psychology*, Vol. 46 (January, 1951), p. 38. The conclusions of these researchers and others are summed up by Robert T. Golembiewski, *The Small Group* (Univ. of Chicago, 1962), pp. 90-97.

network gives him any advantage. In the *line* and the *Y* networks, the symbol *L'* indicates positions of secondary centrality. Results of experiments with nets such as these have revealed the following. Individuals occupying the more central positions tend to be perceived by others as leaders; they do in fact make the bulk of decisions; and they are more satisfied with the process than individuals occupying more peripheral positions. The nets with the more centralized structures—*line, Y,* and *X*—are more efficient in problem solving unless the problems become overly complex, in which case the more diffuse nets show some advantage. Generally, more diffuse nets produce more satisfaction than centralized nets.

Some research by Guetzkow and Simon, however, shows that, regardless of the communication net, groups can become efficient if they learn to use the net efficiently.[15] That is, groups in the circle arrangement can develop a centralized decision-making structure by agreeing to send their communications to one individual.[16]

What does all this mean to small group discussion? Clearly, groups do not normally sit separated by partitions and pass written messages to one another. They sit in a face-to-face situation where everyone can hear everyone else. But to the extent that group members lower in status use pair events rather than set events, the effect is much the same. Other members pay little heed to communications addressed specifically to one or two individuals. For practical purposes such low status individuals might as well be "partitioned off" with their channels of communication open only to the group's leaders. On the other hand, groups that respect and heed the contributions of all members and that use the more open structures can create working relationships characterized by both task efficiency and member satisfaction.

Situational Problems

Three situational problems are present to some degree in every group situation and they reduce communication efficiency. Though each problem has been mentioned already, their significance has not

[15] Harold Guetzkow and Herbert A. Simon, "The Impact of Certain Communication Nets upon Organization and Performance in Task-Oriented Groups," *Management Science,* Vol. 1 (1955), pp. 233-250.

[16] Recall the issue in Chapter 9, pp. 241-243, about the centralized decision-making structure. There we showed that centralized communication structures are not the same as centralized decision-making structures.

yet been identified. These problems are double role (source-encoder and decoder-receiver) complexities, anxiety, and process-task confusions.

Double Role Complexities. Each discussant is, at virtually one and the same time, a source-encoder and a decoder-receiver. The double role complexities should be rather apparent by now. Clearly, if an individual is feeding back privately, jamming, or encoding a message for future transmission, he cannot give his full attention to what someone else is saying. The story is told of a young man who was being sued in court. He had little money so he was able to hire only one lawyer while the plaintiff, a wealthy man, hired two lawyers. After the trial had been under way for a time, the young man called his lawyer aside and said, "I'm afraid we're going to lose the case."

"Why?" his lawyer asked.

"Well," the young man replied, "when one of those fellows is talking, the other is thinking; but when you're talking, no one is thinking for our side."

If discussants aren't careful, they, too, will find that everyone is "talking," aloud or silently, and no one is "thinking." Though the double role cannot be eliminated, it is possible, as the next chapter shows, to do some things to reduce the difficulty and have someone thinking for our side.

Anxiety. Personality characteristics of many individuals, particularly stage 3 individuals, often leave them continually beset by anxiety. They are unable to use feedforward communication productively. Some discussion situations produce a great deal of stress that can create anxiety on the part of the discussants. As might be expected, anxiety and stress, according to research done by Ruth Gynther, reduce communication efficiency.[17] In Gynther's research the subjects were first tested to determine individual levels of anxiety and some were then given instructions that produced considerable stress. They gave speeches that were recorded and analyzed according to measures of communicative efficiency. Since this experiment used individual speeches rather than group discussion, it seems reason-

[17] Ruth Autrey Gynther, "The Effects of Anxiety and of Situational Stress on Communicative Efficiency," *Journal of Abnormal and Social Psychology*, Vol. 54 (1957), pp. 274-276.

able to infer that subjects with high anxiety levels placed in *discussion* situations under stress conditions would probably experience even greater loss of communicative efficiency.

Anxiety is almost certain to be felt by most discussants. If the task is challenging, if something is at stake, if the discussion is anything more than a routine exchange, anxiety will be present. Mature, information-oriented discussants will usually be able to keep anxiety within bounds. But one penalty that must be paid for involving participants and for effectively initiating task requirements is the potential communication disruption caused by anxiety.

Process-Task Complications. Every discussant must be concerned, to some extent at least, with both process and task needs.[18] Evidence from Goldberg's study suggests that individuals will tend to emphasize process communications if they are concerned about how other group members are evaluating them, but they will tend to emphasize task communications if they are concerned with evaluation coming from outside the group.[19]

The communication problem presented by process-task complexities is easily defined but less easily solved. Individuals may tend to do one of three things: (1) emphasize process needs to the exclusion of task needs, (2) emphasize task needs to the exclusion of process needs, or (3) become tongue-tied in attempting to do both. The problem is virtually nonexistent in small cohesive groups; it is aggravated as group size increases and as interpersonal problems become more crucial. Difficulties are reduced as individuals improve their communication skills, thereby allowing them to cope with more, and with more complicated, communications. Difficulties are further reduced by effective leadership and proper planning for participation.

INTERGROUP COMMUNICATION

Intergroup communication is a significant area of concern to the small group discussant. In several places throughout this book the

[18] Refer back to Chapter 9 for explanations of the various conditions that affect process and task demands upon the group.

[19] Alvin Goldberg, "An Experimental Study of the Effects of Evaluation upon Group Behavior," *Quarterly Journal of Speech*, Vol. 46 (October, 1960), pp. 274-283. Goldberg's observation is consistent with the position developed in Chapter 9.

effect of intergroup relations upon the discussion process has been examined. It has been shown how intergroup status, climate, and control affect discussion behavior, and how external task pressures affect groups, but the processes whereby these intergroup influences are communicated have not been examined. However intergroup communication can only be mentioned here because to deal effectively with it would require a study of the characteristics of large group organizations as careful as that of small groups. Recall the warning against attempting to extrapolate from small group research to large group conclusions. Thus intergroup communication is obviously beyond the scope of this book.

Here are some of the questions that a study of large group communications would seek to answer. What are the formal channels of communication? What are the informal channels? At any given level within the organization how many and what kinds of messages are transmitted "upward," "downward," and "laterally"? [20] What is the significance of any communication patterns? What effects do organizational size and complexity have upon communication? What forms of communication are best for transmitting what kinds of messages? What are the effects of organizational philosophy and locus of power upon communication? What is the communicative relationship of small groups within the large organization and with the world outside?

These questions cannot be answered without extensive analysis that space does not permit. We suggest that the reader note some of the sources listed at the end of the chapter which deal with large group communication. Note particularly the books by Blau and Scott, Shull and Delbecq, Haney, and Whyte.

SUMMARY

This book has been concerned throughout with communication, but this chapter and the next focus upon the *process* of communication itself and upon the effects of the discussion situation upon communication. Communication is defined as the process by which

---

[20] Two of our colleagues at the University of Colorado have been especially interested in this question. See Charles Goetzinger and Milton Valentine, "Communication Channels, Media, Directional Flow and Attitudes in an Academic Community," *The Journal of Communication*, Vol. 12 (March, 1962), pp. 23-26.

people interact for the purpose of interpersonal and intrapersonal integration.

Turning briefly from theoretical considerations to value judgments, ten criteria are suggested by which communications can be evaluated. A contribution in a discussion should be relevant to the group's task and personal needs; it should be related to what others are saying; it should be well-timed and of sufficient length to be understood. The problem of clarity is complicated by the fact that words do not contain meaning. Meaning is given to messages by those who use them. Related to the criterion of clarity is the requirement that contributions should be information-oriented. In order to permit evaluation, the seventh criterion, the contributor must show others how they can evaluate his contribution and must show his willingness to be evaluated. Finally, contributions should be internally consistent, provocative, and considerate of the feelings of others.

The first step in building a usable theory of communication is the communication model. It has four basic parts: the source-encoder, the message, the channel, and the decoder-receiver. This model provides us with the means of identifying points or junctures in the process of communication. The information theory approach is one way to study communication. This approach starts with a body of information to be communicated and asks what happens to that information as it goes through the several parts of the model. It concentrates upon barriers to communication and asks how these barriers can be modified or circumvented.

The approach preferred here, however, is the field theory approach which starts with the assumption that man desires to maintain integration. Communication is his means of achieving integration, and thus we must consider how he relates himself, by means of communication, to his environment. The environment considered is, of course, the small discussion group. Three characteristics of interactive communication within a group are identified and all considerations are prefaced with the fundamental fact that each discussant is both source-encoder and decoder-receiver at virtually one and the same time. Feedforward communication is initiatory communication that includes the characteristic of transmitting messages that hint of further directions for communication, road signs, and allow the communicator to "get a reading" on the appropriate-

1ess of messages he would like to send, trial balloon messages.
˚eedback and jamming are two kinds of reactive communication, the
econd characteristic of interactive communication. Intelligent and
pontaneous feedback is essential for checking the accuracy of com-
nunication, but jamming, the tendency to communicate related but
listorting messages, is a temptation that must be rigorously curbed.
Fhe communication structure within a group may account for the
elative influence of individuals who are more central or more peri-
᠈heral in the structure. Groups should learn to develop communica-
ion and decision-making structures which provide both efficiency
and satisfaction. Finally, the double role of source-encoder and
lecoder-receiver, member anxiety, and process-task complications
are three problems that exist to some degree in almost all groups.
Fhe effects of these problems can be mitigated, but usually the
᠈roblems cannot be completely eliminated.

Reluctantly, the nature and complexities of intergroup com-
nunication are only briefly mentioned. Further study is recom-
nended of sources that are able to treat the problem in sufficient
lepth to justify conclusions about intergroup communication.

EXERCISES

1. Arrange for several persons to observe a discussion that can be
ape-recorded at the same time. Have each observer evaluate the contributions of one or two discussants, using the list of Characteristics of
Desirable Communication outlined in the first portion of this chapter.
After an interval of two to three days, arrange to play back the tape and
nave each observer again evaluate the communications of the same person
᠈r persons he observed earlier. Each observer should answer the follow-
ng questions: (a) How would you rate the overall communication for
:he persons you observed? (b) How do your two ratings of the same
ndividual compare? (c) How were you affected by the immediate and
ʋisual stimuli? (d) How are you affected by the delayed and auditory
stimuli? (e) What does this suggest concerning communcation and its
ᵉvaluation?

2. Consider the meanings it is possible to evoke in several persons of
narkedly different ages, backgrounds and orientations by the manner in
ʋhich voice and action may color the following contribution that one
᠈erson made to a discussion group: "good by Joe we're going to think

about that idea." (The reader should apply the capitalization, punctu
ation, force, inflection, timing, and related factors that help convey
meaning.)

3. Plan and carry out a simple experiment to permit observation of
the effects of evaluation and description in two or more discussion groups
For example, it might be possible for a team of three or four individual
to work together in such a manner that two would be members of a socia
discussion group with one deliberately refraining from making any
evaluative contributions and the other deliberately casting the majority
of his comments in evaluative terms. Observers (either external, or per
haps, as members of the group) could note the effect on other group mem
bers, intragroup communication, and reactions toward the two role
players. If the group as a whole happens to be sufficiently mature and
interested, a discussion of the effects may be profitable. The same pro
cedure might be attempted with learning or task-oriented groups. (Ob
viously in all cases the majority of group members should not know tha
an experiment or planned observation is in process until the conclusion
of the discussion.) A variety of other possibilities for experimentation wil
suggest themselves to the reader.

4. Using the communication model described in this chapter, at
tempt to follow the flow of communication in a discussion group. Analyz
the process to determine at which of the major points the most difficulty
appears to exist, and also, at which points the greatest success seems to
appear. Then superimpose the model on the broad context of background
attitudes, and motivations relative to the problem and the persons. What
if any, effect does this have on your analysis?

5. Review carefully the discussion of field theory approach to com
munication and the questions illustrative of such an analysis. Formulate
additional questions to supplement those mentioned on page 410 and then
attempt to analyze communication in a small group using your expanded
list. This exercise may be done as an individual assignment or as a group
project. The results may be reported in written form or discussed as a
group activity.

6. Arrange for a group discussion to explore the implications of the
statement: The purpose of communication is social control and the effec
of communication is learning.

7. Pair yourself with another person whom you know very well and
with whom you feel it is possible to be free and frank. (Make sure tha
your partner shares your feelings regarding the interpersonal relationship.
Plan to engage in a two to three minute conversation for the ultimate
purpose of describing and analyzing the communication process. Selec
a subject on which your beliefs, attitudes, or feelings differ somewhat. A

he conclusion of the exchange, each person should review his thoughts, eelings and behavior (both private and public) making any notes that vill serve either as stimuli to further insight or as aids to memory. Next ooperatively describe what took place both in terms of the communica- ion process and in terms of the reactions of the individuals engaged in his process. One way in which this can be done is to divide a sheet of aper into three columns, heading the first one Individual #1, the second ne Process, and the third one Individual #2. Detailed step by step de- cription of the process that took place can be recorded in the middle olumn. For the other two columns, each person should supply the infor- nation about activities, thoughts, and reactions that were unique to him nd that could come only from his particular point of view. Note: Need ve point out that some hazard is inherent in an exercise such as this, and urther, that its potential is dependent upon the insight, objectivity, per- onal security, and flexibility of the individuals.

8. Observe the communication process in a group for the purpose of lentifying and evaluating feedforward, feedback, and jamming. To what xtent are these present? What individuals provide or engage in each type f response? To what degree are the group members aware of such re- ctions? What are the reactions of the group members to such behavior? s the presence or absence of these reactions related to group structure a any meaningful or causal manner?

9. Organize a brainstorming session to consider one or more of the ollowing problems:

> *a.* What points could be considered when analyzing communica-
> tion from the field theory point of view? (This could precede
> Exercise 5 above.)
>
> *b.* What reactions, signals, or messages should a sender be alert
> to as possible sources of feedback?
>
> *c.* What can the sender do to minimize jamming?

10. Consider the relationship between group norms and communica- on within the group. Observe how such a relationship may or may not e a significant force within a group of which you are a member. With roups of certain composition, background and maturity, this problem ay provide the basis for a profitable discussion.

11. Consider the implications of the statement: Communication pro- uces change and change constitutes communication. How does this late to group discussion? How does it relate to individuals within the roup?

12. Consider the implications of Whitehead's quotation at the begin- ing of this chapter.

424

SELECTED READINGS

Berlo, David K., *The Process of Communication*. New York, Holt, Rinehart and Winston, 1960.

Blau, Peter M., and Scott, W. Richard, *Formal Organizations: A Comparative Approach*. San Francisco, Chandler, 1962.

Cherry, Colin, *On Human Communication*. Cambridge, Mass., Technology Press, 1957.

Haney, William V., *Communication: Patterns and Incidents*. Homewood, Ill., Irwin, 1960.

Johnson, Wendell, *People in Quandaries*. New York, Harper & Row, 1946.

Miller, George A., *Language and Communication*. New York, McGraw-Hill, 1951.

Selected Readings in Management, 2nd series, Fremont A. Shull and Andre L. Delbecq, eds. Homewood, Ill., Irwin, 1962.

Wiener, Norbert, *The Human Use of Human Beings*. Garden City, N. Y., Doubleday, 1956.

Whyte, William Foote, *Man and Organization*. Homewood, Ill., Irwin, 1959.

CHAPTER 16

Improving the Communication Process

A man speaking is four things, all of them needed in
revealing his mind to others. First, he is a will, an intention, a meaning which he wishes others to have, a
thought; second, he is a user of language, molding
thought and feeling into words; third, he is a thing to be
heard, carrying his purpose and words to others through
voice; and last, he is a thing to be seen, shown to the
sight, a being of action, to be noted and read through
the eye.

Charles Henry Woolbert*

The ten criteria listed in the last chapter for measuring the quality
of contributions in a discussion now form the objectives of techniques for improving communication. However, the techniques in
this chapter are not organized according to those criteria for several
reasons. No one-to-one correspondence exists between the techniques and the objectives. Some techniques lay the groundwork for
meeting several objectives; some work directly toward several objectives; and often several techniques are needed to accomplish one
objective. Further, as indicated when discussing the criteria, the
means of accomplishing some of the objectives are apparent or
already covered and hence, need no additional development of

* *Fundamentals of Speech* (New York: Harper, 1920), p. 3.

technique. But before the techniques are developed, a few assumptions are necessary.

First, it is assumed that you and the rest of the group have conscientiously attempted to follow the advice given earlier. Advice about communication techniques is sterile unless prefaced by the principles governing sound thinking about meaningful problems discussed in purposeful and maturing groups. Following the example set by Isocrates, the ancients conceived of speech training as the culmination of education. In one sense it is following this ancient practice to place this chapter here in the book. The second assumption is that obvious advice need not be belabored. It is obviously important to good communication that discussions be as free as possible from outside distraction, that discussants articulate carefully, that members be seated comfortably and in positions where they can readily see one another, but you need not be told what common sense suggests. Finally, it is assumed that you and your fellow discussants understand keenly that discussion is difficult and that effective communication is not easily attained. Improving the communication process requires hard, but fascinating work, that provides many rewards.

Our approach to improving the communication process is to suggest means of facilitating communication rather than to suggest errors to avoid. Concentration upon barriers to communication, pitfalls, traps, blunders, assumes, tacitly at least, that communication would function ideally if the barriers could only be eliminated. That assumption is not sound. Communication is a dynamic process requiring creative input. Further, the "error avoidance" approach tends to make people fearful of making mistakes, and the only sure way to avoid making mistakes is to make the biggest mistake of all—try nothing whatsoever! Therefore, suggestions are made that are likely to improve communication.

From the last chapter recall how each discussant is beset by many, often competing, stimuli which he has to sort out and evaluate. Thus, the basic objective underlying many of the techniques is to reduce complexity and bring the stimuli into manageable proportions. There are stories about high-powered executives who can simultaneously carry on two telephone conversations, read the morning mail, dictate to a secretary, and approve a production plan. But most of us have our hands full carrying on just one conversation at a ime. We need to learn, therefore, how to manage stimuli effectively.

We can learn to handle our communication problems by careful lanning before the discussion and by attention to a limited number f significant techniques during the discussion. The techniques that ollow are arranged in this fashion.

BEFORE THE DISCUSSION

Assuming that you have done your research and have performed he prediscussion analysis suggested in Chapter 11, here are some dditional techniques aimed at improving communication.

Prepare Your Information

You have notes, documents, observations, and ideas. Good. But, unless you are prepared to present the information to the group, your task is only half done. What more remains?

Organize According to Some Pattern. If you have more than one piece of information, you should select some pattern for presentation. If you leave the decision to the spur of the moment, you complicate the decisions you must make and run the risk of confusing the other discussants. Therefore, plan the organization before he discussion, and try to have the organization reflect some pattern. What do we mean by pattern, and how does the advice apply?

Suppose that your group is discussing ways and means of improving public school education, and you have been assigned the task of securing information about teachers' salaries. You have dug out the information and are ready to organize it. You may wish to organize the information according to a *chronological* pattern, showing what has happened to salaries over the years. You may organize it according to a *space* pattern, showing comparative salary figures for different parts of the country. You may use a *cause-effect* pattern, showing what factors seem principally responsible for major changes from time to time. You may use a *comparison* pattern, showing how teachers' salaries relate to those of comparably trained people in other professions.

Other patterns are available, of course, and you may study them at greater length, if you wish, in one or more of the speech texts listed at the end of this chapter. Our suggestion here is to pick some reasonable pattern and stick to it rather than presenting the da◼ helter-skelter. You may have to change the pattern once the actu◼ discussion begins. But if you do, it will be because an alternativ◼ pattern seems to make more sense at the time, and you will be ab◼ to spot that alternative more readily if you have already been thin◼ ing in terms of patterned organization. Also you simplify the listener◼ task if you have organized your information according to som◼ pattern.

Provide Necessary Visual Aids or "Handouts." Some information ◼ better comprehended visually than orally, and some informatio◼ needs to be preserved. If you take the trouble to prepare graphs ◼ charts to assist others in grasping figures, statistics, or complicate◼ relationships, you make your communication responsibilities muc◼ easier. Sometimes you should prepare sufficient copies of summarie◼ of your information, or occasionally complete copies of the infor◼ mation, and distribute them to the other members. Most of us hav◼ access to duplicating facilities, and often the group is so small tha◼ carbon copies will do the trick.

To decide when you need visual aids or "handouts" is not diffi◼ cult. If you are in doubt, try out your strictly oral presentation on ◼ friend and see if he comprehends easily.[1]

Decide When to Present Your Information. This decision must b◼ tentative, of course, since you cannot anticipate precisely the cours◼ of the discussion. But if you take some time to plan before the dis◼ cussion, you are less likely to violate the timing criterion discusse◼ in the last chapter. Of course, it is not recommended that you mak◼ formal speeches during an otherwise informal discussion.

Plan to Perform Functions

On this matter, recall the advice given in Chapter 11.[2] For th◼ purpose of improving communication, planning to perform th◼

[1] Geldard has a long listing of circumstances which call for visual mes◼ sages and another list of circumstances in which oral messages are preferable◼ The bulk of his article, however, discusses possibilities of communicating to th◼ skin. We hasten to add that we see little possibility that skin communicatio◼ will replace the more conventional forms during a discussion. We recommen◼ the article for the visual-oral comparisons. F. A. Geldard, "Some Neglecte◼ Possibilities of Communication," *Science,* Vol. 131 (May 27, 1960), pp. 583-588◼
[2] See pp. 298-300.

functions allows you to concentrate upon communications relevant to the particular functions you intend to perform. If, for example, one of the functions you intend to perform is harmonizing interpersonal conflict, your planning will alert you to feedforward messages hinting that trouble is brewing. You will be able to interpret those messages readily and, thus, be able to respond to them before the situation gets out of hand.

Prepare to Meet Potential Communication Problems

Return again to Chapter 11 to find the model for preparation. At the end of that chapter, a five-step procedure was suggested for developing ability to perform group functions. Here use the same five steps, but adapt them for preparing to meet communication needs.

1. *What Are the Group's Communication Needs?* Have contributions been irrelevant? Has feedback been insufficient or poorly handled? Have there been too many squabbles about the meaning of words? These are a few of the questions you may ask about the group's communication needs. Remember that you are part of the group. The question, What are the group's communication needs? also includes what you see as your own problems. The exercises at the end of Chapter 15 offer a variety of means for developing skill in analyzing communication problems; the whole of Chapter 15 is intended to describe the nature of group communication in order to permit such analysis.

2. *What Have I Done to Meet Those Needs?* Before you can answer this question, and indeed, before you can answer the first question, you must take a sharp look at your own attitudes toward the communication process. An individual's attitudes, as we have seen, can affect his perception of his role in the discussion situation. Here the concern is with your attitudes concerning *what* should be said, to *whom* it should be said, and *how* it should be said. Some interesting insights into this problem are suggested by a study made by Tarnopol.[3] He studied communication attitudes of different managerial levels in an actual business setting, a California public utility. He found significant differences in attitudes toward communication

[3] L. Tarnopol, "Attitudes Block Communications," *Personnel Journal,* Vol. 37 (1959), pp. 325-328.

between top management and foremen. By and large, top management tended to place a high value upon group discussion, the exploration of the views of those working under them, and the interplay of ideas before decision making. Fundamentally, top management revealed less authoritarian tendencies and tended to place more confidence and respect in the opinions of others than did the foremen, who, on the other hand, saw less value in talking things over, in submitting their own ideas to possible change, or in discussing the problems of others.[4] The issue, therefore, is clear. If you believe communication has little value, you will tend to see few problems. If you believe that it is unlikely to be improved, you will tend to be blind to what you have done and what you may do to improve. If your attitudes toward communication are "healthy," you can better describe accurately what you have done—the improvements you have made, and also, the problems you have caused.

3. *What Can I Do Now?* This chapter describes several things to do to improve the communication process. Of course, we would all like to be exceptionally good in all aspects of communicating. But realism tells us that we should expect to focus our attention, at least initially, upon those things we do best. Focusing upon either task or process needs is often the best way of limiting our concern. Some of us, for example, will find it easy to diagnose and improve communications addressed primarily to the group's task needs. Particularly if the subject for discussion is one of our personal projects, we find it relatively easy to cope with problems of relevance, relatedness, and clarity. On the other hand, we may, for any number of reasons, be more inclined to focus upon process needs and will probably concern ourselves more with such problems as creating a permissive climate and making other modifications in the total situation.

4. *What Can I Train Myself to Do?* We must broaden and refine our capacity, and thus we cannot continue focusing upon only a part of the group's communication needs. We will certainly want to train ourselves so that, ultimately, we can successfully perform any com-

[4] We can not help wondering whether this difference in attitudes toward communication might be causally related to the difference in respective positions which top management and foremen occupy in the organizational scheme.

munication functions. Our initial predispositions and the nature of the needs of our particular group may suggest a place to start.

5. *How Do I Intend to Do the Training?* The exercises at the end of this chapter will help. The desirability of courses in speech, listening, general semantics, and linguistics has already been pointed out. Don't wait until next semester or next year to begin, however. Start in whatever ways seem reasonable right now!

These, then, are some suggestions for things to do before the discussion. If you follow these suggestions, you can reduce the communication complexities of the actual discussion situation for three fundamental reasons. First, you will make certain decisions and preparations before the discussion that you need not make during the discussion. Second, you will anticipate communication problems and will, therefore, be in a better position during the discussion to interpret messages indicating their presence. Finally, you will focus your attention upon stimuli that are both important to you and the group and that you feel you can respond to.

DURING THE DISCUSSION

Since discussion is dynamic, all the problems cannot be anticipated, and to assume that any of our anticipations are final answers is, therefore, dangerous. We must be particularly alert to notice whether the grounds for our anticipations continue unchanged during the discussion. We have much to do during discussion. Thus, the suggestions that follow have been selected for two reasons. First, using the techniques is quite likely to improve communication, having been observed to work in actual discussion situations. Second, these techniques have been selected because they strike most accurately at the heart of crucial communication problems.

Unless otherwise indicated, each technique applies with equal force to source-encoder and decoder-receiver.

Assessing Relevance and Relatedness

These were the first two criteria listed in Chapter 15. Three techniques help to meet the twin objectives.

1. *"How Does This Fit?"* Both the one talking and his listeners must keep asking this question, and both must attempt answers. The

problem-solution pattern described in Chapter 4 provides a structure for determining relevance, but this structure often will not be enough.[5] If a speaker strikes out into new territory, he should warn his listeners. If his ideas are vague, but he feels nonetheless that he is beginning to grope toward something valuable, he should ask for help in establishing relevance.

The listeners have special responsibility. They must ask how the speaker's contribution fits, and they must ask how their subvocal reactions fit. If they are feeding back, fine; but if they are jamming, they should catch the tendency quickly.

If a group is brainstorming a topic, and if "anything goes," of course there is no need to worry whether or not the contribution fits.

Be careful, however, of injudicious application of this technique because, improperly used, the question can stifle productive discussion. This may happen in one or both of two ways. If a discussant is struck by an idea, begins to explore it, either publicly or privately, and then discovers that he cannot answer the "how-does-it-fit" question, he may abandon the line of thought before he has sufficient opportunity to examine it. On the other hand, a listener may hear a contribution, ask the "how-does-it-fit" question, decide it does not fit, and *then dismiss the thought without further evaluation.* Let us examine each circumstance a bit more closely.

If we knew more about human thought processes in general and creativity in particular, perhaps we could tell when our minds are simply wandering and when we have the kernel of a promising idea. Considering our ignorance, however, it seems wiser to "play our hunches" when intuition tells us that we may have caught hold of something, rather than to dismiss the thought because we cannot relate it. Even if the idea proves ultimately to be irrelevant to the discussion at hand, it may be an idea we want to pursue privately or with another group at another time. When you are faced with this situation, do one of two things. If there seems to be any possibility that the idea might prove relevant, ask the group's indulgence in allowing you to try out the idea. You may say something like this. "Probably this idea is completely irrelevant, but it struck me while we were talking about . . . that. . . . Now, do any of you see merit in pursuing this further?" Second, if relevance seems highly unlikely,

[5] See pp. 64-68.

pigeonhole the idea, either in a corner of your mind, or on a scrap of paper, for the time being. When you are alone, take the idea out again and turn it this way and that, giving it as fair a trial as possible. Unfortunately, this procedure doesn't guarantee pearls of wisdom every time, if you are a reasonably typical human being. But every once in a while, you may strike gold, and new ideas are so rare that the one chance in a thousand is worth a little added effort.

The listener, who dismisses a contribution out of hand because he cannot see how it fits, is simply shirking his duty. If it does not seem to fit, stay with the contribution until the speaker has finished. Grant the assumption that he senses a relevance or he would not be talking. If, when the speaker has finished, you still cannot fit the idea in, or if you are unsure of the fit, simply ask the speaker, and the others, how the idea fits. You may be the only one who has not found the fit; others may be as puzzled as you; and others may only have assumed that the idea was relevant. In any event, if you are reasonably tactful, you have nothing to lose and everything to gain by sticking with the idea and asking how it fits.

2. *Hook-On.* One way to assure relatedness is to use what we call the "hook-on" technique. Hooking-on consists simply of prefacing a contribution with a reference to the contribution that preceded yours. For example, if the person who just finished speaking has suggested a solution to the problem, you might begin like this. "John has suggested one way of solving the problem, but I would like to go back to the problem itself before we attempt to evaluate solutions. I think we forgot to identify one of the obstacles which is. . . ." Suppose you do not take the trouble to relate your contribution to John's. Others may reasonably infer that you are quarreling with John's proposed solution, when actually your contribution has no direct bearing at all upon *this particular solution*.

To hook-on when you intend to talk directly about the contribution that has preceded yours is easy. Trouble arises when your contribution aims in a different direction. If hooking-on is difficult, either the preceding contribution was out of line or your contribution is out of line. If the other contribution is out of line, your first task should be to try to relate it. If your contribution is out of line, you should either wait until it is appropriate to introduce it or double back as in the example above.

Hooking-on applies to listeners as well. They must seek the bridge between what is *being* said and what *has been* said. If the speaker performs his task well, the listeners' problems are lessened. But if you must discover the bridge yourself, do not assume that all the others have found the same bridge. Feed back your bridge as quickly as possible. If you are right, your feedback will clarify and emphasize the contribution. If you are wrong, you check your own tendencies to jam.

3. *One Point Please.* If a discussant suggests at one time a new goal, an obstacle to another goal, and a solution to meet still a third goal, everyone is likely to become confused. The contribution has become a small oration. But, you may say, if I have three reasons to suggest for adopting a solution, must I give them one at a time? Of course you may give three reasons *for one point* at the same time. This is good policy. Others may agree with one or two of the reasons but wish to disagree with the third. You may need to present all three for any one to have meaning. The important thing is to keep all parts of the contribution related to one main point.

To stick to just one point is often very difficult. Complicated subjects with complicated interrelations tempt us to talk about everything at once. But so far as possible, we should resist the temptation because if contributions are to be properly received and decoded, the contributor must help maintain the focus.

Creating Clarity

"Be clear!" "Be clear!" "Be clear!" These were Napoleon's famous three rules for transmitting messages. But, while this threefold injunction serves to emphasize the importance of clarity, probably it no more helps produce clarity than the injunction, "Be objective!" helps produce objectivity. To guarantee clarity is frankly impossible, as pointed out in the last chapter. Since meaning is a process that involves everyone in the discussion situation, "being clear" must require something more than plain speaking. Weaver and Ness state the problem well: "*Understanding, if it takes place at all, must occur in the mind of the listener;* it is not sufficient that the *speaker* know what he is talking about. The purpose of informational speaking is to produce clear ideas *in the mind of the listener.*" [6]

[6] Andrew T. Weaver and Ordean G. Ness, *An Introduction to Public Speaking* (New York: Odyssey, 1961), p. 89.

There are five specific techniques to suggest, but first a reminder of several rather obvious, but important, techniques. (1) Speak naturally. Informal group discussion calls for natural, not artificial, speaking. (2) Use simple, concrete words. Discussants who say, "But I must use the precise word," are often either throwing up a verbal smoke screen to cover their ignorance or are too indifferent to genuine communication to use words that are more likely to convey their meaning. (3) State the point. As a general rule you should state the point you intend to make and then offer examples, reasoning, and other support to back up the point. If you lead up to the point in the manner in which it first came to you, you run the risk of having your listeners miss connections between ideas because they may miss the main direction. Whether you state it first or last, however, be sure you do state the point rather than leaving your listeners wondering what you are trying to establish. Many more suggestions might be offered, but you probably know most of them already. Let us go ahead with the five techniques that comprise the bulk of this section.

Seek the Purpose. This is different from determining relevance and relatedness. Seeking the purpose requires both speaker and listener to ask this question: What goals does the speaker seek to accomplish as a result of making the contribution? The nature and effects of goal-seeking behavior were already discussed, particularly as they concern problem solving and group climate.[7] They need no repetition here. Important here is how using the techniques of goal-seeking and goal-awareness helps improve the communication process.

If you, in your role of source-encoder, are not aware of your own goal-seeking behavior, you may find yourself preoccupied with creating unnecessary or positively damaging messages. As an example, suppose that everyone in the group has agreed upon some point, and then one of the discussants offers still one more reason to support the agreed-upon position. This is no rare instance; it happens often. The question is, why did the discussant feel obliged to offer the reason? What was his goal? Many goals are possible, but two likely ones might be these: (1) he wanted to further reassure *himself*, or (2) he wanted to "rub salt in the wounds" of someone who had earlier opposed the position. If his reason be the first, he

[7] See Chapter 4, pp. 71-73; Chapter 7, pp. 171-174; and Chapter 13, pp. 358-360.

wastes group time caring for his own insecurity; if it be the second, he is cruel. In either case he clouds the issue because there is no reasonable or apparent goal to be achieved by the contribution.

In your role as decoder-receiver, you must be careful not to allow your own goals to cause jamming. In addition, you must seek the speaker's purpose in order to be able to decode and interpret his message. If you cannot discover the purpose, ask the speaker to explain. Seeking the purpose, for reasons of clarity, is an excellent method of sensitizing others to goals. You may accomplish much more than just clarity, important as that is.

Seek the Pattern. Recall the importance of organizing messages according to some pattern. Your planning before the discussion will help organize thoughts during the discussion, but you must continually keep on organizing ideas. One way is to announce at the beginning of your contribution *how* you plan to develop the rest of the message. For instance: "I see three reasons why we should reject that solution. First. . . ." or "Let me offer one example and one statistic to support that point." Announcing your organizational pattern is one valuable use of road sign messages. You set the bounds of your own message and you alert others to *what* is coming and to *how* they can expect it to arrive.

Seeking the pattern is more difficult for the listener. The listener has little difficulty if the speaker announces a pattern and then sticks to it. But what should the listener do when the speaker neither announces a pattern nor seems to follow one after he gets under way? When this happens, Nichols and Stevens suggest, "the search for any kind of pattern in the talk should end immediately. Such a search is usually fruitless, and engaging in it prevents you from hearing anything of value that might be said." [8] Instead, they recommend that the listener should listen for facts and principles—facts as the building blocks of ideas, and principles as the structure of ideas. The task is not easy, but trying it will help.

What Is HIS *Meaning?* Both source-encoder and decoder-receiver must keep this question uppermost. Your knowledge of purpose and pattern will help answer the question, and your knowledge of back-

---

[8] Ralph G. Nichols and Leonard A. Stevens, *Are You Listening?* (New York: McGraw-Hill, 1957), p. 73.

grounds, habits and peculiarities of other individuals will also help. The total context of the message will help you judge the other person's meaning. When you speak, you should obviously warn listeners if you use a word in a nonconventional manner. When you listen, watch for hints of a word being used nonconventionally.

An amusing incident of the failure to keep this question uppermost happened to the authors one time when they were conducting a training program for a group of businessmen. We gave them copies of a case study. They read it and began to discuss. Something was wrong, however, because the discussion did not go at all in the direction we expected. We discovered the trouble when one of the businessmen said, "What I can't figure out is why the auditors were going over his books." That was it. We had written something about a speaker and his "auditors." By auditor we meant, a listener; by auditor they meant an accountant who "goes over books." Neither we nor they had stopped to think what the other might mean by the word. Little was lost by the error because we were teaching *communications,* and we had a first-rate example of what happens when people do not ask what the other fellow means. Unless you teach communication, however, and can turn such blunders into usable examples, keep asking the question: What is HIS meaning?

Rephrase! The best way to make molehills out of mountains of communicative difficulties is the technique of rephrasing the contributions of others. Rephrasing consists of putting another's idea into a different set of words. Chapter 6, you recall, suggested that every group set as its first operating rule the principle that no one be allowed to disagree with another's argument until he rephrases that argument *to the satisfaction of the originator.* This practice illustrates the use of feedback at its best.[9]

You must ask and answer three questions about rephrasing to learn to use the technique effectively. Who should rephrase? What should be rephrased? How should contributions be rephrased? The "who" question is most easily answered. Anyone who feels unsure of the intended meaning of a contribution may rephrase, and, cer-

---

[9] See p. 152. Some people argue that the term *feedback* must necessarily imply the full and complete reaction on the part of the receiver and terminal reaction on the part of the sender. We believe, however, that this meaning unduly restricts the use of the term.

tainly, anyone who wishes to take issue with a contribution should first rephrase it.

Obviously, we cannot rephrase every contribution made, so we must establish some ground rules for judging which contributions merit rephrasing. If a contribution is unclear to some members, someone should probably rephrase it. But an equally important consideration is the degree to which the contribution is central to the discussion. Some contributions state central ideas that form the core of the talk about a problem. Relatively few contributions are central, but each is important. Other contributions may offer supporting details, questions for exploration, illustrations of a point, and the like. These contributions are essential ingredients in a good discussion, but misunderstanding a few will not cripple most discussions. Therefore, it is wise to rephrase most central contributions, even though you do not seriously doubt their intended meaning, and relatively few of the more peripheral contributions.

When you rephrase another's contribution, keep his meaning uppermost in your mind. Do not extend the argument beyond what he included in his contribution. If you wish to demonstrate the logical consequences of an idea, wait until you have cleared up the problem of meaning.

One useful method of rephrasing that usually pins down the meaning of a contribution is to relate an abstract statement to more specific and observable instances. If you stay on the abstract level, you may find that you simply substitute one set of vague words for another equally vague set with the result that no one is any closer to a workable understanding. For example, suppose a discussant says that the federal government has become too large and powerful. In rephrasing this contribution you might mention certain powers and certain areas of governmental control and ask if he would include these as examples of undesirable size and power. After a few exchanges, you may discover that he does not object to the activities of the Securities and Exchange Commission, the Federal Communication Commission, or the Federal Reserve Board, but he does object to several instances of governmental influence over price and wage settlements. A specific instance might be the rollback of steel prices effected by President Kennedy in the spring of 1962. By using specific instances in your rephrasing attempts, you are able to discover a relatively specific area of control to which he objects. Now you and the rest of the group may examine the implications and validity of his position.

In the example above, the discussants required an exchange of contributions to complete rephrasing. This often happens when we discuss abstract and complicated subjects. If the original contribution is more specific, your rephrasing can usually be a simple preface to your own contribution. In either case, however, stick with the job until the other person acknowledges the accuracy of your rephrasing.

Unfortunately, no way exists to illustrate the spirit in which such attempts at clarification should be undertaken. It can be described, however. It should not be hostile; you are trying to pin down his *meaning*, not *him*. You must put forth some effort too; don't throw out the challenge, "Define your terms!" and then sit back and wait for him to do all the work. It should be in the spirit of genuine helpfulness; you are trying to help him, the rest of the group, and yourself to agree as precisely as possible on just what is meant. Finally, in the process of pinning down the meaning of a contribution, the contributor often begins to see that his original contribution had much sound but little substance. Anyone is embarrassed to discover that his words are empty. Therefore, unless he is capable of making a joke at his own expense, let the matter drop as quietly as possible. Don't be triumphant; don't rub it in. You can do nothing to improve either group thinking or interpersonal relations by making an issue of the matter. Remember also, you may be next!

Watch for the Loaded Word. We all know that words may stir up meanings in addition to literal conventional meanings, and that some words are more loaded with these additional meanings than are other words. Sometimes such words provide humor, as in the well known case of the "declension" of the word *obstinate:* I am firm; you are stubborn; he is a pig-headed fool. More often, however, such words provide communicative troubles because of the feelings surrounding them. If we want to label someone on the faculty of a school, we may call him a teacher, a professor, an educator, a pedagogue, an instructor, a scholar, or a whole host of other names that students may use out of faculty earshot. The literal meanings of the various words are similar, but the loaded (connotative) meanings in each words suggest something different about the attitude of the user and, sometimes, highlight some particular characteristic of the classification. The word *teacher,* for example, may emphasize the classroom functions of a faculty member, while the word *scholar* may emphasize his research functions.

Mathematicians have an easier time of it than most of us because the symbols of mathematics are almost completely stripped of loaded meanings. However, we have nothing to gain by bewailing the fact that words are not so simple and precise as mathematical symbols. We have to use words and we should do so as well as we are able. Three possible ways may help us out of our difficulties:

1. We can create new words—jargon. (Note the way we loaded up the word *jargon.* We do not approve of the extended use of this technique and we are warning you.) When we create a new word or use an old one in a totally different sense, we may solve the problem of loaded meanings *for those who have been given the full definition of our word and for a short time only.* Some people will certainly begin "abusing" the word. But for the uninitiated, our jargon will remain a mystery. One problem of interdisciplinary research, for example, is that the researchers must spend so much time translating their jargon for one another that they have little time left for productive research. Therefore, unless we have discovered something unique, there is little to be gained by using jargon.

2. We can, of course, use big stuffy words that have few loaded meanings. We can talk about circumlocutions instead of talking around the subject. Of course, the reason such words have few loaded meanings is that few people use them. If we use them, our listeners are likely to retort, "Speak English."

3. The wisest way out of difficulty is to use ordinary words whose meanings are as neutral as possible. When conventional loadings are present or when we intend something special by the word, we should be aware of what we are doing and use the vocal equivalents of quotation marks to warn listeners that a special meaning is intended. As listeners we should be alert to the loadings, and, when we feed back and rephrase, we can substitute more neutral words to see whether they work as well.

Promoting Permissiveness

Creating conditions in which people feel free to express their thoughts has been the subject of much of this book. It has been shown that permissiveness is a mark of mature groups, and Chapter 13 showed how group maturity could be hastened.[10] Here are a few techniques that improve the communicative process by promoting permissiveness.

Concentrate upon Content. It has already been suggested that concentrating upon others' motives is unwise. You should concentrate instead upon the content of what others say. Concentrating upon content helps promote permissiveness because it helps you react to *what* is said rather than to *who* is talking. If you concentrate upon content, you encourage objective analysis of ideas and, thereby, reduce your own and others' fear of appearing personally foolish or out of line.[11]

Criticize Your Own Ideas. Just as the person who can laugh at himself sets others at ease, so the person who can criticize his own ideas helps create the permissive climate that allows genuine evaluation. Self-criticism is an extension of the use of *we* recommended in Chapter 11.[12] To criticize your own ideas you must listen critically *when you talk* and you must be willing to be criticized. Self-criticism is basically little different from criticizing others' contributions. If discussion suggests reasons for changing one of your ideas, speak up and suggest the change yourself. If the group reaches the "thinking out loud" stage, and you offer a suggestion that began in promising fashion but ended with that proverbial thud, simply say, "No. I see now, that won't work."

Discussions in a particular group, whose members we know well, are characterized by a high rate of self-rejected ideas. So far as we know, no one has ever tallied self-rejected versus other-rejected ideas because no one really cares who rejects any poor idea. The small group of four people have worked together for a long time and are also good personal friends. The degree of permissiveness is such that a new secretary, working in an outer office, who overheard one of these discussions began to worry that the members were fighting. After she learned to know the people better, she told one of the

[10] See pp. 361-366.
[11] This advice does not contradict the earlier advice to seek the purpose. Recall the distinction in Chapter 4, pp. 61-62, between motives and goals.
[12] See p. 281.

members that she had simply never heard a group of people speak so frankly to one another. Few groups will reach the degree of permissiveness that this one had reached, but none can begin to reach that level if criticism of ideas is avoided. The best place to start evaluating ideas is with your own.

Criticize Specifically. When you criticize ideas of others, criticize specifically rather than "beating about the bush." If you criticize vaguely, you do the other person two injustices. First, you do not show him exactly what you object to; second, you imply that there is more you do not like. We are most concerned here with the second injustice. If others are uncertain of the extent of your criticism, they may become more hesitant and permissiveness you have been trying to build up by "being kind" vanishes. You are not "being kind" when you criticize vaguely.

Avoid Unnecessary Evaluation. Do not busy yourself by correcting another's grammatical slip, mispronunciation, or some other insignificant detail. If the other person's mistake has genuinely impeded communication, you may handle the matter by attempting to rephrase. Otherwise, such corrections are irritating and tend to focus others' attention upon some niceties of expression rather than upon substance. Again, a dampening of permissiveness results.

Praise Generously. Sometimes we become so engrossed in thinking together accurately and completely that we forget to praise good ideas. We act as if the fact that we did not criticize the idea is praise enough. It isn't.

Listen Empathically. Empathic listening is the most important single technique for promoting permissiveness. Note that we did not say "sympathetic"; we said "empathic." What do we mean? The word *empathy* has been introduced before. It is the act of feeling and reacting as someone else seems to be feeling and reacting. When we watch a play on the stage, we empathize with the protagonist. We feel depressed with him; we are elated when he triumphs; we struggle with him. In the old days of traveling tent shows playing the role of the villain required some courage. Apparently more than one excited spectator decided to settle the issue on the spot, pulled out a gun, and began to protect the hero and heroine. A clear example of empathy can be seen today when an especially vicious tackle is made on the football field; one can hear a collective "ooph" go up from spectators empathizing with the tackled player.

What is meant, then, by empathic listening? You should put yourself in the speaker's shoes; struggle with him as he tries to shape words to his thoughts; search mentally with him as he tries to make precise distinctions; in short, imagine that you yourself are speaking. Do not interrupt him; do not give him a word unless he asks for it; but empathize silently.

If you listen empathically, you cannot help revealing by gesture, posture, and expression your concern with the speaker's effective statement. We have yet to hear of a good public speaker who does not hunt for those faces in the crowd that say, "I am with you; keep it up." And when he finds those faces, he keeps looking at them. The same principle is true in the discussion group. Listening empathically helps the speaker, *and it helps you listen more accurately.* Obviously it helps promote permissiveness because it encourages others to express themselves.

Communicating Totally

What do you communicate? Everything that others in the discussion group can see or hear constitutes what you communicate. You must suit the action to the word and the visible expression to the feeling. As you participate in discussion you reveal yourself as a creative, interested, and interesting human being, or you reveal yourself as something less. If what others hear you say and what they see you do complement one another, fine. But if they contradict one another, your fellow discussants will trust what they see. Brigance gives the reason: "Action tells them the real meaning: the false smile, the evasive glance, the grimaces of confusion, the wandering hands. There is the real speech, and the listeners know it." [13]

We do not suggest that you stand before a mirror and practice gesturing. We do suggest that you so involve yourself in what you are saying and feeling that you *want* to communicate totally, and we

[13] William Norwood Brigance, *Speech: Its Techniques and Disciplines in a Free Society*, 2nd. ed. (New York: Appleton-Century-Crofts, 1961), p. 322.

suggest that you become so secure personally that you *can* communicate totally. If you work to develop the skills, insights, and understandings discussed in this book, you can acquire the assurance necessary to total effective communication.

SUMMARY

The best way to improve the communication process is to suggest means of facilitating communication rather than pointing out errors to avoid. Since communication is a complicated process, the bulk of the advice in this chapter concerns methods of reducing the complexities to manageable proportions.

Effective prediscussion planning reduces these complexities. The wise discussant prepares his information before the discussion. He organizes what he has to contribute according to some pattern, provides necessary visual aids or handouts, and decides the best time to present the information. The advice given in Chapter 11 about planning to perform functions helps improve communication because planning alerts discussants to signs of problems they are prepared to meet. Discussants should plan to meet potential communication needs in the same way they planned to perform functions. To plan for communication needs, the discussant must: predict the group's probable communication needs; examine his own attitudes and behavior to judge what he has done to meet those needs; determine what he can do now, what he can train himself to do, and how he intends to accomplish the training.

During discussion, the member has more tasks. He must assess the relevance and relatedness of what he and his fellows communicate by asking how each contribution fits, by hooking-on to what others say, and by confining himself to one main point each time he contributes. There are several rather obvious means of creating clarity: speaking naturally, using simple and concrete words, and stating points clearly. Main suggestions for creating clarity are: both source-encoder and the decoder-receiver must keep the purpose of the communication in mind; both must seek and impose patterns upon messages; both must ask what the other person is likely to mean by what is said; the listener must feed back by rephrasing (the best technique for creating clarity); and both must watch for the loaded word. In order to promote permissiveness, the discussant should concentrate upon the content of contributions, criticize his own ideas, criticize others specifically rather than vaguely, avoid unnecessary evaluation, praise generously, and, most important, listen empathically.

Finally, the discussant must communicate totally, remembering that what others see is probably more important than what they hear.

To conclude this chapter, remember that people are not machines. When we are concerned with machines, we think only of their efficiency and utility. When we think that way about people, we forget that they have feelings, pride, dignity, and compassion. People can be amazingly efficient, but in the long run their efficiency is less important than their humanity. In the first chapter of this book, we contend that people need to be individuals and to relate themselves meaningfully to others. We set forth three steps to accomplish those goals: self-understanding, understanding groups, and understanding and using effective communication. We offered few suggestions for accomplishing the first step; we have offered many for the second and third. We have shown how people can work together effectively and efficiently, but, as we discuss with others, let us not lose sight of the paramount reason—the enhancement of the individual human being.

EXERCISES

1. Develop a personal program for improving your communication, based on the suggestions offered in this chapter. One possible approach is to select one or two aspects or points and direct your efforts toward improving those. Then move on to others in turn. Supplement your own analysis of your strengths and limitations by conferences with a competent colleague, or with your instructor. Remember to continue to build up your assets while correcting your deficiencies.

2. Reflect on your experience as a member of discussion groups, recalling instances where an idea that had significant substantive merit was weakened, disregarded or lost due to poor communication. What factors account most often for such reduction in effectiveness?

3. Pair yourself with a colleague and replay a tape recording of a group discussion in which you both participated. Each should first analyze the other's communication and then immediately replay the tape and analyze his own communication. Compare your self-analysis and

your analysis of your colleague. Do you note any places where your communication behavior during the discussion was significantly affected by your prediscussion preparation for communication? Exchange the analyses you have made of each other and discuss them. What new insights have you gained? Do you anticipate any modifications in your communication behavior as a result of this experience?

4. Analyze your communication behavior in terms of one or more of the following possibilities:

> a. Feedforward—Can you recognize preliminary messages? Can you utilize such communication when it comes from others? Which type, road sign or trial balloon, do you use most frequently? Why? How useful do you find it?

> b. Feedback—To What extent do you provide feedback? How helpful do you feel your feedback is to others? To what degree are you conscious of providing such responses? Do you deliberately attempt to modify your feedback, or is it quite spontaneous? Do you feel that others respond to your feedback? Do you respond to theirs? Do you welcome it?

> c. Jamming—To what extent do you jam the communication of others? What causes you to do this? To what extent do you believe that your jamming has affected adversely your interpersonal relationships, achievement, or progress? (Jamming in interviews, conferences, lectures) How do you think you can reduce your own jamming? Do you have any evidence that others jam your messages? How do you think you can reduce their jamming? Will your proposed course of action be equally effective with all of your receivers?

5. Arrange for a discussion to explore this question: Why do most people seem more willing to admit that they communicated poorly than to admit that they reasoned poorly?

SELECTED READINGS

Barbara, Dominick A., *The Art of Listening*. Springfield, Ill., Thomas, 1958.

Brigance, William Norwood, *Speech: Its Techniques and Disciplines in a Free Society*. New York, Appleton-Century-Crofts, 1961.

Nichols, Ralph G., and Stevens, Leonard A., *Are You Listening?* New York, McGraw-Hill, 1957.

Weaver, Andrew Thomas, and Ness, Ordean Gerhard, *An Introduction to Public Speaking*. New York, Odyssey, 1961.

Name Index

447

Cousins, Norman, (q) 281
Coutu, Walter, (q) 403
Crockett, Walter, 197

Davis, Elmer, 17, (q) 238
Decter, Moshe, 78
Delbecq, Andre L., 424
Denny, Reuel, 4, 19
Deutsch, Morton, 172, 225, 322
Dewey, John, 59, 90
Dickens, Milton, 21
Dickson, William J., 346
Diederich, Paul B., 263
Douglas, Jack, 81
Drury, Alan, 251

Edwards, Allen L., 155
Edwards, Jonathan, 7
Eliot, T. S., (q) 371
Emerson, Ralph Waldo, (q) 114
Ernsberg, Conrad M., 25
Ewbank, Henry L., 51, 154

Fearing, Franklin, 406
Festinger, Leon, 100, 155, 243
Fiedler, Fred E., 195, (q) 316
Finletter, Thomas K., (q) 281
Flint, Austin W., 194
Fouraker, Lawrence E., 100, 168, 185
Frank, J. D., 43
Franklin, Benjamin, 7, (q) 273
Freeley, Austin J., 68
French, John R. P., Jr., 210
Frenkel-Brunswik, Else, 221
Freud, Sigmund, 13
Fromm, Erich, 4, 5, 10, 19, 75, (q) 84

Gaier, Eugene L., 194
Galileo, Galilei, 7
Gardner, Eric F., 160, 181, 200
Garland, J. V., 54
Geis, Irving, 155
Geldard, F. A., 428
Getzels, Jacob W., 76
Gibb, Jack, 404
Gilchrist, J. C., 415
Glaser, Edward M., 74

Glazer, Nathan, 4, 19
Glover, John D., 269
Goethe, Johann, 7
Goetzinger, Charles, 419
Goldberg, Alvin, 418
Goldwin, Robert H., 270
Golenbiewski, Robert T., 30, 415
Gordon, Thomas, 194, (q) 259, 269
Gouldner, Alvin W., 189, 191, 221
Gounod, Charles F., 7
Guetzkow, Harold, 416
Gulley, Halbert E., 155, 242, 308, 389
Gynther, Ruth Autrey, 417

Haeffernan, Marguerite, 21
Haiman, Franklyn S., 54, (q) 81, 89, 154, 172, 185, 189, 267, 314, 340, (q) 389, 393
Haire, Mason, 340
Hamblin, Robert L., 226, 241
Hamilton, Alexander, (q) 265
Hammond, Kenneth R., 58
Hance, Kenneth G., 90
Haney, William V., (q) 94, 123, (q) 401, 424
Hare, A. Paul, 185, 315
Harnack, R. Victor, 172, 202, (q) 231, 355
Hartley, E. L., 27, 39
Harvey, O. J., 76, (q) 106, 123, 221, 232, 251, 374
Hayakawa, S. I., 95, 123
Haythorn, William, 342
Heider, Fritz, 243, 254
Heintz, Roy K., 315
Hellman, Hugo, 4
Hemphill, John K., 192
Hendry, Charles E., 301
Henle, Paul, 60
Hetlinger, Duane F., 319
Hildreth, Richard A., 319
Hinds, George L., 54, 89, 389
Hinkley, R. G., 43
Hogan, H. P., (q) 97
Hollander, E. P., 196
Homans, George C., (q) 169, 185, 224
Hood, William R., 232
Hovland, Carl F., 104
Howard, Robert C., (q) 334
Howell, William S., 155, (q) 188
Hower, Ralph M., 269

Subject Index

451